Materials Development in Language Teaching

CAMBRIDGE LANGUAGE TEACHING LIBRARY

A series covering central issues in language teaching and learning, by authors who have expert knowledge in their field.

In this series:

Materials Development in Language Teaching

Edited by

Brian Tomlinson

CAMBRIDGE
UNIVERSITY PRESS

PUBLISHED BY THE PRESS SYNDICATE OF THE UNIVERSITY OF CAMBRIDGE
The Pitt Building, Trumpington Street, Cambridge, United Kingdom

CAMBRIDGE UNIVERSITY PRESS
The Edinburgh Building, Cambridge CB2 2RU, UK
40 West 20th Street, New York, NY 10011–4211, USA
477 Williamstown Road, Port Melbourne, VIC 3207, Australia
Ruiz de Alarcón 13, 28014 Madrid, Spain
Dock House, The Waterfront, Cape Town 8001, South Africa

http://www.cambridge.org

First published 1998
Fifth printing 2002

Printed in the United Kingdom at the University Press, Cambridge

A catalogue record for this book is available from the British Library

Library of Congress Cataloguing in Publication Data
Materials development in language teaching / edited by Brian Tomlinson.
    p.   cm. – (Cambridge language teaching library)
  Includes bibliographical references and index.
  ISBN 0 521 57418 8. – ISBN (invalid) 0 521 57419 6 (pbk.)
  1. Language and languages–Study and teaching.   2. Teaching–Aids
and devices.   I. Tomlinson, Brian.   II. Series.
P53.15.M38   1997   97–42158
418'.007—dc21   CIP

ISBN 0 521 57418 8 hardback
ISBN 0 521 57419 6 paperback

CE

Contents

Preface

Brian Tomlinson

This is a book of original chapters on current issues in materials development written by well-known contributors to the fields of applied linguistics and TEFL who have made presentations at MATSDA conferences.

MATSDA (The Materials Development Association) is an international materials development association founded in 1993 by Brian Tomlinson to contribute to the development of quality materials for learners of second and foreign languages. It aims to bring together teachers, researchers, materials writers and publishers in a joint endeavour to stimulate and support principled research, innovation and development. It does this by holding conferences, running workshops, providing consultants, publishing a journal (*FOLIO*) and writing books like this one.

For further information about MATSDA and for application forms for membership contact Brian Tomlinson, President of MATSDA, Department of English Language and Literature, The National University of Singapore, 10 Kent Ridge, Singapore 119260.

The main aim of this book is to further the work of MATSDA in providing information, ideas and stimulus which will facilitate the application of current thinking and research to the practical realities of developing and exploiting classroom materials. It also aims to stimulate further experimentation and innovation and thus to contribute to the continuing development of quality materials.

More and more applied linguistics and teacher development courses are including components on materials development (there is even an MA in L2 Materials Development at the University of Luton) and more and more presentations at TEFL conferences are focusing on issues related to the writing and exploitation of materials. And yet very few books have been published which investigate these issues. *Materials Development for Language Teaching* aims to fill this gap by providing an opportunity for researchers, teachers, writers and publishers to communicate their informed views and suggestions to an audience seeking to gain new insights into the principles and procedures which are informing the current writing and exploitation of L2 materials.

Glossary of basic terms for materials development in language teaching

Brian Tomlinson

The following terms are used frequently in this book. Unless they are differently defined by the author(s) of the chapter, they are used with the meanings given below.

Authentic text
A text which is not written or spoken for language teaching purposes. A newspaper article, a rock song, a novel, a radio interview and a traditional fairy story are examples of authentic texts. A story written to exemplify the use of reported speech, a dialogue scripted to exemplify ways of inviting and a linguistically simplified version of a novel would not be authentic texts.

See **simplified texts; text.**

Authentic task (or real world task)
A task which involves learners in using language in a way that replicates its use in the 'real world' outside the language classroom. Filling in blanks, changing verbs from the simple past to the simple present and completing substitution tables are, therefore, not authentic tasks. Examples of authentic tasks would be answering a letter addressed to the learner, arguing a particular point of view and comparing various holiday brochures in order to decide where to go for a holiday.

See **pedagogic task.**

Communicative approaches
Approaches to language teaching which aim to help learners to develop communicative competence (i.e. the ability to use the language effectively for communication). A **weak communicative approach** includes overt teaching of language forms and functions in order to help learners to develop the ability to use them for communication. A **strong communicative approach** relies on providing learners with experience of using language as the main means of learning to use the language. In such an approach learners, for example, talk to learn rather than learn to talk.

Communicative competence
The ability to use the language effectively for communication. Gaining

such competence involves acquiring both sociolinguistic and linguistic knowledge and skills (or, in other words, developing the ability to use the language accurately, appropriately and effectively).

Concordances (or concordance lines)
A list of authentic utterances each containing the same focused word or phrase e.g.:

> The bus driver still didn't have **any** change so he made me wait.
> I really don't mind which one. **Any** newspaper will do. I just
> know what they are saying. **Any** teacher will tell you that it's

See **authentic**.

Corpus
A bank of authentic texts collected in order to find out how language is actually used. Usually a corpus is restricted to a particular type of language use, for example, a corpus of newspaper English, a corpus of legal documents or a corpus of informal spoken English.

See **text**.

Coursebook
A textbook which provides the core materials for a course. It aims to provide as much as possible in one book and is designed so that it could serve as the only book which the learners necessarily use during a course. Such a book usually includes work on grammar, vocabulary, pronunciation, functions and the skills of reading, writing, listening and speaking.

See **supplementary materials**.

Discovery activity
An activity which involves learners in investing energy and attention in order to discover something about the language for themselves. Getting learners to work out the rules of direct speech from examples, asking learners to investigate when and why a character uses the modal 'must' in a story and getting learners to notice and explain the use of ellipsis in a recorded conversation would be examples of discovery activities.

Experiential
Referring to ways of learning language through experiencing it in use rather than through focusing conscious attention on language items. Reading a novel, listening to a song and taking part in a project are experiential ways of learning language.

Foreign language

A language which is not normally used for communication in a particular society. Thus English is a foreign language in France and Spanish is a foreign language in Germany.

Global coursebook

A coursebook which is not written for learners from a particular culture or country but which is intended for use by any class of learners in the specified level and age group anywhere in the world.

Language awareness

Approaches to teaching language which emphasise the value of helping learners to focus attention on features of language in use. Most such approaches emphasise the importance of learners gradually developing their own awareness of how the language is used through discoveries which they make themselves.

See **discovery activities.**

Language data

Instances of language use which are used to provide information about how the language is used. Thus a corpus can be said to consist of language data.

See **corpus.**

Language practice

Activities which involve repetition of the same language point or skill in an environment which is controlled by the framework of the activity. The purpose for language production and the language to be produced are usually predetermined by the task or the teacher. The intention is not to use the language for communication but to strengthen, through successful repetition, the ability to manipulate a particular language form or function. Thus getting all the students in a class who already know each other repeatedly to ask each other their names would be a practice activity.

See **language use.**

Language use

Activities which involve the production of language in order to communicate. The purpose of the activity might be predetermined but the language which is used is determined by the learners. Thus getting a new class of learners to walk around and introduce themselves to each other would be a language use activity; and so would getting them to complete a story which they have been given the beginning of.

See **language practice.**

Learning styles
The way(s) that particular learners prefer to learn a language. Some have a preference for hearing the language (auditory learners), some for seeing it written down (visual learners), some for learning it in discrete bits (analytic learners), some for experiencing it in large chunks (global or holistic or experiential learners) and many prefer to do something physical whilst experiencing the language (kinaesthetic learners).

L2
A term used to refer to both foreign and second languages.

See **foreign language; second language.**

Materials
Anything which is used to help to teach language learners. Materials can be in the form of a textbook, a workbook, a cassette, a CD-Rom, a video, a photocopied handout, a newspaper, a paragraph written on a whiteboard: anything which presents or informs about the language being learned.

Materials adaptation
Making changes to materials in order to improve them or to make them more suitable for a particular type of learner. Adaptation can include reducing, adding, omitting, modifying and supplementing. Most teachers adapt materials every time they use a textbook in order to maximise the value of the book for their particular learners.

Materials evaluation
The systematic appraisal of the value of materials in relation to their objectives and to the objectives of the learners using them. Evaluation can be pre-use and therefore focused on predictions of potential value. It can be whilst-use and therefore focused on awareness and description of what the learners are actually doing whilst the materials are being used. And it can also be post-use and therefore focused on analysis of what happened as a result of using the materials.

Multi-media materials
Materials which make use of a number of different media. Often they are available on a CD-Rom which makes use of print, graphics, video and sound. Usually such materials are interactive and enable the learner to receive feedback on the written or spoken language which they produce.

Pedagogic task
A task which does not replicate a real world task but which is designed to facilitate the learning of language or skills which would be useful in a

real world task. Completing one half of a dialogue, filling in the blanks in a story and working out the meaning of ten nonsense words from clues in a text would be examples of pedagogic tasks.

PPP
An approach to teaching language items which follows a sequence of presentation of the item, practice of the item and then production (i.e. use) of the item. This is the approach currently followed by most commercially produced coursebooks and has the advantage of apparent systematicity and economy. However, many SLA researchers would argue that it is an inefficient approach which creates the illusion of learning. They would say that learning an item takes much longer than this approach suggests and that far more experience of the item in communication is necessary for any lasting learning to take place.

See **language practice; SLA; language use.**

Second language
The term is used to refer to a language which is not a mother tongue but which is used for certain communicative functions in a society. Thus English is a second language in Nigeria, Sri Lanka and Singapore, and French is a second language in Senegal, Cameroon and Tahiti.

See **foreign language.**

Self-access materials
Materials designed for learners to use independently (i.e. on their own without access to a teacher or a classroom). They are normally used by the learner at home, in a library or in a self-study centre.

Simplified texts
These are texts which have been made simpler so as to make it easier for learners to read them. The usual principles of simplification involve reduction in length of the text, shortening of sentences, omission or replacement of difficult words or structures, omission of qualifying clauses and omission of non-essential detail. It is arguable, however, that such simplification might make the words easier to understand but could make it more difficult for the learners to achieve global understanding of a text which is now dense with important information. It might be more profitable to simplify texts by adding examples, by using repetition and paraphrase and by increasing redundant information. In other words, by lengthening rather than shortening the text.

SLA
This is an abbreviation for Second Language Acquisition and is nor-

mally used to refer to research and theory related to the learning of second and foreign languages.

Supplementary materials

Materials designed to be used in addition to the core materials of a course. They are usually related to the development of skills of reading, writing, listening or speaking rather than to the learning of language items.

See **coursebook**.

Task based

This refers to materials or courses which are designed around a series of authentic tasks which give the learners experience of using the language in ways in which it is used in the 'real world' outside the classroom. They have no pre-determined language syllabus and the aim is for learners to learn from the tasks the language that they need to participate successfully in them. Examples of such tasks would be working out the itinerary of a journey from a timetable, completing a passport application form, ordering a product from a catalogue and giving directions to the post office.

See **authentic tasks**.

Text

Any scripted or recorded production of a language presented to learners of that language. A text can be written or spoken and could be, for example, a poem, a newspaper article, a passage about pollution, a song, a film, an extract from a novel or play, a passage written to exemplify the use of the past perfect, a recorded telephone conversation, a scripted dialogue or a speech by a politician.

Workbook

A book which contains extra practice activities for learners to work on in their own time. Usually the book is designed so that learners can write in it and often there is an answer key provided in the back of the book to give feedback to the learners.

For definitions of other terms frequently used in EFL and applied linguistics see:

Crystal, D. 1985. *A Dictionary of Linguistics and Phonetics*, 2nd edn. Oxford: Basil Blackwell.
Ellis, R. 1994. Glossary. In *The Study of Second Language Acquisition*, 692–729. Oxford: Oxford University Press.

Richards, J. C., J. Platt and H. Platt. 1992. *Longman Dictionary of Applied Linguistics*, 2nd edn. Harlow: Longman.

Tomlinson, B. 1984. A glossary of basic EFL terms. In A. Cunningsworth. *Evaluating and Selecting EFL Teaching Materials*, 80–102. London: Heinemann.

Acknowledgements

The author and publishers are grateful to the authors, publishers and others who have given permission for the use of copyright material identified in the text. It has not been possible to identify sources of all the material used and in such cases the publishers would welcome information from copyright owners.

Thompson, G. 1995 *Collins Concordance Cobuild Sampler 3: Reporting*, Collins Cobuild; *Collins Cobuild data sheets* Concordance for 'any', 1986. Collins Cobuild; McDonald, P., Edwards, R. A., and Greenhalgh, J. F. D. *Animal Nutrition*. Reprinted by permission of Addison Wesley Longman Ltd; Gower, R. and Bell, J. 1991. *Intermediate matters*. Reprinted by permission of Addison Wesley Longman Ltd; Nunan, D. and Lockwood, J. 1991. *The Australian English Course*. Cambridge University Press; Burns, A. Joyce, H. and Gollin, S. 1996. '*I see what you mean.' Using Spoken Discourse in The Classroom: A Handbook for Teachers*. NCELTR, Macquarie University (Sydney); Abbs, B. and Freebairn, I. *Developing Strategies*. Reprinted by permission of Addison Wesley Longman Ltd; *Collins Cobuild English Course 1*. Collins Cobuild; Littlejohn, A. and Hicks, D. 1996. *Cambridge English for Schools*. Cambridge University Press; Thomas, R. S. 1963 "*Sorry*" from *The Bread of Truth* HarperCollins Publishers Ltd.; McGinley, P. "*The Adversary*" from *Times Three*. Martin Secker & Warburg; Leon Leszek Szkutnik "*He Never Sent me Flowers*". (Warsaw); Adrian-Vallance and Edge. 1994. *Right Track. Student Book 1*. Reprinted by permission of Addison Wesley Longman Ltd; Gordimer, N. 1991. *My Son's Story*.

Introduction

Brian Tomlinson

This book concerns itself with what we could do in order to improve the quality of materials which are used for the teaching of second languages. I would like to start the book by considering some of the steps which I think we could take and at the same time introducing issues which are dealt with in the various chapters of the book. I should stress that although the contributors to this book are basically like-minded in their approach to the development of L2 materials many of the issues raised are controversial and some of the stances taken in the book are inevitably contradictory. In such cases we hope you will be informed, stimulated and able to make up your own mind by relating the authors' stances to your own experience.

I am going to argue that what those of us involved in materials development should do is to:

1 Clarify the terms and concepts commonly used in discussing materials development.
2 Carry out systematic evaluations of materials currently in use in order to find out to what degree and why they facilitate the learning of language.
3 Consider the potential applications of current research into second language acquisition.
4 Consider the potential applications of what both teachers and learners believe is valuable in the teaching and learning of a second or foreign language.
5 Pool our resources and bring together researchers, writers, teachers, learners and publishers in joint endeavours to develop quality materials.

Terms and concepts

Let me start by clarifying some of the basic terms and concepts which you will frequently encounter in this book.

Introduction

Materials

Most people associate the term 'language-learning materials' with coursebooks because that has been their main experience of using materials. However, in this book the term is used to refer to anything which is used by teachers or learners to facilitate the learning of a language. Materials could obviously be cassettes, videos, CD-Roms, dictionaries, grammar books, readers, workbooks or photocopied exercises. They could also be newspapers, food packages, photographs, live talks by invited native speakers, instructions given by a teacher, tasks written on cards or discussions between learners. In other words, they can be anything which is deliberately used to increase the learners' knowledge and/or experience of the language. Keeping this pragmatic concept of materials in mind can help materials developers to utilise as many sources of input as possible and, even more importantly, can help teachers to realise that they are also materials developers and that they are ultimately responsible for the materials that their learners use.

Materials development

Materials development refers to anything which is done by writers, teachers or learners to provide sources of language input and to exploit those sources in ways which maximise the likelihood of intake: in other words the supplying of information about and/or experience of the language in ways designed to promote language learning.

Materials developers might write textbooks, tell stories, bring advertisements into the classroom, express an opinion, provide samples of language use or read a poem aloud. Whatever they do to provide input they do so in principled ways related to what they know about how languages can be effectively learned. All the chapters in this book concentrate on the two vital questions of what should be given to the learners and what can be done with it to promote language learning.

Although many chapters in this book do focus on the development of coursebook materials (e.g. Jan Bell and Roger Gower in Chapter 5, Peter Donovan in Chapter 7, Hitomi Masuhara in Chapter 10 and Julian Edge and Sue Wharton in Chapter 13), a number of others focus on teacher development of materials (e.g. David Jolly and Rod Bolitho in Chapter 4 and Rod Ellis in Chapter 9) and some suggest ways in which learners can develop materials for themselves (e.g. Jane Willis in Chapter 2 and Alan Maley in Chapter 12).

Materials evaluation

This term refers to attempts to measure the value of materials. In many cases this is done impressionistically and consists of attempts to predict whether or not the materials will work, in the sense that the learners will be able to use them without too much difficulty and will enjoy the experience of doing so. A number of chapters in this book challenge this vague, subjective concept of evaluation and advocate more systematic and potentially revealing approaches. For example, Peter Donovan in Chapter 7 suggests ways in which thorough trialling of materials prior to publication can improve the quality of materials, Andrew Littlejohn in Chapter 8 proposes a more objective, analytical approach to evaluation and Rod Ellis in Chapter 10 argues the need for whilst-use and post-use evaluation of materials in order to find out what the actual effects of the materials are.

All the chapters in this book implicitly accept the view that for materials to be valuable the learning points should be potentially useful to the learners and that the learning procedures should maximise the likelihood of the learners actually learning what they want and need to learn. It is not necessarily enough that the learners enjoy and value the materials.

Language teaching

Most people think of teaching as the overt presentation of information by teachers to learners. In this book the term 'teaching' is used to refer to anything done by materials developers or teachers to facilitate the learning of the language. This could include the teacher standing at the front of the classroom explaining the conventions of direct speech in English, it could include a textbook providing samples of language use and guiding learners to make discoveries from them, it could include a textbook inviting learners to reflect on the way they have just read a passage or it could include the teacher providing the language a learner needs whilst participating in a challenging task. Teaching can be direct (in that it transmits information overtly to the learners) or it can be indirect (in that it helps the learners to discover things for themselves). Most chapters in this book focus on indirect teaching as the most effective way of facilitating the learning of a language. For example, in Chapters 1 and 2 Gwyneth Fox and Jane Willis suggest ways in which learners can be helped to make discoveries about language use by analysing similar samples of language in use, in Chapter 14 Grethe Hooper Hansen looks at ways in which learners can be helped to learn from information which is actually peripheral to the task they are focusing on and in Chapter 15 Brian Tomlinson proposes procedures which could enable self-access learners to learn for and about themselves.

Language learning

Learning is normally considered to be a conscious process which consists of the committing to memory of information relevant to what is being learned. Whilst such direct learning of, for example, spelling rules, conventions of greetings and vocabulary items can be useful to the language learner, it is arguable that much language learning consists of subconscious development of generalisations about how the language is used and of skills which apply these generalisations to acts of communication. Language learning can be explicit (i.e. the learners are aware of when and what they are learning) or it can be implicit (i.e. the learners are not aware of when and what they are learning). Language learning can also be of declarative knowledge (i.e. knowledge about the language system) or of procedural knowledge (i.e. knowledge of how the language is used). Most of the chapters in this book take the position that communicative competence is primarily achieved as a result of implicit, procedural learning. But most of them also acknowledge that explicit learning of both declarative and procedural knowledge is of value in helping learners to pay attention to salient features of language input and in helping them to participate in planned discourse (i.e. situations such as giving a talk or writing a story which allow time for planning and monitoring). Consequently many of the chapters view the main objectives of materials development as the provision of meaningful experience of language in use and of opportunities to reflect on this experience. This is the position taken by Ronald Carter, Rebecca Hughes and Michael McCarthy in Chapter 3, in which they argue for the need to expose learners to spoken English as it is actually used. It is also the position taken by Brian Tomlinson in Chapter 11 in which he proposes experiential ways of helping learners to transfer the high level skill of visualisation from their L1 reading process, by Grethe Hooper Hansen in Chapter 14 when she advocates multi-level experience of language in use and by Brian Tomlinson in Chapter 15 when he suggests an experiential approach to self-access learning of language.

Systematic evaluation of materials

In Chapter 6 Philip Prowse gets a number of well-known materials writers to reveal how they set about writing materials. The remarkable thing is that most of them follow their intuitions rather than an overt specification of objectives, principles and procedures. Obviously these intuitions are informed by experience of what is valuable to learners of a language and in many cases they lead to the development of valuable materials. But how useful it would be if we were able to carry out long-term, systematic evaluations of materials which are generally considered to be successful. I know of a number of famous textbook writers who do sit down and identify the popular and apparently successful features of their competitors so that they can clone these features and can avoid those features which appear to be unpopular and unsuccessful. Doing much more than this sort of *ad hoc* impressionistic evaluation of materials would involve considerable time and expenditure and would create great problems in controlling such variables as learner motivation, out of class experience and learner-teacher rapport. But longitudinal, systematic evaluations of popular materials could be undertaken by consortia of publishers, universities and associations such as MATSDA and could certainly provide empirically validated information about the actual effects of different types of language learning materials.

A number of chapters in this book try to push the profession forward towards using more systematic evaluation procedures as a means of informing materials development. In Chapter 7 Peter Donovan proposes rigorous and representative trialling and evaluation of materials prior to publication, in Chapter 8 Andrew Littlejohn exemplifies procedures for achieving thorough and informative analysis of what materials are actually doing and in Chapter 9 Rod Ellis insists that we should stop judging materials by their apparent appeal and start evaluating them by observing what the learners actually do when using the materials and by finding out what they seem to learn as a result of using them.

Second language acquisition research and materials development

> It seems clear that researchers cannot at present agree upon a single view of the learning process which can safely be applied wholesale to language teaching. (Tarone and Yule 1989)

> . . . no second language acquisition research can provide a definitive answer to the real problems of second language teaching at this point. . . . There is no predetermined correct theory of language teaching originating from second language acquisition research. (Cook 1996)

It is true that we should not expect definitive answers from second language acquisition research (SLA), nor should we expect one research-based model of language acquisition to triumph over all the others; and we must be careful not to prescribe applications of un-substantiated theories. But this should not stop us from applying what we **do** know about second and foreign language learning to the development of materials designed to facilitate that process. What we do know about language learning is a result of thousands of years of reflective teaching and of at least a century of experimental and observational research. If we combined the anecdotal and the empirical evidence available to us we could surely formulate criteria which could contribute to the development of successful materials. From the reports of many of the writers in this volume it would seem that they rely on their intuitions about language learning when they set out to write textbooks. This also seems to be true of many of the authors who have contributed reports on their processes for materials develop-ment to a book called *Getting Started: Materials Writers on Materials Writing* (Hidalgo, Hall and Jacobs 1995). The validity of their intuitions is demonstrated by the quality of their materials. But intuitions are only useful if they are informed by recent and relevant classroom experience and by knowledge of the findings and of recent second language acquisition research. And all of us could benefit from more explicit guidelines when setting out to develop materials for the classroom.

What I am arguing for is a compilation of learning principles and procedures which most teachers agree contribute to successful learning plus a compilation of principles and procedures recommended by most SLA researchers. A marriage of the two compilations could produce a list of principles and procedures which would provide a menu of potentially profitable options for materials developers from the class-room teacher adapting a coursebook unit to the author(s) setting out to develop a series of commercially published textbooks for the global market. Such a list should aim to be informative rather than prescriptive and should not give the impression that its recommendations are supported by conclusive evidence and by all teachers and researchers. And, of course, it needs to be supplemented by information about how the target language actually works (for ways of gaining such informa-tion, see, for example, Chapter 1 in this book by Gwyneth Fox, Chapter 2 by Jane Willis and Chapter 3 by Ronald Carter, Rebecca Hughes and Michael McCarthy).

Of course, one problem is that there is considerable disagreement amongst researchers about some of the main issues relevant to the teaching and learning of languages. Some argue that the main pre-requisite for language acquisition is comprehensible input (i.e. being exposed to language you can understand); others argue that the main

prerequisite is opportunity for output (i.e. situations in which you have
to actually use the language). Some researchers argue that the best way
to acquire a language is to do so naturally without formal lessons or
conscious study of the language; others argue that conscious attention
to distinctive features of the language is necessary for successful
language learning. Try skimming through an overview of second
language acquisition research (e.g. Ellis 1994a) and you will soon
become aware of some of the considerable (and, in my view, stimulating) disagreements amongst SLA researchers. Such disagreements are
inevitable, given our limited access to the actual mental processes
involved in the learning and using of languages and often the intensity
of the arguments provoke additional and illuminating research.
However I believe that there is now a sufficient consensus of opinion for
SLA research to be used as an informative base for the formulation of
criteria for the teaching of languages. The following is a summary of
what I think many SLA researchers would agree to be some of the basic
principles of second language acquisition relevant to the development of
materials for the teaching of languages.

Materials should achieve impact

Impact is achieved when materials have a noticeable effect on learners,
that is when the learners' curiosity, interest and attention are attracted.
If this is achieved there is a better chance that some of the language in
the materials will be taken in for processing.

Materials can achieve impact through:

a) novelty (e.g. unusual topics, illustrations and activities);
b) variety (e.g. breaking up the monotony of a unit routine with an
   unexpected activity; using many different text types taken from
   many different types of sources; using a number of different
   instructor voices on a cassette);
c) attractive presentation (e.g. use of attractive colours; lots of white
   space; use of photographs);
d) appealing content (e.g. topics of interest to the target learners; topics
   which offer the possibility of learning something new; engaging
   stories; universal themes; local references).

One obvious point is that impact is variable. What achieves impact with
a class in Brazil might not achieve the same impact with a class in
Austria. And what achieves impact with ten learners in a class might not
achieve impact with the other five. In order to maximise the likelihood

of achieving impact the writer needs to know as much as possible about the target learners and about what is likely to attract their attention. In order to achieve impact the writer also needs to offer choice. The more varied the choice of topics, texts and activities the more likely is the achievement of impact.

Materials should help learners to feel at ease

> Research has shown . . . the effects of various forms of anxiety on acquisition: the less anxious the learner, the better language acquisition proceeds. Similarly, relaxed and comfortable students apparently can learn more in shorter periods of time.
> (Dulay, Burt and Krashen 1982)

Although it is known that pressure can stimulate some types of language learners, I think that most researchers would agree that most language learners benefit from feeling at ease and that they lose opportunities for language learning when they feel anxious, uncomfortable or tense. Some materials developers argue that it is the responsibility of the teacher to help the learners to feel at ease and that the materials themselves can do very little to help. I disagree.

Materials can help learners to feel at ease in a number of ways. For example, I think that most learners:

- feel more comfortable with materials with lots of white space than they do with materials in which lots of different activities are crammed together on the same page;
- are more at ease with texts and illustrations that they can relate to their own culture than they are with those which are culturally exotic (and therefore potentially alien);
- are more relaxed with materials which are obviously trying to help them to learn than they are with materials which are always testing them. Feeling at ease can also be achieved through a 'voice' which is relaxed and supportive, through content and activities which en-courage the personal participation of the learners, through materials which relate the world of the book to the world of the learner and through the absence of activities which could threaten self-esteem and cause humiliation. To me the most important (and possibly least researched) factor is that of the 'voice' of the materials. Convention-ally, language learning materials are de-voiced and anonymous. They are usually written in a semi-formal style and reveal very little about the personality, interests and experiences of the writer. What I would like to see materials writers do is to chat to the learners casually in the

same way that good teachers do and to try to achieve personal contact with them by revealing their own preferences, interests and opinions. I would also like to see them try to achieve a personal voice (Beck, McKeown and Worthy 1995) by ensuring that what they say to the learners contains such features of orality as:
- informal discourse features (e.g. contracted forms, informal lexis);
- the active rather than the passive voice;
- concreteness (e.g. examples, anecdotes);
- inclusiveness (e.g. not signalling intellectual, linguistic or cultural superiority over the learners).

Materials should help learners to develop confidence

> Relaxed and self-confident learners learn faster. (Dulay, Burt and Krashen 1982)

Most materials developers recognise the need to help learners to develop confidence but many of them attempt to do so through a process of simplification. They try to help the learners to feel successful by asking them to use simple language to accomplish easy tasks. This approach is welcomed by many teachers and learners. But in my experience it often only succeeds in diminishing the learners. They become aware that the process is being simplified for them and that what they are doing bears little resemblance to actual language use. They also become aware that they are not really using their brains and that their apparent success is an illusion. And this awareness can even lead to a reduction in confidence. I prefer to attempt to build confidence through activities which try to 'push' learners slightly beyond their existing proficiency by engaging them in tasks which are stimulating, which are problematic but which are achievable too. It can also help if the activities encourage learners to use and to develop their existing extra-linguistic skills, such as those which involve being imaginative, being creative or being analytical. An elementary level learner can often gain greater confidence from making up a story, writing a short poem or making a grammatical discovery than she can from getting right a simple drill.

The value of engaging the learners' minds and utilising their existing skills seems to be becoming increasingly realised in countries which have decided to produce their own materials through textbook projects rather than to rely on global coursebooks which seem to underestimate the abilities of their learners. See Tomlinson (1995b) for a report on such projects in Bulgaria, Morocco and Namibia.

What is being taught should be perceived by learners as relevant and useful

Most teachers recognise the need to make the learners aware of the potential relevance and utility of the language and skills they are teaching. And researchers have confirmed the importance of this need. For example, Stevick (1976) cites experiments which have shown the positive effect on learning and recall of items that are of personal significance to the learner. And Krashen (1982) and Wenden (1987) report research showing the importance of apparent relevance and utility in language acquisition.

In ESP materials it is relatively easy to convince the learners that the teaching points are relevant and useful by relating them to known learner interests and to 'real-life' tasks which the learners need or might need to perform in the target language. In General English materials this is obviously more difficult; but it can be achieved by narrowing the target readership and/or by researching what the target learners are interested in and what they really want to learn the language for. An interesting example of such research was a questionnaire in Namibia which revealed that two of the most important reasons for secondary school students wanting to learn English were so they would be able to write love letters in English and so that they would be able to write letters of complaint for villagers to the village headman and from the village headman to local authorities.

Perception of relevance and utility can also be achieved by relating teaching points to interesting and challenging classroom tasks and by presenting them in ways which could facilitate the achievement of task outcomes desired by the learners. The 'new' learning points are not relevant and useful because they will help the learners to achieve long term academic or career objectives but because they could help the learners to achieve short-term task objectives now. Of course, this only works if the tasks are begun first and the teaching is then provided in response to discovered needs. This is much more difficult for the materials writer than the conventional approach of teaching a pre-determined point first and then getting the learners to practise and then produce it. But it can be much more valuable in creating relevance and utility for the teaching point; and it can be achieved by, for example, referring learners to 'help pages' before and/or after doing sub-tasks or by getting learners to make decisions about strategies they will use in a task and then referring them to 'help pages'. So, for example, learners could be asked to choose from (or add to) a list of project tasks and then to decide on strategies for achieving their project targets. Those learners who decide to research local documents could be referred to a section in the book which provides advice on scanning whereas those learners who decide to use questionnaires could be referred to a section which deals with writing questions.

Obviously providing the learners with a choice of topic and task is important if you are trying to achieve perception of relevance and utility in a general English textbook.

Materials should require and facilitate learner self-investment

Many researchers have written about the value of learning activities which require the learners to make discoveries for themselves. For example, Rutherford and Sharwood-Smith (1988) assert that the role of the classroom and of teaching materials is to aid the learner to make efficient use of the resources in order to facilitate self-discovery. Similar views are expressed by Bolitho and Tomlinson 1995; Tomlinson 1994a and Wright and Bolitho 1993.

It would seem that learners profit most if they invest interest, effort and attention in the learning activity. Materials can help them to achieve this by providing them with choices of focus and activity, by giving them topic control and by engaging them in learner-centred discovery activities. Again this is not as easy as assuming that what is taught should be learned but it is possible and extremely useful for textbooks to facilitate learner self-investment. In my experience, one of the most profitable ways of doing this is to get learners interested in a written or spoken text, to get them to respond to it globally and affectively and then to help them to analyse a particular linguistic feature of it in order to make discoveries for themselves (see Tomlinson 1994a for a specific example of this procedure). Other ways of achieving learner investment are involving the learners in mini-projects, involving them in finding supplementary materials for particular units in a book and giving them responsibility for making decisions about which texts to use and how to use them (an approach I saw used with great success in an Indonesian high school in which each group in a large class was given responsibility for one reading lesson per semester).

Learners must be ready to acquire the points being taught

> Certain structures are acquired only when learners are mentally ready for them. (Dulay, Burt and Krashen 1982)

Meisel, Clahsen and Pienemann (1981) have put forward the Multi-dimensional Model in which learners must have achieved readiness in order to learn developmental features (i.e. those constrained by developing speech-processing mechanisms – e.g. word order) but can make themselves ready at any time to learn variational features (i.e. those which are free – e.g. the copula 'be'). Pienemann (1985) claims that instruction can facilitate natural language acquisition processes if it coincides with learner readiness and can lead to increased speed and frequency of rule application and to application of rules in a wider range of linguistic contexts. He also claims that premature instruction can be harmful because it can lead to the production of erroneous forms, to substitution by less complex forms and to avoidance. Piennemann's theories have been criticised for the narrowness of their research and application (restricted mainly to syntax, according to Cook 1996) but I am sure most teachers would recognise the negative effects of premature instruction reported by Piennemann.

Krashen 1985 argues the need for roughly-tuned input which is comprehensible because it features what the learners are already familiar with; but which also contains the potential for acquiring other elements of the input which each learner might or might not be ready to learn (what Krashen refers to as i + 1 in which i represents what has already been learned and 1 represents what is available for learning). According to Krashen, each learner will only learn from the new input what he or she is ready to learn. Other discussions of the need for learner readiness can be found in Ellis 1990 (see especially pp. 152–8 for a discussion of variational and developmental features of readiness).

Readiness can be achieved by materials which create situations requiring the use of variational features not previously taught, by materials which ensure that the learners have gained sufficient mastery over the developmental features of the previous stage before teaching a new one and by materials which roughly tune the input so that it contains some features which are slightly above each learner's current state of proficiency. It can also be achieved by materials which get learners to focus attention on features of the target language which they have not yet acquired so that they might be more attentive to these features in future input.

But perhaps the most important lesson for materials developers from readiness research is that we cannot expect to select a particular point for teaching and assume that all the learners are ready and willing to learn it. It is important to remember that the learner is always in charge and that 'in the final analysis we can never completely control what the learner does, for HE (sic) selects and organises, whatever the input'. (Kennedy 1973: 76)

Materials should expose the learners to language in authentic use

Krashen (1985) makes the strong claim that comprehensible input in the target language is both necessary and sufficient for the acquisition of that language provided that learners are 'affectively disposed to "let in" the input they comprehend' (Ellis 1994a: 273). Few researchers would agree with such a strong claim but most would agree with a weaker claim that exposure to authentic use of the target language is necessary but not sufficient for the acquisition of that language.

Materials can provide exposure to authentic input through the advice they give, the instructions for their activities and the spoken and written texts they include. They can also stimulate exposure to authentic input through the activities they suggest (e.g. interviewing the teacher, doing a project in the local community, listening to the radio etc.). In order to facilitate acquisition the input must be comprehensible (i.e. understandable enough to achieve the purpose for responding to it). This means that there is no point in using long extracts from newspapers with beginners but it does not mean that beginners cannot be exposed to authentic input. They can follow instructions intended to elicit physical responses, they can listen to stories, they can listen to songs, they can fill in forms.

Ideally materials at all levels should provide frequent exposure to authentic input which is rich and varied. In other words the input should vary in style, mode, medium and purpose and should be rich in features which are characteristic of authentic discourse in the target language. And, if the learners want to be able to use the language for general communication, it is important that they are exposed to planned, semi-planned and unplanned discourse (e.g. a formal lecture, an informal radio interview and a spontaneous conversation).The materials should also stimulate learner interaction with the input rather than just passive reception of it. This does not necessarily mean that the learners should always produce language in response to the input; but it does mean that they should always do something mentally or physically in response to it.

See in particular, Chapters 1, 2, 3, 11, 12 and 15 of this book for arguments in favour of exposing learners to authentic materials.

The learners' attention should be drawn to linguistic features of the input

There seems to be an agreement amongst many researchers that helping learners to pay attention to linguistic features of authentic input can help them to eventually acquire some of those features. However it is important to understand that this claim does not represent a back to grammar movement. It is different from previous grammar teaching approaches in a number of ways. In the first place the attention paid to the language can be either conscious or subconscious. For example, the learners might be paying conscious attention to working out the attitude of one of the characters in a story but might be paying subconscious attention to the second conditionals which the character uses. Or they might be paying conscious attention to the second conditionals having been asked to locate them, and to make a generalisation about their function in the story. The important thing is that the learners become aware of a gap between a particular feature of their interlanguage (i.e. how they currently understand or use the feature) and the equivalent feature in the target language. Such noticing of the gap between output and input can act as an 'acquisition facilitator' (Seliger 1979). It does not do so by immediately changing the learner's internalised grammar but by alerting the learner to subsequent instances of the same feature in future input. So there is no instant change in the learners' proficiency (as is aimed at by such grammar teaching approaches as the conventional Presentation, Practice, Production approach). There is, however, an increased likelihood of eventual acquisition provided that the learners receive future relevant input.

White (1990) argues that there are some features of the L2 which learners need to be focused on because the deceptively apparent similarities with L1 features make it impossible for the learners to otherwise notice certain points of mismatch between their interlanguage and the target language. And Schmidt (1992) puts forward a powerful argument for approaches which help learners to note the gap between their use of specific features of English and the way these features are used by native speakers. Inviting learners to compare their use of, say, indirect speech with the way it is used in a transcript of a native speaker conversation would be one such approach and could quite easily be built into coursebook materials.

Gwyneth Fox in Chapter 1 of this book and Jane Willis in Chapter 2 exemplify ways of helping learners to pay attention to linguistic features of their input.

Materials should provide the learners with opportunities to use the target language to achieve communicative purposes

Most researchers seem to agree that learners should be given opportunities to use language for communication rather than just to practise it in situations controlled by the teacher and the materials. Using language for communication involves attempts to achieve a purpose in a

situation in which the content, strategies and expression of the interaction are determined by the learners. Such attempts can enable the
learners to 'check' the effectiveness of their internal hypotheses,
especially if the activities stimulate them into 'pushed output' (Swain
1985) which is slightly above their current proficiency. They also help
the learners to automatise their existing procedural knowledge (i.e. their
knowledge of how the language is used) and to develop strategic
competence (Canale and Swain 1980). This is especially so if the
opportunities for use are interactive and encourage negotiation of
meaning (Allwright 1984: 157). In addition, communicative interaction
can provide opportunities for picking up language from the new input
generated, as well as opportunities for learner output to become an
informative source of input (Sharwood-Smith 1981). Ideally teaching
materials should provide opportunities for such interaction in a variety
of discourse modes ranging from planned to unplanned (Ellis 1990:
191).

Interaction can be achieved through, for example:

- information or opinion gap activities which require learners to
  communicate with each other and/or the teacher in order to close the
  gap (e.g. finding out what food and drink people would like at the
  class party);
- post-listening and post-reading activities which require the learners to
  use information from the text to achieve a communicative purpose
  (e.g. deciding what television programmes to watch, discussing who
  to vote for, writing a review of a book or film);
- creative writing and creative speaking activities such as writing a
  story or improvising a drama;
- formal instruction given in the target language either on the language
  itself or on another subject:
  > We need to recognise that teaching intended as formal instruc-
  > tion also serves as interaction. Formal instruction does more
  > than teach a specific item: it also exposes learners to features
  > which are not the focus of the lesson. (Ellis 1990)

The value of materials facilitating learner interaction is stressed in this
book by Alan Maley in Chapter 12, by Julian Edge and Sue Wharton in
Chapter 13 and by Brian Tomlinson in Chapter 15.

Materials should take into account that the positive effects of instruction are usually delayed

Research into the acquisition of language shows that it is a gradual
rather than an instantaneous process and that this is equally true for

instructed as well as informal acquisition. Acquisition results from the gradual and dynamic process of internal generalisation rather than from instant adjustments to the learner's internal grammar. It follows that learners cannot be expected to learn a new feature and be able to use it in the same lesson. They might be able to rehearse the feature, to retrieve it from short-term memory or to produce it when prompted by the teacher or the materials. But this does not mean that learning has taken place. I am sure most of you are familiar with the situation in which learners get a new feature correct in the lesson in which it is taught but then get it wrong the following week. This is partly because they have not yet had enough time, instruction and exposure for learning to have taken place.

The inevitable delayed effect of instruction suggests that no textbook can really succeed which teaches features of the language one at a time and expects the learners to be able to use them straightaway. But this incremental approach is popular with many publishers, writers, teachers and learners as it can provide a reassuring illusion of system, simplicity and progress. Therefore adaptation of existing approaches rather than replacement with radical new ones is the strategy most likely to succeed. So, for example, the conventional textbook approach of PPP (Presentation-Practice-Production) could be used to promote durable learning if the objective of the Production phase was seen as reinforcement rather than correct production and if this was followed in subsequent units by more exposure and more presentation relating to the same feature. Or if the Production phase was postponed to another unit which was placed after further exposure, instruction and practice had been provided. Or if the initial Production phase was used to provide output which would enable the learners to notice the mismatch between what they are doing and what native speakers typically do.

In my view, in order to facilitate the gradual process of acquisition it is important for materials to recycle instruction and to provide frequent and ample exposure to the instructed language features in communicative use. It is equally important that the learners are not forced into premature production of the instructed features (they will get them wrong) and that tests of proficiency are not conducted immediately after instruction (they will indicate failure).

Ellis (1990) reports on research revealing the delayed effect of instruction and in Chapter 9 of this book he argues the need for post-use evaluation of materials to find out what learners have eventually learned as a result of using them.

Materials should take into account that learners differ in learning styles

Different learners have different preferred learning styles. So, for example, those learners with a preference for studial learning are much more likely to gain from explicit grammar teaching than those who prefer experiential learning. And those who prefer experiential learning are more likely to gain from reading a story with a predominant grammatical feature (e.g. reported speech) than they are from being taught that feature explicitly. This means that activities should be variable and should cater for all learning styles. An analysis of most current coursebooks will reveal a tendency to favour learners with a preference for studial learning and an apparent assumption that all learners are equally capable of benefiting from this style of learning. Likewise an analysis of the teaching and testing of foreign languages in formal education systems throughout the world will reveal that studial learners (who are actually in the minority) are at an advantage.

Styles of learning which need to be catered for in language learning materials include:

– visual (e.g. the learner prefers to see the language written down);
– auditory (e.g. the learner prefers to hear the language);
– kinaesthetic (e.g. the learner prefers to do something physical, such as following instructions);
– studial (e.g. the learner likes to pay conscious attention to the linguistic features of the language and wants to be correct);
– experiential (e.g. the learner likes to use the language and is more concerned with communication than with correctness);
– analytic (e.g. the learner prefers to focus on discrete bits of the language and to learn them one by one);
– global (e.g. the learner is happy to respond to whole chunks of language at a time and to pick up from them whatever language she can);
– dependent (e.g. the learner prefers to learn from a teacher and from a book);
– independent (e.g. the learner is happy to learn from their own experience of the language and to use autonomous learning strategies).

I think a learner's preference for a particular learning style is variable and depends, for example, on what is being learned, where it is being learned, who it is being learned with and what it is being learned for. For example, I am happy to be experiential, global and kinaesthetic when learning Japanese out of interest with a group of relaxed adult learners and with a teacher who does not keep correcting me. But I am more likely to be analytic and visual when learning French for examination purposes in a class of competitive students and with a teacher who keeps on correcting me. And, of course, learners can be helped to gain from learning styles other than their preferred style. The important point for materials developers is that they are aware of and cater for differences of preferred learning styles in their materials and that they do not assume that all learners can benefit from the same approaches as the 'good language learner' (see Ellis 1994a: 546–50).

See Oxford and Anderson (1995) for an overview of research into learning styles.

Materials should take into account that learners differ in affective attitudes

> . . . the learner's motives, emotions, and attitudes screen what is presented in the language classroom . . . This affective screening is highly individual and results in different learning rates and results. (Dulay, Burt and Krashen 1982)

Ideally language learners should have strong and consistent motivation and they should also have positive feelings towards the target language, their teachers, their fellow learners and the materials they are using. But, of course, the ideal learner does not exist and even if she did exist one day she would no longer be the ideal learner the next day. Each class of learners using the same materials will differ from each other in terms of long- and short-term motivation and of feelings and attitudes about the language, their teachers, their fellow learners and their learning materials, and of attitudes towards the language, the teacher and the materials. Obviously no materials developer can cater for all these affective variables but it is important for anybody who is writing learning materials to be aware of the inevitable attitudinal differences of the users of the materials.

One obvious implication for the materials developer is 'to diversify language instruction as much as possible based upon the variety of cognitive styles' (Larsen-Freeman and Long 1991) and the variety of affective attitudes likely to be found among a typical class of learners. Ways of doing this include:

– providing choices of different types of text;
– providing choices of different types of activities;
– providing optional extras for the more positive and motivated learners;
– providing variety;

- including units in which the value of learning English is a topic for discussion;
- including activities which involve the learners in discussing their attitudes and feelings about the course and the materials;
- researching and catering for the diverse interests of the identified target learners;
- being aware of the cultural sensitivities of the target learners;
- giving general and specific advice in the teacher's book on how to respond to negative learners (e.g. not forcing reluctant individuals to take part in groupwork).

For reports on research into affective differences see Ellis 1984: 471–83 and Wenden and Rubin 1987.

For specific suggestions on how materials can cater for learner differences see Tomlinson 1996 and Chapter 12 by Alan Maley and Chapter 13 by Julian Edge and Sue Wharton in this book.

Materials should permit a silent period at the beginning of instruction

It has been shown that it can be extremely valuable to delay L2 speaking at the beginning of a course until learners have gained sufficient exposure to the target language and sufficient confidence in understanding it. This silent period can facilitate the development of an effective internalised grammar which can help learners to achieve proficiency when they eventually start to speak in the L2. There is some controversy about the actual value of the silent period and some learners seem to use the silence to avoid learning the language. However I think most researchers would agree that forcing immediate production in the new language can damage the reluctant speaker affectively and linguistically and many would agree with Dulay, Burt and Krashen that:

> . . . communication situations in which students are permitted to remain silent or respond in their first language may be the most effective approach for the early phases of language instruction. This approach approximates what language learners of all ages have been observed to do naturally, and it appears to be more effective than forcing full two-way communication from the very beginning of L2 acquisition. (1982: 25–6)

The important point is that the materials should not force premature speaking in the target language and they should not force silence either. Ways of giving learners the possibility of not speaking until they are ready include:

- starting the course with a Total Physical Response (TPR) approach in which the learners respond physically to oral instructions from a teacher or cassette (see Asher 1977; Tomlinson 1994b);
- starting with a listening comprehension approach in which the learners listen to stories in the target language which are made accessible through the use of sound effects, visual aids and dramatic movement by the teacher;
- permitting the learners to respond to target language questions by using their first language or through drawings and gestures.

A possible extension of the principle of permitting silence is to introduce most new language points (regardless of the learners' level) through activities which initially require comprehension but not production. This was an approach which we called TPR Plus and which we used on the PKG Project in Indonesian secondary schools. It usually involved introducing new vocabulary or structures through stories which the learners responded to by drawing and/or using their first language and through activities in which the whole class mimed stories by following oral instructions from the teacher (see Tomlinson 1990; 1994b).

For discussion of research into the silent period see Ellis 1994a: 82–84; Krashen 1982; Saville-Troike 1988.

Materials should maximise learning potential by encouraging intellectual, aesthetic and emotional involvement which stimulates both right and left brain activities

A narrowly focused series of activities which require very little cognitive processing (e.g. mechanical drills; rule learning; simple transformation activities) usually leads to shallow and ephemeral learning unless linked to other activities which stimulate mental and affective processing. However a varied series of activities making, for example, analytic, creative, evaluative and rehearsal demands on processing capacity can lead to deeper and more durable learning. In order for this deeper learning to be facilitated it is very important that the content of the materials is not trivial or banal and that it stimulates thoughts and feelings in the learners. It is also important that the activities are not too simple and that they cannot be too easily achieved without the learners making use of their previous experience and their brains.

The maximisation of the brain's learning potential is a fundamental principle of Lozanov's Suggestopedia in which, 'he enables the learner to receive the information through different cerebral processes and in different states of consciousness so that it is stored in many different parts of the brain, maximising recall' (Hooper Hansen 1992). Suggestopedia does this through engaging the learners in a variety of left and right brain activities in the same lesson (e.g. reciting a dialogue, dancing to instructions, singing a song, doing a substitution drill, writing a story). Whilst not everybody would accept the procedures of Suggestopedia, most researchers seem to agree on the value of maximising the brain's capacity during language learning and the best textbooks already do contain within each unit a variety of different left and right brain activities.

For an account of the principles of Suggestopedia see Lozanov 1978 and Chapter 14 in this book by Grethe Hooper Hansen.

Materials should not rely too much on controlled practice

It is interesting that there seems to be very little research which indicates that controlled practice activities are valuable. Sharwood-Smith (1981) does say that, 'it is clear and uncontroversial to say that most spontaneous performance is attained by dint of practice', but he provides no evidence to support this very strong claim. Also Bialystok (1988) says that automaticity is achieved through practice but provides no evidence to support her claim. In the absence of any compelling evidence most researchers seem to agree with Ellis who says that 'controlled practice appears to have little long term effect on the accuracy with which new structures are performed' (Ellis 1990: 192) and 'has little effect on fluency' (Ellis and Rathbone 1987).

Yet controlled grammar practice activities still feature significantly in popular coursebooks and are considered to be useful by many teachers and by many learners. This is especially true of dialogue practice which has been popular in many methodologies for the last 30 years without there being any substantial research evidence to support it (see Tomlinson 1995a). In a recent analysis of new low level coursebooks I found that nine out of ten of them contained more opportunities for controlled practice than they did for language use. It is possible that right now all over the world learners are wasting their time doing drills and listening to and repeating dialogues.

Materials should provide opportunities for outcome feedback

Feedback which is focused first on the effectiveness of the outcome rather than just on the accuracy of the output can lead to output becoming a profitable source of input. Or in other words, if the language that the learner produces is evaluated in relation to the purpose for which it is used that language can become a powerful and informative source of information about language use. Thus a learner who fails to achieve a particular communicative purpose (e.g. borrowing something, instructing someone how to play a game, persuading someone to do something) is more likely to gain from negative feedback on the effectiveness of their use of language than a learner whose language is corrected without reference to any non-linguistic outcome. It is very important, therefore, for materials developers to make sure that language production activities have intended outcomes other than just practising language.

The value of outcome feedback is stressed by Brian Tomlinson in Chapter 15 in this book.

To find out more about some of the principles of language learning outlined above you could make use of the index of one of the following books:

Cook, V. 1996. *Second Language Learning and Second Language Teaching* (new edn). London: Edward Arnold.

Ellis, R. 1994. *The Study of Second Language Acquisition*. Oxford: Oxford University Press.

Larsen-Freeman, D. and M. Long 1991. *An Introduction to Second Language Acquisition Research*. London: Longman.

What teachers and learners believe and want

I have argued above that materials developers should take account of what researchers have told us about language acquisition. I would also argue that they should pay more attention to what teachers and learners believe about the best ways to learn a language and also to what they want from the materials they use.

Teachers spend far more time observing and influencing the language learning process than do researchers or materials developers. Yet little research has been done into what teachers believe is valuable for language learning and little account is taken of what teachers really want. In this book Hitomi Masuhara in Chapter 10 argues the need to find out what teachers really want from coursebooks and she puts forward suggestions for how this information could be gained and made use of. Also Peter Donovan in Chapter 7 describes how attempts have been made to find out exactly what teachers think and feel about trial versions of coursebooks so that their views can influence the published versions. David Jolly and Rod Bolitho in Chapter 4 propose a framework which could help teachers to adapt materials and to write materials themselves; and Rod Ellis in Chapter 9 outlines a way in which teachers can improve materials as a result of whilst and post-use evaluation of them.

There have been attempts to involve learners in the evaluation of courses and materials (see Alderson 1985a for an interesting account of post-course evaluations which involved contacting the learners after their courses had finished) and a number of researchers have kept diaries recording their own experiences as learners of a foreign language (e.g. Schmidt and Frota 1986) but little systematic research has been published on what learners actually want their learning materials to do (see Johnson 1995 for an account of what one adult learner wants from her learning materials).

One exceptional example of trying to make use of both learner and teacher beliefs and wants was the Namibia Textbook Project. Prior to the writing of the Grade 10 English textbook, *On Target* (1995), teachers and students all over the country were consulted via questionnaires. Their responses were then made use of when 30 teachers met together to design and write the book. The first draft of the book was completed by these teachers at an eight day workshop and it was then trialled all over the country before being revised for publication by an editorial panel. Such consultation and collaboration is rare in materials development and could act as a model for textbook writing. See Tomlinson (1995b) for a description of this and other similar projects.

Collaboration

The Namibian Textbook Project mentioned above is a classic example of the value of pooling resources. On page iv of *On Target* (1995) 40 contributors are acknowledged. Some of these were teachers, some were curriculum developers, some were publishers, some were administrators, some were university lecturers and researchers, some were examiners, one was a published novelist and all of them made a significant contribution to the development of the book. This bringing together of expertise in a collaborative endeavour is extremely rare and, as one of the contributors to the Project, I can definitely say it was productive. Too often in my experience researchers have made theoretical claims without developing applications of them, writers have ignored theory and have followed procedural rather than principled instincts, teachers have complained without making efforts to exert an influence, learners have been ignored and publishers have been driven by considerations of what they know they can sell. We all have constraints on our time and our actions but it must be possible and potentially valuable for us to get together to pool our resources and share our expertise in a joint endeavour to develop materials which offer language learners maximum opportunities for successful learning. This bringing together of different areas of knowledge and expertise is the main aim of MATSDA and it is one of the objectives of this book. The contributors to *Materials Development in Language Teaching* include classroom teachers, researchers, university lecturers, teacher trainers, textbook writers and publishers and we hope that our pooling of knowledge and ideas will help you to use, adapt and develop materials in effective ways.

1 Using corpus data in the classroom

Gwyneth Fox

Introduction

During the past 20 years there has been a revolution in the way in which language can be studied. Because of the rapid development in the ability of computers to handle large amounts of language data, it is now possible to build language corpora which allow researchers to analyse how the language is being used at the present time, or indeed how it was used at particular times in the past. Before now researchers had basically to extrapolate trends, usages and so on from a small sample of language – their own use, that of people around them, the language they heard and read. The statements made were idiolectal and intuitive. Often they were right – or nearly right – as far as they went; but there was frequently more that could, and should, be said. Dictionaries, grammars, and other reference books compiled before the advent of corpora tended to rely heavily on books that were already published: a new grammar was likely to be based on previously published grammars, a new dictionary likewise. But with the advent of corpora researchers can – indeed should – start afresh, where possible laying aside their intuitions and looking at what the data tells them. The first corpora – which included the Survey of English Usage, established in the early 1960s (Svartvik and Quirk, 1980), the Brown Corpus, completed in 1964 (Kucera and Francis 1967), and the Lancaster-Oslo-Bergen (LOB) Corpus, completed in 1978 (Hofland and Johansson 1982) were, in today's terms, small – but it must be remembered that never before had researchers been able to look at so many examples of the way in which a particular word was used, or the way in which words of a particular grammatical class typically behaved.

Nowadays, computers have developed in such a way that there is no longer any restriction on the size a corpus can be. A corpus is nothing more nor less than a collection of texts input into a computer, and the number of texts will depend upon the uses that will be made of the corpus. For example, if teachers want to know what type of English is likely to be needed by students studying for an accountancy degree, it is possible to build a corpus of the books the students are required to read, plus the lectures they are required to attend; and then to analyse the accumulated data. This would identify the relevant grammar patterns and vocabulary items that students would come across, and would thus provide teachers with material that needs to be taught. This is, of course, only the first stage in the whole teaching-learning process; it would not, for example, identify how the items might be taught or even how they should be built into a syllabus. It should, however, mean that students will understand the relevance of the items to their particular situation, which will assist the learning of them. Specialised corpora of this kind are being built at the present time by teachers in a number of different universities. Further details of specialised corpora of this type will be found in Chapter 2 of this book by Jane Willis.

It is, however, also possible to build a much more general corpus, which is available for research into the language as a whole. For purposes such as these far more data is needed, coming from as wide a variety of sources as possible. For example, The Bank of English, the corpus being built by COBUILD at the University of Birmingham, currently has in it approximately 250 million words of current English: written and spoken, formal and informal, British, American and Australian. 250 million words of running text is a lot of data. Some linguists argue that it is too much. Why then do the COBUILD researchers feel that so much data is necessary for their purposes? And how is this relevant to language teachers in the classroom?

Frequency information

The first important reason for so much data is to do with frequency – the frequency of words and the frequency of individual senses of words. By doing a frequency count, it is possible to find out the relative frequency of words, ranging from the most frequent (always the word 'the' in a general corpus of English) through to the least frequent; indeed there will always be a very high proportion (up to 50 per cent) of hapaxlegomena, words which occur only once. Words which occur only a few times are usually more or less ignored by corpus linguists, as there is not enough evidence as to how they are typically used in the language.

It is easy to discover which is most frequent among words which are near synonyms, for example 'start', 'begin' and 'commence'. In the whole Bank of English, 'start' is about 10 per cent more frequent than 'begin', with 'commence' being very infrequent having just over 1,000 citations as against nearly 125,000 for 'start'. In the spoken data, 'start' is still more frequent than 'begin', but only just. 'Commence' is hardly used at all – there are only 99 examples, including those used in radio broadcasts.

Spelling variants also vary in frequency: 'judgment' is twice as common as 'judgement', and there are approximately five citations of 'inquire' to every four citations of 'enquire'.

Although absolute frequency is not the only criterion for selecting what to teach, it is one important variable. Frequency information of this kind allows teachers, where appropriate, to focus on the most common words, ensuring that students know and can actively use them. It is equally important to know which words are infrequent, as less learning effort need usually be expended on them. Infrequent words are usually topic-specific, and can be acquired when needed. It is the general vocabulary, those words used across the board in a wide range of topics, that is more difficult to acquire, as the meaning is likely to vary according to the context.

It has been argued that the common words are actually the ones which need less teaching as frequency of exposure will do the job for you. This argument seems not to hold water when you read the work of even quite advanced students, or listen to them speak. Their language is often stilted, too formal and too high-level; and when it is analysed it is seen that the most common words are used less frequently, and in fewer contexts, than they would be by native speakers of English. There are many reasons for this, one of which is probably the lack of attention that has been drawn to them in the classroom.

The points made about the frequency of words are equally valid for the frequency of senses. More teaching and learning effort should go into the most frequent senses of words than into rare senses. There is an intransitive use of 'give' as in 'the rope gave', which all native speakers know, but which is rarely used. The contexts it is used in are few and easily predictable. If students come across it, they will quickly under-stand its meaning. However, the transitive use of 'give' in clauses such as 'she gave him a really lovely smile', and 'he gave an extremely boring talk' is so common that many native speakers hardly even notice it. The meaning of 'give' here is easily intelligible to learners, but what they might not realise is how important this particular structural pattern is. Native speakers use it all the time, as it allows us to focus on the event rather than on the action, and also to give as much (or as little) information as we want to about that event. Often there is a related verb that could be chosen instead. For example, 'he gave her a smile' semantically means nearly the same as 'he smiled at her' – although they are potentially very different in what they indicate. Both are relevant to learners, and both should be taught, not merely for understanding but also for active use. Other similar pairs are 'she kicked the door' and 'she gave the door a kick', 'she looked round the room', and 'she gave a look round the room', 'she giggled' and 'she gave a giggle', and so on. Some related verbs on the other hand, are semantically different: 'he gave a talk' could not be replaced by 'he talked', nor could 'he gave an account of his journey' be replaced by the verb 'he accounted'. In English text this structure is extremely common and students should be encouraged to use it in appropriate situations.

A quick look at a number of concordance lines (see the Glossary) for 'give' will show the predominance of this structure (and will probably not show any citations for intransitive 'give'). Students presented with the lines will quickly discover that the sense of 'give' meaning 'hand over' which they have been taught is not nearly as frequent as the delexicalised structures, where most of the meaning is expressed by the noun group rather than the verb. Students might also realise for themselves that an alternative structure could sometimes have been chosen, one where the noun is expressed by a similar verb:

> He gave her a smile – He smiled at her
> He gave the door a kick – He kicked the door

One suggestion for homework is that students can be asked to collect all the examples of 'give' which they see and hear in a 24-hour period. If they then pool these examples, they should find out for themselves how the word is typically used – always providing, of course, that they have not relied too heavily on the classroom and their coursebook! All levels of student can do this, and in many cases a discussion will follow as to why this structure is often chosen in preference to one in which the verb carries most of the meaning.

This is by no means the only instance in teaching where we focus on the concrete meaning of a word, rather than on abstract or figurative ones, in spite of the fact that the word is more likely to be met in a non-concrete context. 'Way' does mean 'direction' or 'route', as in 'Do you know the way?' or 'I drove the wrong way round a roundabout'. But it much more frequently refers to how to do something, as in 'different ways of cooking fish' and 'the only way out of a difficult situation'. Yet the coursebooks examined more frequently focus on the former than on the latter.

The reasons for this are perhaps sound: it is easier to learn a concrete meaning than an abstract one; and most concrete meanings are said to be acquired by native speakers prior to the acquisition of abstract ones. Frequency of use cannot be the sole criterion for selection. But equally, frequency of use should not be ignored in the classroom, especially as students are likely to meet the more common uses out of the class-room.

The word 'thing' is a further example. It does, of course, mean 'object', as in 'What's that thing over there?'. But it is more often used in a less concrete way: We get blamed for all kinds of things.

> Literacy isn't the same thing as intelligence.
> A really strange thing happened yesterday.

And it is also frequently used as a prefacing device to tell the person you are addressing what your attitude is to what you are saying.

into this but obviously the important	thing	is it's the groups you work with <ZFl> i+ if they
write a blockbuster legal thriller. The ironic	thing	is that best-selling legal thrillers generally are
the exotic green peppercorn'. The exciting	thing	is while we have 20 or 30 different foods
these are all very bad songs, but the scary	thing	is: Not one song I've named so far is a winner
long and sometimes torrid session. The sad	thing	is that Geoff Boycott was not there to help him.
running flat out during cold spells. The best	thing	is to replace it as soon as possible. Most boilers
very, very confident but the most important	thing	Is that I am not frightened of winning the Open,'
but no one wanted to know. The stupid	thing	is they all heard Crazy years ago, but not one of
by what my daughter has done. The sad	thing	is she is pregnant and has been for four
some light training, that's all. The frustrating	thing	is he was in such fantastic shape before suffering
for a number of years, but the comforting	thing	is that every year your clay will be getting easier
They're all in midfield and the disturbing	thing	is Ossie doesn't seem capable of recognising it.
evolved a good answer; the intriguing	thing	is the way they did so. The process of evolving
the sun. Nothing odd in that. The strange	thing	is that the star it orbits is a neutron star,
by, let them make their case. The crucial	thing	is to change the law so that the next time a
the world cries out for action. The funny	thing	is, Mr Major has made those choices already. A
are widely misunderstood. The crucial	thing	is to avoid taking the parallel between

Figure 1   *Concordance lines for 'thing'*

Because you can use 'thing' more or less any time when you do not want to specify more precisely what you are saying, it is an extremely useful word, but learners rarely use it as frequently as native speakers do. This sometimes makes their language too precise and therefore it sounds slightly stilted and unnatural. By getting them to study a short concordance of 'thing', they can be alerted to all its uses and can try to use these themselves.

This example points up one of the significant differences between classroom language and language in the real world. Most classroom language is planned (or, at least, semi-planned) and therefore is lacking in some of the common features of unplanned discourse, which include the use of vague language items such as 'something like that', 'something', 'things like that', and, of course, 'thing' itself. Crystal and Davy (1975) pointed out the importance of lack of precision in informal conversation, and Channell (1994) looks in great detail at this whole area, frequently backing up her statements by examples taken from COBUILD data.

Contexts and co-texts

Another reason for analysing a large amount of data is that it allows us to discover the typical contexts and co-texts of words (i.e. the situational and linguistic environments they are commonly used in). Take 'break out' as an example. The subjects of the verb are typically unpleasant, as Figure 2 shows.

should return to Congress should hostilities	break out.	The President had not been given a 'green
the civil war and that fighting would	break out	again as soon as outside troops were
Thus, if Charteris said that strikes were	breaking out	in Germany, Haig predicted an imminent
of the city or another, the fighting simply	breaks out	again and all that may have been gained is
violent and destructive nature. Fighting also	broke out	among the rioters themselves, to such a
from the pilot's head, whilst a small fire	broke out	behind the propeller. Clearly there was a
and London. When the Second World War	broke out,	he was an assistant at the Curtis Institute
36.92. As we left a fierce discussion	broke out	at the table next door about whether Tramp
fall. As long as no serious world conflicts	broke out,	the target was a Reserve force of 600,000
a soldier. As news of the killings spread, riots	broke out	in the West Bank and Gaza strip. The army
to a Bahamas government spokesman, panic	broke out	as the boat was being towed to shore and
with explosives but there was a fire which	broke out	and destroyed whole areas, blocks of this
tried to move them on. A series of fights then	broke out	which developed into running skirmishes
several hundred policemen. The latest clashes	broke out	yesterday, when the Tigers killed at least ten
the company. Toward the end of 1987 a row	broke out	between Eurotunnel and the tunneling firm
day last year when massive demonstrations	broke out	in Bucharest leading to the downfall of the
to become scorched by May and huge fires	broke out,	including a large chunk of the Broadwater
victims have died. Before the epidemic	broke out	Peru had already stocked up on large
to climb Mount Everest when World War II	broke out	and the British put him in a POW camp in
the police to discuss violence which has	broken out	for the past two nights, following the

Figure 2 Concordance lines for 'break out'

As can be seen, it is such things as 'wars', 'fights', 'strikes', 'riots' and 'fire' that break out. If you heard on the radio, 'Peace broke out in Krajuna today' you would notice it because the verb is deliberately being used in an atypical, marked way, with an optimistic subject. This is not a use that you would teach students, although you might point it out to them as being unusual.

Information of this kind about words is not necessarily new. But corpus evidence allows us to make statements with greater confidence than we could if we had to rely totally on our own intuition.

This concordance for 'break out' could be used by the students in the classroom to work out the information for themselves. Once they do, they are unlikely to forget it. Students can then be asked to look out for other words which have restricted subjects. Some are obvious: it is, needless to say, typically 'the police' who arrest someone, or 'a woman' who gives birth to a child; this is real-world information which students bring with them to a classroom. But others are less obvious: why, for example, should it be unpleasant things such as panic, fear, disillusionment, frost and cold weather that set in, rather than pleasant things like certainty, joy, and nice sunny weather? (See Figure 3 below.)

for doctors is that once the infection has	set in, it can spread to the mother's heart, kidney,
wore a cap always now, since the baldness had	set In, wore it even in the house. A loyal fellow,
to return to the place where the disillusionment	set in, even though this may be a favourite painting
at least 10 weeks of good weather before winter	set in, probably more, and . . . much will be done by
would spiral into the pain, depression would	set In, and I would spend the rest of the night in
Many are fit and active; but, as frailty and age	set in, they require Increasing amounts of care and
debris for so long that a polar winter could have	set in, even in the tropics. If it had hit water # more
the Jordanian decline may not yet have	set in, he has surely reached his apogee. <t>
of 1981. In July of that year, as the recession	set in, the monetary measure was at its lowest level
with the detective, and a last-minute panic had	set in. Terry had placed the call, had described the
enfeebled Chancellor because political panic has	set in over rising unemployment levels .<t> In quick
across his stumps to be lbw to Srinath, panic	set in. England lost their last seven wickets for 10
reached [and after which a fairly rapid decline	set in] were 1982 for Germany [58.1 per cent], 1984
20 castles and 30 parishes before decline	set in during the fifteenth century. The last monk left
is that it reveals how rapidly the decline has	set in. Curiously, the decade after the war was a
As the tour wore on, however, some doubts	set In. Boipatong is a tiny place, barely a thousand
worked well far from it. The serious problems	set in when reinsurers lost sight of the original risk

Figure 3   *Concordance lines for 'set in'*

One, perhaps slightly cynical, explanation could be that most pleasant things are ephemeral, and therefore do not have the time to 'set in'. In that case, why do English and French differ? In English we could say 'the cold weather set in' but are unlikely to say 'nice hot weather set in', whereas the French verb 's'installer' can be used for both nasty and nice weather.

There are a large number of words which are typically used of either men or women, but not both. Again, some of these are obvious: real-world knowledge tells us that women are more likely to be nubile and buxom than men. But why are women never described as debonair, and rarely as taciturn? These surely are characteristics which could belong to either sex. Of course, one of the exciting things about language is that you can do anything you like with it, you can play with it and make it fit your needs. But what corpus data shows is how most people use a word when they are not trying to make a point, when they are not trying to be different, but because it is the word that seems to come automatically and naturally to them when they are focusing on the situation they are describing or the topic they are discussing rather than on the language they are using. Again, a lot of examples are needed before we can be sure that the examples we have are of what might be called the everyday, boring use of language, language which is not striving for effect, language which is used in a similar way by a large number of people. If 500 people have used the word 'taciturn' to refer to men, and 20 have used it to refer to women, then the 'unmarked' use, the use that does not call great attention to itself, must be with men rather than women.

Grammar

A central element of language teaching is that of grammar. Indeed, most syllabuses are still grammar-based, whether overtly or covertly. But is the grammar that is taught really the grammar of the language? Are the preoccupations of the coursebooks as important in real life as they are in the classroom? Are the uses of tenses as clear-cut as they are presented as being?

According to the evidence in The Bank of English, the answer to all these questions has to be 'no'. To take one example: for many years teachers taught that there were three conditionals in English. More recently a 'zero' conditional was added – a step in the right direction. When the COBUILD researchers scoured the data for evidence of these four conditionals, they found them – but they also found many more. More or less any permutation seems to be possible – depending on the message the user of the language is attempting to put across, depending on their viewpoint, depending on the shared knowledge between them and their audience. The matter is not as cut-and-dried as the textbooks make out.

Another topic that both teachers and learners agonise over is that of reporting: how do you tell someone something that someone else has told you? It is still sometimes said that the sentence 'I'm coming to see you tomorrow' would be reported as 'He said he was coming to see me the following day'. That's possible, of course. But it's equally possible to report it as 'He said he's coming to see me tomorrow' or 'He said he'd come tomorrow' or even 'He's coming tomorrow'. Yet again, it depends on your point of view, and your time of speaking. If the event has not yet happened, then common sense tells you that the present or future can be used. If the event referred to has happened, then past reference will be used: again, a matter of common sense. See Thompson (1994) for a detailed discussion of the whole topic of reporting based on the evidence of The Bank of English.

In both the case of conditional sentences and that of reported speech, a selection of appropriate lines can be given to students, who can then see for themselves what is happening. They will find sentences exemplifying what is traditionally taught – and that's good: it gives them some rules they can apply and know they will not go far wrong. But they will also find sentences that deviate from what they have been taught – and discussion should help to tease out what is happening: how so much depends on the speakers and their perceptions.

Collocation and phraseology

When even very good learners of the language speak or write English, the effect is often slightly odd. There is nothing that is obviously wrong, but somehow native speakers know that they would not express themselves in quite that way.

The problem is often one of collocation – the words which are frequently used together. For example, the words 'tall' and 'high' are roughly synonymous, but they cannot always be used interchangeably. We can talk about 'a tall building' or 'a high building'; we talk about 'a tall man' but not 'a high man'; we talk about 'a high wind' but not 'a tall wind'. These are very simple examples, and most learners would know they were wrong. But others are much less obvious: we 'do the washing up', but 'make the beds'; we 'do the cooking' but 'make dinner'; we 'do our hair' but 'make a mess'. For students there is no very obvious reason why there should be such variation, but a study of concordances for 'make' and 'do' should help them to see some patterning which might help them to remember when to use which verb.

There are two main uses of the word 'question mark'. One is for the punctuation mark (?); the other, much more common in everyday life, is used to express doubt or uncertainty as to whether something will happen (see Figure 4 below):

the players at all levels are fine but a	question mark	frequently hangs over the precise purpose
exhausted. 'There seemed to be a massive	question mark	hanging over fashion. I lost faith In myself
at the White House. But last night a huge	question mark	hung over his prestigious Washington trip.
was more anti-FLN than pro-FIS. And a	question-mark	must therefore hang over whether the FIS
woman in her own right but a large	question mark	must remain over her understanding of any
er because this gas is sour that puts a	question mark	over the safety factor. But the question of
of growth left in the UK and there Is a big	question mark	over Sainsbury's surprise expansion in the
fault line In southern France has placed a	question mark	over the safety of the Cadarache nuclear
care for many older people, and there is a	question mark	over the future of geriatric care as a result
Douglas Hurd last night placed a dramatic	question mark	over John Major's survival as Prime
City analysts remain sceptical. There Is a	question-mark	over the succession, with Sir Owen Green
won't be on the agenda and there's a big	question mark	over whether the two sides think they're in
to establish Itself, and there is still a	question mark	over that, it is doubtful in the short term at
for the time of year and there was a	question mark	over the strength of recovery. Overall, the
to find spending cuts has put a	question mark	over the future of the extension, especially
and stage partner Maidie; and the only	question mark	over the production concerns Yule's belt-
manager said: 'Medium term there Is still a	question mark	over the dividend. You get the feeling that
to redraw the borders of old Yugoslavia. A	question mark	still hovers over Macedonia. The EC has
one that has been delayed. Another big	question mark	that looms over the new package of
is not away from home overnight is a big	question mark.	Widely unnoticed is the fact that a number

Figure 4 *Concordance lines for 'question mark'*

If you want to emphasise how great the uncertainty is, the most common collocate is 'big', although 'large', 'huge' and 'massive' are also used:

> There's a big question mark over Sainsbury's surprise expansion
> . . .

The word 'question mark' is typically embedded in two phraseologies:

> There's a question mark over. . .
> A question mark hangs over. . .

This gives a theme/rheme variation: again, it is your choice which you use, but once you've made your choice, you are likely to adhere to this phraseology. Although, it is worth noting that you can 'put' or 'place' a question mark over something (often the future).

As can be seen above, even the position of a word in a clause can be important. There are, for example, some intransitive verbs which usually occur as the last element in the clause (see Figure 3 above).

Other verbs are frequently followed by an adverb or a prepositional phrase (see Figure 5 below):

```
                    to get their own way no matter what. We  behave  aggressively when we are sarcastic,
         There is some evidence that boys and girls  behave  differently right from the start, so it seems
          sail. If they do come, Vidin's inspector will  behave  as usual. 'The Danube is an internationall
     none of the children want to go, and they  behave  badly because they resent being there in the first
          must be. I am fond of Maria, but she does  behave  in an extraordinary way, not as though she works
              Services Act, which allowed banks to  behave  like building societies, insurance companies to
              of double standards. All governments  behave  like this. But it doesn't diminish the
        made me think more about training them to  behave  properly and I actually got under my desk for this
             yesterday called on broadcasters to 'behave  responsibly' and reduce the amount of sex and
            not understand why she felt compelled to  behave  so rudely to a friend, but It might well have been
              of ethical standards dictates how we  behave  towards our neighbours. Our advert must
          with such behaviour. She'd much prefer to  behave  well and be liked, I'm sure. But she must be set
           can talk confidently to them and who can  behave  with authority on the world's television screens.
```

Figure 5   *Concordance lines for 'behave'*

A number of nouns nearly always occur after a link verb (see Figure 6 below):

```
             civil war would be much easier be almost a  doddle. The really hard thing laughter # <M01> the
             Italy's mismanaged economy will be a  doddle  compared with cutting out the rot in the political
      and you've got two weeks. It should be a  doddle  for you. You're frightfully good at this sort of
            that their product makes housework a  doddle. Every other bathroom cleaner manufacturer
          our first checkpoint. This seemed such a  doddle  that we even contemplated a few drinks in the
      for those those who think black runs are a  doddle, there's always heli-skiing – where a helicopter
          be too chuffed at finding out that it was a  doddle  compared with the next day's stage to Isola.
            videoplus+ makes timer programming a  doddle, though you'll need to buy newspapers or TV
     but crazy. It was no challenge at all. It was a  doddle, a happy, three-day lark propped between the
                  of a luxury. Grammar, in short, Is a  doddle  and there is no longer any need to call It,
          11th and 12th. In the end, it was not quite a  doddle  but Hockley could afford to drop a shot at the
```

Figure 6   *Concordance lines for 'doddle'*

Other nouns are followed by a particular preposition (see Figure 7 below):

```
                film of the Holocaust Museum. And his  take  on the Natural History Museum gets best visual
             [$4.50]. And then there's Bob Lutticken's  take  on the classic Philadelphia steak sandwich. It's
        # First, will hear a foreign reporter's  take  on the state of some of our democratic
            the film is Jimmy's gleeful, off-the-wall  take  on his own life. Mistaken by the police for the
      we don't really take them that seriously. My  take  on the film Is the honesty in a lot of the
                  <t> Hansen: Sylvia, we'd like to get your  take  on this as someone who has been covering the
           being written about us. Secondly, my own  take  on what's being written about us. It's not very
```

in favor of the plan # First of all, what's your take on the overall plan, and do you think it's actually
didn't believe it.<t> Neary: What's your take on why he is doing all this? Is he sincerely
four partners in this coalition # What's your take on the new government? Do you think it can
is more profound than film # What's your take on that?<t> Rosenberg: Oh, that's a profound
not even nominated for one # What's your take on awards and, I mean, do you feel just a bit
Michael, let's start with you # What's your take on this plan?<t> Wilkes: Well, Liane, I don't think
involved in the Iran-Contra affair. What's your take on this?<t> Page: I think President Bush is
have to start with Kimba Wood # What's your take on what happened?<t> BARNES: Well, for

Figure 7   *Concordance lines for 'take'*

This last example shows that the following preposition is not the only
important structural element. It is obvious from this that the most
common pattern is 'What's your take on . . .?'. It is not the only
phraseology that can be used, but it is so frequent that learners might be
advised to learn that particular chunk of language, knowing that
deviation from this also occurs.

From examples such as this it seems that words are not just slot-
fillers. The more we study the corpus, the more obvious it is that many
words have preferred positions within a clause, and that they attract
other words towards them. The word 'backyard' can mean a place
nearby in which you or, even more typically, a country, wish to have
influence. When it is used in this sense, it is typically found in the
phraseology 'in its/their/your own backyard' (see Figure 8 below):

and that the diamonds were in their own backyard.' Jan and Ian were married for 10 years before
They have a big stockmarket in their own backyard. It works well. They can understand the
not want BA attacking them in their own backyard. There is a good chance that it will block the
I don't want you robbing me in my own backyard. No, I was thinking, there's a real high-rolling
China might choose to do in its own backyard. So the Chinese began testing the water,
<s Baghdad took shape right in its own backyard. Having concentrated so often on citified artists
about these problems, at least in its own backyard. It has totally failed to do that. REP: About 200
call comes as troubles loom in their own backyard. Many papers carry pictures of tens of
often unwelcome change in their own backyard. 'Too fat, too heavy, too dear,' is how
Ayrton Senna in the Brazilian's own backyard. Prost said: 'I am very happy with the car as it is
<t> Imagine if the war were in your own backyard instead of Overseas # For many people living in
would fight the vivisectionists in their own back yard, and use medical science for her own ends.<t>
to stop the grizzly killing in their own back yard. unable even to agree on a common course of
a world away are quickly felt In our own back yard. Kent Hughes [Council on Competitiveness]:

Figure 8   *Concordance lines for 'backyard'*

If something is easily done or accomplished, you can say that it is
'plain sailing'; you can, but typically, you don't: you are much more
likely to use it of something that was not easily done (see Figure 9
below):

Mason would be the last to say it had been plain sailing. He knows from experience that cracking
he said. Picking the All Black side was plain sailing for New Zealand selectors yesterday # The
<t> But Lola makes clear that it wasn't all plain sailing # Someone got him to buy 4 lb of potatoes
all feel it, you know. Only it isn't always plain sailing. Well, goodbye, Mrs Mellanby. Get in touch
heavenly's deal with Sony hasn't all been plain sailing, and earlier this year the major opted out of
to add a sparkle to your life, but it's not all plain sailing, Communication goes haywire on the 6th
to new friends and peers isn't always plain sailing, If you're used to being boss – whether in
at straws, and the world is certainly not plain sailing towards some new Tequila Sunrise on a
a month to remember. Not everything is plain sailing and you do have to watch a tendency to

unsound, but it has not been absolutely	plain sailing	and we have to be a little bit careful.'
Michael Peacock. It was soon clear that	plain sailing	was undoubtedly out. Michael said, and
great. He's the greatest']. The rest was	plain sailing.	One thing to come out of this,' Sir Bernard
round next month. But it's still far from	plain sailing.	Foreign Minister Eduard Shevardnadze,
that five times, but it has not all been	plain sailing	and the horse had a whole year off with leg
crowd went wild. From then on it was	plain sailing	# beautiful, polished and brilliant.<t> The

Figure 9   *Concordance lines for 'plain sailing'*

Pragmatics

An important area of language so far unmentioned is that of pragmatics: the meanings and effects which come from the use of language in particular situations. Words do not just 'have meanings' – if indeed, they have them at all! We use words to communicate, to express our thoughts, hopes and feelings: and in so doing we convey our attitudes to the world around us, and to our discourse. One example already given of this is the prefacing use of 'thing' (see Figure 1 above), where by choosing words like 'interesting', 'funny', 'awful' we are showing our attitude to what follows and also predisposing (we hope) our audience to react in the same way.

Instead of saying 'the interesting thing is', the speaker could in some situations have chosen 'interestingly', or 'interestingly enough' (see Figure 10 below):

very strong academic tradition in the school.	Interestingly enough	the first and the second
police themselves are quite concerned er	interestingly enough	about that and take a so-called
conquest in Milan is an Italian [who also,	interestingly enough,	doesn't speak a word of his native
produced by the endometrium [and,	interestingly enough,	are also found in great
had to date this minor revolution it would be	interestingly enough,	around the time the profligate
of the resident wood boring beetles.	Interestingly enough,	a few days after penning these
without any condemnation or manipulation.	Interestingly enough,	even though I didn't know it would
spores on the caps of smaller companions.	Interestingly enough,	this same metallic blue-black
of menstrual disorders; one used it,	interestingly enough	at that time, for treatments of

Figure 10   *Concordance lines for 'interestingly enough'*

Students could be given a concordance for 'enough' and asked to pick out those lines which showed strong pragmatic intentions.

It is interesting to note – another strongly pragmatic preface – that a pragmatic use of a word is often somewhat at odds with its more semantic uses. To be 'safe' is normally good and desirable, but if you say that someone 'chose the safe option', you are showing disapproval of or disappointment in them because they were not very adventurous or original in their choice. Given sufficient context, students should be able to work this out for themselves. The same is true of 'killer'. To be a killer is bad; to have the killer instinct is something that is widely admired!

A more obviously pragmatic word is 'actually' – one that is quite difficult to capture in, for example, a dictionary entry but one which all native speakers use with a variety of functions (see Figure 11 below):

	actually	
whole of the National Health Service they're	actually	very low. Not only in comparison with other
sure the fish contains some potassium it	actually	contains quite a lot of it. And so if we're to
Even some of the most unorthodox details	actually	have parallels that are rather closer to Wren that
activity or sector which is a high priority may	actually	be reducing the credit availability to that sector
<MO1> to be here. It's an impossible task	actually	to be asked to talk about Shakespearean
not erm automatically say that they are	actually	counselling in that way. As a parent erm I would
you should have invited anybody to come	actually.	But can I commend to you the running bath
Wembley what I can't believe if that you've	actually	done it for us and you've made a lot of people
<MO1> I mean in our college they have got	actually	got a small typing pool of three people.<FO2>
is expected to be below that. So she's	actually	you know getting more in real terms each time
Erm well actually I think th I mean she	actually	used them for another experiment <FOX>
it. I mean I don't know whether they've	actually	made any undertakings to provide [pause] care
Now the biggest structural tr change he	actually	attempted was in the sphere of economic
course of that film there's nothing that I've	actually	sat down and said well what we really need
I am. I think I know who I am but I don't	actually	have the papers to prove actually who I am so I
you know something that you had at home	actually	wouldn't be compatible with that and that has
Yeah not so bad thanks. Erm just a query	actually.	Where does this Friday the thirteenth <ZF1>
would have had the trainer 'cos they were	actually	growling and snarling and being slapped back
over here I'm over here when the water's	actually	the other way. So you actually go in a direction
the means to recompense them. You could	actually	wreck somebody's life and they would not be
I <ZF0> I you know find out whether they're	actually	doing what they were going to say they were
were I suppose. I don't know anyone from	actually	from this village but there were people from
And at the wedding they were terribly good	actually	'cos they were the only children there and erm I
Yeah. I do approve of them. Erm and I think	actually	if it was just for women I think quite a few
the more likely it is that they will want to	actually	do that to relieve them their onslaught of you
should be looking at doing but the onus is	actually	trying to do that in such a way that [pause] you
not in and the central heating's on she'll	actually	make a point of running upstairs as we're going
Yeah. If he was home even Yeah. It's true	actually.	If he was home all the time I don't know if he
a service and that the cost to me was	actually	unimportant that it was my job to actually go
And he couldn't believe that if anybody	actually	needed help they wouldn't ask for it <ZGY>
<ZF0> how young does it go that you could	actually	say the child is participating.<FOX> <ZGY>
in the process there are bits of land that	actually	no-one quite knows who they own.<FO1> Mm.
why we're all the same. Because once we	actually	realize and acknowledge our own differences
setting up new businesses here. Now that is	actually	not a wish-list it's something that's happening
bed watching telly miserable and my dad	actually	broke down in tears and he ways to my mum
means is something about people who	actually	are if you like on an equal level <FO2>
is to do with issues tenants groups that are	actually	campaigning or struggling to survive and it's
because I'm also in touch with staff. And I	actually	think there is an issue there where we have to
pause] But I do think the pay structure is	actually	quite detrimental to women. You don't you do
of patients with neurological problems	actually	will have very little on the whole concept of care
erm if it's external. Because our marks	actually	came out higher than the ones that we'd set
half a degree third a degree we start to	actually	get the get the viscosity below the point where

Figure 11   Concordance lines for 'actually'

Fairly advanced students could be given these, or similar, lines, and asked in groups to try to work out the ways in which 'actually' is being used. There are probably no right answers, because so much depends on context, relationships, and so on. But whenever this exercise has been tried, extremely interesting discussions have ensued.

Other classroom uses of concordances

The uses I have suggested so far have all been of individual concordances which students study in order to find out something about how the word is typically used. It is, however, possible to build exercises around either a single set of concordance lines or two or more sets. The following exercise is based on the word 'pat':

Exercise 1

amazed the number of people who'll stop for a pat and a chat about Fido. Try kicking off a new
BRITAIN'S bosses can give themselves a pat on the back this morning. Most of us think they
[Burma]. The Thai government deserved a pat on the back, too. It ignored a complaint by
Times] that 'no single legislative initiative offers a pat solution to the complex problem of criminal
his most favourite aunt gave him a tight hug, a pat, and a kiss on the cheek. Jasper and Daisy sat
carbon club members the EC and nine others] a pat on the back for setting targets. The quid pro
than steam them lightly and rub them with a pat of savoury butter or drizzle them with warmed
When you've finished with them, give yourself a pat on the back, or better yet a massage. But don't
It was like someone just, you know, gave me a pat on the back and said, 'Everything's OK # Your
minutes to draw out bitter juices, then rinse and pat dry on kitchen paper. Meanwhile, wash rice and
Drain and plunge into cold water, then drain and pat dry, as before. When completely cold, quarter
<CQ0> stage may parrot stock phrases, borrow pat ideas, and seem on the way to becoming less,
times fifty-five the answer would come pat [pause] mentally. So and then we <ZF1> h+
across as one of Job's comforters, dispensing pat answers that don't fit another persons'
it stick, and she replied: 'I have my story down pat and I have friends who will back me up in this.'
You only need to shampoo once, then gently pat your baby's hair dry with a warm towel. When
at him. I believed him, but it seemed a little pat, that a professional accountant would play
sat up, smiled at me and gave my face a little pat. A-ba-ba-ba-ba,' he said sweetly. A pair of
Come on, Miss Pinero." She had the name off pat, a quick study, obviously. 'I'll show you where
manager. Take a cab and have all the points off pat before you get to the hotel, there's a good
the acid. We soon had the ingredients litany off pat: a glass of olive oil, a glass of white wine,
turned it down." I gave her hand a reassuring pat before lifting my glass for a soothing draught,
of 'em had er they used to make it in a round pat and they had a stamp and they just could just
it stick and she replied that she had her story pat and there were friends who would back her up.
was completely bogus. I was bored with the pat socio-economic account of Liverpool music so I
House to play in the pool, or to the stables to pat the horses. Autumn admitted that she would
laugh. He couldn't seem to resist the urge to pat Ella on the rear every time she came within easy
Adelaide, he even insulted a koala, declining to pat it in case it gave him some ghastly disease.<t>
he finds a job in an abattoir, it is almost too pat a metaphor for the way his deranged mind is
development of the artistic personality it is too pat. In what possible direction can these young
You get on really well in this town if you pat people on the back a lot and tell them how
you keep coming in." She gave Lily's shoulder a pat. 'But thanks.' She moved away, half
about $748 million # The package is a kind of pat on the back for Romania which has fallen into
hoe to form a ridge, just like hoeing up potatoes, pat down the top and sow my seed sparingly,
what was coming all right, but even then had to pat her heart to indicate the fluttering pulse

Figure 12   *Concordance lines for 'pat'*

Separate the word 'pat' into noun, verb, adjective, and phrase.
Are any of the senses semantically linked – if so which?
Which parts of the body are likely to be patted?
What other things or people do you pat?
With 'pat' meaning 'touch gently', which is the most common adjective or adverb?
What situations is the verb used in?
When do people get 'a pat on the back'?
Which nouns is the adjective 'pat' used with?
How many senses do there seem to be?
Taking just the cookery context, what other verbs are used?

It is important to make it clear to students that they do not have to painstakingly read every single word of every line. Indeed, they should skim them quickly to start to get a feel for the word, and then go back and look more carefully at how the key word is used.

When students first look at concordances, they often get confused because each line is discrete, often on a completely different subject, and also most of the lines do not even show whole sentences. It is therefore useful to spend some time with students getting them used to looking at concordances.

First, they need to get used to understanding or guessing what a line is about – not in detail, as that is often impossible, but a rough idea is all that is needed. The following is an exercise taken from *Collins Cobuild Concordance Sampler 3*: Reporting by Geoff Thompson (1995):

Figure 13   *From Collins COBUILD Concordance Sampler 3*

EXERCISE 2

Getting used to concordances – understanding the content

When you first look at concordances, it can be confusing because each line has a different example, often on a completely different subject – and many of the lines do not even show the whole sentence. Before you try to use these concordances to find out about report structures, you may find it useful to do a few exercises simply to help you get used to looking at concordances.

First, you need to get used to understanding or guessing what a line is about. You don't have to understand exactly what the topic is (sometimes it is impossible, anyway): you just need a rough idea. For example, where do you think the actions of the following sentences take place? How easy is it to guess? Underline the main words that help you to guess.

1   up a tiny vacant table at the open window of Pierre's cafe, ordered himself an ice-cream and Irish coffee, and sat back
2   n the earlier erroneous FBI reports. Although the judge had ordered all televisions removed from the jurors' motel room
3   he landlord had found out that she had deceived him and had ordered her to vacate her apartment. She had promised this
4   ational, an engine overheated. As a precaution, the captain ordered it shot down. None of the aircraft's passengers wer
5   r bodies to move their thin blood. As dawn broke the guards ordered everyone to their feet. Some didn't get to their fe

Look at any page of concordances. Note down briefly where the action takes place or what the situation is. Write the main words or clues which help you to guess.

		order, promise, proposal, request, suggestion
1	and Ash never knew who had given the	order that he was not to be allowed to leave : the
2	were filed, the judge finally issued an	order that legal investigators of our designation be
3	President Quezon issued an executive	order that $500,000 be transferred from the account of
4	along the sides of hedges, waiting for the	order to attack. The 6th Airborne's commander,
5	deep into the surrounding forest. At the	order to march, the long line of boys set out along the
6	praised was President Jackson's recent	order to the postmasters to destroy any abolitionist
7		
8	questions in time for the Inquiry, despite	promises by Ministers that this would be done. FoE
9	At this point Gorbanevskaya recalled her	promise not to cause suffering to her mother, and
10	twins, returned to England, with vague	promises of presently sending for them, he had left
11	this is to remind you of your	promise of three paintings for my mixed show. The
12	in one of his villas outside Imola, with a	promise that he would recognise any child that might be
13	who had either forgotten his original	promise to buy fish and chips, or was just more
14	Stein was about to add that MacIver's	promise to get Billy a job in the movie industry was a
15		
16	above, there is another issue – say, a	proposal for better street lighting – on which the other
17	for children, the final report contained a	proposal that family allowances should not be paid to
18	was in a bad mood made worse by my	proposal that she move out of Thomas Street. 'Where
19	by the University's opposition to the	proposal that some or all of the colleges should be
20	contentious item,' he says, introducing a	proposal that the number of student representatives
21	that he had refused Mr Feibergerstein's	proposal to send them home to work out the last year
22	have been made on your behalf. A	proposal to study only part-time, for instance at

```
23
24  1972 he approached the Centre with a   request  for assistance in the making of a good quality
25  in the north. With the good news was a   request  from Gates that the bearer be promoted to
26  But there was no verdict at hand, only a   request  from the jury to have some of the evidence
27  Stroganoff to the chef with a courteous   request  that he should try again, and if he is prepared to
28     you are aboard this aircraft, with the   request  that this information be relayed to the Ministry of
29     probable that he would view Julie's   request  to go to Art College with favour, involving as it
30  about her job at NBC to pass on their   request  to me to explain the mission, its purpose,
31
32           went to bed before dawn. So the   suggestion  of a four a.m. meeting was not as outlandish
33  I was thinking seriously of Uncle Sam's   suggestion  of leaving home – going, perhaps, to London,
34     she and Miss Jackson agreed to my   suggestion  that coffee in the sitting-room would be
35  theoretical physics in Vienna, made the   suggestion  that he should give up his chair in Vienna and
36        He spoke stiffly, formally. Gertrude's   suggestion  that he was angry was indeed not far from the
37        and had accepted his Professor's   suggestion  that he write an MA thesis on the juvenilia of
38  instance, in 'How to spend money' my   suggestion  that you try having two purses may help you
39     Spare Rib and allocated shares. The   suggestion  to call the magazine Spare Rib was originally a
40  see.' He's been enthusiastic about a   suggestion  to try the zoo for a possible job and we kept it
```

EXERCISE 3

Predicting missing words

Most concordance lines begin and end with incomplete words. How many of the lines on your concordance page are like this? Think about the content of the whole line – this may help you to guess what the first and last words are. Write down your predictions below, along with a brief description of the content of each line.

Prepositions are difficult for learners of any language. There often seems to be no logical reason why, in for example Spanish, it is 'para' not 'por' in a particular context, or, in French, 'en' and not 'a'. The same is true of English. Showing students a number of lines of one particular preposition may help them to see some thread that links all the uses together (see Figure 14 below):

```
         # Citation: 'Without orders Kelliher dashed   at  the post and hurled two grenades, killing some
25, from Irvinebank, North Queensland, dashed   at  it and with only a revolver killed all but one of the
            We straightened out, turned, and dashed   at  the mountainside for another pass, which we
became more frenzied and more violent, she hit   at  her victim, her rival, again and again with the
head round so the head is in his mouth then hits   at  it with both hands # He does little mouthfuls of
now and again was striking the ground, or hitting   at  stones on the driveway. It was also half singing,
       legs, arms and trunk, which forces you to hit   at  the ball rather than make a fluid swinging motion
her husband by the time she went home. She hit   at  a few balls without a clue as to how to swing a
spent a few years ripping, smashing and kicking   at  the fences that separate you from an otherwise
                 Nick Hart, 18, said: 'They were kicking   at  the door with bare feet to try to get back in. I
felt tears sliding down her cheeks and kicked   at  the water angrily. It seemed to her that all she
keep out the air of that chill summer. She kicked   at  the paper with her foot; her hand decorating an
was not yet fifty, but he looked older. She kicked   at  the door with her foot, to save having to put her
Danlo said. He sipped his coffee while he kicked   at  the steel foot rail and listened to it ring. That
a choking sound. Pagan raised a foot, kicked   at  the shotgun, struck the barrel, but didn't force
the baseball bat threatened to hit me so I ran   at  him with the sword. He decided discretion was
that it was meant as a joke, but at the time I ran   at  him screaming and scratched his face, seriously
'No! It's not her fault! She didn't know!' She ran   at  the demon, shaking her fist in his face. 'She's
about it, but I just grabbed a club and swung   at  it # That was really stupid # He took two more
      was higher and Kuhnen just kept swinging   at  everything, and it worked," he said. <t> Here, he
the serpent, the giant drew his knife and swung   at  the taut quivering line. It split with a resounding
     that he could summon swung his hammer   at  the giant's skull. Such was the violence of
53, refused to give it back and swung a spade   at  neighbour Lionel Sime when he leapt over the
of his Maine Road career for swinging a punch   at  Paul Wilkinson, received no sympathy from
Paul Allott, he was left swinging embarrassingly   at  air like a novice golfer, out for 14.
```

Figure 14   *Concordance lines for 'at'*

In the lines above, 'at' means something like 'towards but not quite reaching'. By seeing them together, students can work this out for themselves, and this should help them to gain more confidence in using this preposition.

Phrasal verbs are a perennial problem for all learners of English. This is partly because the following particle often seems arbitrary. When the particles are focused on rather than the verb, however, there are usually meaning relationships that can be seen. For example, there are a number of phrasal verbs with the particle 'down', where 'down' refers to writing and recording something (see Figure 15 below):

carefully and painstakingly copied the word	down.	Then he said, 'Right. Now wipe your slates
turned around to glare at me as she copied	down	my name from my nametag. At the next break,
I need you to use'em fast # Piaggi copied	down	the information. 'Okay. Our Philly connections
good buddy. Mission accomplished # I copied	down	the entire note and closed the book
instructors read slowly and students copied	down	what was said, word for word.<t> the lecture
go, I always have a pencil and paper and I jot	down	ideas. I could never retire. New things strike me
truck around on a Sunday evening and jotted	down	the address of every house that was adorned
on this page, ' 'TSB' '' here. People always jot	down	initials, abbreviations; I do it myself # <t> I
Turbitt write more music and Mclaren jotted	down	some lyrics, but, says Weltman, <CQ1> they
stop altogether, is to keep a weekly diary. Jot	down	the number of units you drink each day and
patient's condition.<FO1> I will note that	down	or anything that I might want to follow up I note
<t> Just 32 per cent of cardholders note	down	emergency numbers for lost or stolen cards,
in used bills as follows. Please note this	down	carefully. First, one-thousand hundreds.
with whom you experience difficulty and note	down	a typical situation. For example:<ZDY> Asking a
when such visions come, we may note them	down,	but their true value is derived from applying
I confess that was a question I had scrawled	down	here. .<t> Sahl: Oh, please.<t> Simon: 'You
they what they d+ you know they don't write	down	on their application form whether <MO1>
serial number of the bike in order to write it	down.	<LTH> Neuropsychologists have identified
level you must do three things:<ZDY> Write	down	the results [some meters store the result
for travel and entertainment? Don't write it all	down	for someone else to use. Keep some
camera's LCD. <LTH> Then, you could write	down	the exposure information on paper, or, if you're

Figure 15   Concordance lines for 'down'

Students can be given a number of phrasal verbs with 'down', including ones with this meaning, and can be asked to pick out the ones which have a common semantic thread.

By noting the similarities for themselves, they are more likely to recognise other similarities when they come across them. They can then be given a concordance with the particles blanked out, and asked to work out for themselves which particle should be inserted.

The examples given above of the use of concordances in the classroom are but a few of the many possible exploitations. Other ideas can be found in Tribble and Jones (1990), Johns and King (1991), and the *Concordance Samplers* published by Collins COBUILD (1994, 1995). As teachers and students gain confidence in looking at the lines, so other exercises will suggest themselves.

Conclusion

The better students become at a language, the more conscious they need to be of its patterns and uses. One of a teacher's aims must be to instil in students an awareness of what is happening in the language, and a curiosity to find out more: to go beyond the somewhat simplistic language of most coursebooks and most classrooms and to discover how native speakers of English out there in the real world express themselves in their speech and writing. They will hear and see most of what they have learned. But they will also hear and see a great deal that they have not learned, and they need to know how to deal with this.

Corpus analysis has shown us that there are many common features of native speaker use which non-native speakers do not typically pay attention to. Some of these (for example, delexicalised 'give', 'way', and 'thing') have been mentioned in this chapter, but there are many more which students will not have acquired because they might not have been noticed.

Teachers give students many strategies for coping, some of which could be developed through the use of concordances. Students are shown how to look carefully at the particular bit of language being focused on, and are encouraged to work out for themselves how it is being used and what are the reasons for its use. The focus is not merely on the word itself, but on the contexts in which the word is being used.

By studying concordance lines students will become more aware of language, and will note how particular words are used by native speakers. Whilst there is no automatic transfer from awareness of a feature to the ability to use that feature, there is certainly a likelihood that increased awareness will lead to increased proficiency – particularly of features which, once pointed out, are encountered frequently in real-life language situations.

Non-native speakers frequently have difficulty in acquiring new uses of words: once a word has been learned with a particular sense and in a particular context, the tendency is to feel that the word has been 'captured', 'pigeonholed', and that no further learning effort is needed. One value of corpus analysis is to help learners to note the gap between their use of a word and the other way (or ways) it is typically used by native speakers.

By analysing data in this way, students are encouraged to develop further their analytical skills: obviously valuable when learning a language, but it is not too fanciful to say that this is transferable also to other activities. Most people enjoy finding things out for themselves; and the majority believe that learning is enhanced by so doing.

The use of concordances in the classroom is in its infancy as a language teaching technique. My hope is that this chapter will encourage teachers and students to try it.

2 Concordances in the classroom without a computer: assembling and exploiting concordances of common words

Jane Willis

Introduction

The study of language is often corpus-based. Let us imagine that a researcher wishes to study the language of three-year-old children to see if there is any difference between the language of boys and girls at that age. The first step is to gather a corpus, a body of the relevant language, in this case the language of three-year-old boys and girls. This is an obvious step, but it is not an easy one. Decisions must be taken as to the size of the corpus, and care must be taken to see that the corpus is as representative as possible. But in principle the task is a manageable one. Once a researcher has assembled an appropriate corpus, that corpus can be used to answer relevant research questions.

Increasingly nowadays corpora are used to help describe the grammar and lexis of the language. A study may be directed at a particular type of language, spoken as opposed to written, say, or the language of television chat shows or of research articles in medical journals. Corpora can also be used to provide a picture of the language as a whole, but if this is the aim then a very large corpus running into many millions of words is required. One of the best known corpora of this kind is The Bank of English. This corpus provided the basis for the *Collins COBUILD English Dictionary* and many other grammar and usage books (see Chapter 1 of this book for information about COBUILD). The process of gathering a corpus of this kind is extremely complex. Once the corpus has been assembled, however, and has been stored in computer memory, the process of examining it is relatively simple.

Let us say that lexicographers wish to describe a particular word. They can use a computer program to call up a number of *concordances* of that word. Even a limited number of concordances can provide us with some useful insights, as this small set of concordance lines for the word *any* shows. These lines were carefully selected to give a tiny but a representative sample from the original COBUILD corpus. As you read through this set of examples, try to think of what the word *any* actually means. In how many cases do the lines here conform to the commonly given pedagogic grammar rules for *any*?

are interesting to observe. Any child under two is given a bottle
so the young men went for any job they could rather than a farm job
state of affairs could not go on any longer. Someone had to act soon
they hadn't dared to strike any more matches – they were just
the longest open tradition of any of the English links that have
complicated. The closing of any of them would be a major engineering
We work more overtime than any other country in Europe, even
dry. I don't think there was any rain all summer long, was there?
just won't come out. Have we any stain remover? . . . I thought there
at Steve's house. Just turn up any time after 12. It'll go on all afternoon
hard pressed. There was never any time for standing back and appraising

Figure 1   [Source: Cobuild data sheets, 1986]

Although pedagogic grammars and coursebooks often give the rule that *any* is used in negatives and questions, and *some* used in statements, here around half the examples show *any* used in positive statements. In fact, in all its uses, *any* seems to carry a general non-specific meaning of '*It doesn't matter which*' (which is maybe why it is used commonly in questions and negatives where there is often nothing to be specific about). A far larger set of concordances would be needed if we wished to identify common collocations, patterns and pragmatic uses. But this small sample does accurately reflect the balance of uses of the word *any* from the research corpus which in turn reflects typical everyday usage.

The corpus research process, then, involves isolating a particular linguistic feature, a word or a pattern, and studying that feature in detail. From this organised study of the language, researchers are able to produce a description of the language – its grammar and lexis, its collocations, meanings, uses and so on.

Once we begin to view the process of language description in this way it is a short step to applying the process pedagogically. Teachers want to make language description accessible to students. Students need to discover and internalise regularities in the language they are studying. If we can place students in the position of researchers this will accomplish these goals neatly and economically.

This process of language analysis will inevitably lead to particular aspects of the language becoming salient, which is the first aim of any kind of consciousness-raising activity. A rationale for such an approach is outlined in Brian Tomlinson's Introduction to this book. Schmidt (1990) and others argue that 'noticing' features of the target language is

45

a necessary initial stage in the learning process. Ellis (1991a: 241 and elsewhere) argues that 'consciousness-raising constitutes an approach to grammar teaching which is compatible with current thinking about how learners acquire L2 grammar'. Rather than rely on a diet of 'practice activities' which restrict input and expect immediate accuracy in the 'production' of small items of language, we should be giving learners plenty of opportunities to discover language and systematise it for themselves before expecting them to proceduralise their knowledge and put it to use. Performing different kinds of analysis activities based on concordance lines for the most frequent words can highlight a rich array of language features and help students both to recognise and memorise useful chunks, as well as to analyse and make useful generalisations about grammar.

However, we need to offer our students a manageable corpus of the language to study. That corpus will be a set of texts, written and spoken, which students will process receptively through a series of activities. From now on, I will refer to this as the 'pedagogic corpus'. This could, for example, be made up of some or all of the texts and recordings (with transcripts) from the students' coursebook, perhaps supplemented with other materials.

The important thing is that this corpus must be such that it provides sufficient illustrative examples of the language we want our students to learn. It is obviously advantageous if this corpus is made up of 'authentic' texts, i.e. not texts written for language teaching purposes to illustrate a specific language point, or simplified to the point of distorting natural language use. (There is little point in learners studying language that is unnatural or untypical of the language they will meet in real life.) If we can achieve the aim of providing a suitably representative pedagogic corpus, we can then design a series of language analysis exercises based on that corpus, exercises which will enable students, in the role of researchers, to discover typical features of the language for themselves.

The purpose of this chapter is first to see how far this aim is feasible. It is certainly more readily achievable in an environment which offers ready access to computer hardware and software, but we will look beyond that to see how far the aim can be achieved by a resourceful teacher or materials writer without access to expensive technology.

Preparations for concordancing by hand

It is preferable to base language analysis activities on texts familiar to learners i.e. ones they have already read or listened to for some communicative purpose. Having already processed the texts for meaning, students stand to gain more from the study of the forms that carry those meanings. So the first step is to take stock of the texts (both spoken and written) from the pedagogic corpus that learners are currently using or have already used. These are the ones that can be used for concordancing.

The next step is to look through the current texts to see which words appear with some frequency. Knowing which words are likely to be among the most frequent helps here, and this knowledge can be gained from an appropriate word frequency list.

Frequency lists that have been computer generated are now generally available for the use of materials writers and teachers. See Appendix A which contains lists of the top 150 word forms of spoken English and written English. These are compiled from The Bank of English, a large research corpus of over 200 million words of general (non specialist) English. The most frequent 50 word forms actually account for 36 per cent of text (see table in Appendix B), so these highly frequent words make useful starting points for detailed study of a text. These are the words that it is possible to concordance by hand, simply because they are so frequent that examples of them are easy to find. Then, through analysis of the assembled concordance lines, the other areas that Gwyneth Fox in Chapter 1 of this book describes – senses of words, typical collocations, grammatical findings, pragmatics and phraseology and so on – can be explored.

It is, however, worth remembering that not all words will be equally frequent in all texts i.e. not every text will have the same frequency patterns. For example, in spoken English, the words *so, well, think, mean, things* and obviously *yes* and *no* are far more frequent than in written English. Similarly, some words will be more common in spontaneous discourse than in planned discourse. Words will typically occur in different senses and patterns depending on the type of text. And of course specialist or topic words will also appear with higher frequency in a particular text than they would in a general corpus frequency count. But frequency lists can give us a rough indication of words worth looking out for. Better still would be frequency lists giving a break-down of the common meanings and uses of each word in frequency order, such as the data sheets used in designing the lexical syllabus (Dave Willis, 1990: 55–6).

A learners' dictionary can in fact give us this kind of information, especially if it is one derived from corpus research and which gives natural examples and grammatical information for each word. The most frequent words all have several different meanings and uses, and for each main meaning, there will be typical patternings. The dictionary entries for the most common words thus contain a lot of useful information and give some indication of what to look out for in concordance lines once they are assembled. They can be used by teachers and materials writers before preparing activities based on concordances, and by students, selectively, after doing such activities, to consolidate their knowledge of aspects of the word under study.

There are, then, three essentials: the texts themselves, frequency information and a good dictionary.

Assembling and investigating concordances

In this next section, I will describe five sessions where hand-concordancing was used. Each session was based on a different type of text, involved a variety of analytic procedures, and illustrates the kinds of insights that can be gained from using these procedures. The procedures and steps taken will then be summarised.

Sample session 1 – a focus on as for ESP students

I was once invited to a University ESP department in a developing country to lead a workshop on the lexical syllabus and the design of language analysis activities. There was little access to computers but, working with the texts the teachers had brought in, we successfully concordanced, by hand, a number of common words, to see what insights could be gained by doing so. Four teachers had brought in texts on the topic of farm animal nutrition that they were currently using with students studying English for agriculture. After a quick initial glance through these texts, I selected the word *as*, which ranks 16th in the general written frequency lists. While other subject teachers were reading the texts to gain some idea of their subject matter, the four agricultural specialists split up sections of the texts between them and simply wrote up on the board all the examples of *as* they could find in their section, positioning the word *as* in the centre. This took around five minutes. The result looked something like Figure 2 on page 49.

We began by identifying the actual chunks containing the word *as* i.e. deciding where the chunks began and ended. This was harder than it sounds since it involved making decisions relating to semantic units and clause or phrase boundaries. In the case of example 1 (the first line), for instance, most people intuitively felt that the chunk needed to include both verbs: *are decreased proportionately as productivity rises* – to keep the semantic balance. In example 6 (the sixth line), some pairs argued that *as is explained later* should not be separated from the first half of the sentence; when asked why, they were forced to reflect on and try to

Maintenance costs are decreased proportionately as productivity rises
complex activity which includes such actions as the search for food
of blood constituents have been suggested as possible signals including
. . . which receives signals from the body as a result of consumption of food
some agent associated with energy storage acts as a signal for the long term . . .
that signals are received directly from the crop as is explained later.
A variety of aromatic substances such as dill, aniseed, coriander and . . .
food intake and energy requirement suggests that, as with energy, intake should vary
respond to environment temperature in the same way as monogastric animals, in that
This can be considered as an aspect of energy balance in the
Digestibility here is expressed as the coefficient for food energy
appears to be relatively unimportant in grazing as animals will graze in the dark and

Figure 2

explain this meaning of *as*. Very few examples were as straightforward as *in the same way as . . . as a result of . . .* In fact, the whole process of identifying the boundaries of the chunks stimulated both pair and class discussion of meanings and clause relations. Being asked to justify their decisions concerning where chunks with *as* began and ended often forced participants to make explicit things they had only felt sub-consciously before. This is exactly what is meant by the term consciousness-raising activity.

The second task was to try to classify the uses and meanings of the phrases with *as* and to find how many different ways these could be classified. After some discussion, mostly focusing on the meanings and functions of *as*, pairs generally grouped the phrases into around five or six categories, thus:

– referring to time (1)
– introducing examples (2, 7) (Students would know *such as*, but probably not the pattern such + noun + *as* .)
– meaning similar to/same (8, 9 and possibly 6?)
– after verbs like *suggested, acts, considered, expressed* (which also express similarity or something parallel)
– expressing a reason (12)
– left over phrases: *as a result*

For each of these categories, pairs were then asked to suggest a further example that they had met before. They came up with phrases like *functioned as, as you know, As a child, I lived in . . .*

They then felt they wanted to consult a dictionary to find whether their categories were similar to those in the dictionary and to find more parallel examples that might be useful. They did this in groups and then told each other their useful phrases. They particularly liked phrases such as *saving as little as £10 per week, as a consequence of* . . . and those with a more colloquial flavour: *as things stand,* and *as it turned out.*

It was noticeable that two categories of *as* were absent in this set of concordances: the phrase *as if,* and the pattern *as X as.* Maybe these are simply less common in this type of academic text; it would be interesting to take a bigger sample to find out if indeed this was the case.

So far these activities had involved a fair amount of repetition of phrases with *as* (helpful for learners who learn best by memorising), discussion about the various meanings, functions and uses of *as* (helpful to learners with a more cognitive approach). All this was leading to a general broadening of understanding of how and when they and their students could use such expressions. In addition to the word *as,* many other useful words and phrases had been focused on.

Somehow, concordance lines have the effect of enabling us to take a more objective look at the language. They are like tiny snapshots of a linguistic landscape. Just as when looking at a photograph of a familiar scene you often notice something you hadn't realised was there, concordance lines taken from their familiar surroundings seem to make it more likely that we notice new things.

The new things may not just be related to the central word. In this particular session, as a final supplementary activity, we moved the focus of attention outwards from the central word and looked to see what other useful grammatical insights we could gain from looking at other words and phrases in the concordances lines on the board. I thought that this activity might last another two or three minutes, but it proved extremely fruitful. After ten minutes or so the board looked like Figure 3 (see page 51).

The noun groups (underlined above) could be further subdivided into those consisting of noun + noun, and those with adjective + noun:

Maintenance costs	*complex activity*
blood constituents	*possible signals*
energy storage	*aromatic substances*
food intake	*environmental temperature*
energy requirement	*monogastric animals*
food energy	

Participants then went back to the texts themselves to see if they could find more noun + noun phrases, and came up with *body weight, pro-duction costs, control centres, blood glucose, heat increment.* Identifying and exploring the structure and meaning of noun + noun phrases is a good way of focusing on the use of ESP topic lexis in many kinds of text. Noun phrases can be longer and more complex – look out for examples in medical and business text. They also feature commonly in

Maintenance costs are decreased proportionately as productivity rises
complex activity which includes such (actions) as the search for food
of blood constituents have been suggested as possible (signals) including
. . . which reveives (signals) from the body as a (result) of consumption of food
some (agent) associated with energy storage acts as a signal for the long term . . .
that signals are received directly from the crop as is explained later.
A (variety) of aromatic substances such as dill, aniseed, coriander and . . .
food intake and energy requirement suggests that, as with energy, intake should vary
respond to environment temperature in the same way as monogastric animals, in that
This can be considered as (an aspect) of energy (balance) in the
Digestibility here is expressed as the coefficient for food energy
appears to be relatively unimportant in grazing as animals will graze in the dark and

Figure 3

newspaper headlines – try working out the possible meanings of the headline *Christmas Toy Trip Border Wrangle.*

Verbs and verb phrases (with dotted lines in Figure 3) that are not in themselves specialist agricultural terms, but which appear commonly in academic writing, were also noted by participants. These included *includes, have been suggested as . . ., acts as . . ., suggests that . . ., can be considered as . . ., appears to be . . . .*

Other features that could be focused on include:

– General nouns like *aspect, variety, substance, signal, result, way, balance* (circled in Figure 3). These have very little specific meaning on their own and must be further explained, either beforehand, as in *energy balance,* or later, as in *signals from the body, result of consumption of food.*
– phrases with verbs ending in -ed: *are decreased, have been suggested as . . ., associated with . . . .* These can be further classified structurally into passives or adjectival uses, or semantically into subject specialist terms and academic discourse terms.
– nouns formed from common verbs: *maintenance, storage, consumption, digestibility, requirement.*
– adjectives formed from nouns: *aromatic, environmental.*

So, starting with concordance lines assembled by the class, this session stimulated a rich exploration of the meanings, uses and patterns associated with the word *as,* and, in addition, of many other features typical of that type of text which had been captured by chance in the concordance lines.

None of these analysis activities requires advance preparation, since they are general enough to be valid for any text. Such sessions can always be supported by the use of a dictionary should queries arise or more examples be needed.

Summary of activities used

Assembling
- learners identify lines containing the key word, and write them up (on the board or on an OHP transparency), with the key word in a central position.

Analysing
- learners identify the boundaries of the chunks containing the key word,
- learners classify the chunks according to their meaning or use, pattern or grammatical classes they appear to fit,
- learners think of known examples parallel to those they have found and classified.

Extension and consolidation
- learners use dictionaries to consolidate specific areas or uses of the key word (concentrating on the uses occurring in these lines) and share findings,
- they keep a record of useful phrases and examples in their own notebooks,
- learners look at other features that happen to occur in the concordance lines, look for more examples in the original text, and record examples of any useful items.

This first sample session has illustrated some very general, open analysis activities that can be done with any text and with minimal teacher guidance. The next sample session exemplifies some more specific analysis activities, based on categories of word meaning and use, identified in advance by the teacher or materials writer.

Sample session 2: common words in spontaneous spoken narrative

The activities in this session were based on hand-generated concordances assembled in advance by a class of 20 intermediate students who were completing a unit on an incident in an African game park. Recorded materials included an interview and a story about a family's encounter with a man-eating leopard which had been inadvertently released back into the game park. I did a quick scan through the transcripts to find ten words that all occurred a reasonable number of times. These were: *at, had, I, in, of, one, so, that/that's, his, what/ what's.* They were all fairly high on the spoken frequency list – most were above the 50 level.

Students had followed two or three task-based cycles, which entailed listening several times to the story and interview in order to complete the various tasks successfully. I then assigned each of the selected words to two students, and for homework they were asked to read through the transcripts again, searching for examples of the word assigned to them. They wrote out the concordance lines for their word on an OHP transparency and gave these to me a day ahead of the next class.

This allowed time for me to devise different kinds of consciousness-raising activities. With some words, e.g. *one*, I used a dictionary to help identify and describe useful categories. I actually wrote the instructions on the bottom of each OHP transparency, which I then photocopied for future use. Activities for three of the ten sets of concordances are illustrated below.

son. He was just, on, I think about one at the time
And we er – I forget exactly where we went
This is an important detail. I have to make it clear.
first night we were there as I describe we went to
easily scared away. So, I got out of bed,
and the roof. So I lit a hurricane lamp
as the animal came by, I switched the hurricane
And er eventually and I don't exaggerate

Figure 4

- In Figure 4 look at the verb phrases containing the word *I*. Can you divide them into two categories: those which actually tell the story and advance the action (e.g. *I got out of bed*), and those which don't (e.g. *I think*)? Could you then try to find ways to classify the verbs in the second group?

But erm – on this occasion er, we went to Tsavo
connect with the ceiling. This is an important detail. I have
maybe kill – In fact this tig – this leopard that erm, we
In fact – this tig – this leopard that erm, we escaped
I don't exaggerate at this point – it started looking in at the
How old was your son at this time? He was just one.
So, this one already had its er –
And in the case of this one it had been kept in Nairobi

Figure 5

- In Figure 5 find four examples of *this* which probably refer to the leopard.
- Look at the four other phrases with *this*. Which two refer to the time of the actual story and which two refer to the discourse itself (i.e. not the actual story)?
- Choose three phrases with *this* that you think you might find useful. Tell each other.

> Oh, I think about one at the time.
> Er. So eventually . . . One of my plans
> just a bit less than one: Er. So
> we were in danger. One of my plans
> management, you know, if one area hasn't got enough
> and they mixed up one that had misbehaved
> they thought it was just one that they were
> they were moving from one area to another
> so this one already had its
> In the case of this one, it had been kept

Figure 6

- In Figure 6 find two examples where *one* probably refers to the son's age.
- Find four or five examples where *one* means one of two (or more).
- Find four cases where *one* refers to the leopard.
- Find four phrases where the word *one* is definitely part of a larger chunk.
- Which words do you think typically come after *one*? (There are two here.)
- In which single example could the word *one* be made plural (*ones*)?

The class did each set of activities quite quickly, in pairs, and discussed each set as a class before moving on to the next OHP. They wrote down any useful phrases and insights gained for each word. In the case of the first two sets, from *I* and *this*, we all gained several insights into the nature of spontaneous narrative – there is a lot of talk which is not directly telling the story, but relates to the discourse itself, for example emphasising a point (*I don't exaggerate at this point*) or expressing vagueness (*I forget exactly where*). The focus on *so* also drew attention to the way in which phases in the narrative can be signalled, as well as the meaning of other uses of *so*. For this, a translation activity can work well: 'What word/s do you have for each use of *so* in your language?'

Many useful common lexical phrases were identified and practised: *in the case of this one; I have to make it clear, just a bit less than . . .*; phrases with *of* like *and all the rest of it.* Focusing on *in,* learners identified several 'new' phrases: *in an attempt to . . .,* in the (mistaken) *belief that.* Some useful phrases occurred in more than one set of concordances and so were highlighted several times.

Summary of benefits of language analysis activities

From samples 1 and 2, we have seen that by working with concordance lines focusing on frequent words, learners can:

- become aware of the potential different meanings and uses of common words,
- identify useful phrases and typical collocations they might use themselves,
- gain insights into the structure and nature of both written and spoken discourse.
- become aware that certain language features are more typical of some kinds of text than others.

Many people think that this kind of activity is not practicable with elementary learners or near beginners. The next two sample sessions attempt to disprove this.

Sample session 3: real beginners – a focus on that

Beginners will inevitably have a much more limited experience of English, the pedagogic corpus of texts and transcripts will initially be much smaller, and the texts and recordings shorter and briefer. But these will still contain a high proportion of common words. Beginners need to build up a deployable repertoire of useful words and phrases. Some of these can initially be memorised as fixed chunks. But noticing the part that common words play in such phrases will begin to give learners insights into the way the language works, and help them to see how to generate their own chunks for themselves. (See Batstone 1994a, and Skehan 1994.)

Instead of asking beginners to write out complete concordance lines (which may introduce too many additional and possibly distracting features), learners can simply identify and list the chunks or phrases they find containing the key word.

In this early lesson with real beginners, learners first completed a task listing English words that are international (e.g. *football, hotel, disco*). They then listened to a recording of native speakers doing the same listing task, and compared their lists of items. Finally for the language focus activity they read the transcript of the task recording, firstly underlining all the international words, and secondly, circling all the phrases with the word *that*. These included:

> *Taxi? Oh yes, that's a good one.*
> *Picnic. What about that?*
> *Oh yes, that's a good one.*
> *How about that?*
> *Ah, we've done that one!*
> *We've got that, sorry.*
> *Got that!*
> *That's a good one, yes!*
> *Olympics? That's Greek!*

The phrases with *that* are all common phrases and useful for classroom communication, too. Initially they may well be learnt as prefabricated chunks, much in the same way as people acquire language naturally. Many phrases will be naturally recycled later, when the focus falls on another common word, like *got* or *one*.

Because the learners had done the same task, they had probably tried to express the same meanings themselves, so the meanings of these phrases were all fairly clear from the context. Having identified and practised saying the phrases, learners were asked to classify them; for example phrases starting with *that*, and phrases ending with *that* or *that one*. Some learners preferred to group the ones with similar words or patterns together, as shown here.

How about that?   We've done that one.   Oh Yes, that's a good one.
What about that?   We've got that.   That's a good one, yes.
                       Got that.

Figure 7

The final classification is actually less important than the thought processes leading up to it, which involve learners in examining language, looking for patterns and trying to systematise what they find.

Sample session 4: remedial beginners – a focus on the preposition in

This class of weak remedial beginners had done several tasks about where they lived, and had read three short illustrated extracts from the *Guinness Book of Records* about the largest, the smallest and the most expensive houses in the world. They were simply asked to read the texts again and write the whole phrases with the word *in*. The analysis activity was 'Which phrases with *in* refer to place and which to time? Are there any phrases left over?' Note that this three way classification activity (place, time and other) will work with any preposition.

> The examples found in the current texts included:
> *Biltmore House in Asheville, USA*
> *built in 1890*
> *the most expensive house in the world*
> *in 1922*
> *a cottage in North Wales*
> *built in the 19th century*
> *the smallest house in Great Britain*

In this first set of examples, all the uses of *in* were either place or time. However, to give a broader picture of *in*, learners then were asked to look at examples from earlier texts and task recordings and to classify these:

> *Bridget lives in a small top floor flat in London*
> *In fact there are more men in your family*
> *Which room were these people in?*
> *Come in!*
> *Do you know the names of the letters in English?*
> *Do this in groups.*

In the second set of phrases, it can be deduced that *in* can also be used with groups of people, languages, and fixed phrases like *in fact*. It is also interesting for learners to note the examples of the adverbial use of *in* like *Will you join in? Hand your books in* where *in* ends a sentence (this is rare in most other languages).

This session exemplifies how one can begin an analysis activity using texts from the current lesson, and then go back over familiar texts used in previous lessons, both spoken and written. This search for more examples gives a broader picture of the uses of the common word. In other words, it is making full use of the pedagogic corpus so far covered by the learners.

Sample session 5: revision activities based on course materials: intermediate learners

Here are two ways of exploiting the course materials already covered and to encourage learners to review and reread them, and perhaps to prepare for a test:

Select the same number of common words as you have students in the class. Divide them up amongst the class, giving one word to each student, or two words to each pair of students. Ask students to assemble (on an OHP transparency if possible) concordance lines for their word from the texts and transcripts used so far that term.

Students then try to become experts for that word and other features in its concordances, and set an analysis activity for the class to do next lesson. (These could all be written on sheets to be passed around or put on display round the walls.)

Alternatively, students write the concordance lines with a gap instead of the central word, for the class to guess the missing word.

Try this one – the lines are taken from a well-known Intermediate textbook. Cover up the lines with a sheet of paper and then read them one by one. How many do you have to read before you are sure of what the missing word is?

> I suddenly thought of it — eating an animal
> easier to imagine them — whole animals
> that's because I see rabbits — pets
> It seems to me — if they can't make up their minds
> I want a kitten — I'd like its purring
> It's not — if the animals are tortured or anything
> imitating meat which is nearly — bad as having the real thing
> Saturday I buy some cheese — a treat
> him to the funeral. — they went along the road, they passed
> from a button phobia for as long — she could remember
> green leafy vegetables such — spinach, cabbage or lettuce
> cutting down on food such — hamburgers and sausages

Figure 8

Here we find a greater number of uses of the target word than in the previous activity, perhaps because these are taken from a wider variety of texts.

In the same way, students can prepare their own test items. Groups of students (each with concordances for their assigned word) select a set of three or four cloze items to donate to a 'test item bank' kept by the teacher, who can select from the items to assemble a class test. This gives learners a sense of responsibility, as well as motivation to revise and reread, thereby gaining a deeper experience of language. For both the above activities, the whole of the pedagogic corpus covered so far can be used.

Summary of types of concordance based sessions

In this section, I have described five classroom sessions based on the analysis of concordance lines focusing initially on one of the common words of English. The students themselves were asked to find examples and, in all but one case, to write them up as concordance lines.

In session 1, the concordance lines were assembled in the session itself, and the analysis activities were carried out by students with relatively little teacher guidance.

In session 2, the students assembled the concordance lines in advance, allowing time for the teacher to investigate the concordances they have produced, and to set specific analysis activities for each word, based on given categories of the use of that particular word.

In session 3 the beginners simply listed phrases with *that* from a spontaneous task recording, practised saying these phrases, and tried two ways of classifying them.

In session 4, remedial beginners identified and classified phrases with *in* using categories generalisable to all prepositions. They worked first from the current text, and then went back to consider earlier examples from the textbook. In other words, they made full use of the examples that had already occurred in their pedagogic corpus.

We finally looked at concordance lines taken from the coursebook texts and recordings, prepared in advance by learners for an intermediate revision lesson. This gave us a slightly different picture of the word *as* from the one gained in the first sample session which focused on *as* in agricultural text. This shows that focusing on the same common word for a second (or even third) time but using different data will still give us many new insights into the use of that word, its typical phrases and could lead into the study of other features typical of that type of text.

With experience, the techniques illustrated here can be applied to concordance lines from any text, although specific language questions will vary according to the range of meanings, uses and patterns of the actual word being focused on.

Enhancing the process

This section looks at how the process of generating and exploiting hand assembled concordances can be organised, systematised and varied.

Selecting words for concordancing

- Once you become familiar with your frequency lists you will find it easier to scan a text and pick out suitable words. You will probably find that words from the top 50 or so frequency band are generally the most fruitful.
- If you are teaching ESP, try to find frequency lists for your specialist area.
- Try to cover as many of the frequent words as you can; some words can be focused on several times, with different types of text, and learners can still make new discoveries.
- Keep a record (for each class you teach) of words covered, together with the meanings and uses of those words. (By doing this you are, in fact, creating a *post hoc* lexical syllabus.)
- Keep copies of the concordances and activities to use with other classes working with the same pedagogic corpus (and/or to derive test items from).

If, at some point in the future, you can gain access to a computer and a concordancing program, you can aim at inputting the pedagogic corpus. You can ask the concordance program to build a frequency list for each text or group of texts, and use that, together with its concordancing facility, to help you select words from those texts for students to focus on. Alternatively, you can simply print out the concordances for the class to study.

Varying the focus and process

You can vary

- the number of words you focus on in a session.
- the number of texts you investigate each time (single current text, recently used texts or the whole pedagogic corpus covered to date).
- the type of text – spoken, written or both.
- the types of word focused on each time (prepositions, conjunctive items, adverbs etc.) e.g. one type of word every week.
- student groupings e.g. the whole class collecting one word (from different texts), or groups responsible for different words, or on a rota basis, with each student responsible for a different word each week.
- method of display: 'word-sheets' round the walls – one for each word, to be added to (categories can be built up) as more texts are covered; OHP transparencies with overlays presented to the class.
- timing: assembling concordances in lesson or in advance of lesson.
- the analysis activities set on the concordances: general or specific (cf.

sessions 1 and 2 above) with or without given categories. (For more types of consciousness-raising activities see Willis and Willis 1996, Paper 7.)
- extension and consolidation: with/without reference to dictionaries and grammars; students can be encouraged to build up their own dictionaries, and/or to look for more examples in their outside reading/other contacts with the language.
- testing activities: e.g. blanking out common words in mixed sets of concordance lines from familiar texts: lines chosen by student or teacher or picked at random from an item bank built up by the class.

Balancing the pedagogic corpus

The pedagogic corpus will probably consist of the texts and recordings (with transcripts for ease of study) from the class coursebook, plus any supplementary materials used by the class as a whole, in other words texts and transcripts with which they are all familiar. Individual learners should be encouraged to read more widely on their own, and to look out for more examples of specific features from outside data, but since this will be part of the individual learner's corpus, and unfamiliar to other learners, it would not form part of the pedagogic corpus available for concordance analysis.

As I argued earlier, if we are to ask students to study features of language occurring in the texts and transcripts they are familiar with, it is essential that the data forming their pedagogic corpus constitutes a representative sample of the language they will be using in their target discourse communities, in 'real-life' situations.

How can materials writers ensure that their coursebook materials do offer a representative sample of language? How can teachers selecting supplementary materials ensure that these, together with the course-book texts and recordings, will offer a thorough and balanced coverage of the language features, words, meanings, patterns and uses their students need? If, say, you are assembling a general course on spoken English, how can you ensure that the recordings you use offer a balanced sample of spoken English?

A pedagogic corpus is inevitably quite small and needs to be selected in a principled manner. You should ensure, for example, that there is not an overdue emphasis on planned, edited spoken monologue (e.g. radio documentary, rehearsed interviews) or purely transactional talk. There is a danger of including too much data of this kind (often because it is more easily accessible) at the expense of spontaneous spoken interaction, where turn-taking and topic shifting is free and relatively unpredictable.

Ideally what is needed is information derived from a larger research corpus, one that is representative of the type of language the learners will be needing. A large corpus (whether spoken or written, general or specialist) can give us information about the frequency of word forms and their typical patterns and uses. Armed with a checklist derived from a larger corpus, we can then aim to collect a pedagogic corpus which reflects these patterns and uses – a language 'microcosm'. If the pedagogic corpus can then be put on to computer and analysed, the frequency lists can be compared, and typical examples of, say, the most frequent 2,000–3,000 words (as identified by the research corpus) can be selected from its concordances. If words or uses of words are found to be missing, we can try to select additional recordings/texts or design exercises that aim to fill the gaps. It is impossible to achieve a 100 per cent match between the pedagogic corpus and the research corpus, but a principled approach to corpus design is more likely to cover the language that students need than an approach which selects texts and language focus points in a more random fashion.

It is impossible for most language teachers and course designers to assemble their own research corpus for a particular group of learners, unless the learners' target discourse is a very narrow, well-defined area which is readily researchable. But there is a growing range of language corpora with frequency lists already assembled and over the next few years these will be made available for public use. It is, however, possible to aim at assembling learners' own pedagogic corpus, i.e. one that reflects as far as possible their target language needs, even without the insights gained from a computational analysis of a research corpus.

The most frequent words, meanings and patterns are obviously going to be the most useful for learners and give the most efficient coverage of the target discourse. But in addition to the criterion of frequency, we need to take into account factors such as learnability and learners' immediate interests. Thus the syllabus might well include words that are similar in the two languages, and words from topic areas and types of text (e.g. pop songs, magazine pieces) that students find motivating. Such texts would then become part of the pedagogic corpus, and would undoubtedly also serve to illustrate more common uses of common words.

Conclusion

I have attempted to show in this paper that, even without access to an appropriate research corpus or computers of any kind, using hand-generated concordances to focus on common words can provide a wealth of effective learning opportunities for our learners. Even with the small samples of concordance lines illustrated here, learners would, for example, gain insights into the nature of academic text and spoken narrative – all useful for students wishing to write or to speak with more fluency and naturalness.

A full-length lexical syllabus derived from a suitable research corpus might comprise an inventory of, say, 2,000–3,000 words and their meanings and patterns. This could be used as a checklist, and would allow the teacher or materials writer to gain a far more reliable coverage of language that learners needed. But this is the ideal, and without computational facilities, it would take a long time to find and assemble suitable examples of all these words from the pedagogic corpus.

The benefits of focusing on a mere 50 or so very common words may at first sight have seemed somewhat limited in scope. However, because these words occur so frequently in all kinds of text and have so many different uses, they provide the cement for a huge number of fixed and semi-fixed expressions and grammatical patterns. Using these common words as 'bait', learners are likely to catch a wide variety of other useful words, phrases and patterns, and will inevitably gain insights into new aspects of the target language as exemplified by their pedagogic corpus.

The analysis activities encourage learners to process text more closely, to systematise their knowledge and to look out for similar examples. Once attention has been drawn to the meanings, uses and functions of common words in the target language, learners are more likely to notice and reflect on further occurrences of the language items that have been made salient through study of the concordances. This process should lead to the development of the learner's interlanguage. Analysis activities and consciousness-raising procedures can also encourage learner independence and efficient dictionary use (especially with regard to the common words that students often think they know already and don't bother to look up). They help learners to recognise the parts played by collocation and lexical phrases and to realise there is more to language than just words and grammar.

Working directly from the data, searching for patterns, investigating and describing what is actually there, is a secure and relatively unthreatening activity. It is ideal for mixed level classes since, being a learner-centred activity, it allows students to work at their own level, in their own time and in their own ways. It also provides solid benefits for teachers. I have constantly found that language analysis activities inform and enrich my own view of the language. Not only learners but also teachers are likely to gain from an investigative approach to language.

Data collection and materials development

Appendix A Wordlists from a general research corpus

1	the 11110235	51	out 398444	101	world 170293
2	of 5116374	52	about 393279	102	get 168694
3	to 4871692	53	so 378358	103	these 168486
4	and 4574340	54	can 369280	104	how 167461
5	a 4264651	55	what 359467	105	down 166119
6	in 3609229	56	no 342846	106	being 165168
7	that 1942449	57	its 333261	107	before 165119
8	is 1826742	58	new 324639	108	much 164217
9	for 1716788	59	two 308310	109	where 161691
10	it 1641524	60	mr 302507	110	made 161595
11	was 1395706	61	than 297385	111	should 159023
12	on 1354064	62	time 293404	112	off 155770
13	with 1262756	63	some 293394	113	make 153978
14	he 1260066	64	into 290931	114	good 153878
15	I 1233584	65	people 289131	115	still 151889
16	as 1096506	66	now 287096	116	're 151359
17	be 1030953	67	after 280710	117	such 150812
18	at 1022321	68	them 279678	118	day 150684
19	by 980610	69	year 272250	119	know 147052
20	but 884610	70	over 266404	120	through 145920
21	are 880318	71	first 265772	121	say 143888
22	have 879595	72	only 260177	122	president 143502
23	from 872792	73	him 259962	123	don't 142288
24	his 849494	74	like 258874	124	those 142260
25	you 819187	75	do 256863	125	see 141845
26	they 779636	76	could 255010	126	think 140701
27	this 771211	77	other 254620	127	old 140096
28	not 704615	78	my 253585	128	go 137929
29	has 693238	79	last 238932	129	between 137009
30	had 648205	80	also 236350	130	against 136989
31	an 629155	81	just 232389	131	did 135593
32	we 552869	82	your 227200	132	work 131780
33	will 542649	83	years 217074	133	take 131212
34	said 534522	84	then 214274	134	man 130580
35	their 527987	85	most 208894	135	pounds 130095
36	or 527919	86	me 206475	136	too 129804
37	one 522291	87	may 198700	137	long 127660
38	which 513286	88	because 196595	138	own 125299
39	there 501951	89	says 193730	139	life 124047
40	been 496696	90	very 189285	140	going 124018
41	were 485024	91	well 188445	141	today 123869
42	who 480651	92	our 186013	142	right 121995
43	all 478695	93	government 184618	143	home 121052
44	she 469709	94	back 184105	144	week 119115
45	her 448175	95	us 182796	145	here 118177
46	would 430566	96	any 180222	146	another 116325
47	up 428457	97	even 178657	147	while 115963
48	more 422111	98	many 173938	148	under 113114
49	when 404674	99	three 173093	149	London 112310
50	if 401086	100	way 172787	150	million 112138

Figure 9 *The 150 most frequent word forms occurring in The COBUILD Bank of English **written** corpus of 196 million words*

64

1	the 500843	51	are 51775	101	okay 18757
2	I 463445	52	got 51727	102	much 18567
3	and 367221	53	don't 51273	103	didn't 18521
4	you 359144	54	oh 51013	104	thing 18480
5	it 313032	55	then 44372	105	lot 18453
6	to 308438	56	were 41453	106	where 18440
7	that 284422	57	had 41185	107	something 18134
8	a 273009	58	very 41128	108	way 17895
9	of 242811	59	she 38841	109	here 17819
10	in 187523	60	get 38361	110	quite 17470
11	er 178464	61	my 38194	111	come 17089
12	yeah 155259	62	people 37774	112	their 16892
13	they 135084	63	when 37335	113	down 16678
14	was 133022	64	because 37172	114	back 16505
15	erm 132836	65	would 35945	115	has 16017
16	we 124928	66	up 35894	116	place 15888
17	mm 122674	67	them 34766	117	bit 15520
18	is 113420	68	go 34127	118	used 15267
19	know 111741	69	now 33801	119	only 15159
20	but 100648	70	from 33633	120	into 15094
21	so 91836	71	really 33444	121	these 15064
22	what 89364	72	your 33310	122	three 15059
23	there 88938	73	me 33278	123	work 15005
24	on 88456	74	going 32598	124	will 14939
25	yes 87211	75	out 32015	125	her 14286
26	have 84294	76	sort 31555	126	him 14160
27	he 79137	77	been 30405	127	his 14029
28	for 77842	78	which 30334	128	doing 13921
29	do 77207	79	see 30325	129	first 13273
30	well 75287	80	did 30175	130	than 12998
31	think 74543	81	say 29720	131	went 12842
32	right 74191	82	two 28817	132	put 12692
33	be 66492	83	an 27485	133	why 12653
34	this 65424	84	who 27220	134	our 12610
35	like 63948	85	how 26837	135	years 12437
36	've 63160	86	some 26172	136	off 12393
37	at 62654	87	name 26029	137	those 12248
38	with 61289	88	time 25990	138	us 12245
39	no 60885	89	'll 25154	139	course 12211
40	as 58871	90	more 24586	140	mhm 12112
41	mean 58825	91	said 23143	141	isn't 12060
42	all 58360	92	'cos 22345	142	over 11874
43	're 57131	93	things 21982	143	look 11297
44	or 56857	94	actually 21131	144	done 11247
45	if 56774	95	good 20783	145	year 11224
46	about 56321	96	other 20378	146	take 11190
47	not 56109	97	want 20375	147	being 11153
48	just 55329	98	by 20260	148	should 11007
49	one 55189	99	could 19435	149	school 11001
50	can 53090	100	any 18958	150	thought 10786

Figure 10   *The 150 most frequent word forms occurring in The COBUILD Bank of English **spoken** corpus of 196 million words*

Appendix B

This table shows what proportion of general English text is covered by the most frequent word forms. By word forms we mean that *have, has, had,* etc. and singular and plural nouns, for example, each count as a separate item.

Table 1

The most common		
25 word forms account for 29% of written text and 29% of spoken text		
50	36%	36%
100	42%	46%
500	56%	66%

(Source: Cobuild Bank of English: figures based on a written corpus of 196 million words and a corpus of unscripted speech of 15 million words.)

3 Telling tails: grammar, the spoken language and materials development

Ronald Carter, Rebecca Hughes and Michael McCarthy

Introduction

Descriptions of the English language and of English grammar, in particular, have been largely based on written sources and on written examples. This is inevitable since examples of written English are easier to obtain and it is only recently that audio technology has facilitated recordings of the spoken language. One consequence of this situation is, however, that 'correct grammar' has come to mean 'correct grammar as represented by the written language' and that many perfectly normal and regularly occurring utterances made by standard English speakers (of whatever variety – not just standard British English), including, of course, teachers of English, and therefore heard by learners of English, have by omission come to be classified as 'ungrammatical'.

The situation is changing, however, and corpora of spoken English are now being assembled which will allow more precise description of the properties of spoken English and thus enable learners of English to become more aware of a wider range of forms and structures than hitherto. With reference to one such corpus this paper seeks to outline work in the description of spoken English and to discuss some of the implications for English language teaching, and, in particular, materials development.

The corpus which will be referred to is based in the Department of English Studies at the University of Nottingham, and forms part of a joint research project between the University and Cambridge University Press. The working corpus from which examples can be drawn will soon total five million words, though the main aim is to construct a qualitative corpus and not simply a large quantitative corpus. The way the Nottingham Corpus is constructed allows very precise contextualised description of grammar, in particular, and its design allows a discourse-based view of language to prevail in all descriptions (see McCarthy and Carter 1994, and, for more generalised discussion, Crowdy 1993). A contextualised description of grammar means that when a particular form is described, due account is taken of typical contexts of use: for example, differences between 'going to' and 'will' are different speaker choices according to interpersonal and social-context-sensitive factors such as the formality of the situation as much as they relate to strength of prediction.

Consequently, there is a focus on interpersonal communication in a range of social contexts and, wherever possible, differences and distinctions are drawn between the kinds of language used in different contexts. There are thus many examples of English used in informal contexts and comparisons can be made which illustrate speakers making different grammatical choices according to the situation they are in. The Nottingham research team has set out to collect a corpus which shows grammar at work beyond sentence-based contexts of written language and formal spoken contexts such as broadcast talk; its emphasis on grammatical choice according to different communicative contexts is also designed to make it of potential use to language teachers and learners.

Authentic vs. scripted dialogues

When naturally-occurring language is compared with language constructed for the purposes of language teaching, marked differences can be observed. Here are two examples, drawn in fact from Australian English data:

Text 1: scripted text from a textbook

Making a Doctor's Appointment
(telephone rings)

Patient:	Could I make an appointment to see the doctor please?
Receptionist:	Certainly, who do you usually see?
Patient:	Dr Cullen.
Receptionist:	I'm sorry but Dr Cullen has got patients all day. Would Dr Maley do?
Patient:	Sure.
Receptionist:	OK then. When would you like to come?
Patient:	Could I come at four o'clock?
Receptionist:	Four o'clock? Fine. Could I have your name, please?

(Nunan and Lockwood 1991)

Text 2: authentic text

Confirming an Appointment with the Doctor

Receptionist:	Doctor's rooms, can you hold the line for a moment?

Patient: Yes.
Receptionist: Thanks.
(pause)
Receptionist: Hello.
Patient: Hello.
Receptionist: Sorry to keep you waiting.
Patient: That's all right um I'm just calling to confirm an appointment with Dr X for the first of October.
Receptionist: Oh . . .
Patient: Because it was so far in advance I was told to.
Receptionist: I see what you mean, to see if she's going to be in that day.
Patient: That's right.
Receptionist: Oh we may not know yet.
Patient: Oh I see.
Receptionist: First of October . . . Edith . . . yes.
Patient: Yes.
Receptionist: There she is OK you made one. What's your name?
Patient: At nine fift. . .
Receptionist: Got it got it.

(Burns, Joyce and Gollin 1996)

There are a number of general observations which can be made about the second text which marks it off as naturally-occurring discourse. For example, in text 2 speakers interrupt each other and speak at the same time. There are 'unpredicted' sequences such as the opening exchange in which the patient is asked to hold the line and content-less words (*oh*) which serve to indicate surprise or incomprehension. There are phrases which oil the wheels of the conversation rather than contribute any specific content or propositions (*oh I see*; *I see what you mean*). A number of the utterances are incomplete or are completed by the other speaker. And the conversation is terminated without the usual ritualistically polite closing strategies found in much textbook discourse.

By contrast, the language of the coursebook represents a 'can do' society in which interaction is generally smooth and trouble-free, the speakers cooperate with each other politely; the conversation is neat, tidy and predictable; utterances are almost as complete as sentences and no-one interrupts anyone else or speaks at the same time as anyone else. The two texts therefore represent different orders of reality. The scripted text is easier to comprehend but is unlikely to be reproduced in actual contexts of use; the unscripted text is real English but more difficult to comprehend and to produce and therefore likely to be considered less appropriate pedagogically. Pedagogical issues are clearly central and it is thus not our wish in any way to imply criticism of the coursebook material, which is anyway only an extract from a much broader pedagogically rich sequence of material sensitively keyed to learning requirements at a particular stage in language development.

Issues of pedagogy and naturalness in language will be considered towards the end of this paper as they are clearly of major importance for English language teaching. It is first necessary to illustrate features of language and of grammar in particular which a corpus of spoken English reveals and which therefore may be of relevance for syllabus content. The features mentioned in this paper are selected from a much more comprehensive inventory, further examples of which are given in Carter and McCarthy (1995) and McCarthy and Carter (1995). One grammatical feature in particular is given especial consideration as it is our view that the most challenging issues for teaching, learning and materials development can be best illustrated by putting a key feature under a descriptive and pedagogic microscope.

What is a tail?

'Tail' structures are selected here because they are a prominent feature of the Nottingham spoken corpus and because they are not adequately treated in conventional descriptive grammars of English, including some of the most comprehensive grammars of the English language. Tails are almost exclusive to the spoken language and where they do occur in written English they are selected in order to give that written text a markedly spoken character. Such forms present therefore a particular challenge to the materials designer wishing to provide teachers and learners with an opportunity to encounter a key feature of spoken language in use.

Tails: basic examples

Tails are an important feature of a listener-sensitive, affective grammar and occur frequently in informal contexts of language use. Tails allow speakers to express attitudes, to add emphasis, to evaluate and to provide repetition for listeners (see Aijmer 1989). All the examples involve some kind of emphatic recapitulation, either by means of a pronoun or a clarifying noun and can even involve verbatim repetition:

> He's a real problem **is Jeff**
> She's got a nice personality **Jenny has**
> It's too hot for me, **Singapore**
> I'm going to have burger and chips **I am**

It can make you feel very weak **it can flu.**
It was good **that book**
It's a really good film **that one**

Tails, we repeat, are not extensively treated or explicated in traditional grammars, not least because tails only rarely occur in written examples. Quirk *et al.* (1985: 1417) refer to such features as 'tags' but do not offer detailed treatment; Halliday (1985) provides a more detailed discussion of 'tags' in relation to word order.

All the examples of tails above are in bold face. It will be seen that tails perform an essentially recapitulatory function, often necessarily so, as tails are not infrequent in unplanned discourse. They ensure a cohesion which in pre-planned discourse can normally be effectively constructed. Tails are listener-sensitive in so far as they provide orientation and emphasis for the listener, in particular, by means of a clarifying noun, verb phrase or anaphoric pronoun. A tail can also sometimes be especially emphatic in its clarification by combining repetition of both a noun and an accompanying verb or verb phrase:

It can make you feel very weak **it can flu**
He's a real problem **is Jeff**

Tails are one element in what might be described as an *interpersonal* grammar. This 'tails' component of such a grammar is listener-sensitive in so far as the listener gets a clarified and 'expanded' message. But, additionally and more importantly, the speaker attempts to involve the listener by an expression of feelings and attitude. The emphasis is personal and affective and also includes some kind of positive or negative evaluation or signalling of stance on the main proposition contained by the utterance. And it is worth underlining here that tails are not some kind of aberrant, non-standard, regional dialect form; they occur extensively in the standard English dialect and are used by a wide range of speakers irrespective of gender, region, age or any other social, geographical or biological factor. If we are to allow language learners greater choice in the expression of feelings and attitudes and in helping their interlocutors relate to such expression then tails will need to be appropriately embedded within language coursebook dialogues and, ideally, dealt with in the broader pedagogical framework.

Grammar patterns and grammar as choice: some questions

From the examples of tails assembled above it may appear that the rules for tails are relatively straightforward and categorisable. As grammatical forms, embedded within single sentences or utterances, this is to an extent true; and it is not difficult to point to patterns which are ungrammatical. For example:

> Jenny's a good swimmer she is
> *Jenny's a good swimmer she's
> She's a good swimmer Jenny is
> *She's a good swimmer, Jenny's
> ?Jenny's a good swimmer Jenny

from which we may deduce that tails cannot be constructed from contracted forms, and that full noun head subject repetition is not normal.

But in terms of interpersonal values what are the communicative differences and distinctions between the following tails? Thus:

> She's a good swimmer Jenny is
> She's a good swimmer is Jenny
> She's a good swimmer, Jenny.

Are these distinct choices for learners or are the subtleties sufficiently delicate for them to be discounted in a discourse grammar operating at, say, upper-intermediate levels of proficiency?

To what extent are tails available to us as **choices** and what **kinds** of choices are provided by tails in grammar? Clearly, tails enable us to mark an utterance as overtly spoken and interactive but what **is** the precise nature of the choice between the next examples or are such choices simply between written and spoken modes of English?

> It's too hot for me, Singapore
> Singapore is too hot for me.

Such considerations also move us beyond the boundaries of the single sentence in so far as the precise communicative value of each utterance cannot be properly assessed without the evidence supplied by a more extended and surrounding text, for the functions of tails may depend to a considerable extent on **where** they occur in a conversational sequence. It may be relevant therefore to explore tails and, where feasible, to supply learning guidance in respect of tails in extended discourse environments; it is otherwise possible (wrongly) to conclude that tails can be used indiscriminately in every utterance in a sequence. Such a phenomenon would be unusual because it is difficult to envisage a sustained conversation in which every proposition (rather than only selected propositions) were emphatically recapitulated, evaluated or overtly flagged for stance. In the case of narratives, it is difficult to envisage that any tale in which tails were selected to emphasise every event would be judged to be especially telling. Telling tales means drawing attention to key events of the fictional or represented world, foregrounding and highlighting them for the listener within the overall narrative structure.

Sample materials

If we accept that 'tails' are a normal rather than a deviant feature of spoken grammar (our corpus data confirms that tails are distributed across a range of different contexts) and if we accept that learners ought to be introduced to tails as an expressive resource and be guided in their choices of whether, how and in what ways to use tails, then teaching materials will need to address such conditions.

The examples below are drawn from extracts of a draft unit of a forthcoming 'discourse' grammar of English, designed in particular with reference to the principle of grammatical choice and constructed in order to introduce to learners and give them practice in the comprehension and communicative use of spoken grammar including such forms as tails.

UNIT 00: TAILS

A   Introduction

1. Look at these extracts from conversations. Which extracts do you think are particularly informal? In addition to contractions (**he'd**, **it's**, **I'll**), mark the words or phrases which you think make the conversations informal.

   Which of the extracts a–d is the most formal? Rewrite it to make it sound more informal.

a) A: Did Max help you?
   B: Yes, he moved all my books.
   A: He said he'd try and help out.
   B: He was very helpful, Max was.

b) A: It's not a good wine, that.
   B: I'll still try some.
   A: Where's your glass?

c) A: What are you going to have?
   B: I can't decide.
   A: I'm going to have a burger with chilli sauce, I am.
   B: It's a speciality here, chilli sauce is.

---

d) A: That's a very nice road.
    B: It runs right across the moors.
    A: Then it goes through all those lovely little villages.
    B: Yes, the villages are beautiful.

2. Which of the following sentences would be more likely to be used in formal situations and which would be more likely to be used in informal situations? Remember that in informal situations it is often difficult to plan and prepare what to say and therefore to make things clear for your listener. Mark each sentence in the pair (F) formal or (I) informal.

i)   (a) Gandhi was a great leader.   (F)
     (b) He was a great leader Gandhi was.   (I)

ii) (a) He smokes too much, David does.
     (b) David smokes too much.

iii) (a) It's very nice, that road.
     (b) That road is very nice.

iv) (a) You're always getting it wrong you are.
     (b) You're always getting it wrong.

v)   (a) I'm a bit lacking in confidence I am.
     (b) I am a bit lacking in confidence.

vi) (a) Hong Kong is an exciting place.
     (b) It's an exciting place Hong Kong is.

vii) (a) They're not cheap those clothes aren't.
     (b) Those clothes aren't cheap.

viii)(a) That's a very nice beer, Fortuna is.
     (b) Fortuna is a very nice beer.

Answers and Commentary

1. a) **Max was**   b) **that**   c) **I am; chilli sauce is**

    Conversation d) is the most formal conversation. A suggested more informal version is:

    A: It's a very nice road that.
    B: It runs right across the moors it does.
    A: Then it goes through all those lovely little villages.
    B: Yes, they're beautiful the villages are.

2. i)   (a) F (b) I;   ii) (a) I (b) F;   iii) (a) I (b) F;
    iv)   (a) I (b) F;   v)   (a) I (b) F;   vi) (a) F (b) I;
    vii) (a) F (b) F;   viii) (a) I (b) F

In conversation we often want to give emphasis to statements and we can use tails to help us. Tails are single words or phrases which occur at the end of a clause and extend what has already been said. A tail often consists of a phrase which extends a pronoun or demonstrative, it normally occurs as a complete phrase even though the phrase which is put at the front of the clause may be contracted (for example **It's** an exciting place **Hong Kong is**).

Notice that tails often occur in statements in which the speaker is saying positive or negative things rather than saying neutral things. You get tails in sentences in which there are words like **exciting, very nice, great, too much, a bit lacking.**

B Discovering Patterns of Use

> Cover the box opposite until you have completed your observations for B1 and B2

1. Look at the following conversations. What do you observe about the order of words in the tails?

i) A: Did David make it on time?
   B: No, he was late. He was very cross, David.

ii) A: She's a very good tennis player is Hiroko.
    B: I know. She always beats me easily.

iii) A: Did Max help you?
     B: Yes, he was very helpful was Max.

iv) A: Have you heard her sing?
    B: Yes, she sings beautifully, Laura does.
    A: She does, doesn't she?

v) A: Have you visited Singapore?
   B: Yes, but it's far too hot for me, Singapore.
   A: It's not just hot, it's humid as well.

2. Now look at the following sentences. The sentences are all typically spoken sentences. The tails here are repetitions or occur with question tags. What do you observe about the position and order of the tails?

i) I went there early. It would be about seven o'clock, it would. It wasn't dark yet.

ii) It's difficult to eat isn't it, spaghetti? You have to suck it into your mouth.

iii) It'll melt won't it, the ice-cream?

iv) She's a good tennis player Hiroko is, isn't she?

v) You hardly ever show emotion you don't. Don't you have any feelings for her?

vi) She still hasn't finished hasn't Maria.

C   Observations about tails

1. Many tails consist of a noun (or pronoun) and a verb which extend a pronoun (or noun) or demonstrative which has occurred earlier in the clause. The noun can either follow or precede the verb (e.g. He was very helpful **Max was**; He was very helpful **was Max**; she still hasn't finished **hasn't Maria**; she still hasn't finished **Maria hasn't**).

2. When a pronoun comes first in a clause and the tail is formed with a noun then the noun normally makes the comment stronger (e.g. He was a great leader **Gandhi was**).

3. The noun can also be used as a tail on its own (e.g. He was very helpful, **Max**; It's an exciting place, **Hong Kong**).

4. When pronouns occur in tails the word order of the preceding phrase is repeated; otherwise the sentence may be heard as a question (e.g. You're stupid **you are**; (you're stupid are you?); it would take about half-an-hour **it would**; (it would take about half-an-hour would it?))

5. Tails can occur with tag questions and can be placed either before or after the tag (e.g. She's a good player **Hiroko is**, isn't she?; it's not easy to eat, is it, **spaghetti**?)

6. When the tail repeats a verb which is not a verb 'to be' or an auxiliary/modal verb then a **do** verb is used (e.g. She sings very well **she does**; they complain all the time **they do**).

7. Tails always agree with the phrase to which they refer (e.g. **It's not** a good wine **that isn't**; **She'll** never pass the exam, **won't Toni**). Negatives with 'hardly', 'scarcely' etc. keep a negative tail (e.g. He scarcely speaks, **he doesn't**).

D   Follow-up and Summary

1. In this section we will observe more about tails. Once again it can help us to compare formal and informal conversations.

   Rewrite the following dialogues to make them sound a little more informal.

a) A: Here's the menu. What do you fancy?
    B: It's certainly a nice menu.

    A: I'm going to have steak and chips.
    B: I fancy the spaghetti but I always manage to drop it down the front of my shirt.

b) A: I like them. David and Jean make a nice couple.
    B: Do you reckon they'll get married eventually?
    A: David is still lacking in confidence, I suppose, and Jean is a bit too young at the moment isn't she?

c) A: Sophie will never lose weight.
    B: She hardly ever eats cakes or chips.
    A: I should eat less. I'm far too flabby.

2. Re-tell this narrative making use of tails where you consider it appropriate.

It was late at night and typically the last bus had gone. So I decided to walk home. I was really cross with Jeff. He'd left the party early because he had to be up early for work the next day. Anyway, as I walked along our road, I heard a car behind me. It was really dark. I became very frightened and started to run. A man got out of the car and started to follow me. I ran more quickly and then he began to run more quickly too. By the time I reached our house he had caught up with me. I turned round. It was Jeff. He'd come after me to apologise . . .

Where did you put the tails? How many did you use?

3. What do you observe about the use of the tails (in bold) in the following example? Rewrite the sentences so that the tail is the clear subject of the sentence.

i)   It never occurred to me, **the danger I was in**. (The danger I was in never occurred to me.)

ii) That was the book I wanted, **the one with the picture on the front**.

iii) It was a strange feeling, **walking into that place**.

iv) They're far too hot, **those countries where it's all humid**.

Figure 1

Evaluating materials for spoken grammar teaching

The above draft materials are at the time of writing in the process of being trialled in different parts of the world by teachers and by upper-intermediate/advanced students of English. Among the questions being considered, which range from matters of unit design and progression to broader issues of appropriate pedagogy, are the following:

i) To what extent is it appropriate for students to undertake pattern practice tasks **in writing** of forms which are almost exclusively spoken in their contexts of use?

ii) Should tape recordings or CD-Rom support not be integral since intonation and rhythm are essential in the appropriate communicative and interactive delivery of tails?

iii) The expectations of students and their teachers are that grammar is a sentence-based phenomenon. To what extent should materials conform to such expectations, for both pedagogic and possibly commercial reasons, or should expectations be gradually modified? Indeed, if a genuinely **discourse** grammar is to be taught then **texts** should displace sentences; for it is only in extended stretches of language, especially stretches of spoken language in the case of tails, that the communicative value of particular forms are realised in the language, and can be processed, understood and used in different ways by learners. How far can materials go in the introduction of more extended texts?

What are the limits of tolerance both on teacher and learner expectations, and more materially, on page design, length and economy of presentation in a grammar textbook? It will be observed that in the trial material we have adopted a relatively conservative approach by including a significant proportion of sentence-based examples.

iv) What is an appropriate pedagogy for spoken grammar? What are appropriate demands for practice and production? Should greater emphasis be placed on student awareness of the forms in advance of production? Can production be claimed to be faithfully taught until we know more about the phonology, intonation and communicative meanings of the grammatical patterns? What and how much about tails do we teach and what are the most appropriate and effective ways to do it?

v) To what extent do materials writers remain faithful to their corpus? If they seek to reproduce undilutedly authentic texts then the following, more complex examples of tails (and their accompanying lexis) will also qualify for classroom treatment:
'It can lie dormant for years *it can* though apparently *shingles*'
'. . . cos otherwise they tend to go cold, don't they, *pasta*'
– where tails (italicised) cluster with tags, hedging and modalising items (*though, apparently*) and indeed with other tail forms.

Language awareness and consciousness-raising

Recent research in the field of second language acquisition and development has pointed to some advantages in procedures which **raise learners' consciousness** of particular grammatical forms. Such research takes place against a background of communicative language teaching methodology which in a concern for greater fluency has focused on the learner's use of language (rather than on the learner's ability to analyse the language in order then to learn it through processes of structural drilling or of translation or of other more directed, cognitively-based memorisation of the results of that analysis). Communicative teaching, in spite of numerous pedagogic advantages, has not encouraged in students habits of observation, noticing or conscious exploration of grammatical forms and function and the relevant SLA research has sought to some extent to examine the consequences of a (somewhat) re-balanced methodology.

Research by Ellis (1991b) and Fotos (1994), which builds on research in the previous decade by *inter alia* Bialystok (1982), Sharwood-Smith (1981) and Rutherford (1987), reaches the following tentative conclusions in respect of fostering enhanced grammatical consciousness-raising in the EFL/ESL classroom.

i) Properly-sequenced, controlled, conscious attention to target structures is shown to have positive results in terms of students' eventual acquisition of the structures.

ii) Learning can be more effective if learners are required to process the structure without having automatically to produce it; too precipitous an invitation to production is shown to be unhelpful.

iii) Activities should be sequenced so that students first respond to the meaning of the structure through content-based tasks, then are sufficiently encouraged to raise their consciousness to **notice** the form and function of the target structure and then finally engage in some kind of error identification activity (preferably of identifiable learner errors) where incorrect or inappropriate versions of the key structure are presented.

iv) There is some evidence of the benefits of an emphasis on encouragement to students to use their own interpretive skills during the content-based tasks so that there is some initial, personalised purchase on the target structure and its general meanings.

We have already advocated, (McCarthy and Carter 1995; Carter and McCarthy 1995) in respect of spoken grammar teaching, that traditional PPP (presentation; practice; production) methodologies should be replaced by III (illustration; interaction; induction) alternatives and it is interesting to note the correspondences between this advocacy and conclusions reached in SLA research.

There are other reasons, furthermore, why an approach to spoken grammar through language awareness/consciousness-raising activities should be seriously considered and why such an advocacy may be particularly appropriate.

Work in spoken grammar is inevitably in the early stages both of development and of systematic formal identification and description. It is likely, too, that research into grammatical choice will present some areas of grammar not in terms of yes/no alternatives or categorical imperatives but rather in terms of co-occurrence probabilities. That is, learners will learn that particular forms belong in some spoken rather than in written contexts of use and that their selection will entail a more interactive, interpersonal and affective orientation. They will learn that certain areas of grammar are probabilistically appropriate rather than absolutely or deterministically correct; that where the selection of an utterance with a tail may be an appropriate choice, the option will still remain to select a more formal, less interpersonally-orientated alternative.

It will be seen from the presentation of the discourse grammar unit devoted to tails above that one of our main pedagogic approaches is to encourage in learners habits of observation and to help them to use such observation in the comprehension and formulation of rules for the use of tails. We would argue that interaction with the data and the induction of rules is best fostered by the largely discovery-based procedures adopted in the unit. We remain more hesitant and await trialling results in respect of the following:

i) The extent to which the 'illustration' is successful and produces appropriate, motivating responses in the learner.
ii) The extent to which it is proper to talk in terms of **rules** when it is more appropriate, in the case of such areas of grammar, to introduce understanding of **tendencies, variable rules** and **choices** according to context and interpersonal relations; additionally, the extent to which such notions would be unsettling to teachers and learners alike because of their unfamiliarity.
iii) The extent to which the illustrative data can and should be modified for purposes of classroom language learning or left unmodified in the raw forms in which it is collected, transcribed and stored in the corpus.

The sting in the tail: modifying the authentic

One question raised in the previous section merits separate treatment since it bears upon the use of authentic language data in the classroom. The essential pedagogic question is faced by any materials writer with access to a corpus of naturally-occurring data and with a commitment to using such data for purposes of teaching and learning. The basic issue was polarised above when authentic and specifically scripted dialogues were juxtaposed. It seems from such comparison that learners can benefit from exposure to dialogues which are artificially constructed for learning purposes; however, it is regrettable if learners are prevented from accessing the kinds of authentic data from real conversational discourse now being collected as part of the Nottingham project and other similar ones.

As a further illustration of the issues involved, here is a sample of data from the Nottingham corpus selected to illustrate tails in use. A is telling **B** what route he took in his car to get to **B's** house. Both **A** and **B** engage in a kind of phatic exchange, commenting on and reinforcing each other's comments on the journey in a friendly, informal and suitably interactive, interpersonal style. Repeated tails figure prominently in the exchange:

A: And I came over Mistham by the reservoirs, nice it was.
B: Oh, by Mistham, over the top, nice run.
A: Colours are pleasant, aren't they?
B: Yeah.
A: Nice run, that.

On initial inspection the repetition of certain items by the speakers may well serve a pedagogically reinforcing purpose but closer inspection reveals problems of both presentation and preparation. For example: is the final tone group in line 1 (*nice it was*) a tail or is it an example of 'fronting' of the complement *nice* within its own clause – a not uncommon strategy. If the string **nice it was** is in fact a tail then the structure has to be read as an ellipted structure which in its more complete form would be **it was nice it was**, thus paralleling the ellipted (**it was a**) **nice run that** in the final line, where we have a less ambiguous example of a tail. Pedagogically, it could be argued that the co-presence of potential ellipses complicates pedagogic exposure to the basic tail structure. The exchange as a whole is characterised by a pervasive ellipsis. Ellipsis is, of course, a core feature of the grammar of affective interpersonal exchanges (Carter and McCarthy 1995), but to what extent might the presence of ellipsis distract attention from the target structure of **tails**, even though it is to be expected that naturalistic data will contain **clusterings** of features endemic to spoken grammar? Real data does not neatly demarcate structures for attention; it is untidy.

Lexically, too, there is the additional problem that the speakers **A** and **B** create a discourse world of reference which is similarly undifferentiated. 'Mistham' (a place) could be a distracter; the word 'reservoir' may not be known and could need glossing; the word **run** is in a frequent spoken sense of 'trip' or 'journey' but may be known to learners only as a verb; and the use of the preposition 'over' in the sense of 'across high ground from one place to another' possibly needs separate explanation.

One conclusion reached so far in the preparation of discourse grammar materials is that a middle ground between authentic and concocted data needs to be occupied which involves **modelling** data on authentic patterns. (McCarthy and Carter 1994: 197–8) Here is an example of a possible re-modelling of the data above:

> A: And I came over by the village of Mistham. It was nice it was.
> B: Oh you came over the top by Mistham. That's a nice journey.
> A: The colours are pleasant at this time of year, aren't they?
> B: Yes.
> A: It was a nice run that.

The attempt here by the materials developer is to achieve clarity, tidiness and organisation for purposes of learning, but at the same time to ensure that the dialogue is structured more authentically and naturalistically by modelling on real corpus-based English. It remains to be seen whether this is a weak compromise or a viable strategy. (Our editor, Brian Tomlinson, has, for example, commented to us that ellipsis could easily be left in the above modelled data since it is a common feature of such phatic communication and only rarely causes learners any problems in comprehension.)

Heads or tails: towards an interpersonal grammar for learners

Tails occur, as we have seen, at the end of clauses. Heads occur at the beginning of clauses. Here are some representative examples drawn from the Nottingham corpus:

> **The women,** they all shouted.
> **That chap over there,** he said it was OK.
> **That house on the corner,** is that where they live?
> **This friend of ours, her daughter, Carol,** she bought one.

Robert, this friend of mine I work with, his son was involved in a car crash just like that.

Heads (or *topics* as we refer to them in Carter and McCarthy 1995) perform a basically orienting and focusing function, serving to include information which speakers consider relevant to their listeners and attempting to do so economically, even if in some heads the information is quite densely packed. Often by means of a specific reference to people and places, heads also work to establish a framework of knowledge, knowledge which can subsequently be assumed to be shared, so that listeners can respond to questions or to statements without first having to disambiguate or to seek clarification. Heads are also, in a traditional sense, grammatically anomalous, in that they are in a very indeterminate structural relationship with the item they prefigure in the upcoming clause.

Heads orient the listener to what is to follow and function to organise and structure the message before its main ideational content is communicated; tails are a little more directly interpersonal in function since they provide a more personal, attitudinal or evaluative stance towards the message after its main ideational content has been communicated. Heads can of course include attitudinal matter (e.g that **awful** house on the corner, is that where they live?) but the **main** purpose remains one of providing orientation.

Learning how to use heads and tails, selecting heads or tails or both is an important component in competence in the spoken language, and observing and responding appropriately to them is an important component in active listening and appropriate response to much spoken discourse. Learning how to form and to use tails and heads is an important part of learning how to establish and maintain interpersonal relationships in and through language.

Description of grammar in more interpersonal terms represents, therefore, a challenge for research in discourse grammar; an applied linguistic goal would be to help learners to know and to understand the choices available to them when communicating in speech and in writing, more formally or more informally, more or less interpersonally. Work on spoken grammar is, however, in its infancy and it is important to recognise that it will be some time before description can match the degree and delicacy of work based on written sources which has an extensive and centuries-old tradition of scholarly analysis to support it. For example, further data-based explanation is needed before a more precise description of differences in communicative value can be given between the following utterances:

She's a nice girl, Jenny.

> She's a nice girl is Jenny.
> She's a nice girl, Jenny is.
> Nice girl, Jenny.
> Jenny's a nice girl.
> That girl Jenny, she's nice.

Description will need to take account of evaluation, emphasis, formality and listener discourse knowledge and will additionally require some explanatory context-building which goes beyond the confines and limits of a sentence into the formation of meanings across speaking terms. Work on interpersonal grammars is under way, however (e.g. Poynton 1989; Butler forthcoming). For the present we simply argue for the provenance of tails and that learners should learn how to observe them in context, learn how to infer rules for their use and gradually learn how to produce them with general communicative intent.

Rules, probabilities, choices and the hegemony of the native speaker

It is both misleading and disturbing to learners of English to suggest that grammar is simply a matter of choices. Grammatical rules exist; they have been extensively codified and form the core in the structure of the language, both spoken and written. Rules exist, for example, that prescribe in Standard British English that a plural subject has to be followed by a plural form of the verb and it is simply and unequivocally incorrect for us to write or say therefore that 'the buildings is very high'. Within a central core choices are not possible.

As we have seen, however, there are areas of meaning which are selected within the grammar. The choice of a correctly formed active or a correctly formed passive allows, for example, different forms of representation to be communicated and there is an extensive literature, particularly within the tradition of systemic-functional linguistics, devoted to grammar and language as choice (e.g. Halliday 1994; Hasan and Perrett 1994). Within the domain of spoken grammar we have also seen that it may be more accurate to speak in terms of variable rather than absolute rules for certain choices.

The notion of variable rules is a familiar notion within traditional sociolinguistics, stressing as it does how different, equally correct, forms of language can be selected according to the audience, purpose and context in which meanings are communicated. Because of the direct, face-to-face nature of most spoken encounters, the notion applies to such communication with particular force as speakers select from options which are themselves in turn functionally and communicatively derived. An interpersonal grammar of English will need to specify such options, arranging them with the kind of information and examples which will enable learners to know what are the most likely forms to be chosen in a particular context and what is the probable expressive range (of attitude, evaluation or emphasis) allowed by the chosen form. Spoken grammar will figure prominently in developing interpersonal analysis of grammar. An interpersonal grammar will contain rules but it will also be a probabilistic grammar, motivated by a view of language as choice.

It can be argued that the pedagogic provision in the EFL/ESL class-room of variable, probabilistic rules is a preoccupation rooted in native-speaker modelling of target language learning. Do non-native speaking learners want to or even need to have such options? Why should they want to acquire the expressive resources of a native speaker when most communication undertaken in English is with other non-native speakers, is often primarily utilitarian in orientation, and interpersonal choices may not need to extend much beyond a range of ritualistic politeness formulae? The concern for spoken grammar on the part of native-speaker pedagogues could simply be dismissed as an extension of native-speaker hegemony in English language teaching and learning contexts.

A counter-argument to this position may be simply to say that teachers and learners can always choose not to learn those areas of language where rules are more probabilistic than determinate but that they have no choice at all if such options are not made available. Learners should not be disempowered and syllabuses should not be deliberately impoverished. Learning a language should also, in part at least, involve developing something of a 'feel' for that language. The folk-linguistic term 'feel' has been around for many years in language teaching, but it has remained a largely unanalysed concept. Learners who concentrate on the more rule-bound and referential domains are unlikely to develop that kind of sensitivity, personal response and affect which probably underlies 'feel' and which goes some way to helping them discover, understand and begin to internalise the expressive as well as the referential resources of a language.

Conclusions

The following conclusions might be drawn from current explorations into the description for pedagogic purposes of spoken English:

i) The development of such work is in its initial stages.

ii) A description of features of language is not the same as the pedagogic classroom presentation of those features (Owen 1993). Concocted, made-up language can be perfectly viable but it should be modelled on naturalistic samples.

iii) A discourse-based view of grammar underlines the importance of grammatical choices; particularly in the domain of spoken grammar it is better therefore to work with the notion of regularities and patterns rather than with absolute and invariable rules.

iv) Learners need to be helped to understand the idea of variable rules. Classroom activities should therefore encourage greater language awareness and grammatical consciousness-raising on the part of the learner and try to stimulate an investigative approach so that learners learn how to observe tendencies and probabilities for themselves.

v) Ideological factors cannot be left in the background. Corpora constructed so far are based on the discourse of native speakers. Do teachers want to teach and do learners want to learn native speaker English? Is the native speaker the most appropriate paradigm? Is it unrealistic to expect non-native speakers to be able to or even want to express feelings, attitudes, interpersonal sensitivity in the target language? The term 'native speaker' in itself is not without problems of definition (Davies 1991). In this regard it is important that corpora become extended to include greater international representativeness and data involving interaction between non-native speakers; without such a dimension it will be difficult in future to defend an exclusively British English, native-speaker-based corpus against charges of narrow parochialism.

vi) Research so far is beginning to contribute some answers to questions such as: what is successful communication in a second or foreign language? What is the precise linguistic nature of interpersonal language use?

Further reading

Descriptions of spoken corpora – Rundell 1995a and b.
Heads – Geluykens 1992.
The case for and against teaching spoken grammar – Prodromou 1990; Pennycook 1994.
Consciousness-raising – Aston 1988; James and Garrett 1991; Batstone 1994b; Bygate *et al.* 1994; Van Lier 1995; Woods 1994.

Comments on Part A

Brian Tomlinson

The basic message which comes across from the three chapters in Part A is that many L2 learners have been disadvantaged because, until very recently, textbooks have been typically based on idealised data about the language they are teaching. Some have taught a prescriptive model of how their authors think the learners should use the target language, many have been based on the authors' intuitions about how the target language is used, most have been informed by a model of the target language based on information from reference books rather than from actual data, and nearly all have taught learners to speak written grammar. None of this is too surprising given that until very recently textbook writers had no access to comprehensive and representative data of authentic language use. They had to make use of reference books based on rules and constructed examples rather than on instances of language use. Or they based their books on their own abstract awareness of how they, as typical educated users of the language, expressed themselves in the target language. Such awareness was inevitably biased towards the norms of planned discourse (e.g. essays, lectures) as it is difficult to be aware of how we use language in unplanned discourse (e.g. spontaneous informal conversation) in which by definition we do not plan what to say and are not usually aware of exactly what we have said. So we had, for example, the ridiculous situation of writers insisting that learners use complete sentences in their conversations when the writers rarely did so themselves. Now we have no excuse. We have access to data which tells us how the target language is typically written and spoken and we know for a fact that language use is variable and depends on the context in which it is being used. We know that the grammar of the spoken language is distinctively different from that of the written language, that the degree of intimacy and of shared experience between the participants are crucial determinants of the lexis and the structures used in discourse, that all language use is subjective, attitudinal, purposeful and strategic and that the purposes of a communication will exert a strong influence on the language which is actually used. In grammar books and textbook dialogues language use tends to be neutral and cooperative, and grammatical rules tend to be constant (or at best to be allowed a few exceptions). In real life language use tends to be biased and competitive and grammatical patterns are variable.

A question frequently asked these days (and at least implied in all three chapters in this section) is how much of the reality of language use do learners really need to be faced with? It can be argued that pedagogic simplifications of real language use are necessary in order to protect the learner from the apparent chaos of reality and to provide the security of apparent order and systematicity. Learners need to start learning what is simple; learners need rules; learners need to get things right. But learners also need to be prepared for interaction in the real world. They need to be aware of the intentions as well as the meanings of the speakers and writers they interact with; and they need to be able to produce language which is not only accurate and appropriate but which is effective too. They need, therefore, materials which are designed to facilitate systematic progress but which at the same time provide them with encounters with the reality of target language use. In my experience, learners have no problem with this if they are first helped to reflect on the variability of grammatical patterns in their first language, if they are not duped at the beginner stage into thinking that the target language is constantly rule-bound and if they are helped to see how languages follow principles and develop patterns rather than obey rules.

All three chapters in this section argue persuasively for the need for language learning materials to be informed by data from a corpus of authentic language use; all three warn that it is not enough to present samples of the data to learners and hope that they learn from them; and all three consider a language awareness approach to be the most profitable way of helping learners to gain from exposure to the reality of language use. I would agree with all three points and would particularly endorse the value of helping learners to invest energy and attention in discovering patterns and tendencies for themselves from guided investigations of samples of authentic language. In my experience, learners can gain confidence and curiosity by making discoveries for themselves from the earliest stages of language learning. The awareness they gain can then make them more attentive to salient features of their input and this can facilitate language acquisition.

One very effective way of helping learners to make use of their language discoveries is to help them to write their own grammars of the target language. The teacher provides language awareness activities from which learners make generalised discoveries and then record them with illustrative authentic instances under pattern headings in a loose leaf folder (or better still on a disk). The learners are encouraged to revise and develop their generalisations as they encounter further evidence during and outside the course and occasionally their developing grammars are monitored by the teacher. At the end of the course each learner has a grammar of the target language written by themselves which they can take away and develop, if they want to, from their post-course encounters with the language.

To date, published language awareness materials have tended to use constructed examples to lead learners to discoveries about the grammatical and semantic systems of languages (e.g. Bolitho and Tomlinson 1995). Useful though these materials are in encouraging learner investment and facilitating learner discovery there is a strong argument for the development of materials which help learners to develop pragmatic awareness (Tomlinson 1994a) through critical analysis of authentic discourse, and in particular of the strategy use of the participants in the discourse. Learners need not only to know what the grammatical and lexical options are but also what strategies are effective in what situations. Such strategic awareness activities can be devised for classroom use but even more profitable can be activities which guide learners to make discoveries from real world exposure about how users of the target language achieve their intended effects.

The focus of Part A is on analysis of authentic language data but it is very important that learners experience language in use as well as investigate it. In other words, there should be times when their attention is on meaning and on their communicative role in an interaction rather than on the language being used. If there is no target language use in their environment then they will need their teacher and/or materials to involve them in meaningful encounters with the target language in authentic use (possibly in communication activities which are subsequently analysed by the learners to help them to develop language awareness). This is true for all learners but especially so for those many learners whose preferred learning style is experiential rather than analytic. Language awareness activities can be extremely valuable but they can never be sufficient.

4   A framework for materials writing

David Jolly and Rod Bolitho

Introduction

In this chapter we offer the reader a practical idea of the different aspects of the process of materials writing for the classroom. This is achieved through case studies illustrating the process.

The starting point for this practical overview derives from the thoughts and feelings of those most involved with language materials: the comments boxed below are the authentic voices of students and teachers of English as a foreign language. Each statement appears to have materials-writing implications.

Exercise

As you read through the boxed remarks, you may like to cover the commentary beneath each one and make a brief note about what you feel the materials-writing implications to be.

> 'I have noticed that the coursebook I use doesn't seem to deal with "real" English.'
> (Italian secondary school teacher)
>
> 'My demand is becoming a reporter of the English football and I need, so, much familiarity . . .'
> (Danish upper intermediate student on full-time intensive course in British school)

There are many sources of real English within language-learning publications but clearly our Italian teacher is working with materials, perhaps prescribed, that fail to employ authentic language or texts. She has thus **identified** a need for materials. Similarly, though in a different context, the second quote identified a need for new materials, particularly a variety of text-types for listening and reading, since there is no book or set of materials known to the authors that caters for the precise needs of this Danish student.

> 'The textbook my institute has written says that you use "please" and "would" for simple requests and "would you mind" for more polite requests. I have heard lots of other things such as "could you possibly . . ."'
> (Yugoslav evening institute teacher)
>
> 'I get very confused with all these noughts and zeros and nothings in your language . . .'
> (Argentinian part-time student on low intensity course in Britain)

The evening institute has identified a need for materials that practise making requests but clearly the Yugoslav teacher feels that she does not know enough about the language of requests to teach it as effectively as she would like to do. Textbooks inevitably and necessarily make pedagogical selections of exponents used for specific language functions which do not suit all learners or satisfy all teachers. This teacher will have to engage in some linguistic **exploration** of the functional area of 'requests' in order to produce more informative materials for her classes. The implication of the word 'confusion' in the second quotation is that here too the materials-writing teacher will find it necessary to do some linguistic and semantic exploration before she attempts to respond to the Argentinian's request. Even the experienced native-speaker would be hard-pressed to locate and contextualise spontaneously all the uses of 'nought', 'nil', 'nothing', 'love', 'zero', 'o', etc.

> 'It's a very nice book and very lively, but in the section on "processes" for example all the exercises are about unusual things for our country. We are a hot country and also have many Muslims. The exercises are about snow, ice, cold mornings, water cisterns; writing and publishing EFL books and making wine. I can tell you I can't do making wine and smoking pot in my country!'
> (Experienced school teacher from the Ivory Coast)
>
> 'Previous materials were not based on life in Brazil which is why I don't think they worked very well . . .'
> (Brazilian teacher of English in school)

> 'Sir. . . what is opera?'
> (Iraqi student in mixed nationality class using materials
> designed to practise reading narrative)

The implications of these three quotations are not linguistic; rather, they address the problem of appropriate **contextual realisation** for materials. For the teacher in the Ivory Coast, the materials offered on 'processes' would be outside the cultural experience of his students and thus effectively useless; conversely, for the Brazilian teacher, the choice of Brazilian settings and familiar mores had clear advantages over alien contexts as they are essentially more motivating. The quote from the Iraqi student suggests that complete unfamiliarity with the notion of opera is likely to reduce the efficacy of the reading exercises.

Degrees of certainty: past

Uncertain	More certain	Certain
Perhaps she's lost the way. She might/could have lost the way.	She's probably lost the way. She must have lost the way.	I'm sure she's lost the way.

1. **Richard went shopping yesterday and lost his wallet.
Suggest where and how he might have lost it.**

Here are his movements in detail:

– he went shopping at the local supermarket
– he paid for the goods and put his wallet on top of the shopping trolley
– he doesn't remember what he did with the wallet after that
– he packed the goods into a cardboard box
– he carried the box to the car and put it on the back seat
– he drove to the dry-cleaner's, got out of the car and left the car unlocked
– he went to the dry-cleaner's but they told him that his cleaning wasn't ready
– he walked across the road to the greengrocer's to buy some vegetables
– when he came to pay for the vegetables, he couldn't find his wallet.

Work in pairs and make your suggestions, like this:

He Somebody The cashier A person in the shop	might could must	have	put dropped left found	it ...

Figure 1   From Developing Strategies (Abbs and Freebairn, 1980)

Exercise 1   (Students in British language school classroom
doing exercises in pairs as suggested)
PAIR 1 A: His wallet must have fallen down the trolley . . .
        B: He must have forgotten it there . . .
PAIR 2 C: Perhaps he left it on the shopping trolley. . .
        D: Perhaps he left it on the car. . .
        E: No, perhaps he drop it in the cleaner's . . .

In the exercise illustrated above the students are asked to make statements about the relative likelihood of events given the information. However, since no basis for any one hypothesis is stronger than any other basis, students doing the exercise end up making correctly-formed but random statements. In terms of recognising a need, exploring the language required to meet the need and finding a reasonable context for practice, this exercise may be said to pass muster; what has clearly failed is the **pedagogical realisation** of the materials, i.e. if these materials were intended to provide meaningful practice whereby students would make statements of greater or less certainty, they clearly fail. Part of the materials-writers task must be to provide clear exercises and activities that somehow meet the need for language-learning work initially recognised. Some would say that this is the core of materials writing. Part of effective pedagogical realisation of materials is efficient and effective writing of instructions, including the proper use of metalanguage; poor instructions for use may waste a lot of valuable student time as this second example reveals:

'But Paola, I didn't intend you to copy out the whole text word for word – you should just have corrected the summary version . . .'
(British FE lecturer to assiduous part-time intermediate Italian student using self-access listening materials)

'I can't use this book – it's very crowded with its double columns; I just can't see the point of any page and I'm sure the students can't . . .'
(British teacher on an intensive language course in a British language school: referring to Collins COBUILD English Course 1 – see Figure 2)

---

54 What kind of home?

Bridget lives in a small top floor flat. It is quite modern and has two bedrooms, a sitting-room, a kitchen and a bathroom. She shares it with her flatmate.

Find a new partner and find out about their house or flat.

▶ Write about it.
Also write about your own flat or house. ◀

Let your partner read what you have written. Did you say the same things?

55 The largest... the smallest... the most expensive...

Bridget's flat has five rooms. Most family houses in Britain have two or three bedrooms, a bathroom, kitchen, sitting-room and dining-room – about six or seven rooms altogether. Prices vary.

A small family house about 20 miles from London cost about £70,000 in 1987. In other parts of Britain the same kind of house would be much less, perhaps as little as £20,000. But in London, the same house could be £150,000.   JDW

a How many rooms do most family houses have in your own country?
How much do small family houses cost?

b Read about the houses below. Which one is:

the most expensive house in the world?
the largest private house in the world?
the smallest house in Britain?

_____ is Biltmore House in Asheville, North Carolina, USA, belonging to the Vanderbilt family. It was built in 1890 at a cost of US$4,100,000. It has 250 rooms and stands in an estate of 48,100 hectares.

_____ is the Hearst Ranch at San Simeon, California. It was built for the newspaper owner, William Randolph Hearst in 1922–39 at a cost of US$30,000,000. It has over 100 rooms and a garage for 25 cars.

_____ is a cottage in North Wales built in the nineteenth century. It is 10 feet (309 cms) high, and measures only 6 feet (182 cms) across the front. It has a tiny staircase and two tiny rooms.

c Look at the photographs. Write one or two more sentences about each of the houses. Begin: 'It...' Check your sentences carefully.

Give your sentences to other students to read. Can they say which house each sentence is about?

56 *Grammar words*

in

Can you find six phrases with the word *in* in the texts about the houses in section 55 above? When is *in* used with time, and when with place?

How many of these examples are about place? What about the others?

In fact there are more men in your family.
Bridget lives in a small top floor flat in London.
Which room are these people in?
Good morning, please come in!
The largest private house in the world is in Asheville.
It was built in 1890.
Do you know the names of the letters in English?

57 The old flat

a David lives by himself in a ground-floor flat. It's quite small but it's near the shops and it's got a small garden.

Bridget asked him about his flat, then she asked him:

BG: Where did you live before you lived in your flat now?

57a Which flat do you think David likes best, and why?

b Bridget had to move out of her old flat because the owner came back from America and wanted to live there again. David asked Bridget which of the two flats she liked better – her old one, or the one she lives in now.

57b Which flat did Bridget like better? Why?

Figure 2   From *Collins COBUILD English Course 1* (Willis and Willis, 1988)

> 'This picture . . . is dog or is . . . funny animal . . .'
> (Spanish student, using teacher-made worksheet)

The **physical appearance and production** of materials is important both for motivation and for classroom effectiveness. Teachers engaged in writing materials need to develop the same care and attention to presentation that one would expect of good publishers, though the first quote reveals that even very good publishers also fall down on the job.

> 'I wish I could just write materials and not teach at all . . .'
> (British teacher at Technical School in the Middle East)

The implication of this remark is that materials writing, to this teacher, is regarded as an end in itself. However, we take an entirely different view, believing that materials writing as a process is pointless without constant reference to the classroom. In short, a need arises, materials are written, materials are **used** in the classroom to attempt to meet the need and subsequently they are **evaluated**. The evaluation will show whether the materials have to be rewritten, thrown away, or may be used again as they stand with a similar group. Writing the materials is only a part of the activity of teaching.

Exercise

You may now like to examine the quotations that follow.

Think about the implications of each one for materials writing; you may feel that some of the quotations carry more than one implication. If possible discuss the implications with a colleague; no notes are appended this time.

a) 'The book *Welcome 3* really works well in my experience because there are modern topics, and good tapes that go with the book.' (Swiss schoolteacher)
b) 'These listening comprehension tapes have too much noise on them, it is difficult to understand the speaker.' (Secondary schoolteacher)
c) 'My students find the speaking (fluency) drills in the lab confusing.' (Austrian schoolteacher)
d) 'The materials that in my experience don't seem to work very well are coursebooks based on communicative methods only, with a few

exercises because students find it difficult to follow the book.'
(European schoolteacher)

e) 'I think, Rafid, there's been a misunderstanding about what you
were supposed to have written in this task . . . the pictures tell you
what to do in order to change a bicycle wheel and I expected you to
write a set of instructions to do that . . . but you've written about
how you changed your bicycle wheel last week . . . why?' (English
teacher in Britain marking the work of an Armenian student of
academic English)

f) 'Schon wieder so ein dummes Übungsgespräch!' ['Another stupid
practice conversation!'] (Young German learner referring to a
tourist/policeman dialogue in an elementary secondary school
coursebook)

g) 'In our English textbook we only read about film stars and pop stars
and famous people. I want to know how the English people live.'
(Turkish university student who has never visited the UK)

The process of materials writing

It would be appropriate at this point to attempt to summarise the various
steps involved in the process of materials-writing in the form of a flow-
diagram. Figure 3 on page 97 reveals in a simple although undynamic
way how the implications raised in the statements on the previous pages
may be arranged into a simple sequence of activities that a teacher may
have to perform in order to produce any piece of new material.

Most materials writers move in this direction, and use some or all of
these steps, if not always precisely in this order: a movement from the
identification of a need for materials to their eventual use in the
classroom. Some such simplified version of the materials-writing
process is also clearly how most publishers are constrained to work.
The one-directional simplicity of this model, however, may be what
makes so many materials, whether published or found in one's own or
a colleague's filing-cabinet, lack that final touch of excellence that many
teachers appear to wish for. In fact, the excellence of materials lies less
in the products themselves than in the appropriate and unique tuning
for use that teachers might be better engaged in. The simple sequence in
Figure 3 fails to illustrate the extent to which materials writing can be a
dynamic and self-adjusting process.

In the first place, by ending with use in the classroom, it equates
materials production and use of materials with effective meeting of need
identified. What is lacking is a stage beyond use in the classroom:
evaluation of materials used. The act of evaluation at least in theory,
turns the process into a dynamic one since it forces the teacher/writer to

IDENTIFICATION by teacher or learner(s) of a need to fulfil or a problem to solve by the creation of materials

EXPLORATION of the area of need/problem in terms of what language, what meanings, what functions, what skills etc.?

CONTEXTUAL REALISATION of the proposed new materials by the finding of suitable ideas, contexts or texts with which to work

PEDAGOGICAL REALISATION of materials by the finding of appropriate exercises and activities AND the writing of appropriate instructions for use

PHYSICAL PRODUCTION of materials, involving consideration of layout, type size, visuals, reproduction, tape length etc.

Figure 3   ς USE in the classroom

examine whether s/he has or has not met objectives: furthermore, a failure to meet objectives may be related to any or all of the intervening steps between initial identification of need and eventual use. (Failure may, of course, be attributed to poor or inadequate use of perfectly adequate materials but that becomes a matter of classroom management rather than materials evaluation except where poor use is directly related to faulty production.)

Secondly, the human mind does not work in the linear fashion suggested above when attempting to find solutions to problems. For example, a proposal about what form a particular language exercise could take may very well generate spontaneous second thoughts about the language being exercised; wondering about the physical production of a piece of material may well spark off thoughts about contextual-isation and so on. Thus, in addition to evaluation as an essential component of writing materials, we must also imagine a variety of optional pathways and feedback loops which make the whole process both dynamic and self-regulating. These then will allow us to deal in a concrete way with the reasons for the failure of language materials and provide us with clues to their improvement, both during the writing and after their use. See Figure 4.

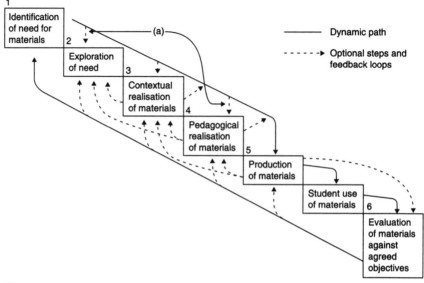

Notes

a) Even in the creation of entirely new materials, it may be the case that some of the steps envisaged have already been done for the writer.

b) Materials may be produced and evaluated without student use, e.g. by a colleague or professional. Most publishers work this way. This does not reduce the need for evaluation after use by specific groups of students.

Figure 4 *A teacher's path through the production of new or adapted materials*

Case studies

The case studies which follow illustrate, from different teaching contexts, how the steps in the path are taken into account in actual samples of material.

Case study 1

Materials produced for a class at upper intermediate level

IDENTIFICATION OF NEED

In reading a text, students come across the sentence: 'It's time the Prime Minister listened more carefully to her critics.' They are puzzled by the apparent clash between the past **form** and the actual **meaning** of the verb 'listened'. They ask for an explanation and further examples.

| EXPLORATION OF LANGUAGE | Teacher promises to respond and consults the *Communicative Grammar of English* (Leech and Svartvick) pp. 283–7 on **Fact, Hypothesis and Neutrality.** 'It's time . . .' is one of several expressions involving hypothesis. |

| CONTEXTUAL REALISATION | Teacher decides to produce worksheets on 'Hypothetical Meaning' to try to anchor the concept and the related language in students' minds. Decides to provide simplified contexts for practice, and to refer to students' own experience. Worksheet is for class use, to reinforce actual teaching. The names used in **Step three** of the worksheet are those of students in the class and of a co-teacher. |

| PEDAGOGICAL REALISATION | Teaching decides on *contrastive* approach (facts vs hypothesis) initially with an exercise focusing on the distinction, and on the verb forms involved. Enough examples provided to establish a 'code' to work from.

Once basic **notions** are recognised, **communicative functions** of sentences involving hypothetical meaning are elicited. Focus on unspoken meaning and speaker's attitude. Provision of references for further practice/ study. |

| PHYSICAL PRODUCTION | Handwritten worksheet xeroxed and distributed to learners. |

| USE | Introduction in class, followed by completion of worksheet at home and checking in the next class. |

| EVALUATION | Student comments and difficulties with worksheet, e.g. |

1 'In Step one there is a fact **and** a hypothesis in the sentences. It's confusing.' (This sent the teacher back to 'Peda-

gogical Realisation' and led to the changed instructions and underlinings in Version 2.)

2 'Can't the "if" sentences also be positive, do they only express regret?' (This student had noticed an important oversight which took the teacher back to the exploration stage and led to the inclusion of two further examples in Step two of the revised version of the worksheet.)

3 Teacher noted problems with 'I wish you would finish . . .' vs. 'I wish you had finished . . .'
Further exploration led to production of follow-up worksheet on 'possible vs. impossible wishes'.

4 The class liked Step three and enjoyed making up similar sentences about other members of the group.

Version 1

HYPOTHETICAL MEANING: WORKSHEET

STEP ONE

a)   Fact or hypothesis? Tick the right box for each statement

	FACT	HYPOTHESIS
1 I'm pleased that you've finished the work		
2 I wish you would finish the work		
3 It's time you finished the work		
4 I wish you had finished the work		
5 If only you had finished the work		
6 I see that you've finished the work		
7 If you had more time you would soon finish the work		
8 I'm surprised that you've finished the work		

b) Now underline the verb forms of 'finish' in each sentence. What do the <u>facts</u> have in common? What do the <u>hypotheses</u> have in common? What is the <u>paradox</u> about some of these verb forms?

Here are some more examples, from the press, to help you with the answers to these questions.

1 It's time the Americans substituted action for words.
2 If I were the Prime Minister I'd think hard before trying to impose Conservative policies in Scotland.
3 Many Alliance politicians wish the parties had gone into the election united under one leader.
4 Economic experts are puzzled to see that the pound has not risen on world markets.
5 If only England had a player of Maradona's calibre.

STEP TWO

There is an idea 'behind' many of these sentences with hypothetical meaning. Look at these examples:

It's time you had your hair cut. (It's too long)
I wish my brother were here with me. (But he isn't)
If only I had worked harder. (But I didn't)

a) Now provide the ideas behind each of these statements.

1 I wish you didn't smoke so heavily. (   )
2 It's time we went home. (   )
3 Just suppose you had dropped the bottle. (   )
4 If only you had listened to your mother. (   )
5 I'd have bought the car if it hadn't been yellow. (   )
6 It's high time you got rid of that old jacket. (   )
7 If I were you I'd catch the early train. (   )
8 He looked as though he'd seen a ghost. (   )

Which of the above examples expresses (a) regret?
                                      (b) advice?
                                      (c) strong suggestion?
                                      (d) a wish?
                                      (e) reproach?

b) Now try to explain the difference <u>in the speakers' minds</u> between these pairs of statements:

I (a) 'It's time to leave.'   II (a) 'It's time to get up.'
  (b) 'It's time we left.'   (b) 'It's time you got up.'

III (a) 'It's time for us to take a break.'
    (b) 'It's high time we took a break.'

The process of materials writing

Make statements to respond to or develop these situations, using the instructions in brackets in each case.

1 It's 9.30 and René still hasn't arrived in class. (Comment reproachfully on this.)
2 Adrian's hair is rather long. (Advise him to have it cut.)
3 Nathalie hasn't done her homework. (Advise her to do it next time.)
4 You haven't worked very hard during the course. (Express regret.)
5 Pauline is still teaching at 12.45. (Reproach her.)
6 Thomas asks to borrow your rubber for the tenth time. (Make a strong suggestion.)
7 You went out last night and Robert de Niro was on TV. (Express regret or relief.)
8 It's 8 pm and your landlady still hasn't put dinner on the table. In fact, she's painting her toenails. (Use a question to make a strong suggestion.)

REFERENCES

Look at:
Murphy, R. 1996. *English Grammar in Use* (new edn.) Units 37 and 38. Cambridge: Cambridge University Press.
Swan, M. 1996. *Practical English Usage* (new edn.) 606 and 632.2. Oxford: Oxford University Press.

Figure 5 *Version 1 of hypothetical meaning worksheet*

Version 2

HYPOTHETICAL MEANING: WORKSHEET

STEP ONE

a) Fact or hypothesis? Look at the verb forms underlined and then tick the right box in each case.

	FACT	HYPOTHESIS
1 I'm pleased that you've finished the work		
2 I wish you would finish the work		
3 It's time you finished the work		
4 I wish you had finished the work		
5 If only you had finished the work		
6 I see that you've finished the work		
7 If you had more time you would soon finish the work		
8 I'm surprised that you've finished the work		

b) What do the <u>facts</u> have in common? What do the <u>hypotheses</u> have in common? What is the <u>paradox</u> about some of these verb forms?

Here are some more examples, from the press, to help you with the answers to these questions.

1 It's time the Americans substituted action for words.
2 If I were the Prime Minister I'd think hard before trying to impose Conservative policies in Scotland.
3 Many Alliance politicians wish the parties had gone into the election united under one leader.
4 Economic experts are puzzled to see that the pound has not risen on world markets.
5 If only England had a player of Maradona's calibre.

STEP TWO

There is an idea 'behind' many of these sentences with hypothetical meaning.
Look at these examples:

It's time you had your hair cut. (It's too long)
I wish my brother were here with me. (But he isn't)
If only I had worked harder. (But I didn't)

a) Now provide the ideas behind each of these statements.
1 I wish you didn't smoke so heavily. (   )
2 It's time we went home. (   )
3 Just suppose you had dropped the bottle. (   )
4 If only you had listened to your mother. (   )
5 I'd have bought the car if it hadn't been yellow. (   )
6 It's high time you got rid of that old jacket. (   )
7 If I were you I'd catch the early train. (   )
8 He looked as though he'd seen a ghost. (   )
9 If I hadn't screamed we'd have crashed. (   )
10 Suppose you hadn't had your cheque book with you. (   )

Which of the above examples expresses (a) regret?
(b) advice?
(c) strong suggestion?
(d) a wish?
(e) reproach?
(f) relief?

b) Now try to explain the difference <u>in the speakers' minds</u> between these pairs of statements:

I (a) 'It's time to leave.'   II (a) 'It's time to get up.'
(b) 'It's time we left.'   (b) 'It's time you got up.'

III (a) 'It's time for us to take a break.'   (b) 'It's high time we took a break.'

The process of materials writing

Make statements to respond to or develop these situations, using the instructions in brackets in each case.

1 It's 9.30 and René still hasn't arrived in class. (Comment reproachfully on this.)
2 Adrian's hair is rather long. (Advise him to have it cut.)
3 Nathalie hasn't done her homework. (Advise her to do it next time.)
4 You haven't worked very hard during the course. (Express regret.)
5 Pauline is still teaching at 12.45. (Reproach her.)
6 Thomas asks to borrow your rubber for the tenth time. (Make a strong suggestion.)
7 You went out last night and Robert de Niro was on TV. (Express regret or relief.)
8 It's 8 pm and your landlady still hasn't put dinner on the table. In fact, she's painting her toenails. (Use a question to make a strong suggestion.)

REFERENCES

Look at:
Murphy, R. 1996. *English Grammar in Use* (new edn.) Units 37 and 38. Cambridge: Cambridge University Press.
Swan, M. 1996. *Practical English Usage* (new edn.) 606 and 632.2. Oxford: Oxford University Press.

Figure 6 *Version 2 of hypothetical meaning worksheet*

Case study 2

IDENTIFICATION OF NEED	Materials to practise the description of development and change over time.
EXPLORATION OF LANGUAGE	Not carried out.
CONTEXTUAL REALISATION	Simple, universal context of an isolated island seen at four stages in its history.
PEDAGOGICAL REALISATION	Introduction to information. Instructions to student. Four labelled diagrams, showing development in pictorial form and notes.
PHYSICAL PRODUCTION	Introduction and instructions at top. Pictures hand-drawn and hand-written, xeroxed.

USE OF MATERIALS

With European, Asian and North African students on academic writing course. Drafting and as much time allowed as desired.

EVALUATION OF MATERIALS

This revealed that

1 The need had been correctly **identified.**

2 That other needs remained unfulfilled because no adequate **language exploration** had been done, e.g. language of time duration.

3 The **contextual realisation** was very good and well understood but in some ways factually inaccurate.

4 There were flaws in the **pedagogical realisation** which had led to poor practice by students: (i) writing was distorted through lack of a sense of audience (ii) the instructions were confusing (iv) some labelling was confusing.

5 There were flaws in the **physical production,** particularly in the visual aspects which confused students.

Rewriting of Materials

The evaluative feedback led to a revamping of the materials and the production of Version 2 in which changes were made on the basis of (3), (4) and (5) above.

VERSION 1

Writing   DEVELOPMENTAL NARRATIVE

THE VOLCANO ON HEIMAEY

Introduction   Heimaey is an island near Iceland. Volcanoes which have been inactive (dormant) for a long time may erupt violently, blowing out previously solidified material and scattering volcanic ash.

Writing   Study the following pictures carefully and then write a description of the development of the island of Heimaey during the last 1000 years.

The process of materials writing

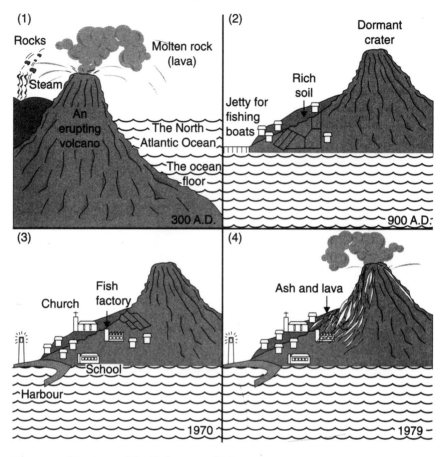

Figure 7   *Version 1, The Volcano on Heimaey*

VERSION 2

DESCRIBING DEVELOPMENT AND CHANGE IN THE PAST

Writing   THE ISLAND OF HEIMAEY

Introduction Heimaey is an island near Iceland, in the North Atlantic Ocean. It is a volcanic island, formed in the year 300. Volcanoes which have been inactive for a long time may erupt violently, blowing out volcanic ash and previously solidified material.

Writing Task Study the following pictures carefully. They show the changes on Heimaey from its formation to 1973. Write a description of this development, on the page opposite, using the notes given to you.

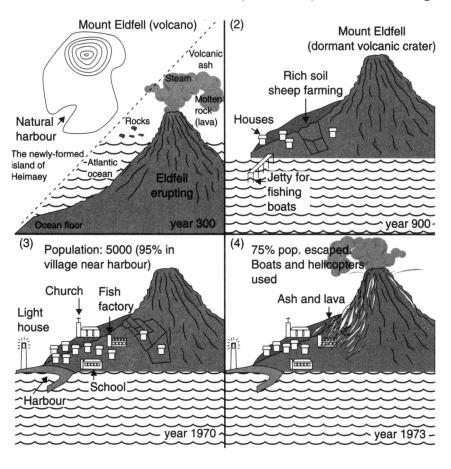

(2) Mount Eldfell (volcano)
Volcanic ash
Steam
Molten rock (lava)
Natural harbour
Rocks
The newly-formed island of Heimaey
Atlantic ocean
Eldfell erupting
Ocean floor
year 300

(2) Mount Eldfell (dormant volcanic crater)
Rich soil sheep farming
Houses
Jetty for fishing boats
year 900

(3) Population: 5000 (95% in village near harbour)
Church
Fish factory
Light house
School
Harbour
year 1970

(4) 75% pop. escaped. Boats and helicopters used
Ash and lava
year 1973

Before the year 300 AD, the island of Heimaey did not exist.
At about that time, _____

_____

_____

_____

_____

In approximately 900 AD, people came from Iceland and
settled on Heimaey.

_____

_____

_____

_____

_____

_____

In the next thousand years, _____

_____

_____

_____

_____

_____

_____

A few years ago, Heimaey's peaceful development was suddenly
disrupted when _____

_____

_____

_____

_____

_____

_____

_____

_____

Figure 8   *Version 2, The Volcano on Heimaey*

Case study 3

With this case study we intend to highlight the fact that the writing of
materials is rarely a neat self-contained linear process, but an activity
which is intimately bound up with all questions that teaching itself
raises: learners' needs, syllabus, schemes of work, lesson plans, classroom management, resources, outcomes and assessment, the relation of
learning/teaching to real life and so on.

English teacher's evening reverie

EVALUATION	. . . that session on shopping with group 4 today was a bit flat . . . in fact, can they shop effectively at all . . . I mean, can I really say, hand on heart, that Duda or Kristina could get a small sachet of lemon shampoo from Boots, . . . or
IDENTIFICATION OF NEED	Miguel his cotton shirts? . . . I'll have to give it another go tomorrow, but I can't have them sitting in pairs doing an A-B exercise . . . what do I want? . . . They must be able to
LINGUISTIC EXPLORATION	ask for an item, and ask about size, colour, amounts, quantities . . . The contents of the book were OK, perhaps
CONTEXTUAL REALISATION	a bit too diverse . . . Shall I concentrate on food, clothes, newsagents and general personal items you can get from Boots? . . . But sitting in pairs was very flat, no urgency,
LINGUISTIC EXPLORATION	. . . they weren't really . . . Now what happens when they need to go and shop for something, what is going on? Yes, you've got an idea of what you want, say bananas or apples and you also have other things in your head, like how many you want and you also want to find things out
PEDAGOGICAL REALISATION	like where the apples come from, whether they are sweet or less sweet . . . so . . . so . . . what I can produce is a set of cards, cue-cards which they can work from . . . the
PHYSICAL PRODUCTION	cards should be analogous to what would be in their heads as they went into the shop. I can put a picture or draw one on each card to represent the items and on the right-hand side I can put various cue words to indicate what needs to go on in the shop. I'd better go over the cue words in a quick exercise before we start . . . what sort of cues . . .
PEDAGOGICAL REALISATION AND USE	you need some general clues such as 'sizes' or 'colours' so that they can ask 'What colours do you have?' and so on . . . and you also need specific cues, such as 'small' or 'red' so that they have to ask things like, 'Have you got a small one?' . . . What I need is some card divided into two
PHYSICAL PRODUCTION	by three inch rectangles . . . I could colour code it so that blue cards are newsagents items and red ones are for food shopping and so on . . . should be easy enough. Perhaps
PEDAGOGICAL REALISATION AND USE	they can do it in groups first . . . one group doing the food cards and one doing the clothes and one for Boots and so on. . . then I can shuffle the cards and they can practise on me as the British shop assistant . . . not a bad role if you work it up . . . they can take random cards further . . .
further EXPLORATION after IDENTIFICATION	hang on . . . they were having problems with containers and things so maybe I'd better do a preliminary exercise on that . . . box, packet, sachet, tube, tub, can, tin, ball, packet, carton, bundle . . . any more. . .? I'll go and look in the cupboard downstairs . . . yes bottle, mustn't forget that
PEDAGOGICAL REALISATION	one! . . . yes I'll give them a simple list of items and they can give me the right containers . . . or do it with each other and then have me check them . . . now, I'd better make some notes on all this before I forget it . . .

NOTES MADE

language exploration	FOOD:	Special questions – quantity/amount General questions – types? sizes?
	CLOTHES:	Special questions – colours, sizes, materials General questions – colours? materials? (Items: jeans, blouses, shirts, skirts, socks . . .)
pedagogical realisation	signs on cards	! = REQUEST ? = QUESTION

Examples of materials written

physical production

material? blue? grey? sizes? 2!	Chianti? £? 1½ litres!	cotton? colours? sizes? cost? 1!	Irish? cost? 1½ kilos!

Figure 9

Conclusions

In this article we have outlined and illustrated a framework for materials writing. Underlying this framework are some beliefs and working principles which we'd like to make explicit and comment on here.

1 **Materials writing is at its most effective when it is turned to the needs of a particular group of learners.**
Sooner or later, every teacher of any subject comes up against a need to write materials. How they respond to this need depends on many variables: the prevailing norms in a specific educational context, the amount of time available, the availability of reprographic facilities, the teacher's background and training, etc. In some contexts, teachers are expected to adhere rigidly to a prescribed coursebook; most teachers are too busy to contemplate writing their own material from scratch, though there are a few who don't adapt their textbooks in some way; photocopying and other forms of reproduction depend on the availability of technical back-up and supplies of paper; materials evaluation, adaptation and production are often neglected or under-emphasised on initial training courses.

British publishers do great business in many parts of the world with mass-market English language coursebooks. In Eastern and Central Europe, for example in the years immediately after the collapse of Communism, the welcome given to *Discoveries*, the *Cambridge English Course, Headway* and similar courses was, after decades of restriction, understandably warm. Yet, in many countries in the region, the initial enthusiasm was quick to wear off, and a number of them are now involved in producing their own school textbooks. The logic is inescapable. A 'home-produced' coursebook, if it is well-produced, stands a much greater chance of success locally simply because the authors are more aware of the needs of learners in that context, and are able to design the materials in such a way as to fit in with their own learning and teaching traditions, and with the conceptual world of the learners. Put another way, the further away the author is from the learners, the less effective the material is likely to be.

To sum up, the most effective materials are those which are based on a thorough understanding of learners' needs, i.e. their language difficulties, their learning objectives, their styles of learning etc. This implies a learning-centred approach to materials writing, rather than one which is driven purely by the subject through syllabus specifications, inventories of language items etc.

2 **Teachers understand their own learners best.**
They understand their needs and their preferred learning styles. The more they become sensitive and responsive to these needs, the more they become involved in researching their own classrooms. Indeed, we believe that the teacher as materials writer belongs firmly in the (recent) tradition of the teacher as researcher.

3 **All teachers need a grounding in materials writing.**
It is not until a teacher has attempted to produce her own materials that she finally begins to develop a set of criteria to evaluate materials produced by others. Only then does the full range of options, from blind acceptance of other materials, through adaptation and supplementation, to the production of 'purpose-built' materials, become clear. The process of materials writing raises almost every issue which is important in learning to teach: the selection and grading of language, awareness of language, knowledge of learning theories, socio-cultural appropriacy; the list could be extended. And to extend point 2 above, the the current emphasis on action-research in teacher education programmes needs to be backed up by the establishment of materials writing as a key component on initial training courses and a regular feature of in-service training programmes. Teachers need to

be enabled to write their own materials in order to reduce their dependency on publisher materials and as a means of professional development.

4 All teachers teach themselves.
Teachers teach specific groups of learners, as discussed above. They also, inevitably, 'teach themselves' and this has powerful implications when it comes to the materials they are to teach with. All the evidence suggests persuasively that 'teaching against the grain' leads to dissatisfaction, loss of confidence and learning failure. Enabling teachers to produce their own effective materials minimises this possibility and helps them to 'teach themselves'.

5 Trialling and evaluation are vital to the success of any materials.
Learners are the users of materials, and we have to need their opinions and listen to their feedback. This is easy enough for the teacher-writer, working with her own group of learners. Yet it is a message which many publishers have been slow to take on board. Even when trialling takes place, it is most often teachers' feedback, rather than learners', which is sought. In presenting our framework, we hope to have demonstrated how evaluation, by both learners and teachers, based on learning objectives, can cut down on wasted time and effort and result in clear pinpointing of the steps which require attention in the subsequent process of revision.

Part of our purpose in writing this chapter has been to help to empower the teacher-reader to write her own material within a principled framework arising from our experience. Learning to write materials is, inevitably, a matter of trial and error. We hope that the steps we have described will at least provide a generative model which will cut down on some of the risks involved and help the reader to feel more secure while experimenting.

Appendix

A materials writer's kitbag

The list below is neither a conventional bibliography nor a set of references. It consists of books, procedures and thinking prompts which we have found useful at each stage of the materials-writing process. Readers may wish to add to it from their own experience.

Stage	Support, resources and procedures
1 Identification	Questionnaires; feedback from students in class; formal or informal diagnosis of errors and shortcomings in learners' competence; analysis of existing course materials; pre-course needs analysis Dubin, F. and E. Olshtain. *Course Design* (CUP) Hutchinson, T. and A. Waters. *English for Specific Purposes* (CUP) Munby, J. *Communicative Syllabus Design* (CUP) Nunan, D. *Syllabus Design* (OUP) Yalden, J. *Principles of Course Design for Language Teaching* (CUP)
2 Exploration	*Cobuild English Language Dictionary* (Collins) *Dictionary of Contemporary English* (Longman) *Advanced Learner's Dictionary of Current English* (OUP) *The Language Activator* (Longman) *Roget's Thesaurus* (Penguin) McArthur, T. *Lexicon of Contemporary English* (Longman) Quirk, R. *et al. Grammar of Contemporary English* (Longman) Leech, G. and J. Svartvik. *A Communicative Grammar of English* (Longman) Close, R. *A Reference Grammar for Students of English* (Longman) Other descriptive and pedagogical grammars Syllabus models (e.g. in the books under 'Identification' above) A copy of your own syllabus Text typologies Van Ek, J. *Threshold Level and Waystage* (Pergamon/Council of Europe) Alexander, L. G. *et al. English Grammatical Structure* (Longman) Bolitho, R. and B. Tomlinson. *Discover English* (2nd revised edition) (Heinemann) Blundell, J. *et al. Function in English* (OUP) Bowers, R. G. *et al. Talking About Grammar* (Longman) Swan, M. *Practical English Usage* (OUP) Swan, M. and B. Smith. *Learner English* (CUP) HMSO. *Discover Britain* (Cultural background material) Wright, T. *Investigating English* (Edward Arnold)
3 Contextual realisation	Access to as much published/unpublished material as possible Exponentially expanding, organised and assorted collection of visuals Large collection of written texts, conveniently organised (e.g. by text-type, topic, degree of complexity etc.)

Large collection of listening material, similarly organised
Video material, too, if equipment is available
Crystal, D. and D. Davy. *Advanced Conversational English* (Longman)
Maley, A. and F. Grellet. *The Mind's Eye* (CUP) (Students' Book and Teacher's Book)
Nunan, D. *The Learner-Centred Curriculum* (CUP)

| 4 Pedagogical realisation | Access to as much published/unpublished material as possible |

4 Pedagogical realisation

Access to as much published/unpublished material as possible
Exercise and activity typologies
Familiarity with as many generative frameworks as possible
Ideas magazines, e.g. *Modern English Teacher*
Select bibliography for this stage:
Baddock, B. *Scoop*; *Press Ahead* (Prentice Hall International)
Brandes, D. and H. Phillips. *The Gamester's Handbook* (Hutchinson)
Brandes, D. *The Gamester's Handbook 2* (Stanley Thornes)
Byrne, D. *Teaching Writing Skills* (Longman)
Candlin, C. (Ed.). *The Communicative Teaching of English: Principles and Exercise Typology* (Longman)
Collie, J. and S. Slater. *Literature in the Language Classroom* (CUP)
Ellington, H. and P. Race. *Producing Teaching Materials* (2nd edition) (Kogan Page)
Frank, C. and M. Rinvolucri. *Grammar in Action Again* (Pergamon)
Gairns, R. and S. Redman. *Working With Words* (CUP)
Grellet, F. *Developing Reading Skills* (CUP) (exhaustive typology of reading activities)
Harmer, J. *Teaching and Learning Grammar* (Longman)
Hedge, T. *Writing* (OUP)
Jolly, D. *Reading Choices* (CUP)
Jolly, D. *Writing Tasks* (CUP)
Jones, K. *Simulations in Language Teaching* (CUP)
Kennedy, C. and R. Bolitho. *English for Specific Purposes* (Macmillan)
Klippel, F. *Keep Talking* (CUP)
Lavery, M. *Active Viewing Plus* (Modern English Publications)
Leach, R. *Making Materials* (National Extension College)
Murphey, T. *Music and Song* (OUP)
Nunan, D. *Designing Tasks for the Communicative Classroom* (CUP)
Ellington, H. *et al. A Handbook of Educational Technology* (Kogan Page)
Pincas, A. *Teaching English Writing* (Macmillan)
Rinvolucri, M. and J. Morgan. *Vocabulary* (OUP)

Rixon, S. *Developing Listening Skills* (Macmillan)
Sexton, M. and P. Williams. *Communicative Activities for Advanced Students of English. A Typology* (Langenscheidt-Longman)
Shepherd, J. *et al. Ways to Grammar* (Macmillan)
Hall, N. and J. Shepherd. *The Anti-Grammar Grammar Book* (Longman)
Trimble, L. *English for Science and Technology* (CUP)
Ur, P. *Grammar Practice Activities* (CUP)
Ur, P. *Teaching Listening Comprehension* (CUP)
Wallace, M. *Teaching Vocabulary* (Heinemann)
Wright, A. *et al. Games for Language Learning* (CUP)
Wright, A. *Visual Materials for Language Teaching* (Longman)

5 Physical production

pens/inks/pencils/rubbers/Tipp-Ex® fluid/'luminous' text markers/scissors/knife/typewriter/word processor/ruler/glue stick/paste/stencils/Letraset
cards/card/labels/laminating/roll or laminator/polythene envelopes
Access to a photocopier/thermal copier/duplicator/print shop
Extra copy of text, source material etc. for first draft
Secure systems for storing masters
Ellington, H. and P. Race. *Producing Teaching Materials* (2nd Edition) (Kogan Page)
Leach, R. *Making Materials* (National Extension College)
Rowntree, D. *Teaching through Self-Instruction* (Kogan Page) Chs. 8–12

6 Evaluation

Files containing single copy of all materials in which updating and revision notes can be made
Phials containing small doses of courage and honesty enabling writer to throw away materials that do not work or cease to enchant
Feedback from students and colleagues on quality, effectiveness, and interest value of materials
Rea-Dickens, P. and K. Germaine. *Evaluation* (OUP)

5 Writing course materials for the world: a great compromise

Jan Bell and Roger Gower

Introduction

Coursebook writers may set out to write materials they would want to use themselves if they were teaching in a particular situation but their role has to be to collaborate in the publication of materials for *others*. They need to cater for a wide range of students, teachers and classroom contexts which they have no personal acquaintance with, even though they might be familiar with the *general* pedagogic situation which the material is intended for.

Textbook writers have to try to anticipate the needs and interests of teachers and students and to modify any initial ambitions they may have as a result of what they continue to learn about those needs and interests. The focus of this article is on that process of modification and whether the inevitability of compromise is a positive or negative force upon the writers' pedagogic principles. We will use our own experience to illustrate and assume that readers will, despite our conclusions, make up their own minds.

Coursebooks in general: confronting the issues

In recent years there has been renewed debate about the desirability of coursebooks – indeed by many of the authors to be found in this book. The debate has tended to be polarised between those who object to coursebooks in principle, whether they see them as instruments of institutional control supported by a range of commercial interests or as implicitly prescriptive and destroyers of teacher and learner creativity; and those who argue that coursebooks provide teachers and learners with a range of professionally developed materials within tried-and-tested syllabus structures and allow teachers to spend their valuable time more on facilitating learning than materials production. The arguments in favour of coursebooks are often made by those with vested interests – writers, publishers and distributors – and are therefore open to the accusation of special pleading.

Some also accept the need for coursebooks but argue that the quality of many of those that are published is poor – not only because they are often produced too quickly with too little piloting but because they do not sufficiently reflect what we know about language learning and thus fail to meet the true needs of learners.

As coursebook writers ourselves we obviously accept that there is an important role for a coursebook in many classes. It would be impossible for us to write if we thought otherwise. Coursebooks *can* provide a useful resource for teachers. Providing they are used flexibly, we think they *can* be adapted and supplemented to meet the needs of specific classes. But it would be foolish to ignore many of the questions raised by the debate. These are some of the more important ones.

1 If one of your pedagogic principles is that creativity is important in the classroom, then how can you make sure that your coursebook does not take away investment and responsibility from teachers and learners?
2 If coursebooks are sometimes used by schools to maintain consistency of syllabus, how can you at the same time make sure they reflect the dynamic and interactive nature of the learning process?
3 Although it is true no coursebook can cater for all the individual needs of all learners all of the time, can you provide enough material to meet most of the needs most of the time and build in enough flexibility to enable teachers to individualise it?
4 If the language presented in many coursebooks bears little relationship to real language use and more to coursebook convention are you sure your samples of use are as natural as possible?
5 If coursebooks are frequently predictable in format and content how can you bring to your material a feeling that it is not boring and predictable?

We cannot pretend that when we started out we were fully aware of the significance of all these questions but in different ways at different times of the process they were all asked.

There were other issues. In our situation we were writing what is sometimes misleadingly called a 'global' coursebook – which means a coursebook for a restricted number of teaching situations in many different countries rather than all teaching situations in all countries. And those who dislike coursebooks feel they have an even stronger case against the global coursebook: the singing-and-dancing, glitzy (expensive) multi-media package, usually produced in a native-speaker situation but destined for the world with all language in the book (including rubrics) in the target language. Words like 'imperialist' and 'new colonialist' are sometimes used to criticise such books. Some of those who favour this line of argument feel that many teachers without the 'benefits' of a native-speaker situation are resentful and unwilling victims of a situation manipulated by an alliance of local institution and foreign publisher. On the other hand those who argue in favour of the global coursebook – again, often those making money out of it – point out that good sales world wide ensure a high production quality and enable publishers to finance interesting but less commercially viable publications on the backs of the big success stories.

From a pedagogic point of view we knew that one of the dangers of this kind of publication is that many of the cultural contexts in the materials and the text-topics can seem irrelevant to the learners. The material inevitably lacks the targeting to specific learning situations in a particular culture. We were also aware that many classes do not have the advantages of others. Not all of our potential users would be like the private language schools in the UK (one of our potential users) with their small classes, courses of 19–25 hours a week and the support of the native-speaker environment. On the other hand, the UK situation has the disadvantages (as well as some advantages) of the multilingual classroom with the teacher frequently unable to speak the learners' own languages and minimally aware of their cultures.

The notion of compromise

With international materials it is obvious that the needs of individual students and teachers, as well as the expectations of particular schools in particular countries, can never be fully met by the materials themselves.

Indeed, most users seem to accept that what they choose will in many ways be a compromise and that they will have to adapt the materials to their situation.

This is a reasonable approach – indeed it prevents the illusion that situation-specific materials can do the job without the teacher having to adapt the materials to a particular group of individual students at a particular time. In other words, contrary to many current arguments about the inhibiting role of coursebooks, international course materials can actually encourage individualisation and teacher creativity rather than the opposite. It all depends on the relationship that a user, in particular a teacher, has or is allowed to have with the material. Coursebooks are tools which only have life and meaning when there is a teacher present.They are never intended to be a straitjacket for a teaching programme in which the teacher makes no decisions to supplement, to animate or to delete.The fact that course materials are sometimes treated too narrowly – for example, because of the lack of teacher preparation time, the excesses of ministry or institution power, the demands of examinations, or the lack of professional training – should not be used as a reason to write off global coursebooks.

Obviously no publisher is going to make a substantial investment unless there is a prospect of substantial sales. Material has to be usable by teachers and students alike or publishers lose their investment – hype can encourage a teacher or school to try a course once but no amount of hype can encourage the same course to be readopted. It has to work, at least in the eyes of the school. In order to work, the material up to a point has to be targeted – targeted to a particular type of student, in a particular type of teaching situation, and a particular type of teacher with a particular range of teaching skills and who has assumptions about methodology which he/she shares with his/her colleagues.

There is no point in writing a course for teachers of adult students and expect it to be used by primary teachers. These teaching contexts are different anywhere in the world. And yet adult teaching in most countries has a lot in common – particularly these days with far greater professional integration than ever before (thanks to conferences, courses, professional magazines etc.). We felt that many of the situations around the world in which teachers would want to use our materials *did* have a lot in common: for example, teachers used to organising groupwork and aiming for improved communicative competence in the classroom and young adult students very similar to the ones we were used to in the UK.

The publisher's compromise

Compromise is not just something that is shared by users. Publishers also compromise – otherwise they would not get the material they want, i.e. material that they can not only be proud of when exhibiting against other publishers but which sells because users want to use it. Publishers will fail, and have failed, if they try to go for every market and produce something which is thereby anodyne and anonymous. The Eastern, Middle Eastern, Latin American, European, UK-market may have certain things in common (they may all be prepared to commit themselves to the same grammar syllabus, for example) but their differences (for example, whether or not they use the Roman script or whether or not speaking is emphasised in the secondary school system) will ensure that publishers are cautious if they aim to sell globally. And are there many examples of an over-cautious coursebook succeeding commercially? Most successes (as in recent years *Strategies*, *The Cambridge English Course* and *Headway*) are usually seen to be breaking new ground at the time they are published.

Which is not to say a publisher is going to be a great innovator either – such courses, too, rarely succeed. (See Hopkins 1995 for some of the reasons why.) Indeed many of those courses that are felt to be new are in fact successful because they have something which is 'old' about them. One of *Headway*'s successes was that it reverted to a familiar grammatical syllabus when many other coursebooks were considered to have become too functionally oriented. The sensible balance – a compromise of principle – will surely be between innovation and conservatism, a blend of the new and different with the reassuringly familiar.

It may also be true that materials in which designers have too great an influence are also weakened commercially in the long-run. In our experience what is good design for a designer is not necessarily a good design for a teacher. We ourselves have heard designers severely criticise the design of successful books that teachers seem to regard as well-designed books and praise the design of books that are not thought by teachers to be well-designed. Does it matter to a teacher whether there are one, two or three columns on a page and whether a unit is of uniform length in its number of pages? In our experience, what matters to teachers is that it is absolutely clear on the page where things are and what their purpose is and that the balance (and tone) of visuals and text is right for their students. While publishers would undoubtedly agree with this in principle and argue that the number of columns and pages per unit affects usability there is sometimes a worrying gap between the aesthetic principles of a designer and the pedagogic principles of the writers.

Also there are real and necessary pedagogic constraints which designers have to accept as well as design constraints that authors have to accept. Sometimes it is necessary pedagogically to sacrifice illustration for words (texts, rubrics etc.) in order to make a series of activities work in the classroom just as it is sometimes necessary to cut back on say a practice activity to make it fit in with an adequately-spaced visual. This is not to decry the role of designers. They have an essential (and integral) function in making sure that the authors' ideas are properly and attractively presented. They also need to make the students and teachers feel they are using materials with an up-to-date but usable look. Compromise has to be a benefit.

The authors

And what of the authors? They too find themselves compromising – and indeed they often feel themselves compromised by publishers, particularly authors who are teachers with a strong sense of the ideal combined with what works for them in the classroom. This is hardly surprising if a publisher who has done little real research of their own (with their only input coming from the hunches of marketing managers and conventional publishing wisdom) relies on the authors' own experience and then later tells them they cannot put their ideas into practice.

But teachers who are authors also have to compromise. Their teaching experience is often different from that of many intended users and their ideas might not work in a majority of classrooms. They have to beware of being too much the teacher trainer and look also at what students want rather than concentrate on new ideas for teachers. It is very tempting to try and impose your views about what *should* happen in a classroom when the learning experience for different learners is so diverse. This is a common problem in coursebooks (possibly our own included) where the writers are used to working in a privileged learning environment with videos, study centres, small motivated classes etc.

It is not for nothing that most global coursebooks aim to be eclectic in their approach. Also what may work in the context of a particular lesson for the writer – or work in a skills and supplementary book – does not necessarily work in a coursebook where a range of syllabuses are operating, where balance of activity and skill is necessary and where there is often one eye on recycling and revision. And another major, often overlooked consideration is that your material has to fit on the page so that students can actually see it!

Authors who are not teachers also have to compromise. While there are writing skills which not all teachers have – such as structuring a sequence of activities and balancing it with usable visuals – and there are skills which experienced writers have which teachers need if they are to write (see Waters 1994 for a light-hearted view) so there are teaching realities which authors long out of the classroom have to recognise if they are to produce materials that teachers want to teach with. In a lesson of 50 minutes the register still has to be taken, homework given back, announcements made and revision undertaken with students who have just come in tired from work and an irritating traffic jam. And that activity in your coursebook cannot work unless you allow an hour for it!

So all authors find themselves compromising and having compromise forced upon them.

A case study

At this point we are going to be anecdotal and talk about our own experience. A few years ago we were asked to write an intermediate-level course for adult students both in the UK (15–21 hours a week) and in private schools overseas (2–3 hours a week) called *Intermediate Matters*. The assumption was that teachers would have been trained to do things like set up communicative activities in the class, work with texts to develop reading and listening skills and be able to use coursebooks flexibly.

However, the brief itself indicated a need for compromise:

1 The multilingual intensive UK situation and the monolingual far less intensive situation are, as we have already seen, not the same. What is needed in the context of 25 hours a week in the native speaker environment is not necessarily needed in the 1–3 hours a week in the non-native speaker environment. For example, the latter may need (but it has to be said, not necessarily want) a lot more focus on listening and speaking than the former.

2 Monolingual situations differ. For example, can you write for both Europe and the Middle East when the shared knowledge and cultural assumptions are so different? All coursebook writers know the dangers of assuming that all students will know who the (usually Western) cultural icons are.

3 The material was also likely to be used by less trained, untrained or differently-trained teachers. It cannot be assumed that a type of communication activity familiar to a trained teacher will be familiar to an untrained teacher. Things have to be spelt out to the inexperienced teacher without patronising the experienced teacher.

4 What is an adult? It was likely that the material would be chosen by some schools when it is inappropriate for their situation and used by learners who are too young to identify with the cultural content of the material. But could we really worry about that – no matter how keen the publishers might be on extensive sales?

5 It was likely that the materials would be used in some schools where the language syllabus and indeed the whole programme of study are framed by the coursebook even though the aim was to try to produce materials which could be used flexibly.

Principles

We decided on a set of key principles:

1 Flexibility

We wanted an activity sequence that worked pedagogically. But it was important that teachers should feel they could move activities around, cut them out or supplement them according to need. In other words we wanted to produce a coursebook with a strong resource book element. Indeed we saw the Workbook as a potential extra classroom resource for the teacher as well as a self-study book for the learner.

2 From text to language

Because of the needs of intermediate students, we wanted to provide authentic texts which contained examples of the focus language, rather than construct texts of our own. 'Language in a global context' we called it and we hoped we could draw language work out of the texts.

3 Engaging content

We wanted to provide human interest texts from a specific British context and stimulate cultural and personal comparisons. We wanted the texts to engage the students *personally*. At the same time we wanted them to be used as a resource for language and the basis for speaking and writing. We felt that *some* of the texts could be serious in tone but not too many. Too many texts on the environment, vegetarianism and race relations would not appeal. While quite a lot of students seemed to be interested in money, relationships, clothes and food, far fewer students in general language classrooms were interested in the worthier topics to be found in the *Guardian*. There needed to be a balance of serious and 'fun' articles. We realised that coursebooks are written partly to appeal to teachers; but teachers are hardly likely to accept material that bores their students.

Overall we felt that the main criteria for the texts was that they should be generative in terms of language and would motivate students to want to talk or write. Inevitably, this meant choosing texts which focused on many old, favourite topics (relationships, clothes, money etc.) but it also meant that we had to find new angles on those topics.

Of course, we recognise that even these decisions made cultural and situational assumptions. Some students may well prefer intellectual topics and indeed it was subsequently found by many British and American teachers working in post Cold War 'Eastern Europe' that *their* students regarded 'fun' material as trivial!

4 Natural language

We wanted spoken texts to be authentic as far as possible and 'real' people (not actors) to do the recordings. We felt that exposure to real and unscripted language was important at this level to motivate students and help get them off the learning plateau. 'Old' language which they had already had presented at lower levels would at intermediate level be embedded in new and natural language – from native speakers communicating naturally.

5 Analytic approaches

We wanted a variety of approaches to grammar but decided to place great importance on students working things out for themselves – an analytic approach. After all our target students were adults and the conscious mind has a role to play in language learning as well as the acquisition device. This was particularly true for grammatical structures students were familiar with but needed more work on – the difference between the Present Perfect and Past Simple, or *will* and *going to* for example.

6 Emphasis on review

We felt the need to review rather than present a lot of grammar at this level. We assumed students already 'knew' most of the grammar and had practised it at lower levels. Yes, sometimes we felt something should be re-presented but in general at intermediate level fluent and accurate use was what we decided to focus on rather than trying to get across the 'meaning' and use of the structure.

7 Personalised practice

We wanted to provide a lot of practice activities at this level. We felt that where oral practice had to be mechanical (e.g. pattern repetition) it should as far as possible be personalised. So for example, when practising *if* structures for imaginary situations learners would draw on their own experience, as in the activity below.

Complete the following sentences:
a) I'd be very miserable if . . .
b) I'd be terrified if . . .
c) I'd leave the country if . . .

8 Integrated skills

We believed that the four skills should be integrated throughout and that the 'receptive skills' of reading and listening should not be tagged on after the language work. Language use is a combined skill where everything depends on everything else – at the very least we listen and speak together, and read and write together. And we felt that, like playing tennis, communicating in language is something you only improve with practice. *Knowing* about the language can be helpful for adults in learning to use it but overemphasis on the *knowing about* – usually the grammar – is useful for traditional exams but less useful in real-life communicative situations. We believed that both language work and the productive skills should come out of work on listening and reading texts. We believed in the value of texts being slightly above the level of the students and in the possibility of acquisition of language whilst focusing on content.

9 Balance of approaches
We wanted a balance in our approaches. We wanted inductive, deductive and affective approaches to grammar. We wanted fluency → accuracy work (i.e. 'process' approaches) as well as traditional accuracy → fluency work in speaking and writing because we believed that drawing on what the students can do and improving upon it was a valid aim. And in general we would provide opportunities for both controlled practice and creative expression.

10 Learner development
We regarded this as very important but we thought it best to integrate learner development work throughout rather than make it 'up-front' training. Nevertheless we decided to have up-front work on vocabulary skills, to get students to analyse grammar for themselves and to provide a language reference for students at the end of each unit. We also wanted to encourage students to start their own personalised vocabulary and grammar books.

11 Professional respect
We wanted to produce something that gave us professional satisfaction and was academically credible to our colleagues, something we could be proud of. We also wanted a course that looked 'cool': adult and sophisticated with a clean look about it.

Pressures

The publishers
As inexperienced coursebook writers we were soon confronted by not only the harsh realities of commercial publishing but by some of the diverse needs of potential users.

The publishers were encouraging and allowed us a lot of creative freedom. They shared many of our aspirations and also wanted something that would give them academic credibility as well as healthy sales. Nevertheless they had an eye on markets they had to sell to and did not want spiralling production costs. There was no open-ended budget for colour photographs or permissions for songs sung by famous pop singers. At the same time we sometimes felt – not necessarily justifiably – that they gave more attention to first impressions the material would make (the 'flick-test') than its long-term usability. We also felt they overemphasised the need for rubrics to be intelligible to students when we were writing a classbook which would be mediated by teachers. In fact to us teacher mediation was vital or we would end up prescribing the methodology too much (a real problem this: should you ever say

'Work in groups' when the teacher may want to do an exercise in pairs, or 'Write these sentences' when the teacher may want the students to say them?).

Schools and institutions

One of our problems was to sort out the real from the illusory in this area. A lot was made by the publishers of the fact that the main book had to be the right length, there had to be so many units, so many pages per unit – linked to so many hours of work, the syllabus had to include this and that grammatical item, there had to be tests. And yet when it came to it our instincts told us that there was a lot more freedom in our market to do what we liked in terms of overall structure, providing our material was usable and motivating for the level of students. This was confirmed when we talked to teachers informally. Indeed many teachers seemed not to notice how many pages there were in a unit or what was in the syllabus!

Institutional needs nevertheless imposed perfectly proper constraints on our writing: the material should not be inappropriate to the context, the topics should be interesting to their students, the material should not date, it should be 'user-friendly', it should be usable alongside and sometimes integrated with other materials and should enable students to make rapid progress. On the production side it should be good quality but cheap and all components – coursebook, workbook, tapes, teacher's book – should be available locally on launch!

Teachers

We felt teachers wanted a book they could sympathise with in terms of its pedagogic principles. It would need to have a fresh and original feel to it and yet be reassuringly familiar. At the same time teachers are very busy and they naturally wanted an easy life: not too much preparation, usable and motivating materials, fun activities that worked in terms of improving the students' communicative skills, transparent methodology, up-front grammar and a flexible approach which allowed teachers to use the materials more as a resource than a prescriptive course.

Students

Students would want material that they could enjoy and in which they could find things they could identify with and learn from. Language needed to be comprehensible but there did need to be 'new' language there on the page. They needed a lot of revision, a lot of material they could use to study on their own. They needed supplementary materials such as workbooks.

Principles compromised

With all these factors at work it is not surprising that the issue of compromise was central to our work. Having said that it is surprising how many of our grand principles above more or less survived. The main areas of compromise were these:

Overall structure

It was clear that the idea of a flexible coursebook was not (at that time) fully understood by our potential users. We were aware from initial feedback that some teachers felt they had to cover everything in the book in the order presented. Our idea of using the Workbook as part of the classroom resource was not universally accepted since many students did not have access to the Workbook. In other words the material ended up being less flexibly organised than we would have liked. However, at that time it is true that we were not sufficiently aware of the potential of the Teacher's Book to go beyond declaring intentions and suggesting ideas to providing its own resources in terms of extra photocopiable practice activities – a situation we remedied in later editions. This facility very visibly puts into practice the principle of aiming to supply teachers with a resource to help them build up *their* programme.

Originally we wanted to start the book with a 'deep-end' approach and so we flagged our first four units as review units – to activate language students had already been presented with and do remedial work on it if necessary. But many markets did not like or understand this approach and wanted straightforward presentation of the main language items. Should we have compromised and provided this presentation?

Lack of space caused us great frustration at the editing stage when we saw many of our practice activities disappear or get pruned. We had to make a decision whether to cut whole activities or cut back on the number of items within an activity. The fault was probably ours for having too great an ambition for too few pages. So the compromises that were made met with some complaints from users and we have had to provide extra material in the Teacher's Book in later editions.

Methodology

We did manage to get away from a traditional PPP approach in terms of Unit structure since we started each unit with a skills activity rather than a language presentation but our original ambition to draw target language out of authentic texts failed at the intermediate level, partly because of the difficulty of finding texts which contained clear examples of the focus language together with interesting content. We got nearer to our ambition at the upper-intermediate level.

As for our approach to grammar we found the analytic exercises were not very popular in some parts of the world – they were seen to be too serious and to expect too much from students – and perhaps we should have compromised more by having fewer such exercises. And our learner development tasks might have been too worthy and in need of even more integration.

Texts

We resisted publisher pressure to make our texts more intellectual. We still think we were right – this has been supported by subsequent feedback; in fact, we perhaps should have resisted more. But it was clear there were going to be problems with unadapted authentic texts. Finding texts with a generative topic of the right length and the right level of comprehensibility for the level (i.e. comprehensible input + 1) as well as an accessible degree of cultural reference and humour was not easy. So we compromised on this ambition and wonder now whether we should have compromised more and simply gone for texts which were interesting. Here the compromise was one of logistics, publisher pressure and student expectation as well as our own greater realisation that some of our initial ambitions were unrealistic.

We also wanted our listenings to be natural and as authentic as possible – we believed you learn to listen to real English by listening to real English – but we did compromise and use some actors. On reflection, given the response of some non-UK markets to the difficulty of some of the authentic texts we wonder now whether we should have compromised more. We put in a lot of effort to make sure the listenings were authentic but it was not appreciated universally. Perhaps we should have made more of them semi-scripted – or at least made the authentic ones shorter and easier and built in more 'how to listen' tasks.

Content

In terms of content we realised we could not please everyone. We did compromise and not include some texts we would have used with our own students, on the grounds that they would not go down well in such and such a country. We did not want to fight shy of sex, drugs, religion and death (still THE taboo subjects in EFL coursebooks) but found ourselves doing so and being expected to do so. (At the higher level we got away with more.) There was also the great influence of political correctness at that time, particularly in the men vs. women debate, which was US/UK-teacher/publisher driven rather than student-driven. Certain texts were avoided, others were encouraged – women in important jobs, for example – and others toned down.

Piloting

There was a pilot edition of the material which proved to be good training for us as writers but most of the material in the pilot edition did not get used except in parts of the Workbook. The process helped our thinking but not all the feedback was as helpful as we had hoped. We also taught some of the pilot material. But for the final edition direct piloting was difficult if schedules and budgets were to be met. We relied more on our own experience and the experience of advisers.

Conclusions

This is a personal account and yet it is undoubtedly typical of most writing teams in one way or another. Compromise almost by definition is a subtle art if all sides are to be satisfied with getting less than they originally wanted and it has not always been possible to tease out and identify all the compromises that were made when and by whom. We know we compromised our ambitions and we have no doubt our users have had to compromise theirs. We were lucky in that the publishers respected our lead in terms of the content and methodology and also compromised.

I think if we are to make a conclusion it has to be that compromise is not only inevitable it is probably beneficial. At least it was for us. Without certain compromises we would have produced worse materials. If we had made other compromises – and been more aware of the areas where we should have compromised – we might have produced better materials.

6 How writers write: testimony from authors

Philip Prowse

Introduction

A group of ELT materials writers from all over the world met in Oxford in April 1994 for a British Council Specialist Course with UK-based writers and publishers. The personal accounts of the writing process which make up this article are taken from questionnaires and correspondence with course participants and tutors, and their friends.

The accounts are presented as they were written, and are grouped thematically.

Writing together

Most of the contributors have written at some time, or always, as a member of a team. Their accounts of collaborative writing highlight the importance of team building, as well as divergences in working practice. Writing teams are often put together by publishers and considerable 'getting to know you' needs to take place before writing can start. A rough rule of thumb is that team-working on supplementary materials is like an affair, team-working on a coursebook is more like a marriage! 'Getting to know you' works on different levels, and the human one of shared response to experience is as important as shared methodological pre-suppositions. Teams who have taught together are common, and have a head-start on both levels, although it can be argued that to actually start writing at once and to get to know each other as you write is equally effective.

> 'Writing together means what it says: sitting down at a table together. We meet for a whole evening at a time and are very strict with ourselves – no gossip or chatting, just work. Ideas come to you at any time, and collecting materials you can do on your own, but the actual writing process is something we have to do in the same room.'

> 'What we do is each draft a unit (we work in separate rooms),

consulting with the other only if there is some knotty problem. Then each reads the other's unit and criticises: sometimes there is very little to change, sometimes a radical overhaul is necessary. We have never had any ego-problems in this area; it must be awful (and awfully time-consuming) if you do.'

'There's no fixed pattern. But the actual writing definitely takes place individually, at a distance. Ideally the team of writers must first meet and agree on an overall approach and methodology. Then they go away to write their own chunks, which could be thematically related or unrelated. Then they meet regularly to comment on each other's work, and go away to improve their chunks with the benefit of the feedback. Needless to say, we need good team-players – who are confident, but not arrogant, so that they can react positively to criticisms. When it comes to finalising the manuscript, it takes someone with a bit of authority to edit everything. Here I'm talking about the development of classroom materials for an institution, like the university I'm working at. When it comes to published materials, the authors can write pretty independently. I just finished writing an exam practice book with two colleagues and we hardly met over the book.'

'Our textbook team is made up of 13 members, six working for lower secondary level and seven for upper secondary level. The size of the team is rather unusual and lots of people, teachers, inspectors, trainers and ourselves doubted the results of a "mob-at-work".

There are of course, drawbacks: mismatch between individual working styles, individual writing styles, unstandardised units, a longer than usual time for decisions as we must give credit to everyone's idea in order to reach solutions agreed, if not by all members, but by a large majority. If, however, this formula still works it is because we have found a lot more advantages than downsides: variety of ideas (both "triggers" and "template" type), wider range of information and methodological sources, the benefits of getting together people from different parts of the country, which means different areas of interest, conceptions, ideas, and the certainty that once an idea is accepted it has to be a good one.

The major decisions about the content of the book, the topics to be covered, the balance of skills, the treatment of vocabulary and grammar, and the culture and civilisation input are taken from the whole team. Planning, setting up deadlines and seeing that these are met, updating all members and persons related to the project on progress of work and results, organising piloting of the materials, ensuring standardisation, avoiding overlap, reviewing the materials, workshops (organisation, management and reports), and relationships with the publishers are the project co-ordinator and UK consultants' job.

The mode of working we've agreed on is the following:

- During a first workshop: the group decides on topics, functions, skills focus, treatment of grammar, vocabulary, format of a unit and a lesson. Then units are allocated to each member.
- Writers go back to their hometown and devise units accordingly. They send them to the project co-ordinator for checking. The consultants get them for suggestions as well.
- In about three months the group meets again with the project co-ordinator and the consultants and common agreement for all lessons is obtained.'

'I write a first draft which I give to my co-author to comment on and adapt if necessary. If I am stuck for an appropriate activity my co-author often supplies it. Ditto for authentic materials. We work at a distance as we find that this avoids serious disagreements and both of us work better and faster when alone.

The final decision as to approach and content is with me as initiator of the work with a clear overall picture of the methodology, the progression and the "soul" of the book. The responsibility for revising the materials is mine, partly for the reasons just outlined and partly because the materials are trialled at the institute where I work.'

'My only experience of co-authoring was when I wrote part of the Teacher's Book for an exam course and someone else did the rest. The problem was that I was up against deadlines both for the coursebook and for the Practice Tests Book, with one or two other crises going on at the same time! Living abroad also meant that communications (pre-fax) were dire: I never actually managed to discuss the book with my co-author and in the end it became the product of what editors in the UK chose from both our contributions. A real dog's breakfast, in other words.'

'My colleague and I decide on the topic to work on and we get together in the same room and try to find appropriate materials and ideas (in our library). We also bring materials from home and the bookstore, pool it and then "disperse" to get activities prepared. Then we come together again, order our parts, decide together about order and usefulness, and after trying things out we reverse them (each looks at the other's part). Then our colleagues try the material out and give us feedback.'

'For us collaborative writing is team work. We discuss a great deal, decide what we will include in our writing in advance, make an outline and then start writing. The written materials, if they are developed separately, are discussed again. We all agree on the language, content and presentation before they are okayed. Revision is done in the same way.

Very often a member of the team becomes a scribe, and writes what others dictate to him or her after elaborate discussions.

The most senior colleague usually has the final say in case we have disagreements.'

'In general, I find it best to agree on a division of labour that reflects each person's interests and strengths and agree a deadline. Then drafts are exchanged, comments made and the draft re-worked. Perhaps I have been lucky in my co-authors, but this pattern has worked extremely well for me. It does necessitate openness (the willingness to be frank and the willingness to accept constructive criticism), of course, but the benefits are enormous.'

'I have had negative experiences in working with co-authors who are virtual strangers and who are representing the country for whom the book is intended. This is often a relationship full of stresses and strains which result from approaching the project from totally different angles. Then changes made to a manuscript are often guided by motives unconnected to pedagogical considerations.'

'With EFL materials it is a matter of deciding which types of task or which unit you will take responsibility for. Each of you should produce a draft for the other to read and comment on. (Final decisions rest with whoever keys in the final version!) "Co-writing" is ambiguous in English: "co-writing" proper (like team-teaching) I find difficult; I suppose what I do is co-authoring.'

'We have had a few different gos at seeing which approach works best vis-à-vis working in a "team" of two. So far we have tried:

- working together (at home, in long-hand) on the outline of a couple of units at a time. This will include basic structure, a "pot" of ideas, suggestions for texts, but no detail. Then each of us would take a unit and write it, passing it over for comment and/or rewriting afterwards.
- dividing up the book into the first half and the second half. Having macro meetings to discuss syllabus, topics, texts, and then basically getting on with it. Obviously each draft of the unit would be commented on by the co-author.
- one person doing the "macro" sketching out (basically the "creative" bit) and the other one doing the filling in of exercises, detailed artbriefs, wording of Language References and other "micros".

We have not yet found a perfect solution!'

'Recently two of us have been working on some pilot materials for a publisher. We've both got compatible computers so the way it worked was that after lots of preparatory meetings we each started work on a different lesson. Then we would post the disks containing the rough draft to each other, and instead of commenting on it, as we used to do when it was all paper, would simply rewrite the lesson, adding or cutting, quite a lot sometimes, and send it back. In this way we ended up with a unit of lessons which weren't anyone's property. Then we sat down together at one computer and got it all in order, standardising layouts and rubrics and so on. It was a really good way to work, and would have been even quicker if we'd had e-mail.'

How to work together is clearly something which occupies materials writers. In the accounts given here we can distinguish pairs who work closely together, pairs who complement each other, and larger teams where management of the writing process becomes as important as the writing itself. As a writing team gets larger the benefits it receives from diversity are often rapidly outweighed by the negative effects of personal and professional disagreements. There is, however, a tension between having as small a writing team as possible and coping with the demands of a large project. This tension is sometimes resolved by 'sub-contracting' elements of the project, typically workbooks and test or resource packs, but also now teachers' books, to other authors working under the direction of the lead authors.

The creative process

In the production process of a modern coursebook, which can take three to five years from initial idea to copies in the classroom, the actual creation of the lessons, paradoxically, can take up less time than all the other aspects of authorship. These accounts of how writing 'happens' emphasise the creative nature of the process.

'The only work which counts as real work for me – as opposed to meetings, presentations, revising, proof-reading etc. – is a day spent in front of the word processor, originating the first draft of a lesson. No day involves such hard work, but no work is more rewarding. But even this day begins perhaps some months before, at the stage when the whole course design is worked out and elaborated. This stage is essential; it takes time, maybe a week or so, but it means that on the happy day of "real" work, there's no such thing as writer's block, only bad planning.

The process begins as I check the course design requirements for the lesson to be written, and then I begin a fairly lengthy process of deciding in which authentic contexts the target structures or vocabulary are likely to be heard or read. When I've thought about this, I look for input texts, which will be used as either listening or reading material in the lesson. This may involve rereading a lot of old newspapers, going to the library or just going through the bookshelves in my study.

Once I have selected the main input material, I decide on the stages of the lesson, just as a teacher might draw up a lesson plan. Although the principal syllabuses will focus on the target structures or vocabulary, the secondary syllabuses of reading, writing, speaking, listening, pronunciation, socio-cultural training, among others, have to be covered as well. I like to ensure that everything occurs in activity sequences with a beginning, a middle and an end, so that a communicative context is established, and this usually involves a little ingenuity. I put on screen all kinds of possible exercises and activities, type in the input material and then just spend a lot of time thinking about the most suitable choice and order. I often do this thinking during some exercise around the middle of the day, and by the time I get back, it's miraculously clear what the activity sequence is.

By the time I start to write the lesson, most of the significant decisions have been made, and everything usually goes very quickly. It will take me a couple of hours to finish a lesson – for my present series, a lesson corresponds to a double page spread. So, in all, two pages will take me about a day to originate.

Of course there's a lot of polishing, revising and finishing to do, which is usually done in collaboration with my editor. There are also tapescripts to prepare, answers to check and the teacher's book to write, which often throws up further flaws. But all this is done later in the writing/editing process, and the certainty that these tasks remain to be done does not impinge upon the pleasure I feel at the end of this day of "real" work.'

'Some people just sit down at the table and work. It has never been this way with me. My ideas and intentions boil inside me for a long time, even details take quite a while to mature, then at some point I feel I can start writing. Usually after this moment everything pours out in a gulp. And later on for quite a long time I may be reluctant even to look through what has been done, postpone indefinitely working over the text, editing . . .

- writing is fun, because it's creative.
- writing can be frustrating, when ideas don't come.
- writing brings joy, when inspiration comes, when your hand cannot keep up with the speed of your thoughts.
- writing is absorbing – the best materials are written in "trances".
- writing improves with practice, but everybody needs a bit of a push to face up to their first writing assignment.
- writing is addictive – after you've completed your first job you keep asking for more.'

'When I feel inspired the writing comes easily, but when the first idea has been put on paper I tend to lose interest. I nevertheless want the work to be "mine", and get tense when my co-author seems less committed to the storyline and the relationships between the characters than I am.'

'Writing, for me, is a tortuous activity. I think a lot, or, in a way, worry a lot, not about the mechanics of writing, but about making a bonafide beginning, and then about keeping things organised while I write.

Thinking, or what others would call "planning", takes place everywhere – in the bus, on walks, while shopping, anything which keeps me occupied. So if I see you around Kathmandu and don't recognise you, you should not worry. I will go a little distance, remember you, and come back to say hello to you.'

'Sometimes it's hard to stop writing. Carrying on into the night – long after you're past your best and you seem to be working on auto-pilot – can bring on insomnia and reduced efficiency the day after. Meals get postponed, as does time with the family and with friends.

Why do we do it? In my case I can't offer any better reason than the "buzz" . . . I'd like to think that I write to help students learn, or even help teachers teach, but if I'm really honest with myself it's difficult to believe that I'd put in 100-hour weeks for that purpose alone.'

'In materials writing mood – engendered by peace, light, etc. – is particularly important to me and the process is also rather different from that involved in other kinds of writing. The main difference, perhaps, is that in materials writing I need to start from the germ of an idea. When I've got that, I might just let it simmer away, give it a stir from time to time, and then at a certain point have a closer look at it. I draw heavily on my own experience. I might look through what other people have done, but I basically rely on my own intuition. This suggests that I work quickly and surely. I think I do work quickly, but since I often leave gaps (for the rather tedious bits that need to be filled in later), and since I also feel the need to shape and polish, I go through endless drafts before I am more or less satisfied.'

Most of the writers quoted here appear to rely heavily on their own intuitions, viewing textbook writing in the same way as writing fiction, while at the same time emphasising the constraints of syllabus. The unstated assumption is that the syllabus precedes the creation. An alternative view is to base lesson materials on topics and activities which are of interest and value in themselves, and derive the actual syllabus from the materials, using checklists where necessary to ensure sufficient 'coverage'. 'Coverage' is another unspoken assumption, as if teaching materials can encapsulate the whole of the language, rather than offer a series of snapshots of it.

The materials described in this section are, in the main, student materials, and where reference is made to a teacher's book it is assumed to be written afterwards. Some authors, however, prefer to create the teacher's and student's books at the same time. This approach is clearly essential with primary school materials, where the material on the student page may be entirely visual, but can be adopted at all levels. A possible practical drawback is that continuing revision and editing of the student material can necessitate the rewriting of the teacher's book a number of times. For adult learners it can be argued that student lesson material should be so clear that it could be taught 'off the page', without reference to a teacher's book which will mainly contain extra ideas and activities.

Working with publishers

Major coursebook series these days are usually commissioned by publishers rather than suggested by authors, and the account below reflects a not untypical writing process. Missing, of course, are the endless meetings and discussions before a project is commissioned, and the post production pressure (welcome as it is) to travel and promote the series.

Initial stage
- Research on new level – what is needed/gaps in market/ weaknesses of other materials – by talking to teachers (students sometimes), looking at/teaching other materials. My co-author and I do this independently with follow-up meeting/sharing of opinions and findings.
- Meeting with co-author (at home) to discuss and draft our basic rationale. This will include book and unit structure, and a draft grammar syllabus and usually takes some time. Initially done in long-hand.
- Creation of draft unit (usually Unit 1). Planning of unit usually done together, and then divided up and worked on individually with lots of batting to and fro. Done on computer and faxed backwards and forwards for comments. Editors not involved at this stage.
- Submit rationale/draft unit/proposed grammar syllabus to publisher. This is then sent out to readers – an "inner sanctum" of people, and a wider net to catch diverse opinions from "the market".

Meanwhile
- Myself and co-author continue to build up ideas for other syllabuses – vocabulary, writing, pron., etc. in terms of activity types and topic. We also build up a bank of authentic texts which we feel we can use or adapt. This is usually done separately, with follow-up meetings to discuss and decide.
- There is often a meeting with the designer and art editor at this stage to discuss the "look" we want from the book, and how we can make it look different from other levels.
- When reports come back on draft unit and rationale there is a

meeting (at a "neutral" spot like a country hotel) with the publisher and project manager, to share views and "take a stand" on what changes. This is where sparks usually fly!

First draft

At first draft stage we don't worry about writing to the page, detailed artbriefs, recordings, keys etc. We send the first draft out to about 14 readers and triallers and feedback on the first draft is again followed up by a mega-meeting with publishers, when changes in content and philosophy may occur. At this point readers are encouraged to focus on the big issues rather than the "toddlers".

Otherwise during the first draft stage the publisher and editor keep pretty much off our back, apart from helping to find texts and researching song permissions etc. More and more, they (and we) are getting involved in "research visits" to schools in the UK and abroad to find out "what the market really wants" and this is fed in, where possible.

Second draft

This is usually done over a relatively intensive period and will often involve quite a lot of change – finding new texts, cutting out presentations, adding other activities etc. At this point, we become much more critical, and start to write much more "to the page", with an eye on design and layout.

This is also sent to readers, but by this stage (hopefully) they are commenting much more on the micros.

At this stage we also have to get involved in briefing the person writing our Workbook and Teacher's Book. This always involves more work than we remember – as the decisions for what to include rest with us.

Third draft

Usually within a very limited time, and has to involve making our own recordings, too, as well as the key. At this point the publishing team are very involved, and as we are writing, "finished" units will be copy-edited and sent back to us, usually requesting drastic cuts. There are also meetings with designers and editors.

Finally

From the day we finish writing there is, on average, six months of non-stop follow-up production work, particularly in the area of design, cuts and rubrics. This is, perhaps, the most stressful time, perhaps because of the continual liaison with the whole team, rather than just us two.'

The writer refers to the publishing team which may typically consist of a publisher in overall charge, a commissioning editor, whose project it is, one or more desk editors who work on the material in detail, and a designer (although much design work is now freelanced). Supporting this team will be a recording studio producer and actors for audio tapes, artists and photographers, picture researchers, copyright clearers, and proof-readers. There will be a number of 'readers' who give feedback on the material at various stages, and 'pilot' teachers who check the material in classroom use.

Two relatively new developments are worth noting: input from marketing, and the rise of the freelance editor. For most UK publishers the influence of the marketing team over almost every aspect of materials production is now paramount, particularly as more market-specific courses are being produced. It is input from marketing which sets the parameters within which the writer operates.

Just as important as the relationships within the writing team is the relationship between writers and editors. Typically in the past materials were produced by the publisher's own staff. Cost pressures and 'down-sizing' have led to the increasing use of freelance editors and designers working under the overall control of a commissioning editor. This is neither good nor bad in itself, but in a major project can lead to the authors having to relate to an increasingly large number of 'new' people, with the consequent inevitable and vital 'getting to know you' phase occupying more and more time.

Designer and illustrators

While a number of the contributors complained of lack of involvement with the design of their books, the account which follows accurately reflects the current awareness of the importance of design. Frequently a design for the look of the student page is finalised before much of the writing is done, and authors write to fit the design.

> 'We have always been very involved in the design process. This can be highly rewarding if you have a good and congenial designer; it can be murder if you and the designer have different agendas. Of course, to some extent, you and the designer always have different agendas in the sense that she or he wants the design to be aesthetically pleasing and you want it to be pedagogically effective. We have always had a general meeting with designers before they begin working on the book, to try and communicate both ways our ideas for the book, and, for

instance, to look over samples of illustrators' work to come to some kind of consensus about what we feel comfortable with. We also write a general brief covering points that are important to us, e.g. having a spread of age, race, sex, ability, social class in the people depicted in the illustrations; we request that the designer bear this in mind, and that each illustrator see it as well.

Some of the problems with designers may also come from the fact that they are operating on a tight budget and can only employ third-rate illustrators. They won't tell you this: they will try and convince you that the illustrations you are getting are actually very good.

There are sometimes problems with the artbriefs for illustrators. These come from two sources:

1 My maxim of illustrators: any one illustrator can either read or draw. So either s/he reads your artbrief carefully and takes care to observe it, in order to produce a boring pedestrian illustration that your seven-year-old could have done; or s/he produces a wonderful illustration that will really draw your learners in and make the page striking and attractive . . . but the learners won't be able to do the corresponding exercise because some of the elements of the illustration are wrong or missing.

2 Suspension of Gricean maxims. You can't assume anything with an illustrator. If you say "desert scene", it is best to specify that there should be no igloos in it. If you don't, and you complain about the igloos in the art rough, you will be told it is your fault. Learning to write a tight artbrief may be the most difficult subskill of the EFL writer's trade.'

It would be interesting to compare the reactions of learners from different cultures to today's highly designed full colour coursebooks. Does the expenditure of so much time and money increase the effectiveness of learning, or merely ensure that one book is purchased rather than another? To what extent is a fashionable design a barrier rather than an aid to learning?

Technology

Submission of text on disk as well as paper is the norm now rather than the exception. Ironically, publishers' desire to set text direct from disk and eliminate errors from rekeying means that the disks have to be submitted without any of the wonderful features of design and layout which modern word processing packages allow. The first of the contributions below raises the question of the extent of progress through technology.

'I write on an Apple Mac, which I enjoy, and I'm fortunate that my co-authors use the same word-processing program so it's simple to exchange disks. Sometimes we work together over cups of tea at the kitchen table, but more often we communicate by phone, post and fax. And now my editors and most of my co-authors use e-mail, so there is increasing pressure for me to follow suit. I certainly recognise the practical advantages of being able to transmit material from screen to screen when deadlines are pressing.

But the advance in electronic communication doesn't appear to have speeded up the publishing process. And there are psychological implications that worry me. If the publisher faxes me a document rather than posting it, I feel I should respond immediately. Instant transmission seems to demand instant response, constant accessibility. The medium is the message. It's easy, it's fast and it's very beguiling. Yet sometimes I don't want to be instantly accessible – I value my time and space.'

'What I write with matters a lot to me. I always start with pen and paper and my first plan (pre-draft) is usually a "mind map", with lots of balloons and arrows and crossings out. I often use different coloured pens to help me remember to include particular exercises or quotations at particular points in what I am writing. I recently rediscovered (3,000 miles away and 15 years later) a favourite fountain pen I thought I had lost, and now I find myself using it a lot. It sounds pathetic, but I really feel more comfortable writing with it than with any other pen.'

'I write with pen and paper. Usually I use ball pens and plain A4 size paper.'

'I invariably use scrap paper (i.e. unused handouts or the blank side of previous typed drafts) – I feel less guilty about covering sheet after sheet.'

'I used to write with a pen in a thick notebook. I now have a lap-top Toshiba computer. It is an old one, but good enough for my work.'

'Most of the writing process takes place on paper. I still cannot get my mind around the typewriter/computer kind of writing.'

'I wrote my first books (early 1980s) on a typewriter, but then moved on to a personal computer. I've never written books by hand. I touch-type, so I've always been able to type faster than I can think, and get thoughts down more efficiently that way. I do remember, though, the difference it made when we moved from typewriters to word processing.'

'I usually go straight to the computer and compose at the keyboard except (1) when I am not in my office or at home, like when I'm in a café (2) when it's a very demanding writing task, say, when I have to use a lot of tact, in which case I would do a draft on paper (3) when I need to lay out words in tabular form, e.g. when I'm designing a car hire record form, in which case I'll do a pencil sketch on paper.'

'I write straight on to the screen, no paper, no favourite pens.'

Throwing out a 15-year-old manuscript composed on a manual typewriter, covered with Tipp-Ex® blobs, and glued on extra bits, emended in coloured pen and pencil is a salutary experience for today's author: none of us would like to go back to that time. Nevertheless it is interesting to speculate on how different the contributions to this article might have been if I had asked for them on disk, rather than handwritten on a questionnaire.

A time and a place to write

Another reassuringly divergent set of views, this time on when and where to write. The final contribution may represent a dream, rather than reality!

'Usually when the kids are away. I need complete peace when I write. Distractions break my flow of ideas.'

'In my daughter's bedroom, late at night for two–three hours. The room is small, homely, and cramped, with a parrot.'

'I need solid blocks of "private" time to do any serious writing of materials for classroom use or publication. This usually means after 10 pm after my son has gone to bed, up to 1 am or 2 am, until I start fading, or if I fade after sitting at the computer for, say, half an hour, I'll try to get up early in the morning like 5 am, to meet my own quota, or more often, publisher's deadlines.'

'When I was in the "peaceful" position of just being a writer my best working time was evening and into the night, in my study at home, with masses of books around, and the computer in front of me and the curtains pulled.'

'I usually write in my study, at the desk, by the window. My bulldog always comes to sleep and snore near me when I work. I can never work at night, my most efficient time is morning.'

'I write mostly at night. I prefer that time as it is comparatively quieter here and I can concentrate more. I write in the family study room. When my children go to bed I come and work at my table.'

'I do my best creative writing (I think) in the morning (have to get up at 6.30 to put my young son on the school bus) and mid-afternoon. I've got a small flat about a mile away from the house where I do all my writing work. Marital harmony has followed the decision to make a total separation between family and writing.'

'I usually write at night in my sitting room-cum-study. I begin writing after supper, say between 7.30 and 8.00 and continue until 11.30 or midnight.'

'I write in a room overlooking the garden, so the only distraction out of the windows are the movements of cats and squirrels. I sometimes long for a view of the street to watch the schoolchildren, students and passers-by, but maybe I'd get less work done.'

'In a study at home, and this has its pros and cons. You don't waste time travelling, and everything is in its place. But at the beginning it took a while to train other people, neighbours, friends, that during the day I was actually working and not available for chatty phone calls or drop-in visits; with some people I would have to say on the phone "I'm afraid I'm in a meeting just now." And the worst aspect, I think is that it's always there: especially if you're worried about being late for a deadline, it is so easy to go and do a few more hours' work in the evening, or to get up early in the morning, and never escape from the work. This can be very stressful.'

'Somewhere quiet, comfortable, bright (ideally sunny). An armchair by the fire suits me very well for certain kinds of writing, at the drafting stage, anyway. I also like a sunny window-seat.

One particularly productive period was spent on my own on a secluded beach, just letting ideas for exercises float to the surface of my barely conscious mind. I jotted these down and worked them up into exercises later.'

Conclusion

A different set of prompts and questions would certainly have elicited different responses, and it would have been interesting to see if these had focused more on learning principles and objectives, and less on syllabus, ideas, and procedures. It would also be interesting to learn more about the relationship between writers and the classroom: how many still teach regularly, visit schools and observe classes, and work with groups of teachers. Then there is the publisher's view of writers, the teacher's view of materials, and the learner's perception of the whole process. What does come through strongly in the range of views presented here is the apparent centrality of writing to the contributors' lives, and the seriousness with which they take it.

One of the delights of the course in Oxford was the sharing of experience, and the realisation that one was not alone. It is to be hoped that the above accounts will strike chords with other writers around the world, and lead to a little more understanding between writers and publishers.

An aspect not touched on above is the extent to which writers make use of 'displacement activities', doing everything except sit down and write. Perhaps this article should be considered to be such an activity!

With heartfelt thanks to the contributors:
Wendy Ball (UK), Jan Bell (UK), Elisabeth Fleischmann (Austria), Judy Garton-Sprenger (UK), Ram Ashish Giri (Nepal), Simon Greenall (UK), Shamsul Hoque (Bangladesh), Marina Larionova (Russia), Tony Lynch (UK), Peter May (Belgium), Ian McGrath (UK), Olga Nikolaeva (Russia), Ruxandra Popovici (Romania), Naina Shahzadi (Bangladesh), Keith Tong Sai-tao (Hong Kong), Catherine Walter (UK).

Further reading

Hidalgo, A. C., D. Hall and G. M. Jacobs. 1995. *Getting Started: Materials Writers on Materials Writing*. Singapore: SEAMEO Regional Language Centre.

Comments on Part B

Brian Tomlinson

The three chapters in this section offer very different perspectives on the process of creating language teaching materials but they do share some themes and they do raise similar issues.

All three chapters stress the dynamic nature of materials development and reveal how materials, whether they be for publication or tomorrow's lesson, need to be constantly evaluated and revised. Materials should keep changing, and, in fact, I even change my own published materials every time I use them in class. Ideally materials need to be monitored by the author(s), by other 'experts' not involved in the writing team and by typical users of the material. This is the process commonly adopted on textbook projects these days and which, in my personal experience, has been very successful in increasing the learning potential of books written recently for schools in Bulgaria, Morocco and Namibia (Tomlinson 1995b) and for universities in China. The Namibian Textbook Project is a particularly interesting example of dynamic development of materials. A team of 30 writers (teachers, curriculum developers and advisers) worked together for eight days to develop a book (*On Target* 1995). During that time the team used responses to teacher and student questionnaires plus their pooled experience and expertise to determine the content and approach of the book and then to draft, revise and write it. Later it was trialled by teachers throughout the country, monitored by 'experts' and then finalised. This collaborative, interactive approach is one I would recommend whether for global coursebooks, local textbooks or even institution specific material.

Another theme common to the three chapters is that of meeting the needs of all the interested parties (a theme also discussed by Peter Donovan when he focuses on the trialling of materials in Chapter 7 and by Hitomi Masuhara when she considers the needs of teachers in Chapter 10). While most people would agree that meeting the needs of the learners should be the primary target, it is obviously important to meet the needs of the teachers, the writers and the 'sponsors' too. If teachers are not enthused by materials their dissatisfaction is always apparent to the learners, the materials lose credibility and the learners' motivation and investment of energy are reduced. If writers do not enjoy writing the materials and are not proud of them this deficiency is detected by the users and the credibility of the materials is diminished. If the publishers, Ministry or other sponsors are not satisfied with the materials then they will not be active in promoting them. In my experience the way to satisfy all the interested parties is not compromise but collaboration at all stages of the project. In the Namibian Textbook Project representatives of the Ministry of Education, the Examination Board, the publishers, the teacher trainers and the teachers were present throughout the development of the book. They gave advice, they gave feedback and they gave positive encouragement to the writers to enjoy the process of developing the book.

One of the issues touched on by all three chapters concerns the question of whether to pre-determine the syllabus of the materials or to let the syllabus develop organically from the materials. In some cases the authors are writing to a specific brief and must follow an imposed syllabus absolutely. But one of the things we know about language acquisition is that most learners only learn what they need or want to learn. Providing opportunities to learn the language needed to partici-pate in an interesting activity is much more likely to be profitable than teaching something because it is the next teaching point in the syllabus. And deriving learning points from an engaging text or activity is much easier and more valuable than finding or constructing a text which illustrates a pre-determined teaching point. My own preference is for a text-driven approach to syllabus development. If the written and spoken texts are selected for their richness and diversity of language as well as for their potential to achieve engagement then a wide syllabus will evolve which will achieve natural and sufficient coverage. If the materials are constrained by an external syllabus then a text-driven approach with constant reference to a checklist (as suggested by Philip Prowse in Chapter 6) is the most profitable approach. This is how *On Target* (see above) was written, with the writers focusing on learning points which suggested themselves from their texts but also with the writers constantly checking to see if a particular point was receiving too much attention in the book so far or not enough.

Another of the issues raised by these chapters is the question of to what extent materials should be and can be driven by learning prin-ciples. One argument is that principles are subjective and diverse and that different participants in the materials development process will follow differing principles. Compromise is therefore necessary to satisfy the different parties and also to cater for different learner styles and expectations. A counter argument is that compromised principles are no longer principles and that they can lead to an eclectic mishmash of activities which are perceived by both teachers and learners alike to lack consistency and conviction: good materials are those which are consistently informed by the same set of believed-in principles. The danger of this second argument is that closed principles can lead to inflexible procedures which cater for a minority of learners only. So a belief that listening is the primary skill in early language acquisition can lead to an edict that beginners should not see the target language written down; or a belief that practice makes perfect can lead to a plethora of mechanical drills which fail to engage the energy or attention of the majority of users of the materials. The answer is not easy; but I think it lies in the overt establishment of agreed and justifiable principles followed by procedural compromises which cater for differing preferences, providing they are driven by one or more of the established principles. In other words, an approach to materials writing in which the on-going evaluation of the materials being developed is constantly informed by a checklist of agreed principles. This worked on the Namibian Project and can work on any materials project providing one of the agreed principles is that different learners learn different things and in different ways.

7 Piloting – a publisher's view

Peter Donovan

Introduction

There is a range of situations in which teaching materials are trialled in the course of their development. Individual teachers often prepare exercises or sets of material for their own classes, which can be refined over a period of time on the basis of 'how it went' with a number of classes. Rather than trying to arrive at a final, definitive state for the materials, such development is often a continuing open-ended process of refinement and adaptation to different groups of learners. In some situations, a group of teachers may prepare materials for use by themselves and by other teachers in their own institution, which may then be finalised in a more permanent state for ongoing use after a trialling period. In larger scale materials development projects, a pilot or trialling phase may be built in before the materials are revised and disseminated more widely and formally.

This chapter attempts to describe the issues involved in piloting on a wider and more formal scale, during the course of development of materials leading up to their commercial international publication. Several characteristics of this process distinguish it from the situations described above. Firstly, the original authors of the material are frequently physically distanced from the piloting event. While they might be able to teach some or all of the materials themselves (and it is undoubtedly desirable that they do so), the pilot material will be channelled through the publisher's editors and marketing staff to teachers who will not know the authors, nor their intentions except as they are expressed and realised in the materials themselves. The authors will therefore typically have no direct influence over most of the piloting situations or regular contact with them. (Although large-scale piloting projects where authors move between teaching and materials writing do exist, these are less common and tend to be focused on requirements for a particular educational sector, often sponsored by a ministry, a publisher, an aid agency, or a combination of partners.)

Secondly, the piloters themselves will usually have a free choice as to whether to use the materials or not (unlike teachers who may be required by their institution or their peers to use material being specially produced for their benefit). Thirdly, and related to the latter point, the piloters may not directly need the pilot materials as part of their teaching programme. Institutions typically have their own requirements satisfied through their choices of existing published material. Pilot materials are offered as an optional extra, which teachers may decide to incorporate in their programmes for a given period out of interest, for variety, because of a relationship with a publisher, or because they might fill a need which is not currently catered for. It would be difficult for a publisher to coerce individual teachers into participating in a piloting project, although individual teachers might not be able to resist the decision of a head of department or institution to take part.

Pre-publication piloting is usually for a specific, limited period, which has to reconcile the requirements of the publisher's development schedule with the constraints of the teaching situation – the period in which the materials can be used during the teaching year, term or semester, and the number of teaching hours which can be devoted to it. It will involve the teacher providing feedback in the form of answers to a questionnaire, and sometimes in addition a written report of the pilot experience. This may, optimally, be supplemented by informal inter-views with the authors, editors, or marketing staff, for more detailed and anecdotal comment. A final distinction is that in some situations payment or some other benefit such as books or materials may be offered to the teacher or institution involved in the piloting, usually in return for particularly detailed reporting on the material and the experience over and above the completion of questionnaires.

What therefore distinguishes the process of piloting materials in preparation for their formal publication, as opposed to other modes of piloting or trialling, can be summarised in terms of factors of proximity, channels of communication, volition, time and benefit.

What is piloted?

Given that the piloter is usually at a distance from the author and publisher, it follows that what is supplied for piloting should be a clearly presented, coherent package, providing all the components needed for the particular project – printed and recorded student material for class and self-study use, with teacher's guides, etc. (Video and multimedia may also be piloted, and this is dealt with below.) The teacher must be able to divine the intention of the material and how it is to be used from the pilot package itself, without the intervention of the author or editor, making the teacher's book an essential part of the package. There will need to be clear indications of the intended audience, ages, level, teaching time, needs and expected outcomes, and so on. The learners must have clear printed pages and audio material to work from, and so the work must have gone through at least a preliminary editorial stage before release. Ideally, as much of this material as possible should be in the teacher's hands when making a decision on whether to pilot. The teacher should also have the questionnaire for the pilot from an early stage – either when making a decision, or from the start of the pilot programme – in order to be able to see what the aims and scope of the pilot are, and to be alert to the issues on which feedback is required.

Whilst pilot materials around ten years ago might have been made up of a 'cut and paste' version of the author's typescript, rising expectations from users and the widespread use of 'desk-top publishing' packages on authors' personal computers have led to pilot materials appearing in more professional form, sometimes laid out in ways reflecting the design of the final materials, and incorporating representative artwork scanned into the pages. Pilot materials are, however, likely to be provided in black and white only, for reasons of cost. Exceptions might be some types of material for younger learners, or specific pages on which colour is essential for teaching purposes. (While the reasons for a basic level of presentation are accepted by the majority of piloters, feedback often contains references to the standard of design, and hopes that the final production will be of higher quality, in colour, with improved layout, etc.)

Examples of piloted materials

Below are examples of pages from two different types of pilot materials, and an example of how one of them has appeared in final published form. Figure 1 is an example of a current supplementary (grammar) pilot, for learners aged around 11. Figure 2 consists of some pages from the pilot of *Cambridge English for Schools*, again for learners aged around 11, which was produced in the early 1990s. Figure 3 shows the corresponding material in its final published form, in 1996. As you look at the materials notice the differences between the pilot and the published versions.

5B What's in your fridge?

Kim! Where are you?

Kim's mum is angry. There is orange juice and water on the kitchen floor. The dirty glasses are on the table. The dirty jug is in the sink. The bowl is under the table. There's an orange behind the door, the empty sugar bag is next to the bin and there's an orange between the oven and the fridge ...

1. Read the description and answer the questions.

1 Where's the knife?
It's under the table.

2 Where's the jug?

It's .... the sink.

3 Where are the dirty spoons?

They're .... the fridge.

2 Write the correct words for the diagrams.

① ② ③ ④ ⑤

on ....

⑥

........../ by/ beside in front of above

Check your answers on page 60.

**3. Write the questions.
Use *Where is ...? / Where are ...?***

1 ....

It's under the TV.

2 ....

It's in the bin.

3 ....

They're by the telephone.

4 ....

It's above the oven.

5 ....

They're between the crisps and the salad.

4. Look at the picture and finish the sentences.

1 The post office is .... the river.

2 The seats are .... the bridge.

3 The tennis court is .... the park.

4 The book shop is .... the bank and the police station.

5 The bus stop is .... the bank.

5. Look at the fridge. Write sentences. Use the words below and *There is ... / There are ...*

on   in   under   between   behind
next to/by/beside   in front of   above

1 *There is a fish next to some milk.*

2 ....

3 ....

4 ....

5 ....

6 ....

6. Now look at the fridge. What's different? Write sentences. Use *The ... is/are ...*

1 *The fish is*...

2 ....

3 ....

4 ....

5 ....

6 ....

7. What's in your fridge? Write 6 sentences.

1 ....

2 ....

3 ....

4 ....

5 ....

6 ....

Puzzle

There are some ducks on a pond. There are two ducks in front of a duck, two ducks behind a duck and one duck between the ducks. How many ducks are there?

....

Figure 1

UNIT
11

Natural forces

> The weather; frequency adverbs; much/many;
> (un)countables; comparatives and
> superlatives; present simple revision;
> curricular links with Science and Geography

Take a look at Unit 11!

What things in nature can you learn about? What grammar can you revise?
What is Part C about? What do you need for Part C?

PART A: THE WEATHER

1 **What's the weather like?** | music, and types of weather |

🔊 Listen to the cassette. You can hear part of Beethoven's 6th Symphony,
about the weather. Do you like the music? Why/why not?

Which of the pictures below best describes the music?

stormy winds	warm weather	rain
thunder and lightning	cold weather / snow	hot weather

What type of weather do you like? Look at the pictures again and tell the class.

I like <u>warm weather</u>   *I don't like* .....   *I don't mind* .....

2 **Where does the weather come from?** | Reading |

Why do we have rain? Why are there winds? Why do we have thunder and
lightning? Tell the class what you think.

Now work in a group of four. Two of you read Text A and the other two read Text
B. Put the pieces of information in the correct place. Then, in your language, tell
the other pair what your text says.

TEXT A: WHY DO WE HAVE RAIN?

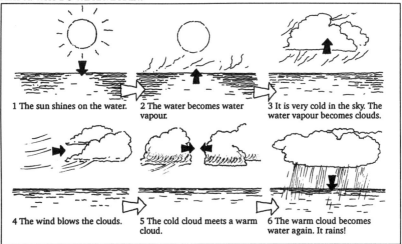

1 The sun shines on the water.
2 The water becomes water vapour.
3 It is very cold in the sky. The water vapour becomes clouds.
4 The wind blows the clouds.
5 The cold cloud meets a warm cloud.
6 The warm cloud becomes water again. It rains!

TEXT B: WHY DO WE HAVE WINDS?

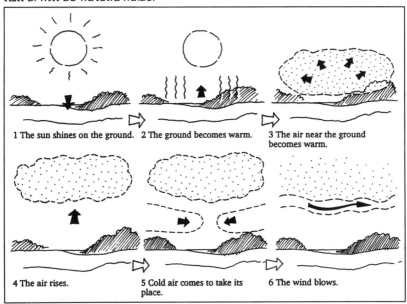

1 The sun shines on the ground.
2 The ground becomes warm.
3 The air near the ground becomes warm.
4 The air rises.
5 Cold air comes to take its place.
6 The wind blows.

📟 **Listen to the cassette to check your answers.**

155

The process of materials evaluation

3 What makes lightning?

vocabulary

Here is another 'natural force' – thunder and lightning. Can you put in the missing words? Work with your neighbour.

cloud   rises   colder   goes down   expands   make   jumps

1. A heavy rain ....

2 Water vapour .... in the air.

3 Inside the cloud, the water vapour becomes .... It changes into ice.

BANG!

4 The ice is heavier than the water vapour and so it ....

5 More water vapour is rising inside the cloud but the ice is going down. When they meet, they .... static electricity.

6 The static electricity .... to the ground and makes lightning.

7 The lightning warms the air. The air .... very fast and makes a bang!

156

4 What's the weather like in your country?

| Frequency adverbs and months |

Look at the calendar. What weather do you have in your
country each month? Copy the calendar into your book and make some notes.

January	February	March	April
		\	
		strong winds and rain	
May	June	July	August
September	October	November	December

strong winds   rain   warm weather   cold weather   hot weather
thunder and lightning   snow   hot weather

Tell the rest of the class your ideas.

We	always usually sometimes never	have .... in ....

5 We never have snow in June!

| writing |

Work in pairs. Look at the calendar again. Write 10 sentences about your
weather. Make some true and some untrue.

Give your sentences to another pair. They have to put the untrue sentences right.

1 We always have snow in June.   *Not true! We never have snow in June.*
2 We sometimes have rain in July and August.   *True!*
3 It is colder in June than in February.   *True!*
4 It is hotter in May than in ...

6 What's the weather like?

| listening |

Look at the pictures below. When do you have weather like that
in your country? What type of day is today?

Listen to the people on the cassette. What type of day are they talking about?

    Cambridge English for Schools Pilot Edition Level 1 Student's Book

The process of materials evaluation

7 How many rainy days do they have?

Work in pairs. Look at the chart below about the weather in Norway in June and December. Ask each other questions, like this:

How many sunny days do they have in December?
How many rainy days do they have in June?
How many windy days do they have in December?

THE WEATHER IN NORWAY

'A normal week in December'

	Mon	Tues	Wed	Thur	Fri	Sat	Sun
Hours of sun	3	3	4	3	3.5	3.5	3
Rain/snow in mm	150	0	0	0	30	0	0
Windspeed (kph)	5	10	5	8	0	0	5

'A normal week in June'

	Mon	Tues	Wed	Thur	Fri	Sat	Sun
Hours of sun	20	20	20	20.5	20.5	20	20
Rain/snow in mm	0	0	0	0	0	0	0
Windspeed (kph)	5	10	5	8	0	0	5

Compare your answers with other students in the class. Do you agree what 'sunny' 'rainy' and 'windy' mean?

Can you answer these questions? Calculate the answers!

1 How much rain do they have in December?
2 How much rain do they have in June?
3 How much sun do they have in December?
4 How much sun do they have in June?

8 Decide ...

In a small group of 3 or 4, decide what you want to do next:
  practise your vocabulary about the weather and write an exercise (see 8A)
or read about hurricanes and draw some pictures (see 8B)
or something else. Decide what you want to do and then ask your teacher.
(Use the Ideas List on page 139 to make an exercise for your class Exercise Box.)

8A What's the word?

vocabulary

1 Join the word halves together and match them to the meaning. Write the complete word.

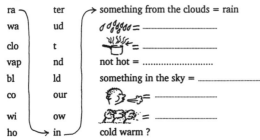

ra	ter	→ something from the clouds = rain
wa	ud	
clo	t	
vap	nd	not hot = ...
bl	ld	something in the sky = ...
co	our	
wi	ow	
ho	→ in	cold warm ?

2 Now look at exercises 1–4 and make another word exercise. (You can also put the meanings in your language.) Give your exercise to another group to do.

Figure 2

158

24 Topic The weather

The weather; curriculum
links with Science and
Geography; frequency
adverbs

hot weather

1 Musical weather

*Music, and types
of weather*

🔲 Listen to the tape. You can hear part of Beethoven's
6th Symphony, about the weather. Do you like the music? Why/Why not?

Which of the pictures describes the music best?

warm weather

strong winds

thunder and lightning

cold weather

snow

What type of weather do you like?
Look at the pictures again and tell
the class.

rain

I like warm weather. *I don't like …* *I don't mind …*

2 What's the weather like in your country?

strong winds
and rain

*Frequency adverbs
and months*

*Extra practice • WB
Exs. 1, 2, 6*

Look at the calendar. What weather do you have in your country?
Copy the calendar and
make some notes.

rain
warm weather
hot weather
cold weather
snow
strong winds
thunder and lightning

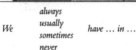

January	February	March	April
May	June	July	August
September	October	November	December

Tell the rest of the
class your ideas.

| We | always
usually
sometimes
never | have … in … |

159

The process of materials evaluation

3 We never have snow in June!

Work in pairs. Look at the calendar again. Write six sentences about your weather. Make some true and some untrue.

Give your sentences to another pair. They have to correct the untrue sentences.

Writing
Extra practice • WB
Exs. 1, 2

1. We always have snow in June.   *Not true! We never have snow in June.*
2. We sometimes have rain in July and August.   *True!*
3. It is colder in June than February.   *Not true! It is colder in February.*
4. It is hotter in May than in October.

4 What's the weather like?

Look at the pictures below. When do you have weather like that in your country? What type of day is today?

Listening
Extra practice • WB Ex. 3

a chilly day

a windy day

a sunny day

a rainy day

a foggy day

a cloudy day

Listen to the people on the cassette. What type of day are they talking about?

5 Sing a song! Singing in the rain

Listen to 'Singing in the rain' and sing it with your class. The words are on page 155.

6 Where does the weather come from?

Why do we have rain? Why are there winds?
Tell the class what you think. Are these sentences true or false?

Reading
Extra reading • WB Ex. 4

1 Hot air rises.

4 High up in the sky, it is very hot.

3 We have winds because trees move.

2 Cold air rises.

5 Clouds are water vapour.

Unit 24 Topic   107

160

7 Why do we have rain?

Work with your neighbour. Read the diagram.
Put the pieces of information in the correct place.

The cold cloud meets a warm cloud.
The water becomes water vapour.
The wind blows the clouds.

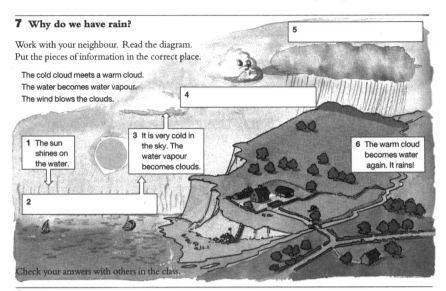

5

4

1 The sun shines on the water.

3 It is very cold in the sky. The water vapour becomes clouds.

6 The warm cloud becomes water again. It rains!

2

Check your answers with others in the class.

8 Why do we have winds?

Work with your neighbour again. Put the pieces of information in the correct place.

The wind blows.
The ground becomes warm.
The air rises.

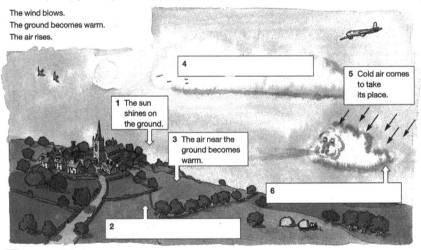

4

5 Cold air comes to take its place.

1 The sun shines on the ground.

3 The air near the ground becomes warm.

6

2

Listen and check your answers.

The process of materials evaluation

9 Decide ...

You can work by yourself, with a partner or in a small group. Choose an exercise.

Exercise 9.1 gives you vocabulary practice.
Exercise 9.2 gives you reading practice about lightning.

Or you can do **something else.** Talk to your teacher and decide what to do.
(You can use the *Ideas list* on pages 150–151 to make an exercise.)

9.1 What's the word?   *Vocabulary*

Join the word halves together and then match them to the meaning.
Write the complete word.

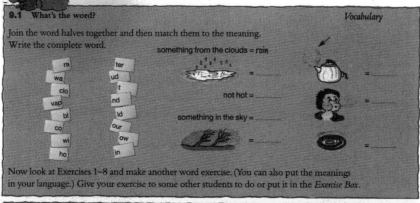

something from the clouds = *rain*

ra | ter
wa | ud
clo | t
vap | nd
bl | ld
co | our
wi | ow
ho | in

not hot = ...

something in the sky = ...

Now look at Exercises 1–8 and make another word exercise. (You can also put the meanings
in your language.) Give your exercise to some other students to do or put it in the *Exercise Box.*

9.2 Why do we have lightning?   *Reading*

Can you put in the missing words? Draw the missing picture.

cloud rises colder falls expands make jumps

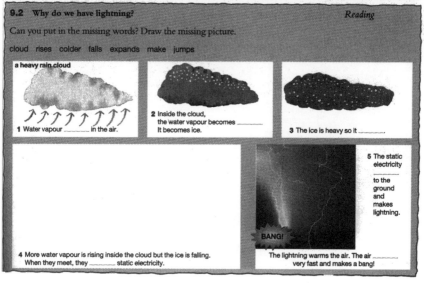

a heavy rain cloud

1 Water vapour .... in the air.

2 Inside the cloud, the water vapour becomes .... It becomes ice.

3 The ice is heavy so it ....

4 More water vapour is rising inside the cloud but the ice is falling. When they meet, they .... static electricity.

5 The static electricity .... to the ground and makes lightning.

BANG!

The lightning warms the air. The air .... very fast and makes a bang!

Figure 3 Cambridge English for Schools Level 1: Student's Book

Some factors in determining what to pilot

Pilot materials are provided free of charge by the publisher, their cost of production being absorbed into the overall development cost of the project. In the case of a main course, the cost of the pilot phase can be considerable, since copies of all components, including audio recordings, have to be provided in some quantity. The economics of print production can result in the unit manufacturing cost of a black and white pilot book being as much or even more than the manufacturing cost of the final full-colour version, as the pilot is printed in smaller quantities. The number of copies produced will generally depend on the type of material and its purpose. Supplementary material, English for special purposes material, skills material and so on may be piloted in quantities of a few hundred. This would enable them to be used with 15–20 classes of between 15–30 students, depending on the types of institutions. Use with fewer classes than this would not yield very useful results, particularly if the material is designed for an international audience and needs to be piloted in several countries. Production on this scale can be handled quite simply by photocopying or limited-run printing, and can be quite readily managed by an editor.

Projects with a larger investment, such as main courses, grammars, reference materials, etc. are usually piloted more widely. This adds not only to the cost, but also to the responsibility for editing, production, distribution and coordination of the piloting itself. These projects involve more staff and systems over a longer time, and may be piloted with thousands rather than hundreds of learners. Cambridge University Press's *Cambridge English for Schools* was used in pilot form by around 5,000 learners over two years, in classes in various countries.

The ideal would be to pilot complete levels of material, with all components, over a complete teaching cycle such as a school year. This can be done, with both smaller and larger scale pilots. Piloting a complete year's material clearly impacts on to the development schedule, as time has to be allowed for writing a whole level and preparing this for pilot, which together might take a year or more in themselves. Added to this is the piloting year, followed by a period for revision, making a total of at least two and possibly three years. Piloting a complete level would probably add at least a year and a half to an overall development schedule, and the publisher has to be prepared to accommodate this in the publishing plan, with implications for finance, return on investment, and the timing of publication compared to their competitors who may be bringing similar material to market earlier.

The option of piloting parts of material is therefore an attractive one for the publisher, which will speed up the development process. This is done with both course and supplementary material, and a decision would have to be taken on any given project on the route to follow. If the materials have a high degree of regularity in unit design, content, task type, etc., then piloting parts may indeed yield useful information about the whole. If users are unlikely to be able to devote the whole of their programme to the pilot, then having a section of the whole will enable them to combine it with their existing course material, with minimum disruption to their classes. This may well be an attractive option for the pilot centre, which has the stimulus of trialling new material and adding variety to existing programmes, without the risks to themselves involved in turning over a whole year or cycle to untried material. Material which forms part of a series in which other levels are already published and established could also be limited to partial piloting. Material which is more innovative, is less susceptible to being broken down into discrete chunks, contains unusual or controversial content, is the first level of a new approach, or represents an entry into a unfamiliar sector, would call for fuller piloting.

Who pilots and why?

Piloters are drawn from a range of teaching situations. Contacts are most often made by publishers' marketing staff or teaching consultants within a country, who will know a range of teachers personally, and be able to invite them to pilot when a suitable opportunity arises. Details of likely piloters are supplied to the editorial centre, where these are held on file or database. Frequently, teachers make contact with local or central marketing or editorial staff and express interest in piloting. When launching piloting programmes, editors will contact a range of suitable potential piloters in relevant institutions and markets, either directly or through local representatives. Pilot centres may be judged as suitable on a number of criteria, such as willingness to pilot, quality of previous feedback, availability at the right time, and being representative of the target learners, teaching situations, and so on.

Different teaching situations and different types of material place differing constraints on piloting activity. It is often reasonably easy to arrange piloting of, say, material for adults in private language schools, where teaching programmes are relatively flexible, teachers have a free choice of materials, and there are fewer internal and external conditions of syllabuses or examinations to be satisfied. In such cases, piloting can often be set up fairly informally, by direct contact with teachers or directors of studies a few weeks in advance, materials distributed and integrated into the overall programme, and feedback supplied within a period of time suitable for the publisher's needs.

However, there are drawbacks. Learners who are paying for or being funded to attend a private course will demand a high level of professionalism with a good standard of presentation in any materials used. They will also expect course materials to be part of a coherent package, perhaps with a main course element supplied by a published text in full colour. They will not necessarily take well to being presented with a substitute with lower production values in an incomplete form. Such a situation can be mediated by skilful intervention of the teaching staff in alternating use of published material with sections of pilot material, and by explaining that both teachers and learners are being asked to participate in a trialling and validation exercise which should have benefits for future generations of learners. Often, the publisher will supply sections of material, such as a representative selection of units rather than a complete course, partly to make piloting more manageable in such situations.

In the area of teaching children and young students in full-time education, piloting takes on an altogether more sensitive aspect. Supplementary material can indeed be integrated into the main teaching programme fairly easily; but with declining funding for education and increasing economic pressures on parents who may have to buy books, the market for supplementary materials has declined very substantially in recent years. What publishers are going to want to pilot in schools is therefore likely to be main course material. Whether this takes place in the state school or private education sector, the constraints will be similar. Teachers will want to choose a course which they can commit to for at least a full teaching year, if possible moving on to the next level in the following year. Books will be required for all students, with complete sets of related teacher's material and cassettes, etc. Usually the choice will be between using an established published course in full colour, and an unknown, untried and largely unseen pilot edition in black and white. In some situations, individual teachers will be able to choose the material for their classes. But more often the decision will need to be made across a group of teachers, by a director of studies or by a head teacher, or any combination of these parties, frequently in consultation with, or with the approval of, parents.

Again, goodwill, trust and a constructive relationship between piloters and publishers is needed. Teachers are often motivated to pilot material out of a sense of involvement in a new enterprise, and an expectation that using new materials will reflect most recent good practice and therefore benefit themselves and their learners. But they will need to see samples at least of the pilot material before making a decision, to be satisfied that it is likely to suit their needs, and be able to consult with superiors, managers, decision-makers and parents (not to mention the learners themselves) in making the decision. The choice of what material to use in a school year is usually made in the previous school year, so that such samples will need to be available well in advance of the start of the pilot programme, and potential piloters will need to be identified and approached equally far in advance (frequently a minimum of six months ahead of the start of the programme).

The most effective piloting and feedback come from an arrangement entered into freely on the part of the teacher and class. When, infrequently, teachers have (sometimes unsuitable) material foisted on them by superiors, the results can be predictably unproductive. Some initial hesitation and scepticism can however be healthy, as this might replicate the situation with adoptions of the final material, where the decision is not always taken by the teacher. If the pilot material can survive some initial reluctance and reservations, or the feedback can point out the source of this to the writers, this will be to the benefit of the process. The actual piloting activity, and the relationships this implies between the new material, the teacher, the class and the publisher can generate both negative and positive reactions. Sometimes there can be (at least) initial frustration that the materials are not as glossy or attractive as alternative published courses, that they have rough edges and a degree of provisionality. On the other hand, the teacher and class can generate a lot of enthusiasm for being involved in what they see as worthwhile activity, in being privileged first users, and being able to influence part of the teaching and learning environment over which they normally have no control. Sometimes some very positive professional relationships can result.

Replacing a complete programme of established teaching material for a body of work in progress is very much an act of trust, and should be recognised as such by the publisher. Personal support and contact should be offered wherever possible, ideally by local representatives such as editors and marketing staff, and certainly by the organiser at the centre. With increasing moves by the main international ELT publishers to localise their operations and publishing, this personal contact becomes more feasible. The more informal and regular it can be, the better. Simply knowing that certain teachers in a representative's area are piloting certain material is vitally important, so that the representative can make regular informal inquiries about progress and glean any relevant anecdotal information for the organiser. The process is greatly helped if the responsible or commissioning editor can meet a majority of piloters during the course of a project, and even more so if the authors can do so. All such formal and informal contact can serve to reinforce the teacher's feeling of being involved in a dynamic relationship in which their experience is valued and taken seriously.

The element of teacher care and involvement is central to the piloting relationship. It is easy to assume that individual teachers are supported by a network of their colleagues, the infrastructure of their institution, and a wider professional environment. Experience over many years of piloting in different situations has indicated that all too often this is not the case. Due to a variety of professional and societal factors, teachers frequently have inadequate opportunities to interact professionally with their colleagues, may be unsupported by their institution and lack any wider professional framework in which to operate. In many situations the teacher regards him or herself as an individual, striving to do the best for their students, often in spite of the surrounding educational and social environment. Piloting can offer such a teacher an opportunity for professional experience which transcends their normal routine, and puts their experience into a wider context, and gives them a chance to make a contribution to a wider enterprise outside their own classroom.

Clearly, however, there is a need to involve a range of teachers who best represent the likely audience for the final materials. It is relatively easy to identify the active, involved teacher who goes out of their way to make contact with publishers and other professionals, and takes part in professional activities, conferences, and on. But such a teacher will probably not represent the majority of likely users of the materials. It is the successful involvement of the relatively 'average' teacher in an 'average' institution which is the key to an effective piloting programme, as the trialling and feedback is less likely to be influenced by the enthusiasms or ambitions of the more high-flying teacher.

Benefits – who gets what from piloting?

Looked at honestly, it is not always apparent what the pilot centre (teacher, learners, institution) stands to gain in concrete terms from piloting. The sense of involvement in a new enterprise has been mentioned. Receiving the attentions of a publishing house and their authors and staff can also be attractive to some institutions. For a private institution this might have commercial overtones which might be beneficial, but also a state-funded institution might feel it reflects well on them to have such wider contacts. On a mundane level, provision of sets of free materials can be attractive to parents, students and institutions, but this is not likely in itself to influence a decision. Significant financial reward is rarely, if ever, a potential benefit to anyone concerned. It does seem as though the main motivational factors may be affective ones such as the chance to use something new which might be stimulating to the class and the teacher, the opportunity for contact with people outside the day to day world of the classroom such as publishers and authors, the sense of being valued for one's work and opinions by outsiders, as well as the more altruistic aim of making a contribution to the success of future generations of material. Certainly, piloters will normally be acknowledged formally in the final publication, either by their own name or that of their institution, and this can give strong professional satisfaction, particularly in the case of a publication which becomes established and successful.

Despite the quantity of new material being continually published in language teaching, the involvement of pilot centres is still relatively limited. It is probably true to say that the more prestigious and well-known private institutions, British Council teaching centres and key institutions with extremely large regular enrolments are all targeted regularly by publishers with requests for piloting. In these cases, it will have been necessary for the publisher to build up a relationship over a period of time, and to have established an understanding of what will constitute an acceptable piloting relationship. It may actually be the case that such an institution has very little to gain from piloting, and more to lose in the form of disruption to teaching patterns and the provisional nature of pilot material.

State schools, or private institutions offering mainstream education in which languages are a component of general education, are however much more numerous, and represent a highly important market for publishers. The very number of these makes it easier to identify those which have not been subjected to 'saturation piloting', and therefore see certain benefits of the type outlined above in becoming involved in the process.

Publishers, authors and their material, on the other hand, stand to benefit considerably from piloting, and they do so on several levels. Firstly, there is the opportunity to validate materials before publication. At the time of writing, to develop one level of a main course through all the stages of research, writing, editing, design and production up to publication can require an investment in the region of £300,000 or more for components consisting of a student's book, workbook, teacher's book and recordings. This figure then needs to be multiplied by the number of levels in the course. If the materials are to be in any way innovative or more than a clone of existing successful courses, the results of piloting can give the publisher the confidence to commit the necessary investment to complete the development. Being able to report the results of successful piloting when launching new material can also add to the credibility of the publication. There is also the general profile and relationship with the teaching profession to be taken into account, which can be enhanced through piloting activity.

Piloting will typically yield information on two levels. At a macro level, this includes: the suitability of the overall approach for the target audience, the level and progression within the material, how well it fits into the number of hours available, its suitability for the age and interests of the learners, the success of the internal organisation into units, lessons, sections, etc., how easy it is to prepare and teach, and so on. Crucially, it should give feedback on how well the materials contribute to learning aims, and how much progress the learners are able to make. However, learning is a particularly slippery parameter to measure, and this is one of the most difficult to assess in piloting. Sometimes progress tests might be included in a course pilot, but often tests are only produced after development of the main materials in order not to have too many variables to assess at once. If teachers can use the pilot materials with one or more classes while also using their regular materials with other classes, this can provide a useful indicator of learning progress with the new materials against existing norms. Experienced teachers will have expectations of what they expect their classes to master at given points in the programme, and will be able to relate progress using the pilot material against their expectations of achievement.

Measuring learning achievement and progress in piloting is however subject to all the qualifications and reservations which apply to language acquisition in general: what does it mean to have 'mastered' a language point, what provision is made for innate patterns and sequences of acquisition, has allowance been made for differences between learners, how much 'learning' is transferred into language use outside the classroom, has the possibility of late acquisition of some items despite classroom practice been considered? Measuring these factors is as difficult with pilot materials as with any other teaching and learning materials. However, the experienced teacher can usually give a good impressionistic 'feel' of whether the materials are suitable for the learners, whether they are pushing them to achieve or stretching them too far and too fast, whether they are intrinsically motivating, and how they compare with other materials and fit expectations of the teaching programme. Questions about learning and progress should therefore form part of the questionnaire, for both quantitative and qualitative responses.

Since learning is only measurable effectively over a period of time, such questions apply best to pilots of complete levels of courses. It is more difficult to apply them to piloting of supplementary material, which might be used in a fragmented way alongside other material. It is however important to ask them where the material is aiming to break new ground, through a progressive methodology or content, or a different approach, where comparisons can be made between existing expectations and the results of using the pilot. Material which is specifically aimed at exam preparation should be more susceptible to evaluation in terms of achievement norms (but the risk attached to using completely new materials for an area of high personal investment such as exam preparation might deter users from using exclusively pilot materials on such courses).

The authors and publisher will also be looking for information on a micro level, which will enable them to 'debug' the material at the next stage of editing. They will therefore be looking for feedback on the success of individual tasks and exercises – both in terms of the effectiveness of the learning outcomes, and whether there were any problems or inaccuracies in design and execution of the tasks. The type of material being piloted and its degree of innovation will determine the level of feedback being sought. There is also clearly a relationship between the amount of material being piloted and the level of feedback which can be obtained, with a macro level of response requiring extensive stretches of material to be used over a prolonged period of time, and a micro level being possible with sections or selections of material.

The piloting process

The piloting process will begin with a conscious decision to pilot certain materials, and with a view of what and when this is to be done. Publishers differ in their policy on piloting, some only piloting relatively major publications, and others attempting as far as possible to ensure all of their teaching materials – supplementary as well as main courses – are piloted in some form. In general, all materials are capable of being piloted, and stand to benefit from this: courses, supplementary material, photocopiable resources, grammars, tests, reference works, material for special purposes, and so on.

Occasionally, authors will have used material in their own and colleagues' classes during its development, and in the case of supplementary material or material with specialised interest, this may have provided sufficient information to enable it to be revised effectively. However, for reasons of objectivity and breadth of response, piloting with users at a distance from the author is usually to be preferred.

The planning process is crucial to effective piloting. With major projects there is the need to set up piloting quite far in advance. Contacts need to be made with piloters, samples may need to be produced, quantities will need to be established, and material produced and distributed to a range of countries. Only in certain cases can the author's material be used directly for piloting; it will often require artwork, an element of design layout, and production of audio recordings. A pre- liminary editorial stage is therefore required to prepare a pilot edition.

This process will clearly have an impact on the overall development schedule of the project, quite apart from the piloting period itself, which will need to be built into the overall schedule. The publisher therefore needs to balance the need for and extent of piloting with the commercial necessities of publishing by a certain date, and the financial impact of extending the development period to incorporate effective piloting. Piloting of a main course can add an extra year or more to the development schedule, and publishing companies which are driven by a need to show a return on investment within a specific period may find these pressures particularly difficult to reconcile.

Once a network of piloters has been established, and the materials prepared, these will be distributed in the quantities required together with a questionnaire and a clear indication of the time available for piloting. The questionnaire is clearly a crucial instrument in effective piloting, the form of which will vary according to the purposes of the pilot. In some cases, more than one questionnaire will be distributed, or one questionnaire may contain two sections. One section may deal with overall responses to the material: level, suitability of topics, pace, syllabus, and so on. The other section would then deal with specific parts of the material, and may ask detailed questions about individual units, exercises and tasks, their difficulty, level of interest, time taken, student response, teacher observations, and so on.

Questionnaires are often a balance of objective questions requiring limited answers, and scope for more open-ended responses. While the objective answers can be useful for establishing a basic profile of feedback on certain areas, experience has shown that the subjective, descriptive responses of users are particularly valuable in judging the effectiveness of the material, its 'feel', the degree of success in class interaction and motivation, its success in promoting learning, its contribution to achieving learning norms, etc. If the questionnaires can be combined with interviews by the publisher's representatives, editors or authors, then a particularly useful profile can result.

Feedback can also be gathered from the learners themselves in a number of ways. At more intermediate and advanced levels, specific questionnaires for learner responses can be distributed. At lower levels the teacher may be asked to gather responses to a number of questions, or to translate a limited questionnaire for the learners. Teachers are often willing to permit observation of classes using pilot materials, and to set up a class discussion or interviews with students.

Figures 4 and 5 are some examples of questionnaires which demonstrate the range of possible types from a simple form to accompany supplementary material to more elaborate questionnaires to accompany main courses. Figure 4 is the questionnaire for the grammar material in Figure 1, and Figure 5 is the questionnaire (in two parts) for the pilot in Figure 2.

The process of materials evaluation

GRAMMAR WORKS 1 - *Pilot Questionnaire*

Thank you very much for your help on this project. Please answer the questions below. Use a separate sheet where necessary.

Name ....
School name/ address

....

....

BACKGROUND
1. How many classes did you try out this material with?

....

Please give details for each class:
Class A: Age range ....
                Nationality ....
                Number of students ....
                Is this their first year of English?.................................

                ....

Class B: Age range ....
                Nationality ....
                Number of students ....
                Is this their first year of English?.................................

                ....

2. Which coursebook(s) do you usually use with the above classes?

....

Do you use any other supplementary books with these classes? Which?

....

GRAMMAR WORKS 1 - Student's Book

3. The author has written *Grammar Works 1* so that within each unit, the exercises get more and more difficult.
Do you feel that this approach works?...
Please comment on the success of particular exercises you have used. ....

....

4. The student is expected to refer to the back of the book for grammatical information.
Did this happen in your class/ for homework? ....

....

Was it successful? ....

....

Why do you think this was? ....
....
....

5. Are there any grammar points in the material which you feel should not be covered at this level? ....
....
....

6. Would you like to add any grammar points to this level?
....
....

TIMING
7. How long did each unit take on average?..

Did any unit take much longer/ shorter than the others? ....
Please comment. ....
....
....

GRAMMAR WORKS 1 - Teacher's Book

9. Was the grammatical information at the beginning of each unit helpful?...
If 'Yes' please give examples. ....
....
....

10. Would you like any more grammatical information to be included?................
If 'Yes' please give examples. ....
....
....

11. Do you feel any of the grammatical information should be excluded?.............
If 'Yes' please give examples. ....
....
....

12. Was the phonological information at the beginning of each unit helpful?...
If 'Yes' please give examples. ....
....
....

13. Would you like any more phonological information to be included?..
If 'Yes' please give examples. ....
....
....

14. Do you feel any of the phonological information should be excluded?

....

If 'Yes' please give examples. ....

....

15. Were the *Classwork Suggestions* helpful? ....
Please comment on particular units. ....

....

....

16. Would you prefer more detailed instructions on how to use the material in class?...
Please comment on particular units. ....

....

....

17. Think of other Teacher's Books that you have used. Which one(s) do you find most useful?..

....

Why?...

....

....

18. What would you expect to find in the Teacher's Book for a Grammar Work book of this kind?..

....

....

Do you feel that this Teacher's Book meets your requirements?

....

....

....

FINAL COMMENTS
19. What did you like most about the material? ....

....

....

20. Was there anything you didn't like? ....

....

....

21. Would you use this material in its final published form
    a) as an adopted text ....
    b) as a recommended text ....
    c) for homework ....
    d) for classwork ....
    e) other. How? ....

....

22. Do you think *Grammar Works 1* should be published in colour or black and white? ....

Figure 4

Cambridge University Press

Cambridge English for Schools Level 1. Pilot Edition

QUESTIONNAIRE

Completed questionnaires (for Sections A and B) should be returned to CUP by 20 December 1993, based on the work covered up to that date.

SECTION A: REPORTS ON INDIVIDUAL UNITS

Please fill out <u>one sheet for each unit</u> as soon as you have taught it.

Your name: ....

Unit number: .... Unit title: ....

1. Which exercises did you do with your class?

....

....

2. How long did it take you to complete the unit (in lessons of about 45–50 mins.)?

....

3. Do you think this unit was: successful ❑ , acceptable ❑ , not successful ❑ .

Please state your reasons: ....

....

....

....

4. Did you experience any particular problems with the exercises? If so, why do you think that was? ....

....

....

5. Which exercises were most successful/enjoyable? Why?

....

....

....

....

6. Do you have specific comments on particular sections/parts of the unit?

....

....

....

....

7. Do you have any ideas or suggestions on how the unit can be improved?

....

....

....

....

....

8. What were your students' opinions about the unit? (Perhaps you could ask them to complete a brief questionnaire or to discuss it in small groups.)

....

....

....

....

....

9. Other comments:

....

....

....

....

....

....

....

....

Cambridge University Press

Cambridge English for Schools Level 1. Pilot Edition

QUESTIONNAIRE

Completed questionnaires (Sections A and B) should be returned to CUP by 20 December 1993, based on the work covered up to that date.

SECTION B: BACKGROUND AND GENERAL COMMENTS

I: YOU, YOUR SCHOOL, AND YOUR STUDENTS

1. Your name: ....

Name and address of your school: ....

....

....

....

Country: ....

Type of school *(e.g. state secondary, private language school, etc.)*

....

2. Your class: Number of boys [   ] Number of girls [   ]

Age range ....

Level of English when starting CES ....

Approximate amount of English studied before starting CES. ....*(years/months)*

Number of lessons (around 45–50 minutes) of English a week [   ]

Number of weeks in a term: [   ]; in a school year: [   ]

Are there any observations you would like to make about the class *(ability, motivation, background, etc.)*:

....

....

....

....

....

3. Have you been using CES by itself? Yes/No

If no, what other book(s) have you been using?

....

....

....

....

How much of the time have you been using CES, and how much any other material?

....

....

....

....

4. How far have you got with CES at the time of completing this questionnaire?
Unit ....

How many lessons (around 45–50 minutes) has it taken to get that far? [   ]

5. Have you been using (please tick):

      the Student's Book ❑
      the Workbook ❑
      the Teacher's Book ❑
      the Class Cassette ❑
      the Student Cassette ❑

II: YOUR GENERAL IMPRESSIONS OF CAMBRIDGE ENGLISH FOR SCHOOLS

1. In general, is the level of the material appropriate for your students? Please comment.

....

....

....

2. Is the syllabus appropriate for your needs at this level, in terms of coverage and organisation? Would you recommend any changes?

....

....

....

....

3. What is your opinion of the organisation of the material in the Student's Book (in themes, units, parts of units, Culture Matters, Revision and Evaluation)?

....

....

....

....

4. Is the pace of language development appropriate? Is the balance of skills appropriate? Please comment.

....

....

....

5. How do your students react to the topics and the tasks?

....

....

....

6. Did you find the material easy/OK/difficult to work with as a teacher? Please comment.

....

....

....

7. Is there sufficient/too much/not enough material? Please comment.

....

....

....

....

8. How does it compare to other courses you have used for this age range of students? ....
....
....

9. Do you have any specific comments on:

* the Student's Book ....
....
....

* the Workbook ....
....
....

* the Teacher's Book ....
....
....

* the Class Cassette ....
....

* the Student's Cassette ....
....

10. Do you think the learners have made acceptable progress in their learning while using the material? Please comment.
....
....
....

11. In summary, what is your general impression of Cambridge English for Schools, Level 1? ....
....
....

12. Do you think the Rationale as set out in the Teacher's Book is valid, and is it achieved in the materials? Please comment.
....
....
....

13. Do you think anything should be changed during the revisions, to make it more suitable for your needs?
....
....
....
....

III: YOUR VIEWS ON SPECIFIC SECTIONS/PARTS OF THE MATERIALS

Please comment in general on the following sections of the materials.

Unit 1 (Welcome to English)

....
....
....
....
....

The 'Core' Units (the first two units in each theme)

....
....
....
....
....

Part A (topic)

....
....
....
....

Part B (language study)

....
....
....
....

Part C (activity)

....
....
....
....

The Language Records

....
....
....
....

The Culture Matters Units

....

....

....

....

The Revision and Evaluation Units

....

....

....

....

The 'Parcel of English' (How did you use it?)

....

....

....

....

The Exercise Box and Ideas List

....

....

....

....

The A–Z Reference Section in the Teacher's Book

....

....

....

....

Thank you for taking the time to complete this questionnaire. Please return it to the local CUP representative who is coordinating the piloting, or if this is not possible to:

CES, Cambridge ELT, Cambridge University Press, The Edinburgh Building, Shaftesbury Road, Cambridge CB2 2RU, England.

Fax: ++44 223 315052

Figure 5

What can go wrong?

It should be clear from the above account that much of the process of piloting relies on clear communication by the providers about expectations and practical arrangements, willingness and goodwill on the part of teaching staff, school heads, parents and students, and both sets of parties keeping to their side of the undertaking. Since the advantages for the institution are largely intangible, they have much to lose if the process does not go smoothly. Pilot materials which fail to arrive by the required time can leave whole classes and years without suitable material. This can be due as much to the vagaries of postal systems as to any delay by the publisher. Pilot materials which fall short of expectations in presentation, extent or quality will also cause significant problems.

For the publisher, a poor response in terms of quantity or quality of feedback, or lateness of feedback, will seriously affect the effectiveness of the exercise, particularly when a set time has been built into the development schedule for revision. This is where a network of piloters who are known to the publisher through their local operations is particularly valuable, and where personal contact can be invaluable. However, a restricted set of piloting centres can also be a disadvantage, if certain institutions are repeatedly approached to pilot materials by the same or sometimes different publishers, generating a form of fatigue which is unproductive for both parties.

A problem restricted to the private sector is the lack of predictability of course composition. Often an institution is keen to pilot on an upcoming course, particularly more specialised material, only to find that the course does not materialise through lack of numbers, or that students are not of the level predicted or do not have the interests or needs which were originally foreseen. State and private institutions catering for more core primary, secondary and tertiary education can therefore also provide more stable as well as wider populations.

What can result from piloting?

A successful pilot is one in which the process has gone according to plan, and a body of useful feedback has been assembled. Whether the feedback is negative or positive is independent of the success of the pilot itself (although of course teachers and students who are satisfied with the outcome and publishers with a set of positive feedback will be a bonus). Piloting provides publishers and authors with immensely valuable information on many levels, with all types of materials.

In general, piloting provides a feel for whether the material actually 'works' or not; whether the aims of the materials are fulfilled; whether it is appropriate in level, content, and approach; whether it is suitable for particular ages and groups of learners; whether it relates well to teachers' expectations and stages of development, and whether it successfully promotes learning. Reactions can be gauged in relation to other materials of a similar type – is it more effective or better liked than competing material? Or, if it is breaking new ground, is it doing so effectively, do learners make satisfactory progress, and is the material easy for teachers and learners to use?

The scale of investment in new course production in financial terms has been mentioned above. Added to this are the human resources which go into researching, writing and developing materials through to production, and all the overheads involved throughout the process. The greater the investment, the greater the temptation to 'play it safe', to repeat successful formulae, or attempt only incremental variations, in order to publish commercially viable materials. But there is also an educational and pedagogical imperative to produce materials which break new ground, to cater for new educational conditions and needs, as well as to fill niches which have been identified as vacant in the market. If published materials are to attempt to move the profession on or reflect changes in the teaching environment, then there is a responsibility to innovate, and this innovation could be extremely risky without a piloting phase which enables the writing and publishing team to get some things wrong within a controlled environment in which they can be put right without endangering the whole enterprise.

Many publishing projects certainly emerge from authors' own teaching situations, where they are producing materials to suit a particular set of needs, have the chance to use these with their and their colleagues' learners, modify them in the light of experience and prepare them for a wider audience. Even so, care should be exercised over the 'it-works-very-well-with-my-students' syndrome, as materials will usually benefit considerably from wider and more objective assessment. Less experienced authors will undoubtedly learn much from the process, which will contribute to their own professional development as well as to the viability of the materials. More experienced authors may possess a stronger repertoire of writing skills but be further from the classroom, in which case they and their work will also benefit from the process.

New materials can be researched thoroughly before and during development in terms of needs, aims, approaches, level, number of hours, and so on. But such factors can often only be defined in terms of what is already available: course X is thorough but unexciting, course Y is more inventive but difficult to handle, course Z is very good on listening and speaking, but takes up too much time and does not have thorough grammar coverage, and so on. Establishing what approach materials should take, how their educational objectives should be framed, which techniques might be most effective, how skills can be balanced and integrated, how grammar and vocabulary presentation and review should be handled, exactly which topics and what content will be successful, and so on, is not something which is reducible simply to questionnaires and data input. Interviews, questionnaires and other surveys will play a part, as will attention to stated educational or training objectives, and the prevailing or aspirational orthodoxy. But successful materials writing is at its core a creative activity, and one which is reliant on the skills of the writers to synthesise all the external factors, information and requirements, and create materials which will engender successful teaching and learning events. Only through trialling these materials will it be known if this creative process is actually working, and if things can be put right if it is not.

In addition to the general feel for the effectiveness of the materials, piloting will reveal much in detail about the components for success. If the approach is innovative, has it been implemented in practical terms which are accessible to teachers and learners? Can teachers and learners follow what is required of them? Is the material organised into suitable and realistic chunks of lessons, sections, units, etc.? Does it require undue amounts of preparation and inventiveness by the teacher, who may not have time or resources available? Does it fit the number of hours available? Does the material result in learning outcomes which are satisfactory, and measurable if necessary? Is there a suitable sense of progress for learners, teachers, parents and any external validators or sponsors?

Does the syllabus meet expectations? Is the balance of skills appropriate? One of the most frequent outcomes of piloting is a need to re-order units or sections in order to achieve a better balance and progression of material. This can have considerable implications for reconnecting all the links backwards and forwards in the course, and can be a major undertaking. During the pilot of the original *Cambridge English Course* in the early 1980s it became clear that leaving the past simple tense until late in level one, which is often the case in courses for younger learners which may even leave it until level two, was not appropriate for the adults with whom the course was being piloted. They wanted the past at an earlier stage in order to speak effectively about themselves and their lives, and so this level was duly unravelled and re-knitted.

Often the amount of material comes in for special criticism. This seems to be particularly the case in materials which are attempting to be consciously innovative, where the authors' ideas may be running away with them, but where students and teachers have a clear sense of the pace at which they can proceed. Organisation of material is equally important, and often what seems reasonable on paper needs breaking down into smaller sections for use in the classroom. Again, the implications for revision can be significant. Sometimes, however, piloting can reveal that users are spending much more time on sections or particular tasks than the authors intended, perhaps because of unfamiliarity, or because the intention is not clear. This can happen, for instance, with listening exercises in which the activity should be listening for specific information or gist, but where teachers and students are more used to trying to process all listening material in great detail. In such cases the intention of the activity needs to be highlighted clearly both to the student and the teacher, or the activity changed to make it more successful in its aim.

Topics and content, as well as the exercises and tasks themselves, can only really be judged when the materials are actually in use. A contents list which might look prosaic and predictable can come to life in the actual material through the skill of the writers in selecting or constructing suitable texts and tasks. Only by using these in class will we know if they actually appeal to the learners, are relevant to their needs, and stimulate their interest and involvement. Readers' reports and the expert opinion of educators, teachers and language teaching professionals are always an essential and extremely valuable part of materials assessment. But only trialling in the classroom will yield the authentic reactions of learners, who after all should be the central focus of criteria of success, as well as demonstrating success or difficulty with the material in practical classroom terms.

In terms of the materials themselves, then, it should be clear that they stand to benefit considerably from piloting, if they are then modified in response to all the feedback. Clearly, judgements have to be made as to what should be revised in the light of feedback, according to the relative importance of items raised, time available, and the complexity involved. If the materials benefit, then so does the teaching and learning associated from them, which is the main aim of the process.

But the publisher also benefits very strongly from a successful piloting project. There is the confidence that the materials work, or if they do not work in some respects that sufficient steps have been taken to put these right before major investment is put into final editing, design, artwork and production.

When launching any new materials, and particularly publications with considerable investment involved, it is clearly an advantage to know that they are already tried and tested on a certain scale, and therefore likely to meet with success on a larger scale.

The publisher can therefore turn the piloting into a marketing advantage, making it clear that potential customers will be purchasing materials which already have a track record. In some cases, word of mouth will have spread news about the course before publication, which is always a particularly effective form of promotion. There will be a cadre of teachers who have used the material, who might be willing to participate in seminars or more direct promotion, or at least provide quotes for promotion material. There will also be evidence of students' work and achievements with the pilot to demonstrate successful learning. Such benefits can outweigh any potential risks a publisher might run in piloting by revealing too much of future materials and plans ahead of actual publication. The security of knowing that material is as good as it realistically can be at the time of publication can also compensate for the longer development times required by including a piloting phase.

The future of piloting

Given these benefits, it could be assumed that the future of piloting is not in doubt. But financial and marketing realities are always likely to constrain the possibilities. Longer development times mean longer periods of investment, before the material is earning income for the author and publisher. In the increasingly stringent corporate world in which many publishers operate, the case for piloting may be hard to make in purely financial terms. The advantages of refining the publication through piloting have to be weighed against bringing the material to market before the competition, or in time for anticipated changes in the market. But each publisher has to decide where their competitive advantage lies, and the case for or against piloting is bound up in whatever attitude the publisher takes in this area.

The size of publishers' investment in main courses and major support material is such that it is well worthwhile to keep the material up to date and responsive to user feedback by producing new editions of successful publications. A successful first edition actually represents a very wide-scale pilot, from which extensive feedback can be collected in order to prepare the new edition. The pattern of revisions of successful main courses and supplementary material has become well established in recent years, and is likely to continue well into the future.

Educational reform in different countries can also be the spur to pilot material, in order to find a way of satisfying new requirements with material which is acceptable and practicable to teachers and learners.

'New' media – video, software, and multimedia – present new challenges for piloting. Video is costly to develop, and to change in response to piloting. But new developments in electronic editing of video are making it easier and cheaper to change the shape of the final edit, which can be done in response to trialling even if none of the material can actually be re-shot. It is sometimes possible to detach one or more sequences of video recording from the main shoot, and get these out for pilot reaction before proceeding with the rest of the recording. Piloting of samples at least of videos is therefore possible, and likely to have beneficial results in fine-tuning the main production and editing.

Software of most kinds generally does go through at least one piloting, or beta-testing, phase in which responses are collated and the programme is crash-tested to try to discover any lurking bugs before publication. Good practice should dictate that language learning software should undergo the same process.

Multimedia is even more costly to develop. But once the material has been assembled it is again becoming cheaper to produce small quantities of CD-Roms with samples of part of the programme, for limited trialling and response. The complexity of such products makes it essential to trial them fully before publication, and so growth in this area is likely to lead to an increase rather than a decrease in piloting activity.

'Desk-top publishing', which has revolutionised working practices in the publishing and printing industries, has also had a significant impact on the possibilities for piloting, and will continue to do so in future, making it easier for authors to present material in ways which reflect their intentions and their vision of the publication, and for the publisher to take this over into the pilot material and on to the final publication.

New distribution channels such as the Internet and World Wide Web will certainly have strong implications for piloting, whether in seeking centres to pilot, collecting feedback, or in the distribution of pilot materials themselves. Responses can be immediate, even over long distances, and material could be drawn down in quantities or forms which suit piloters' needs, rather than the delivery of pre-packaged sets of books.

But piloting essentially involves a relationship – between the publisher (editorial and marketing), the author, the pilot centre (teachers, classes and the institution), and the materials. The tangible and intangible benefits of piloting have been set out above, and publishers will continue to make their own decisions on whether and how much piloting is justified, in overall policy terms, and on a project-by-project basis. For those publishers who do choose the piloting option, the conditions and the opportunities have probably never been better than they are now or will be in the future.

8 The analysis of language teaching materials: inside the Trojan Horse

Andrew Littlejohn

Introduction

In the field of language teaching, we have become accustomed to regular 'revolutions' as one syllabus model gives way to another, or as methodological innovations supplant the practices of the past. My starting point in this chapter, however, is the suggestion that one of the key issues has been under-explored, and that it is not so much *what* ideas are being expressed which is important, but *how* it is that these ideas become widespread and – however temporarily – take root. Conferences, journals, and workshops have all played their part in spreading new ideas and in shaping practice, but, I would argue, the most powerful device in this has been one of the main 'tools of the trade' of language teaching: the published coursebook.

In recent years, materials design has become characterised by two important developments. Firstly, the use of published materials is now more widespread than ever before, evidenced, for example, by the presence of UK publishers in all corners of the world. This has meant that those at the 'centre' (Littlejohn 1992: 52ff) have been able to disseminate ideas to further points of the 'periphery' (or, in other words, members of the target language culture have inevitably spread their cultural norms to learners of the language from other cultures). Secondly, and it is this which makes the spread of materials so significant, materials themselves have evolved into much more complex objects. In the early days textbooks contained mainly readings, perhaps with some questions and sentences to translate. Now materials frequently offer complete 'packages' for language learning and teaching, with precise indications of the work that teachers and students are to do together. The extent to which materials now effectively structure classroom time has thus increased considerably.

The issue which I wish to address in this paper, however, is not whether this phenomenon is good or bad (and there are points for both arguments, depending on what individual materials contain) but that these developments necessitate even more than ever before a means by which we can closely analyse materials. We need to be able to examine the implications that use of a set of materials may have for classroom work and thus come to grounded opinions about whether or not the methodology and content of the materials is appropriate for a particular language teaching context. We also need to be able to test out the claims now being made for materials: Do they truly help to develop autonomy? Do they truly involve problem-solving? Are they truly learner-centred? We need, in short, a means of looking inside the Trojan Horse to see what lies within (as the use of materials, like the Trojan Horse, may imply more than is immediately apparent).

My concern, then, is with the analysis of materials 'as they are', with the content and ways of working which they propose, *not*, it must be stressed, with what may actually happen in classrooms. Analysing materials, it must be recognised, is quite a different matter from analysing 'materials-in-action'. Precisely what happens in classrooms and what outcomes occur when materials are brought into use will depend upon numerous further factors, not least of which is the reinterpretation of materials and tasks by both teachers and learners. This paper, then, is concerned with the analysis of what Breen and Candlin (1987) and Breen (1989) describes as *tasks-as-workplans*, those predesigned tasks which are offered to teachers and learners as a 'frame' for learning and teaching opportunities. This is distinct from *tasks-in-process*, the point when teachers and learners bring their own personal contributions, and *tasks as outcomes*, the learning that may derive from their use. A discussion of how effective materials may be in promoting learning, therefore, is beyond my discussion here.

My concern is to enable a close analysis of materials themselves, as a support to designing materials, and as a preliminary step to materials evaluation and classroom research.

One of the most obvious sources for guidance in analysing materials is the large number of frameworks which exist to aid in the evaluation of a coursebook (e.g. Harmer 1991: 281–4; Williams 1983; Cunningsworth 1984; Doughill 1987; Nunan 1991). Whilst recognising that such frameworks frequently serve a useful purpose in guiding the selection of materials, one of the principal problems in their use is that they usually involve making general, impressionistic judgements on the materials, rather than examining in depth what the materials contain. Typically, they also contain implicit assumptions about what 'desirable' materials should look like. Thus we have features listed such as an 'up-to-date methodology of L2 teaching' (Williams, *ibid.*: 252) and questions such as 'Is it foolproof (i.e. sufficiently methodical to guide the inexperienced teacher through a lesson)?' (Doughill, *ibid.*: 32) and 'Is the language used in the materials realistic – i.e. like real-life English' (Harmer, *ibid.*: 282). Each of these areas, however, will be debatable – being 'up to date' is not *in itself* a good thing; 'foolproof' materials will reflect particular views of the role of the teacher and ideas about the best route to teacher development; 'real-life' English may lead to an emphasis on authenticity at the expense of pedagogic good sense; and so on. There are further problems, too, in establishing whether the materials are indeed 'foolproof' or 'up to date'. How can the teacher-analyst know, other than by making impressionistic, unguided judgements?

What is required, then, is a framework which separates assumptions about what is desirable, from an analysis of the materials. We need, in other words, a general framework which allows materials to 'speak for themselves' and which helps teacher-analysts to look closely into materials before coming to their *own* conclusions about the desirability or otherwise of the materials. This suggests three separate questions which we need to consider carefully:

1 *What aspects* of materials should we examine?
2 *How* can we examine materials?
3 *How* can we relate the findings to our own teaching contexts?

It is to these three questions which I now turn.

A general framework for analysing materials

What aspects of materials should we examine?

There are very many aspects which one can examine in a set of materials. It would be possible, for example, to describe materials in terms of the quality of the paper and binding, pricing, layout, size, typeface and so on. One might also look closely at the artwork and texts in the materials to see, for example, how the sexes are represented or how different races are portrayed. Each of these will be important aspects, depending on the purposes one has in looking at the materials. My focus here, however, is on materials as a *pedagogic* device, that is, as an aid to teaching and learning a foreign language. This will limit the focus to aspects of the *methodology* of the materials, and their *content*. To this end, there are a number of established analyses of language teaching which can guide us in identifying significant aspects of materials (e.g. Mackey 1965, Corder 1973, Breen and Candlin 1987 and Richards and Rodgers 1986). Each of these models, however, was evolved for a specific purpose and so will not, on their own, be suitable for an analysis of *any* set of teaching materials. The framework which I propose (summarised in Figure 1 below), draws extensively on these models in an attempt to provide the basis for a more comprehensive listing of the aspects which, from a pedagogic viewpoint, need to be taken into account when analysing materials.

1 Publication
  1 Place of the learner's materials in any wider set of materials
  2 Published form of the learner's materials
  3 Subdivision of the learner's materials into sections
  4 Subdivision of sections into sub-sections
  5 Continuity
  6 Route
  7 Access

2 Design
  1 Aims
  2 Principles of selection
  3 Principles of sequencing
  4 Subject matter and focus of subject matter
  5 Types of learning/teaching activities:
    – what they require the learner to do
    – manner in which they draw on the learner's process competence (knowledge, affects, abilities, skills)
  6 Participation: who does what with whom
  7 Learner roles
  8 Teacher roles
  9 Role of materials as a whole

Figure 1 Aspects of an analysis of language teaching materials

The framework consists of two main sections: *publication* and *design*. *Publication*, relates to the 'tangible' or physical aspects of the materials and how they appear as a complete set or book. Here we will be concerned with the relationship that may exist between the student's materials and any other components (e.g. whether answer keys are only available in the teacher's book, how the student's material relates to any tapes and videos, and so on) and the actual form of the material (e.g. durable vs. consumable, worksheets vs. bound book), all of which may have direct implications for classroom methodology. We may also look inside the materials to determine how they are divided into sections and sub-sections, how a sense of continuity or coherence is maintained and whether the order in which the material can be used is predetermined. This final aspect suggests one further element: how access *into* the materials is supported – for example, whether there are contents lists, wordlists and indexes.

The second section in the framework, *design* (following Richards and Rodgers 1986) relates to the thinking underlying the materials. This will involve consideration of areas such as the apparent aims of the materials, how the tasks, language and content in the materials are selected and sequenced and the nature and focus of content in the materials. Also of central importance in this will be the nature of the teaching/learning activities which are suggested by the materials. An analysis of materials will need to focus closely on what precisely learners are asked to *do*, and how what they do relates to what Breen and Candlin (*ibid.*) call learners' 'process competence'. Process competence refers to the learners' capacity to draw on different realms of *knowledge* (concepts, social behaviour, and how language is structured), their *affects* (attitudes and values), their *abilities* to express, interpret and deduce meanings, and to use the different *skills* of reading, writing, speaking and listening. Teaching/learning activities are also likely to suggest modes of classroom participation – for example, whether the learners are to work alone or in groups – and, from this, the roles that teachers and learners are to adopt. Finally, we may examine the materials to determine what role they intend for themselves. Do they, for example, attempt to 'manage' the classroom event by providing detailed guidance on how teachers and learners are to work together, or do they only aim to provide ideas that teachers and learners are actively encouraged to develop or reject?

Taken together, the areas listed in the framework should provide a comprehensive coverage of the methodological and content aspects of any set of materials. Armed with such an analytical description of a set of materials, teachers, materials designers, educational administrators and, indeed, learners, would be in a good position to take decisions about the usefulness and desirability of the materials. We are, however, faced with an immediate problem: how can the listings be used in practice? How can we examine the materials to find the information required? In the next section, I would like to consider these questions and propose some practical solutions to guide the detailed analysis of materials.

How can we examine the materials?

Levels of analysis

Looking through the framework set out in the previous section, we can see that some of the aspects will be relatively easy to identify (for example 'published form of the materials' and 'division into sections') whilst others appear more abstract and difficult to establish (for example 'aims' and 'learner/teacher roles'). It is also clear that some of the listed aspects will involve examining different parts of the materials before coming to a general conclusion. 'Principles of sequence', for example, may require looking at the language syllabus and the precise nature of the types of teaching/learning activities (materials may, for example, become methodologically more complex in later parts).

On its own, therefore, the framework has very limited use since it is not able to guide the teacher-analyst in examining the materials to any depth. The principal problem is that some aspects in the framework actually entail coming to a conclusion about other aspects in the framework. This means that in building up an analysis of a set of materials, teacher-analysts will not only have to examine different sections of the materials but, more importantly, move through different 'levels' of analysis, making more and more inferences – and subjective judgements – as they move from a consideration of the more easily identifiable aspects to the more abstract and complex. Figure 2 outlines the levels which may be involved, from the most objective (what is physically there in the materials, Level 1), through deductions about the demands likely to be made of teachers and learners (Level 2), to conclusions about the apparent underlying principles and 'philosophy' of the materials (Level 3).

---

1 'WHAT IS THERE'
– statements of description
– physical aspects of the materials
– main steps in instructional sections

---

2 'WHAT IS REQUIRED OF USERS'
– subdivision into constituent tasks
– an analysis of tasks: What is the learner expected to do? With whom? With what content? Who determines these things?

---

3 'WHAT IS IMPLIED'
– deducing aims, principles of selection and sequence
– deducing teacher and learner roles
– deducing demands on learner's process competence

Figure 2 Levels of analysis of language teaching materials

Level 1: What is there?

At the top of Figure 2 lies the 'explicit nature' of the materials, where we would expect little disagreement in describing the materials. We might begin, for example, with statements found within the materials. These might cover, for example, the publication date, the intended audience, the type of materials (e.g. 'general' or 'specific purpose', 'supplementary' or 'main course'), the amount of classroom time required, and how the materials are to be used (e.g. for self-study, in any order, etc.). Beyond this, we can also look at the physical aspects of the materials such as their published form (for example, durable books or consumable worksheets), number of pages, use of colour, and the total number of components in a complete set (for example, student's book, workbook, cassettes, etc.). Looking inside the materials we can see how the material is divided into sections (for example, 'units', tapescripts, answer keys and tests) and the means of access into the materials that are provided (for example, an index of vocabulary items). We might also wish to see how the various sections and means of access into the materials are distributed between teacher and learners, since this may provide data for conclusions about teacher–learner roles. Looking further into the materials we can examine how the 'units', 'chapters' etc. are subdivided, their length, and if there is any standard pattern within them.

As a support for recording this kind of 'explicit' information about a set of materials, Figure 3 provides a schedule which teacher-analysts may use to guide their investigation. As an example, the schedule presents an analysis of the 'explicit' nature of a coursebook which I have co-authored, *Cambridge English for Schools 1*. The precise categories of information recorded would, however, depend on the particular materials being analysed and what information is explicitly provided. Since the length of most materials would make it impractical to analyse their entire contents in any further depth, Part B in the schedule records the proportion of the material examined and the main sequence of activity within that extract. Depending on the purpose the teacher-analyst has in mind, an in-depth analysis might be made of the students' or teachers' materials. For a 'snapshot' impression of the general nature of a set of materials, I have found it useful to analyse about 10% to 15% of the total material, ideally chosen around the midpoint. (For example, in a work consisting of 20 'units', this might involve an analysis of Units 9, 10, and 11.)

Title: *Cambridge English for Schools SB 1* **Author:** *Littlejohn and Hicks*
Publisher: *CUP*

A. BOOK AS A WHOLE

1 *Type*: 'General', 'main course', class use for post beginners

2 *Intended audience*
  age-range: 12–16   school: secondary schools   location: world-wide

3 *Extent*
  a. *Components:* durable 'Student's Book' and consumable 'Workbook'
    Student's cassette. Teacher's Book, Class cassette, video
  b. *Total estimated time* 1 school year

4 *Design and Layout*
  4 colour SBk, 160pp; 2 colour WBk, 96pp; 2 colour Teacher's Bk 176pp

5 *Distribution*

a. *Material*	teacher	learners
cassettes	[X]	[X]
tapescript	[X]	[_]
answer key	[X]	[_]
guidance on use of class material	[X]	[_]
b. *Access*		
index/wordlist	[X]	[X]
detailed contents list	[X]	[X]
section objective	[X]	[X]

6 *Route through material*
  specified   [X]
  user determined   [_]

7 *Subdivision*
  6 'Themes' of 5 'units' each: with some standardised components according to type:
  Topic: Tasks about the topic, song, 'Decide. . .' exercise, Time to Spare?, Language
  Record
  Language Focus: Language tasks, 'Out and About' social English, Time to Spare?
  Language Record, Revision Box
  Activity: steps of an activity, evaluation
  Culture Matters: no recurring pattern
  Revision and Evaluation: self-assessment, revision exercises/practice test and test
  design; evaluation on learning process

B. OVERVIEW OF AN EXTRACT

1 *Length*: 1 'Theme' out of 6, 16.5% of the Student's Book

2 *Sequence of activity*
  Topic Unit: 1 class discussion, 2 listening to sounds, 3 brainstorming and reading, 4
  brainstorming 5 poster design, 6 song, 7 reading, 8 Decide. . . (exercise choice), 9
  Poster work, 10 Language Record
  Language Focus 1 Discussion, 2 listening, 3 grammar discovery and practice, 4
  grammar discovery and practice, 5 Out and About, 6 Language Record
  Activity: 1 research at home, 2 writing (family tree), 3 writing about family, 4 comparing
  work, 5 evaluation of work done.
  Culture Matters: 1 discussion, 2 reading, 3 reading, 4 comprehension and discussion
  Revision and evaluation 1 self-assessment, 2 test, 3 designing own test, 4 evaluation
  of learning process

Figure 3   *Level 1 – A schedule for recording the explicit nature of a set of
materials*

Level 2: What is required of users?

Whilst Level 1 was mainly concerned with the 'objective' nature of the materials, the next level in the framework moves the teacher-analyst on to a slightly deeper level of analysis to what is probably the most important aspect of materials. Here, we need to draw deductions about what exactly teachers and learners using the materials will have to *do* (assuming they use the materials in the manner indicated). In order to come to these conclusions, we will need to divide the materials into their constituent 'tasks', and then to analyse each task in turn. It is thus important to establish as precisely as possible a definition of what 'a task' is.

One commonly encountered use of the term 'task' sees it as referring to meaning-focused work, such as projects, problem-solving and simulations (e.g. Nunan, 1985). For a general framework to analyse *any* set of language learning materials, however, this definition will be too narrow, since it will be inapplicable to materials which are not meaning-focused (for example, grammar drills, dictations, and so on). An alternative broader definition (based on Breen 1987) which I propose, then, is to say that:

> . . . 'task' refers to any proposal contained within the materials for action to be undertaken by the learners, which has the direct aim of bringing about the learning of the foreign language.

Such a definition has the virtue of recognising that there are many different routes to classroom language learning, from simulations to choral repetition, whilst at the same time excluding work that is not directly related to language learning – for example, copying a chart as a preparation for a listening comprehension exercise, the latter *in itself* not directly related to language learning. In practical terms, however, it is not always easy to determine the aim of a proposed classroom action and it is for this reason that we are now at a second level of inference. Here, then, we are talking about what the teacher-analyst understands as the aim, guided perhaps by a rationale contained in the materials.

A definition as broad as the one above, however, needs further detail in order to enable us to focus on the various aspects within tasks. Drawing on the ideas outlined above we can identify three key aspects of tasks:

- a *process* through which learners and teachers are to go
- *classroom participation* concerning with whom (if anyone) the learners are to work
- *content* that the learners are to focus on

Using a detailed definition of this kind, it will now be possible to go through an extract of a set of materials and divide it into tasks. Figure 4 lists the 'questions' that we can put to each task, reflecting the three aspects of process, participation and content.

I **What is the learner expected to do?**
   A Turn-take
   B Focus
   C Operation

II **With whom?**

III **With what content?**
   A Form
      – input to learners
      – output by learners
   B Source
   C Nature

Figure 4 *Questions for the analysis of tasks*

The first question concerning *process,* contains three sub-sections which allow us to focus in detail on what precisely learners are expected to **do**. *'Turn-take'* relates to the role in classroom discourse that the learners are expected to take. Are they responding to direct questions, using language largely supplied by the materials (e.g. comprehension questions, or drills), are they asked to 'initiate', using language not supplied (e.g. 'free writing', or asking their own questions), or are they not required to take any direct role at all (for example, only to take note of a grammar explanation)? 'Focus' refers, for example, to whether the learners are asked to focus on the meaning of the language, its form or both. *'Operation'* refers to the mental process required – for example, repetition, deducing language rules, and so on.

The second question asks about classroom participation: *'With whom?'* – are the learners to work alone, in pairs/groups, or with the whole class? Finally, the third question asks about the *content* of the task. Is it written or spoken? Is it individual words/sentences or extended discourse? Where does it come from – the materials, the teacher or the learners themselves? And what is its nature – is it, for example, grammar explanations, personal information, fiction, general knowledge and so on?

Each of these questions can be applied to each task in an extract from the materials, and, with the aid of the Teacher's Book where appropriate, help to build up a detailed picture of the classroom work that the materials propose. Figure 5 provides a further schedule to support the teacher-analyst in doing this, while Appendix 1 provides an example analysis of two extracts from the coursebook mentioned earlier

(*Cambridge English for Schools*). Appendix 2 provides example definitions of aspects of materials.

Working through materials in this detailed manner is likely to be very revealing of the underlying character of the materials. It is precisely in the nature of classroom tasks that materials designers' assumptions about the best route to classroom language learning become clear, and in consequence, teacher and learner roles become defined. It is also through an analysis of tasks that we can most effectively test out the various claims made for the materials. If, for example, the materials claim to be 'learner-centred' yet we find that by far most of the tasks involve the learners in 'responding' and in working with content supplied by the materials, there would appear to be a serious mismatch. Similarly, if the materials claim to promote cognitive work and problem-solving, but we find that this forms a very small part of the 'mental operations' required and that the rest of the tasks involve simple 'repetition', then we would have reason to doubt the accuracy of the claim. To assist in gaining an overall picture of the materials, percentages for each feature can be calculated, such that, for example, we can say that X per cent of tasks involve 'writing', Y per cent involve 'discussion and negotiation', Z per cent involve 'repetition' and so on.

Task Analysis Sheet

Task number:							
I What is the learner expected to do?							
A TURN-TAKE							
initiate							
respond							
not required							
B FOCUS on							
language system (rules or form)							
meaning							
meaning/system relationship							
C MENTAL OPERATION							
II Who with?							

III With what content?

A FORM							
a input to learners							
b expected output from learners							
B SOURCE							
materials							
teacher							
learner(s)							
C NATURE							

Figure 5 *A schedule for analysing tasks (see also Appendix 1 for an example)*

Level 3: What is implied?

The final level of analysis draws on findings at Levels 1 and 2 to come to some general conclusions about the apparent underlying principles of the materials. Working from a description of the explicit nature of the materials (Level 1) and an analysis of tasks (Level 2), it will now be possible to make statements about the overall *aims* of the materials and the basis for *selecting* and *sequencing* both tasks and content. Also at this third level of description, we should now be able to come to a conclusion about the *roles proposed for teachers and learners*. We may do this partly by examining how various sections of the material are allocated to teachers and learners (for example, who has answer keys, tapescripts, etc.) but we are likely to find greater evidence for this in the analysis of tasks, particularly under *turn-take* and the various categories under *source*. Here, also, we will be able to produce a general statement about the demands placed upon learners, particularly in relation to what Breen and Candlin (1987) term 'process competences' of knowledge, affects, skills and abilities. Finally, at this level, we will be able to come to a conclusion about what appears to be the *role of the materials as a whole* in facilitating language learning and teaching – does it appear, for example, that they endeavour to guide all classroom work or do they simply intend to stimulate teachers'/learners' creative ideas and own decision-making?

To draw this together, Figure 6 page 203 summarises the various aspects set out above, and how the schedule for recording the explicit nature of materials (Figure 3) and the schedule for an analysis of tasks (Figure 5) can help to find the required information. Appendix 3 shows an example of a description of a set of materials which was arrived at using the two schedules.

How can we relate the findings to our own teaching contexts?

Taken together, the three levels of analysis and the two schedules for examining a set of materials provide a very powerful means of revealing the underlying nature of materials. They provide a thorough basis for testing out how far both aims and claims in materials are met and thus will aid anyone involved in their design and use to take more control of the materials with which they are involved. At the design stage of materials, the greater depth of understanding that the framework will provide should aid materials designers in identifying any mismatches between aims and the actual nature of the materials they are working on. Similarly, at the implementation stage of classroom use, the framework can potentially help teachers and students to examine materials and to decide on further courses of action. Whilst, however, the framework will reveal the underlying nature of materials, a next step towards fully evaluating them (that is, deciding their relative pedagogic worth) will in principle require an equally careful prior analysis of what teachers/students/institutions expect from materials, to see how far the two (that is materials and expectations) relate to or match each other. Figure 7 on page 204 provides a brief outline of how this may work.

At the heart of Figure 7 lies a clear distinction between an analysis of the materials, an analysis of the proposed situation of use, the process of matching and evaluation, and subsequent action. By clearly dividing the various stages involved in this way, careful account can be taken of each element in materials evaluation. As we have seen in this paper, materials may be analysed and described so as to expose their internal nature and, at the same time, make the analyst's subjective interpretations more easily visible. Similarly, the nature of the situation in which the materials would be used and the requirements which are to be placed on the materials can also be analysed and described independently. Matching and evaluation can then follow in which an evaluator would need to set out precisely which aspects of the materials are appropriate or inappropriate and why. In practice, this, for example, might involve a group of teachers *first* identifying what they require of

Levels of inference	What: Aspects of the material	How: Source of data (schedules)
	Publication	
Level 1: 'What is there'	Place of learner's materials in set	EN/A3 Extent, A5 Distribution
	Published form of learner's materials	EN/A3 Extent, A4 Design and layout
	Subdivision of learner's materials	EN/A7 Subdivision,B2 Sequ. of Act.
	Subdivision of sections into sub-sections	EN/A7 Subdivision,B2 Sequ. of Act
	Continuity	EN/A7 Subdivision,B2 Sequ. of Act
	Route	EN/A6 Route
	Access	EN/A5b Access
	Design	
Level 2: 'What is required of users'	Subject matter and focus	AoT/III With what content?
	Types of teaching/learning activities	AoT/I What is the Lr expected to do
	Participation: who does what with whom	AoT/II Who with?
Level 3: 'What is implied'	Aims	syllabus, Sequ. of Act. (EN/B2), nature of tasks (AoT/I-IV),
	Principles of selection	sequence of tasks
	Principles of sequencing	distribution (EN/A5), turn-take (AoT/IA),
	Teacher roles	source (AoT/IIIB)
	Learner roles (classroom)	demands on process competence (AoT/I-IV)
	Learner roles (in learning)	deductions from levels 1 – 3
	Role of materials as a whole	

EN = schedule for recording the explicit nature of the materials; AoT = schedule for the analysis of tasks; A3,A4, I, II, III etc. = item/question on the appropriate schedule

Figure 6   Summary of What and How – using the schedules

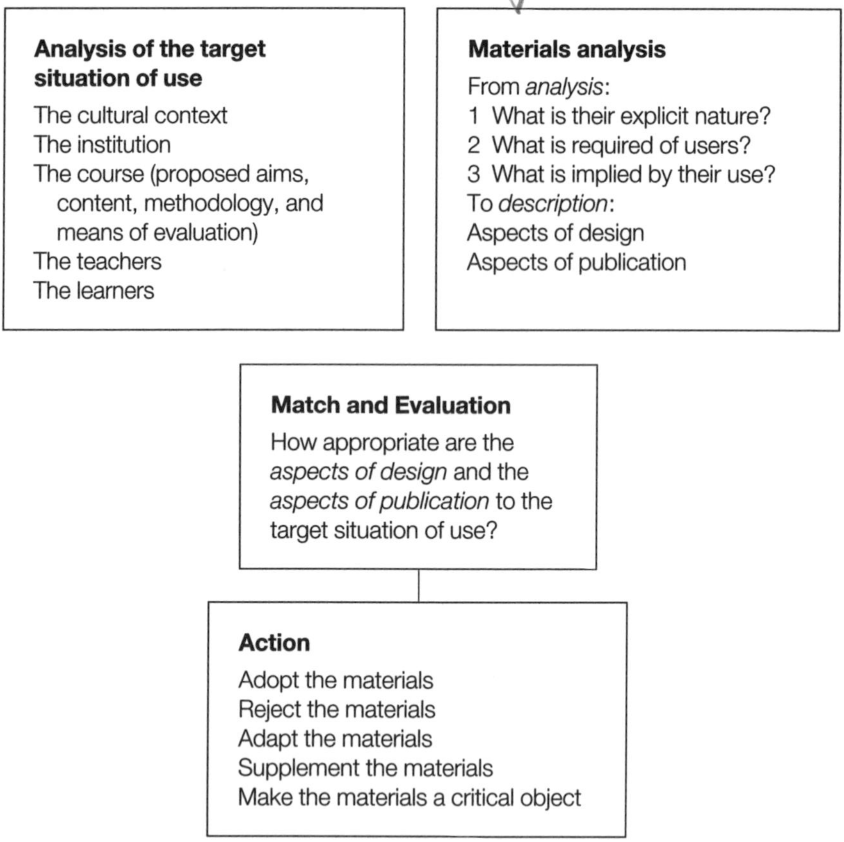

Analysis of the target situation of use	Materials analysis
The cultural context The institution The course (proposed aims, content, methodology, and means of evaluation) The teachers The learners	From *analysis*: 1 What is their explicit nature? 2 What is required of users? 3 What is implied by their use? To *description*: Aspects of design Aspects of publication

Match and Evaluation

How appropriate are the *aspects of design* and the *aspects of publication* to the target situation of use?

Action

Adopt the materials
Reject the materials
Adapt the materials
Supplement the materials
Make the materials a critical object

Figure 7 *A preliminary framework for materials analysis, evaluation and action*

materials, perhaps talking through what they see as 'desirable' answers to the categories shown on the two schedules and the examples (in Appendix 1 and 2) presented in this paper as way of raising their own consciousness. The materials may then be analysed in detail so that the extent of match between the teachers' expectations and the nature of the materials can be seen.

The final stage in Figure 7, 'action', involves evaluators in making decisions over what to do next in the light of matching and evaluation. A number of conventional responses are listed here but there is also the possibility of adopting a set of materials in order to make it an object of critical focus. In this way, the contents and ways of working set out in the coursebook can be viewed as *proposals* which may be open to critical examination and evaluation by teachers and learners. In much the same way as Freire's (1972) 'problem posing' approach to education, a critical focus would aim to analyse and question the proposals contained in the materials (Littlejohn and Windeatt 1989).

By viewing the processes of materials analysis, evaluation and implementation in this way, the 'hidden assumptions' of the evaluation guides I referred to in the introduction (Harmer 1991; Doughill 1987; and so on) can be lessened. In its place, an open procedure is proposed in which evaluators can investigate the internal character of the materials and the situation in which they will be used, make clear their own personal judgements and act accordingly. In this way, the analytical framework may be seen as potentially empowering educational administrators, teachers, learners and others to voice their needs and to take more control over the materials with which they are involved.

Conclusion

I began this chapter by suggesting that the complex nature of modern-day materials, and the extent to which their use is now widespread, necessitates a means of closely analysing materials so that we can see 'inside' them and take more control over their design and use. As one of the main 'tools of the trade' in language teaching/learning, it is important that we understand the nature of the materials with which we work. One of the downsides of the professional production of contemporary materials is that, for many teachers and learners, materials appear as *faits accomplis,* over which they can have little control. One of the aims of this paper has been to endeavour to dispel that myth.

Appendix 1: Example analyses

This appendix includes two short extracts from two units of a coursebook for secondary school students, *Cambridge English for Schools, Student's Book I* (Littlejohn and Hicks 1996). The extracts have been divided into 'tasks' according to the definition given earlier in this paper, and numbered sequentially.

Following the extracts, an analysis of tasks is given, also according to the framework outlined in the paper. This was completed using the information supplied in the student's materials and, where necessary, notes in the Teacher's Book. Definitions of the features specified in the analysis are given in Appendix 2, where further example definitions of tasks, drawn from a larger sample of materials, can be found.

The process of materials evaluation

29 Topic The cavepeople

Cavepeople, cross curriculum links with History and Social Studies

1 15,000 years ago ...

15,000 years ago, people lived in caves.
Look at the picture. How was
life for cavepeople?
Tell the class your ideas. **①**

exciting boring horrible
nice dangerous safe
hard easy difficult
happy unhappy

Extra practice •
WB Ex. 1

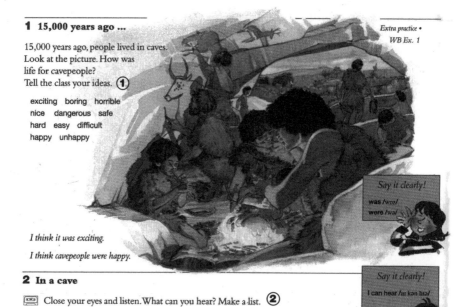

Say it clearly!

was /wɒz/
were /wə/

I think it was exciting.

I think cavepeople were happy.

2 In a cave

Say it clearly!

I can hear /aɪ kən hɪə/

Close your eyes and listen. What can you hear? Make a list. **②**

I can hear ...

Compare your list with your neighbour and with the class. Do you think the cave is a
nice place? Is it dry or wet? Is it cold or warm? **③**

3 A dangerous life for cavepeople!

Life was very dangerous for cavepeople.
④ Why? Brainstorm your ideas
with your neighbour.

Reading

Extra practice • WB
Exs. 2–3

It was very cold in winter

A dangerous life for cavepeople

⑤ Now read the text. How many dangers
can you find? Can you add any more to your ideas above?

126 Theme F

206

Nogoba – the cavegirl

Nogoba was a cavegirl. She lived in a cave with about 40 other people. Cavepeople lived in big groups to help each other. Their lives were very dangerous. There were many wild animals near the caves – lions, tigers, bears and elephants. The cavemen hunted. They killed the animals for food.

The children's jobs were dangerous, too. Nogoba and her friends went to the river every day to get water. Sometimes, the river was very deep. Sometimes, there were animals near the river.

For many months of the year, Nogoba was cold. There was ice and snow everywhere. It was difficult to be warm. The children sometimes went to sleep by the fire. Sometimes they were too near the fire.

Sometimes Nogoba and her friends went to find fruit and nuts to eat. Sometimes the fruit and nuts were poisonous and everyone became ill. There weren't any cave doctors or cave hospitals!

 You can listen to the text on the cassette.

4 A dangerous life today   *Writing*

There are many dangers in modern life. Brainstorm your ideas with the class. **⑥**

A dangerous life today

5 Differences Poster   *Making a poster*

How is life different today? Make a 'Differences Poster'. **⑦**

Write your sentences on the poster.

Put your poster on the wall. During the next lessons write some more sentences on your poster.

Differences

Food and Drink

Houses

Clothes

Free Time

Life 15,000 years ago
People lived in caves
People lived in dark places
People walked to different places

Life today
We live in flats and houses
We have electricity
We travel by car

Say it clearly!
lived
walked

The process of materials evaluation

Language focus

Introducing the Past tense:
'be', 'have', 'go', 'make' and
some regular past forms

1 Your own past: your first day at school

Discussion

① Tell the class what you can remember.

What was the name of your first school?	*My first school was …*
Was it big or small?	*It was a small/big school.*
Can you remember your first classroom?	*The classrooms were …*
How many children were there?	*There were …*
Who was your teacher?	*My teacher's name was …*
How old were you?	*I was … years old.*

2 Sophie's first day

Listening

🔊 Barbara is asking Sophie about her first school.

② Listen and answer the questions.

Where was Sophie's first school?
Was it big or small?
What was her classroom like?
How old was she?

BARBARA: Sophie, where did you go to school before?
SOPHIE: I went to a school in Scotland.
BARBARA: Was it nice?
SOPHIE: Yes, it was a very small school. It had 86 pupils.
BARBARA: That's very small!
SOPHIE: Yes, but there were a lot of children in each classroom. There were 32 in my classroom. There were only three classrooms.
BARBARA: Was it an old school?
SOPHIE: Yes, it was very old. It was more than 200 years old. We were in the best classroom. In the other rooms, in the winter, there was ice inside the rooms!
BARBARA: Oh! When did you start school?
SOPHIE: At nine o'clock.
BARBARA: No, I mean, how old were you?
SOPHIE: About four and half.
BARBARA: Oh. I was five, I think …

③ Was your first school bigger or smaller than Sophie's?
Was it older or newer? Were you younger or older than Sophie?

208

3 Were you older? Was it newer?

'was' and 'were'
Extra practice • WB
Exs. 1, 2
Extra practice • TB
Ws. 30.1

3.1 'Was' and 'were'

When do you say 'was'? When do you say 'were'?
Look at these sentences from Units 29 and 30 and complete the table.

It was a small/big school	It was very cold.
The classrooms were	Life was very exciting.
I was four years old.	Cavepeople were happy.
It was exciting.	Cavemen were hunters.
It was dangerous.	It was difficult.
Cavepeople were vegetarians.	Sometimes, everyone was ill.
Cavepeople were farmers.	How old were you?
Nogoba was a cavegirl.	Were you happy there?
The river was very deep.	We were in the best classroom.

I	....	
You	....	older.
He + She+ It +	....	happy. 12 years old. very cold.
We They	....	
There	....	32 children in my classroom.
There	....	ice in the classroom.

3.2 Was it cold?

Choose the best question to continue each conversation.

a I went swimming on Saturday.	1 Was it a long way?
b I went to the cinema at the weekend.	2 Were you excited?
c I went to bed at 6 o'clock last night.	3 Was the film good?
d I went in a helicopter yesterday.	4 Were you tired?
e We walked home last night.	5 Was it difficult?
f My mother helped me with my homework yesterday.	6 Was the water cold?
g I cooked a meal yesterday.	7 Was it good?

3.3 Spot the differences

Look at these pictures. Can you find eight
differences between the morning and the
afternoon? Write a sentence about each one.

The process of materials evaluation

Analysis of two extracts from: Units 29 and 30, Cambridge English for Schools I

Task Analysis Sheet

	Unit 29: 1	2	3	4	5	6	7	Unit 30: 1	2	3	4	5	6
I WHAT IS THE LEARNER EXPECTED TO DO?													
A TURN-TAKE													
Initiate	/	/	/	/		/	/			/			/
Respond					/			/	/		/	/	
Not required													
B FOCUS on													
Language system (rules or form)										/			
Meaning	/	/	/	/	/	/	/	/	/	/			
Meaning/system relationship												/	/
C MENTAL OPERATION													
Retrieve from LT memory	/	/		/		/	/			/			/
Build text	/	/		/		/	/			/			/
Draw on prior knowledge	/	/		/		/	/			/			
Relate sounds to objects		/											
Compare			/		/								
Decode semantic meaning					/			/		/			
Select information					/			/					
Repeat with expansion					/			/					
Deduce language rule					/			/		/			
Apply language rule					/			/			/	/	/
II WHO WITH?													
Learner to class	/					/		/		/			
Learners individually simultaneously		/			/			/		/	/	/	
Learners in pairs/groups			/	/		/							
III WITH WHAT CONTENT?													
A FORM													
a input to learners													
Graphic	/						/					/	
Oral words/phrases			/										
Oral extended discourse													
Written words/phrases	/					/		/		/	/		
Written extended discourse					/		/		/				
Sounds/music		/											
b expected output from learners													
Oral words/phrases		/						/	/			/	
Oral extended discourse	/		/		/					/			
Written words/phrases											/		/
Written extended discourse					/		/						
B SOURCE													
Materials				/					/		/	/	/
Teacher													
Learner(s)	/	/	/	/		/	/	/		/			
C NATURE													
Personal opinion	/					/							
Fact		/	/	/		/	/						
Fiction					/					/			/
Personal information								/		/			
Metalinguistic knowledge						/		/			/	/	

Appendix 2: Aspects of tasks – some definitions

This list comprises examples of aspects of tasks found through an analysis of extracts from materials aimed at secondary school learners. It is not an exhaustive list of all possible task aspects (see Littlejohn 1992).

I WHAT IS THE LEARNER EXPECTED TO DO?

FEATURE	DEFINITION	EXAMPLE
A TURN-TAKE	the learner's discourse role and discourse control	
1. Initiate	the learner is expected to express what he/she wishes to say without a script of any kind	free discussion
2. Respond	the learner is expected to express him/herself through language which has been narrowly defined	guided writing
3. Not required	the learner is not expected to initiate or respond	listen to explanation
B FOCUS	where the learner is to concentrate his/her attention	
4. language system	a focus on rules or patterns	substitution tables
5. meaning	a focus on the message of the language being used	comprehension qs
6. meaning-system relationship	a focus on the relationship between form and meaning	tracing anaphora
C OPERATION	what the mental process involves	
7. repeat identically	the learner is to reproduce exactly what is presented	oral repetition
8. repeat selectively	learner is to choose before repeating given language.	dialogue frames
9. repeat with substitution	the learner is to repeat the basic pattern of given lang. but replace certain items with other given items	substitution drills
10. repeat with transformation	the learner is to apply a (conscious or unconscious) rule to given language and to transform it accordingly	change statements into questions
11. repeat with expansion	the learner is given an outline and is to use that outline as a frame within which to produce further language	composition outlines
12. retrieve from STM	the learner is to recall items of language from short term memory, that is, within a matter of seconds	oral repetition
13. retrieve from ITM	the learner is to recall items from intermediate term memory, that is, within a matter of minutes. Here taken up to the length of the lesson (approx. 50 mins.)	recall vocabulary within lesson
14. retrieve from LTM	the learner is to recall items from prior to the present lesson	recall vocabulary from last lesson

The process of materials evaluation

FEATURE	DEFINITION	EXAMPLE
15. formulate items into larger unit	the learner is to combine recalled items into, e.g. complete sentences, necessitating the application of consciously or unconsciously held language rules	discussion
16. decode semantic/ propositional meaning	the learner is to decode the 'surface' meaning of given language	read a text for its meaning
17. select information	the learner is to extract information from a given text	answer questions by reading a text
18. calculate	the learner is to perform mathematical operations	solve maths problem
19. categorise selected information	the learner is to analyse and classify information selected through operation 17	sort information into groups
20. hypothesise	the learner is to hypothesise an explanation, description or meaning of something	deduce meanings from context
21. compare samples of language	the learner is to compare two or more sets of language data on the basis of meaning or form	compare accounts of the same event
22. analyse language form	the learner is to examine the component parts of a piece of language	find the stressed syllable in a word
23. formulate lang.rule	As 20, but learner is to hypothesise a language rule.	devise gramm. rule
24. apply stated language rule	the learner is to use a given language rule in order to transform or produce language	change direct to reported speech
25. apply general knowledge	the learner is to draw on knowledge of 'general facts' about the world	answer questions on other countries
26. negotiate	the learner is to discuss and decide with others in order to accomplish something	in groups, write a set of instructions
27. review own FL output	the learner is to check his/her own foreign language production for its intended meaning or form	check own written work
28. attend to example/ explanation	the learner is to 'take notice of' something	listen to a grammar explanation

II WHO WITH?

29. teacher and learner(s), whole class observing	the teacher and selected learner(s) are to interact	a learner answers a question; other learners listen
30. learner(s) to the whole class	selected learner(s) are to interact with the whole class, including the teacher	learner(s) feed back on groupwork
31. learners with whole class simultaneously	learners are to perform an operation in concert with the whole class	choral repetition
32. learners individually simultaneously	learners are to perform an operation in the company of others but without immediate regard to the manner/pace with which others perform the same operation	learners individually do a written exercise
33. learners in pairs/ groups; class observing	learners in pairs or small groups are to interact with each other while the rest of the class listens	a group 'acts out' a conversation
34. learners in pairs/ groups, simultaneously	learners are to interact with each other in pairs/groups in the company of other pairs/groups	learners discuss in groups

FEATURE	DEFINITION	EXAMPLE
III WITH WHAT CONTENT?		
a input to learners	form of content offered to learners	
35. graphic	pictures, illustrations, photographs, diagrams, etc.	a world map
36. words/phrases/ sentences: written	individual written words/phrases/sentences	a list of vocabulary items
37. words/phrases/ sentences: oral	individual spoken words/phrases/sentences	prompts for a drill
38. extended discourse: written	texts of more than 50 written words which cohere, containing supra-sentential features	a written story
39. extended discourse: oral	texts of more than 50 spoken words which cohere, containing supra-sentential features	a dialogue on tape
b expected output	form of content to be produced by learner	
40. graphic	pictures, illustrations, photographs, diagrams, etc.	a plan of one's house
41. words/phrases/ sentences	individual written words/phrases/sentences	write sentences using a specified word
42. words/phrases/ sentences: oral	individual spoken words/phrases/sentences	response to a drill
43. extended discourse: written	texts of more than 50 written words which cohere, containing supra-sentential features	a story in writing
44. extended discourse: oral	texts of more than 50 written words which cohere, containing supra-sentential features	an oral account of an event
c source	where the content comes from	
45. materials	content (or narrowly specified topic) supplied by the materials	dialogue/text in the coursebook
46. teacher	content (or narrowly specified topic) supplied by the teacher	teacher recounts own experiences
47. learner(s)	content (or narrowly specified topic) supplied by the learner(s)	learner recounts own experiences
d nature	type of content as required in the operation (sec. Ic)	
48. metalinguistic comment	comments on language use, structure, form or meaning.	a grammatical rule
49. linguistic items	words/phrases/sentences carrying no specific message	a vocabulary list
50. non-fiction	factual texts ('other facts')	a text about a foreign culture
51. fiction	fictional texts	dialogue between imaginary characters
52. personal information/opinion	learner(s) own personal information or opinion	details of learner's interests

Appendix 3: An example of an analytical description

This description relates to *Cambridge English for Schools Student's Book 1*. Since the author of this paper is also one of the authors of the book, the description cannot be be considered impartial. It is provided here simply as an example of how an overview of a set of materials may be expressed.

1 Publication

1 Place of learner's materials in the set
   - part of a 'complete' package
   - means of access into the materials provided for teacher and learners; support facilities (answer keys, transcript etc.) provided for the teacher only
   - learner's materials may be used independently of the teacher's materials
   - learner's materials form focal point for classroom work

2 Published form of the learner's materials
   - monolingual throughout
   - durable and consumable materials for the learner
   - focal point for classroom work provided by learner's durable materials
   - four-colour for learner's durable materials; two-colour for other components of set

3 Subdivision of the learner's materials
   - subdivided into 6 'Themes' with 5 'Units' within each theme. Standardised number of pages for each Theme and each Unit type, suggested estimated time to complete each unit
   - patterning across Themes; loose pattern within unit types

4 Subdivision of sections into sub-sections
   - patterning within Themes: 'Topic' units provide fluency type activities, drawing on students' own experience/ideas of a cross-curricular topic; 'Language focus' units focus on structure/functions of language raised in the 'Topic' units; 'Activity' units provide a larger 'language product' task related to the Theme; 'Culture matters' units provide cross-cultural information related to the Theme; 'Revision and evaluation' units revise language presented and evaluate the process of learning

5 Continuity
   - provided by a 'Theme' structure to the book
   - Units relate to different aspects of the Theme
   - an incremental syllabus

6 Route
   - one route through material proposed: to use the material in the order presented
   - Teacher's Book suggests ways route may be shortened/extended

7 Access
- means of access into the materials: a listing of unit/lesson names, a listing of unit/lesson objectives; index and wordlist

2 Design
1 Aims and objectives
- to develop learner's linguistic competence in all four skills
- to develop cross-curricular and cross-cultural knowledge
- to raise metalinguistic knowledge
- to develop learner's decision-making abilities

2 Principles of selection
- types of tasks: brainstorming activities, drawing on student's knowledge/ideas, decision-making concerning planning/evaluating learning; reproductive language practice
- content: cross-curricular and cross-cultural topics; learner's personal information/ideas; little fiction
- language: common language patterns and semantic meanings; language relevant to topic

3 Principles of sequencing
- tasks: movement from student ideas/opinions, to text presentation of information/language knowledge, to choice of practice exercises to larger 'whole task' activities
- content: no clear principle for the sequence of content
- language: simple to complex in terms of surface structure

4 Subject matter and focus of subject matter
- input and output content mainly cross-curricular topics
- virtually all content is factual
- source of content: students' ideas/opinions/prior knowledge, and materials themselves
- metalinguistic comment in 'Language focus' units

5 Types of teaching/learning activities
- learners called on to provide ideas, knowledge in an 'initiate' position
- materials direct classroom interaction for both teachers and learners;
- demands for student creativity characterise most tasks
- general range of operations required: retrieve, formulate, decode semantic meaning, select information, compare, formulate language rule, hypothesise, negotiate
- mother tongue called upon to compare with foreign language
- emphasis on learners' prior knowledge, (deducing) knowledge of language structure
- high frequency of tasks requiring learners to share ideas with the class
- emphasis on language production rather than reception; speaking rather than writing and reading rather than listening; extended discourse in most cases

6 *Participation: who does what with whom*
- three basic modes of classroom participation evident: learner to class and teacher, learners individually simultaneously, and learners in pairs/groups simultaneously

7 *Classroom roles of teachers and learners*
- 'decision-making' weighted towards the teacher by the materials (guidance on using the materials and provision of answer keys for teacher)
- both teachers and learners, however, are expected to follow directions of the materials
- teacher's role: to manage the classroom event, elicit learners' ideas, monitor language output
- learners' role: to contribute and share ideas, to make decisions over what/when/how to learn

8 *Learner roles in learning*
- undertake tasks as directed by the materials
- produce language tasks for self/others
- learning as the gradual accumulation of items, as deducing language rules and comparing with mother tongue/prior knowledge

9 *Role of the materials as a whole*
- to structure the teaching and learning of English, classroom time and classroom interaction
- to provide a route for teaching and learning English
- to provide a stimulus for learners' own creative language use
- to involve the students in classroom decision-making

9 The evaluation of communicative tasks

Rod Ellis

Introduction

Murphy, writing in 1985, could legitimately complain that 'the necessity for evaluation is not understood and recognized' (p. 10). However, this is not the case today. There has been a strong surge of interest in the goals, roles and methods of evaluation in language teaching over the last few years (e.g. Alderson and Beretta 1992; Rea-Dickens and Germaine 1992; Weir and Roberts 1994). Acceptance of the need for evaluation – both to determine to what extent a programme has 'worked' and, more broadly, to facilitate the whole process of curriculum development – is now widespread.

This change has been brought about in part by applied linguists paying more attention to mainstream educational theory (the influence of Stenhouse [1975] has been of particular significance) and in part by the need to carry out large-scale programme evaluations for outside agencies responsible for funding programmes (e.g. United Kingdom agencies such as the Overseas Development Administration and the British Council and United States agencies such as USAID).

In general, however, the growing interest in evaluation has manifested itself in a concern for macro evaluation of programmes and projects (or, according to Weir and Roberts (*op. cit.*: 3), of organised educational activities offered on a continuing basis and 'activities funded to achieve a particular task'). A brief look at the evaluation case studies in Alderson and Beretta (*op. cit.*) and in Weir and Roberts (*op. cit.*) demonstrates this concern. There is one report of a micro-evaluation, Slimani's (1992) study of uptake in relation to classroom interaction (included in Alderson and Beretta [*op. cit.*] but referred to as 'not an examination of a programme but ... rather an examination of a classroom technique'); but all the other studies are of macro-evaluations. For example, Alderson and Beretta include a number of case studies of programmes and projects. Alderson and Scott (1992) report an evaluation of a national ESP project in Brazil. Lynch (1992) discusses an evaluation of the Reading English for Science and Technology Project at the University of Guadalajara. Mitchell (1992) summarises her work on a bilingual education project in Scotland. Palmer (1992) examines a first-year German course at the University of Utah. Ross (1992) evaluates a 70-hour course in a Japanese junior college. Coleman (1992) looks at a Key English Language Teaching Project in an Indonesian university and Beretta (1992) reviews his evaluation of the Communicational Language Teaching Project in India. The primary focus, then, has been on **macro-evaluation**.

Macro-evaluation can be defined as evaluation that seeks to answer one or both of the following questions:

1 To what extent was the programme/project effective and efficient in meeting its goals?
2 In what ways can the programme/project be improved?

The first of these questions relates to what Weir and Roberts (1994) refer to as 'accountability evaluation' and the second to 'development evaluation'. In order to carry out a macro-evaluation of a programme/ project, the evaluators need to collect various kinds of information relating to one or both of the following:

1 Administrative matters (i.e. the logistical and financial underpinnings of the programme)
2 Curriculum matters, which, in turn can be broken down into a consideration of:
   a) Materials
   b) Teachers
   c) Learners

A macro-evaluation, then, is an evaluation carried out for account-ability and/or developmental purposes by collecting information re-lating to various administrative and curricular aspects of the programme.

While there is an undoubted need for macro-evaluations of the kind reported in Alderson and Beretta (*op. cit.*), it might be argued that such an approach to evaluation does not accord with the perspective which many teachers have about what evaluation involves. Teachers are obviously concerned with whether they are accomplishing their goals and whether they need to make changes to their programme. However, their attention is likely to focus less on the programme as a whole and more on whether specific activities and techniques appear to 'work' in the context of a particular lesson. In other words, any macro-evaluations that teachers make are likely to be the result of a whole series of micro-evaluations carried out on a day-by-day and lesson-by-lesson basis. If this argument is right, a teacher-oriented approach to evaluation will emphasise **micro-evaluation**.

A micro-evaluation is characterised by a narrow-focus on some specific aspect of the curriculum or the administration of the programme. Each of the curricular and administrative aspects referred to above lend themselves to a micro-evaluation. Thus, in the case of teachers/teaching one might focus on the kinds of questions teachers ask in a lesson (see Ellis 1994b). In the case of learners one might focus on which learners participate productively in a lesson. In the case of materials, we might ask whether a particular task is effective or efficient. These questions may be informed by a desire to obtain information that will speak generally about the effectiveness and efficiency of the learners, the teachers and the materials in achieving learning goals (i.e. they may be shaped and directed in top-down fashion by an attempt to collect information for a macro-evaluation) or, as I suspect is often the case, they may be informed by more local, on-the-spot considerations. It is quite likely, of course, that a macro-evaluation may eventually emerge, bottom-up, from repeated micro-evaluations.

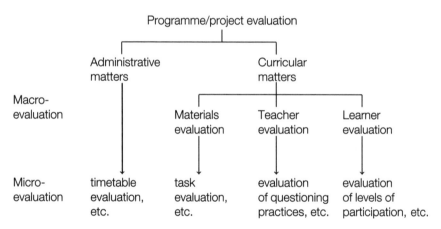

Figure 1 *Macro- and micro-evaluation in language teaching*

The view of evaluation that informs this paper is reflected diagrammatically in Figure 1. It suggests that one way of profitably adding to our understanding of evaluation in ELT and of helping teachers to undertake evaluation that accords with their own perspective might be to adopt a micro- rather than macro-perspective.

How then should a micro-evaluation be carried out? I want to address this question with reference to the idea of materials for tasks. I want to show how a systematic and principled approach to task evaluation can provide a means of approaching materials evaluation and, thereby, programme/project evaluation. As my focus is 'materials', I will start by providing a brief account of work in materials evaluation in general. I will also consider a number of general issues relating to the kinds of decisions that evaluators need to make. This will be followed by an outline of a proposed procedure for conducting a task evaluation and an example of how to design a task evaluation.

Materials evaluation

Brown (1994) makes the important, if obvious, point that any evaluation can be carried out before the programme commences or after or, of course, on both occasions. In the case of published work on materials evaluation the focus of attention has been before-programme evaluation. This is somewhat surprising given that there is widespread recognition that 'the ultimate evaluation of text comes with actual classroom use' (Daoud and Celce-Murcia 1979: 306).

A before-programme evaluation of published coursebooks is motivated by the need to choose materials that will be relevant and appropriate for a particular group of learners and possibly also by the need to identify specific aspects of the materials that require adaptation. In a before-programme evaluation the evaluator identifies a set of criteria which are used to reach a decision regarding which book to adopt and how it needs to be adapted. To this end a number of questionnaires, checklists and guides have been produced (e.g. Cunningsworth 1984; Breen and Candlin 1987; Skierso 1991; McDonough and Shaw 1993). Frequently these instruments are organised into two or more levels or stages to reflect the decision-process teachers need to go through. For example, Breen and Candlin (*op. cit.*) organise the questions in their evaluation checklist into two phases that address the overall 'usefulness' of the materials and that provide for 'a more searching analysis . . . with your particular group of learners and your actual classroom situation very much in mind' (p. 18). Breen and Candlin also recommend soliciting learners' views about learning and teaching so that these can be considered in the final evaluation.

McDonough and Shaw (1993) suggest that teachers begin with an 'external evaluation', consisting of an examination of the claims made on the cover of the student's and teacher's books, the introduction and the table of contents. This, they suggest, will help teachers to determine the intended audience, the proficiency level, the context in which the writers of the materials intend them to be used, the way the language has been organised into teachable units and the writer's views on language and methodology. This should be followed by an 'internal evaluation', which requires an in-depth look at two or more units in order to investigate such aspects as the presentation of skills in the materials, the grading and sequencing of the materials, the kinds of texts used and the relationship between exercises and tests. Skierso (*op. cit.*) envisages a three-step procedure:

1 identification of relevant contextual information relating to the students, the teacher, the course syllabus and the institution,
2 analysis of the features of the textbook followed by an overall rating of the text, and
3 the actual judging of the acceptability of the textbook, involving both the rating and weighting of specific evaluative criteria.

The goal of these textbook survey guides is to provide a systematic and principled approach to materials evaluation. Although the guides may be of practical use to teachers, they raise many questions relating to such issues as what aspects of the materials should be considered and, crucially, how one aspect should be weighted in relation to another. For example, many of the guides specifically ask whether the materials contain authentic texts, but as Widdowson (1979) has pointed out, the whole question of authenticity in language teaching is a complex one with authenticity being determined by what the learners do with the text. Also, a positive rating on a criterion of authenticity (i.e. the materials contain authentic texts) may be matched with a negative rating on the criterion of vocabulary load (i.e. the number of new words introduced is excessive). How is the materials evaluator to reconcile these conflicting ratings? Faced with such questions, which remain unresolved in the existing literature, it is hard not to agree with Sheldon (1988: 245) that 'coursebook evaluation is fundamentally a subjective, rule-of-thumb activity, and that no neat formula, grid, or system will ever provide a definite yardstick'. It is pertinent to ask whether greater objectivity is achievable in a micro-evaluation focused on a particular language learning task.

The same guides that have been designed for before-programme materials evaluation can be used for after-programme evaluation. There are, however, very few published accounts of such evaluations. The *ELT Documents* issue devoted to 'ELT textbooks and materials: problems in evaluation and development' (Sheldon 1987) disappointingly does not contain a single after-programme evaluation.

Why have there been so few? One possible reason is that teachers see no need for a systematic and principled post-programme evaluation. They feel they know whether the book 'works' or not as a result of their day-by-day experiences of using it in their teaching. Even if they acknowledge a need for detailed evaluation, teachers may be daunted by the size of the task; carrying out an empirical evaluation of a textbook is an enormous undertaking. The desirability of engaging teachers in a careful evaluation of language teaching materials after they have been used is widely acknowledged, however (see, for example, Rea-Dickens and Germaine 1992; 30). Such an evaluation provides an appraisal of the value of specific teaching activities for particular groups of learners and, perhaps more importantly, serves as encouragement to teachers to adopt a 'reflective approach' to their own teaching (Richards and Lockhart 1994). One way of encouraging the systematic evaluation of materials after use may be to engage in micro-evaluation by focusing on particular tasks. Such an approach to the empirical validation of teaching materials may prove more manageable and therefore less daunting to teachers.

What kind of evaluation?

Before we turn our attention to the evaluation of language learning tasks, it is pertinent to ask what kind of evaluation will be required. I shall attempt to answer this by examining a number of dimensions of evaluation: (1) approach, (2) purpose, (3) focus, (4) scope, (5) the evaluators, (6) the timing and (7) types of information. These dimensions are discussed in the existing literature in relation to macro-evaluation (i.e. programme/project evaluation) but they are equally applicable to micro-evaluation (e.g. the evaluation of a specific task).

The literature on educational evaluation distinguishes two broad **approaches**; the 'objectives model' and 'responsive evaluation' (see Norris 1990). The former belongs to the psychological tradition of educational research and is nomothetic in approach (i.e. it employs quantitative data to make statistical generalisations with a view to establishing general 'laws'). It requires that curricula be expressed in terms of precise objectives, the achievement of which can be determined by tests that measure learner behaviour and learning outcomes. Responsive evaluation belongs more to the sociological tradition of educational research and is idiographic in approach (i.e. it proceeds by means of intensive studies of individuals or particular cases). Whereas the 'objectives model' approach is concerned with determining whether the programme/project has achieved its goals, the 'responsive evaluation' approach aims to illuminate the complex nature of the organisational, teaching and learning processes at issue. The recent history of educational evaluation can be seen as a debate between the rival claims of these two approaches. Increasingly, however, evaluators are recognising the need for a broad-based approach to evaluation that incorporates both the objectives model and responsive evaluation (see Weir and Roberts 1994, for example).

These two approaches to evaluation reflect two general **purposes** for carrying out an evaluation: (1) accountability and (2) development. Where accountability is at stake, the purpose of the evaluation is to determine whether the stated goals of the programme have been met. In the case of development, the purpose may be either (a) to improve the curriculum or (b) to foster teacher-development or both. In general, evaluation for accountability will require an 'objectives model' approach, while evaluation for development will require a 'responsive' approach. However, it is not quite so simple as this, as the methods employed by either approach can yield information that is of value to both accountability and to development. For example, summative test scores can be used to determine whether the goals of the programme have been met but they can also be used to help teachers understand what parts of the curriculum need further attention.

In addition to overall purpose it is useful to consider the **focus** of the evaluation. Two principal foci can be identified: effectiveness and efficiency. It is much easier to focus on effectiveness as the question that needs to be answered is simply 'Is the programme effective in meeting the needs of the learners?' It is much more difficult to address the efficiency of a programme, where the key question is 'Does the programme meet the needs of the learners more effectively than some alternative programme?' To address effectiveness the evaluator needs to compare what the learners knew and were able to do before the programme started with what they know and are able to do at the conclusion of the programme. If the learners show gains in those aspects of language proficiency which were the stated goal of the programme, then the programme can be considered 'effective'. To investigate efficiency, however, it is necessary to compare the learning gains evidenced by one programme (the programme being evaluated) with the gains evidenced by another programme that differed in some way from the target programme. It is not always possible to carry out a comparison of this kind.

Evaluators also need to determine the **scope** of their evaluation. The important decision to be made in this respect concerns whether the evaluation will examine the programme in terms of its stated goals (i.e. ask 'Did the programme meet its goals?') or whether it will also examine the goals themselves (i.e. ask 'Are the goals appropriate for the learners in question?'). In other words, the scope of the evaluation can be 'internal' in the sense that it uncritically accepts the goals of the programme or it can be 'external' in the sense that it submits the goals of the programme to critical scrutiny. This distinction between 'internal' and 'external' evaluation is important in another way. An internal evaluation will focus narrowly on whether the learning predicted by the goals of the programme has been achieved, while an external evaluation will also enquire into whether any unpredicted learning (i.e. learning not catered for explicitly by the curriculum) has taken place. There is, in fact, a growing recognition of the need to consider unpredicted learning (see Allwright 1984, for example).

Consideration needs to be given as to who the **evaluators** of the programme should be. Evaluation need not – and in the eyes of many should not – be restricted to outside evaluators. Where the overall purpose of the evaluation is development, there is obviously a critical need to involve all the 'stakeholders' who have some investment in the programme (i.e. organisers, curriculum designers, teachers and learners). Whereas an outsider evaluator is more likely to offer a 'fresh' perspective and may give the evaluation credibility, stakeholders will be able to bring an insider's perspective to the evaluation (see Alderson 1992: 279). If it is accepted that a completely objective evaluation is an impossibility, a strong case exists for 'advocacy evaluation', where various parties argue the case for their own biases and stances. It can also be argued that involving stakeholders in the evaluation is more likely to foster 'development', if that is the goal of the evaluation.

Where **timing** is concerned, a common distinction is made between a 'formative' evaluation, which takes place as the programme is being developed and taught, and a 'summative' evaluation, which takes place at the end of the programme. This is a distinction that appears to be more relevant to macro- than to micro-evaluation, however. Micro-evaluations are likely to be essentially summative in nature. That is, the evaluation will take place when a piece of teaching has been completed. Indeed, a formative programme evaluation might be viewed as a series of ongoing summative micro-evaluations.

Finally, there is the question of the **types of information** to be collected for an evaluation. An evaluation based on an objectives model approach traditionally relies on one type of information: (1) learners' tests scores. A responsive evaluation, particularly if it is directed at curriculum or teacher-development, will require a greater variety of information, including (2) documentary information (e.g. syllabuses and materials), (3) information collected by means of self-report by different stakeholders and (4) observation of actual classrooms. There is now a general recognition that even an accountability-oriented evaluation requires varied and extensive information.

As a way of identifying the kinds of decisions that need to be taken in planning an evaluation, Figure 2 summarises the various dimensions discussed above. It provides a checklist which evaluators can run through when they wish to conduct an evaluation of a task.

Dimension	Key questions	Answers
Approach 1 Objectives model 2 Responsive evaluation	Is the approach to be one evaluating the task in terms of its objectives or is it to be one of developing an understanding of how the task works for language learning. Or both?	

Purpose
1 accountability
2 development
  a) curriculum
    improvement
  b) teacher
    development
	Is the evaluation directed at determining whether the task 'works' or is it directed at improving the task for future use or encouraging teachers to reflect on the value and use of this kind of task?	

Focus 1 Effectiveness 2 Efficiency	Is the focus of the evaluation on the effectiveness or the efficiency of the task? If the focus is on the efficiency of the task with what is the task to be compared?	
Scope 1 Internal 2 External	Will the evaluation of the task be in terms of its stated objectives or will it consider the appropriateness of the objectives themselves? Will the evaluation of the task consider predicted benefits or will it also consider unpredicted benefits as well?	
Evaluators 1 Insiders 2 Outsiders	Who will evaluate the task? What biases do the chosen evaluators have?	
Timing 1 Formative 2 Summative	Will the evaluation of the task take place as it is being used in the classroom or on its completion?	
Type of information 1 Test scores 2 Documentary 3 Self-report 4 Observation	What kinds of information will be used to evaluate the task? How will the information be collected?	

Figure 2   *A checklist of questions for evaluating a task*

Tasks in language pedagogy

There has been a growing interest in the idea of a task as a unit for developing language curricula. This interest has been stimulated by work in second language acquisition which supports Corder's (1967, 1981) early claim that learners have their own 'built-in syllabus' which is 'in some way more efficient than the instructor-generated sequence' (p. 9). Thus, a syllabus that specifies the linguistic content and the order in which it is to be taught may not accord with the learner's built-in syllabus. One way round this problem is to specify the content of the syllabus in terms of 'tasks', which indicate in broad terms what learners will communicate about and the procedures they will follow to do so, but which do not attempt to specify explicitly the actual language that is to be used or learnt.

Task-based language teaching, therefore, is predicated on the principle that having learners perform tasks will help them to develop knowledge and skill in the second language in accordance with the way their own language learning mechanisms work. Tasks function as devices for creating the conditions required for language acquisition. There is still uncertainty and disagreement, however, regarding what these conditions are. According to one body of theory, learners need opportunities to engage in meaning negotiation in order to obtain the kind of input that works for acquisition and to experience occasions when they are 'pushed' to use the second language more precisely and appropriately. Pica (1994) reviews the arguments and research in favour of such meaning 'negotiation'.

What exactly is a 'task'? There are many definitions available but perhaps the most helpful is that provided by Richards, Platt and Weber). A task is:

> . . . an activity or action which is carried out as a result of processing or understanding language (i.e. as a response to verbal or non-verbal input). For example, drawing a map while listening to a tape, listening to an instruction and performing a command, getting a partner to draw a concealed picture from instructions, group completion of a demanding jigsaw puzzle, may be referred to as tasks. Tasks may or may not involve the production of language. A task usually requires the teacher to specify what will be regarded as successful completion of the task. (1985: 289)

From this definition, we see the following criterial features of a task: (1) it involves an activity of some kind (e.g drawing or performing an action), (2) it has a specified outcome that determines when it has been completed and (3) it may require language comprehension or language production or both. I wish to add a fourth criterion, taken from Nunan (1993); (4) a task requires that learners focus their attention principally on meaning rather than form. This then excludes from consideration activities such as traditional grammar exercises, which require a primary focus on form (but could include language awareness activities which involve learners discovering and discussing linguistic phenomena from evidence provided for them). My concern is with how *communicative* tasks can be evaluated.

Following Breen (1989), we can view tasks from three different perspectives: (1) tasks as workplans, (2) tasks in process and (3) tasks as outcomes. When we view tasks as workplans, we are concerned with the actions and learning that the task is designed to bring about. We can determine these by examining the objectives of the task and procedures for implementing the task (see next section). When we view tasks in process we need to examine what actually takes place as a task is used with a particular group of learners. This will require careful observation. Finally, when we view tasks as outcomes, we need to consider what actions and learning are actually accomplished as a result of performing the task. Clearly, the evaluation of a task requires all three perspectives, as Breen makes clear.

Conducting an evaluation of a task

We have already seen in Figure 2 the major dimensions that the evaluator of a task needs to consider in conducting an evaluation. We also need to consider the steps involved to ensure that the evaluation is systematic and principled. A suggested procedure is outlined in Figure 3. An example of a task evaluation follows in the subsequent section.

Description of the task

The evaluation of a task requires a clear description of the task to be evaluated. This can be achieved by specifying the content of a task as follows:

1 Input (i.e. the information that the learners are supplied with). Input can be in verbal form (e.g. a series of directions) or non-verbal (e.g. a diagram or a picture).
2 Procedures (i.e. the activities that the learners are to perform in order to accomplish the task).
3 Language activity (i.e. whether the learners engage in receptive

language activity, listening or reading, or productive language activity, speaking or writing, or both).

4 Outcome(s) (i.e. what it is that the learners will have done on completion of the task): again, the outcome may be verbal (e.g. performing a role-play) or non-verbal (e.g. drawing a diagram).

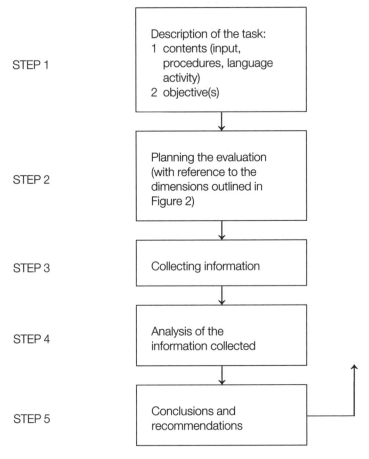

Figure 3   Steps in conducting an evaluation of a task

A full description of the task also requires consideration of the objectives of the task. To this end, the distinction that Nunan (1989) makes between 'real-world' and 'pedagogic' tasks is important. A real-world task is one which requires learners to approximate in class the kinds of tasks required of them in the real world. In such cases, the *teaching objective* and the *student's target* are one and the same. An example might be 'Writing a Cheque'. A pedagogic task is one that requires learners to perform some language activity which is not found in the real-world but which is believed to facilitate language acquisition. In such cases, the *teaching objective* and the *student's target* are not the same. For example, 'Making a Model Aeroplane' has as its student target the making of the aeroplane, but the teaching objective is different (perhaps 'encouraging the students to clarify written instructions').

It is obviously much easier to specify the teaching objective of a real-world task; the objective is to enable learners to perform whatever the real-world task is. It is much more difficult to specify the objectives of pedagogic tasks as these are essentially vague (e.g. to enable the students to acquire new linguistic knowledge or to enable the students to improve their fluency). In the context of a micro-evaluation of a single task it will be very difficult to establish whether learners have acquired new linguistic knowledge or improved their fluency as a result of accomplishing the task. For this reason, it may be necessary to focus the evaluation less on whether the objectives have been met and more on whether the kinds of language behaviour hypothesised to bring about language acquisition (e.g. meaning negotiation) have been achieved.

Planning the evaluation

It is probably true to say that normally teachers who engage in task-based language teaching do not give prior consideration to how they will evaluate the effectiveness or efficiency of the task. Yet, arguably, this is just what is required, because without prior planning it may prove impossible to achieve a systematic and principled evaluation. Also, the very act of carrying out the planning of a task evaluation may have a beneficial impact on the choice and design of a task. The various dimensions listed in Figure 2 serve as a guide for the kind of prior planning that is needed. Various decisions will also have to be made about what information to collect, when to collect it and how to collect it. These are considered under 'Collecting information'.

Collecting information

A task evaluation will need to consider collecting three types of information: (1) information about how the task was performed, (2) information about what learning took place as a result of performing the task and (3) information regarding the teacher's and the learner's opinions about the task.

There are various types of instruments available for collecting information. Figure 4 lists some of the main ones. A detailed discussion of the main instruments can be found in Weir and Roberts (1994).

Information can be collected (1) before the task is used, (2) while the task is being used and (3) on completion of the task. (1) will be particularly useful in the case of real-world tasks. It will supply data on whether and to what extent the learners are able to perform the desired action (e.g. writing a cheque) before they do the task. However, it may not be necessary to collect prior information when evaluating a pedagogic task as a single task is unlikely to result in measurable gains in fluency or knowledge. Information about what occurs while the task is being performed, however, is likely to be of crucial performance in evaluating this kind of task, as it will enable the evaluator to determine whether the task results in the kind of interactional behaviour considered important for language acquisition. For example, if the task performance is recorded, it will be possible to determine to what extent the task afforded opportunities for the kind of meaning negotiation hypothesised to facilitate language acquisition. Irrespective of the nature of the task, information collected on the completion of the task will be crucial. The collection of two kinds of information should be considered; (1) information relating to the outcome of the task that is the focus of the evaluation (e.g. the cheque the learners have written or the model aeroplane they have made as a result of completing the task) and (2) information relating to whether the learners can perform the task (or a similar task) without any pedagogic support (e.g. ask them to write a cheque on their own or make another aeroplane based on similar instructions to those used in the task). (1) helps to answer the question 'Did the students accomplish the task?' and (2) enables the evaluator to investigate whether any general learning has taken place.

	Before	During	After
Documentary information	Teacher's record of work Journals		Task products (e.g. a map, written story)
Tests	Achievement test Pre-task		Achievement test Post-task
Observation		Interactional analysis Recording of task performance	
Self-report	Questionnaire Interview	Think-aloud	Questionnaire Interview Conferences Uptake report

Figure 4   Sources of information in a task evaluation

Analysis of the information collected

One of the major decisions facing the evaluator at this stage of the evaluation is whether to provide a quantitative or a qualitative analysis of the data or both. A quantitative analysis involves the use of numbers. For example, it might be possible to develop a scale for rating the outcome of the task (e.g. the cheque the learners have written or the model aeroplane they have made). The results of this rating could be presented numerically in terms of the number of learners achieving the highest, middle and lowest ratings. This then provides a quantitative way of assessing whether the task has been accomplished successfully. A qualitative analysis involves a more holistic and, perhaps, impression-istic approach. For example, the evaluator might seek to represent the learners' own evaluation of the task in terms of representative responses to open questions in the questionnaire they had completed on finishing the task. Both types of analysis are useful. Brown (1994) points out that qualitative data can sometimes be converted into quantitative data. For example, one might try to find a way of quantifying the learners' responses to the questionnaire. Attempting some kind of quantification is wise because it serves as a way of checking the reliability of more qualitative analyses.

Conclusions and recommendations

It is helpful to make a clear distinction between 'conclusions' and 'recommendations'. Conclusions relate to what has been discovered as a result of the analysis. For example, the analysis might have shown that, as a result of doing the task, 75 per cent of the learners were able to write out a cheque correctly but 25 per cent made errors by omitting key information such as the date. Recommendations concern proposals for future teaching. They cover such issues as whether the task should be used again or abandoned, what changes need to be made to the task (in terms of input and/or procedures) and what kinds of follow-up work is needed with the learners in question. Each recommendation should be supported by reference to relevant conclusions. Separating conclusions and recommendations, however, enables a user of the evaluation to determine whether the recommendations are valid in the light of the stated conclusions. It also allows the user to agree with the conclusions but to disagree with the recommendations.

Designing a task evaluation: an example

As indicated by the procedure outlined above, the design of a task evaluation requires the evaluator to (1) describe the task to be evaluated, (2) make a number of general planning decisions, (3) decide what information is to be collected and how and (4) consider how the information to be collected will be analysed. There is, of course, no one way of conducting a task evaluation. What Rea (1983: 90) said about programme evaluation is equally applicable to task evaluation: 'Different areas of evaluation are important to different people, at different times, and for different reasons'. The following example of a task evaluation is intended to provide information about the use of a listening task which the learners (third year senior high school students in Japan) had had no previous experience of.

Description of the task

The task to be evaluated is of the information-gap kind in which learners need to gain new information from the input in order to complete the task successfully. It takes the form of a set of directions about where to place different kitchen objects (e.g. an apple, a scouring pad) in a matrix picture of a kitchen. The materials for the task are attached. The learners are required to listen to each direction, identify the object referred to and try to indicate where it should go by writing the number of the picture of the object in the correct location in the matrix picture. In this task the learners are allowed to request clarification if they do not at first understand a direction. To assist them in this, a number of formulas are written on the board (e.g. 'What is ___?' and Could you say it again?').

The task is of the pedagogic rather than real-world kind. However, a special feature of this task is that the directions include a number of words labelling kitchen objects that are unlikely to be known by most of the learners. Thus, although the task is communicative in nature (in that it requires the learners to focus their attention on comprehending the directions rather than on learning the new words), it also has an identifiable linguistic content.

Using the framework for describing a task outlined above, the main features of this task can be summarised as follows:

Input

Numbered pictures of kitchen objects; matrix picture of a kitchen; oral directions.

Procedures

The teacher says each direction; students request clarification as needed;

students attempt to locate objects in the matrix picture; students write in numbers in the matrix picture.

Language activity

Students listen to directions; students perform requests for clarification.

Outcome

A picture of a kitchen with numbers written on it to indicate where the individual objects should go.

The task was designed with a number of objectives in mind: (1) to improve the students' ability to understand detailed directions, (2) to encourage students to request clarification when they do not understand something and (3) to provide incidental exposure to the English names of a number of kitchen objects so that the students have an opportunity to learn them.

Planning

In planning the evaluation of this task, the following decisions were taken:

Approach: A dual approach was adopted. An attempt would be made to follow the objectives model approach by determining to what extent the objectives of the task had been met. In addition, it was decided to undertake a more responsive evaluation of how the teacher and the learners felt about the task.

Purpose: In accordance with the decision to adopt a dual approach, the evaluation would have an accountability function (i.e. seek to ascertain whether the task 'worked' in terms of its objectives) and a development function (i.e. seek to understand how the task might be improved for future use).

Focus: The focus of the evaluation was the effectiveness of the task. No attempt would be made to determine the efficiency of the task.

Scope: The evaluation would be internal (i.e. no attempt would be made to evaluate the appropriateness of the objectives). However, an attempt would be made to examine unpredicted as well as predicted learning outcomes.

Evaluators: The task would be evaluated by both the teacher and an outside evaluator.

Timing: The evaluation would be summative.

Collecting information

The information to be collected consists of data on how the task was performed, what learning took place and what opinions the teacher and the learners formed of the task. To this end, the following instruments will be used:

Before task: teacher interview
The teacher will be interviewed to ascertain the learners' experience with tasks of the kind being evaluated and any problems the teacher has previously encountered with such tasks.

Achievement test
An achievement test will be used to determine to what extent the learners know the target words. The test will take the form of a set of pictures of kitchen objects which the learners will be required to label by selecting from a list of words provided.

During task: interaction analysis
Observation of the lesson will take place by the external evaluator. The observation will consist of keeping a record of the number of times each learner requests clarification.

After task: task product
The completed matrix picture will be collected from each student.

Uptake chart
Immediately the task has been completed, each student will be given a piece of paper and asked to write down any new words they learned as a result of completing the task (see Slimani 1989).

Achievement test
The students will complete the same achievement test used before the task was performed.

Learner questionnaire
The learners will be given a simple questionnaire to complete (see Figure 5). Such questionnaires could themselves be considered as tasks (Potts 1985).

Teacher interview
A unstructured interview with the teacher will take place, focusing on:

– her views as to how successful the task was,
– her views about any problems with the task,
– her views about how the task might be improved for future use.

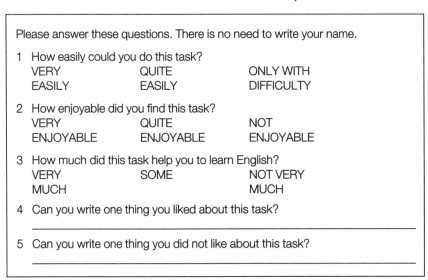

Please answer these questions. There is no need to write your name.

1   How easily could you do this task?
    VERY   QUITE   ONLY WITH
    EASILY   EASILY   DIFFICULTY

2   How enjoyable did you find this task?
    VERY   QUITE   NOT
    ENJOYABLE   ENJOYABLE   ENJOYABLE

3   How much did this task help you to learn English?
    VERY   SOME   NOT VERY
    MUCH   MUCH

4   Can you write one thing you liked about this task?

    _____

5   Can you write one thing you did not like about this task?

    _____

Figure 5   *Learner questionnaire*

Analysing the information

The analysis of the information will need (1) to determine whether the objectives of the task have been met (an accountability evaluation) and (2) to indicate ways in which the task might be improved (a development evaluation).

To deal with (1), a number of quantitative analyses will be carried out. First, the learners' level of comprehension of the directions will be determined by deriving a comprehension score for each learner from the matrix picture they completed. This will provide information to indicate to what extent the learners were successful in comprehending the directions (objective (1)). Second, the number of times each learner requested clarification will be tabulated. This information will be used to determine to what extent the objective (2) was met. This information, together with that provided by the uptake chart and achievement test, will also enable the evaluator to examine whether learners who did not actually request clarification themselves were able to gain from the clarifications sought by other students. Finally, the differences between each learner's score on the pre-test and the post-test will be calculated to provide an indication of whether the learners have learnt the names of kitchen objects which they did not know prior to the task. In addition, the learners' uptake charts will be inspected to identify which words the learners thought they had learnt from the task. This provides a means of investigating unpredictable learning. These analyses will be used to determine whether objective (3) has been met. Of course, these analyses do not show that the learners *retained* the words in the long term. For that, further achievement tests, administered weeks after the lesson, would be needed.

To investigate ways in which the task might be improved, both quantitative and qualitative analyses will be carried out. First, the number of learners who comprehended each direction will be calculated. This will provide an indication of which directions were very easy and which ones were very difficult. Second, quantitative information relating to the learners' own evaluation of the task will be provided, based on their answers to the questionnaire. This can be used to provide a general indication of the overall difficulty of the task and, importantly, the level of motivation generated by the task. Third, the two interviews with the teachers (the one before the task and the one after) will be analysed qualitatively to determine to what extent the teacher felt this particular task had 'worked'. Finally, the learner questionnaires and the teacher post-task interview will be analysed qualitatively to identify their views about any problems with the task.

Clearly, a task evaluation such as this is costly in time and effort. It is intended not as an example of the kind of evaluation that should always be undertaken but as an example of the kind of comprehensive evaluation that is possible and that might be undertaken occasionally. Teachers wishing to evaluate the tasks they use on a regular basis will need to undertake narrower evaluations, focusing on either accountability or development, and thereby, limiting the kinds of information that need to be collected and analysed.

Conclusion

This chapter has examined the case for carrying out evaluations of communicative tasks. It has been argued that evaluation in ELT has been primarily concerned with macro-evaluation (i.e. the evaluation of complete programmes or projects through the evaluations of materials, teachers and learners) and that attention also needs to be given to micro-evaluations. A task evaluation constitutes an example of a micro-evaluation. Such evaluations, it has been suggested, accord more with teachers' own ideas of what evaluation entails and can contribute to teacher development by promoting reflection on teaching.

As yet there are few published evaluations of language learning tasks, one of the few being Murphy 1993, which reports an evaluation of tasks used by 20 Malaysian teachers of English. There is, however, a substantial body of published research that has investigated the relationship between the design features of tasks and the language use that results from them (e.g. Long 1981; Pica and Doughty 1985; Gass and Varonis 1985; Duff 1986; Berwick 1990). It is pertinent to conclude this paper, then, by considering in what ways this published research differs from the kind of task evaluation I have proposed.

It is not possible to draw a clear distinction between research and evaluation. As Rea-Dickens states:

> Distinct boundaries do not operate between educational evaluation on the one hand and educational research on the other. (1994: 71)

It is not surprising, therefore, to find that task-directed research and task evaluation have much in common. For example, they share a common set of procedures for collecting data. All the procedures listed in Figure 4 can be used in task-directed research. There are, however, differences in the goals, design and outcomes of research and evaluation.

Task-directed research has been typically theory-driven. In particular, researchers have been concerned to discover what effect varying task features has on the negotiation of meaning that Long (1983) has hypothesised to facilitate second language acquisition. In contrast, task evaluation, like all educational evaluation, is motivated by the desire to contribute to the effectiveness of pedagogy. It is, as Norris (1990: 98) puts it, designed 'to elucidate a problem in action'. Of course, task-directed research may also be motivated in part by a desire to increase the effectiveness of pedagogy, but, its primary purpose has been theory development. It does not *directly* address pedagogic problems. Evaluation, as Rea-Dickens (1994) points out, is concerned with 'immediate practical use rather than ultimate use'.

This difference in goal is reflected in design differences. Task-directed research has sought to control extraneous variables in order to examine the effects of particular design features on output. In contrast, task evaluation accepts the inevitability of the uncontrolled variation that arises when tasks are used in real classrooms. It is concerned with the outcomes of task use in natural, not experimental or pseudo-experimental, environments.

Finally, there are differences in the outcomes of task-directed research and task evaluation. The former provides information that is used to frame general laws to account for how task variables affect language use. Subsequently, of course, these general laws can be applied to pedagogy but problems of application may arise because the information on which they are based was not derived from an actual teaching context. Task evaluation, in contrast, is directly concerned with the effectiveness and efficiency of particular tasks in particular contexts. As Glass and Worthen (1971; cited in Norris 1990) point out, the outcomes of research are judged in terms of reliability and validity while the outcomes of an evaluation are judged in terms of utility and credibility.

The distinction between task-directed research and task evaluation need not be as sharp as I have described, however. Much depends on the *kind* of research. As Norris (1990) points out there are obvious similarities between much contemporary educational research and evaluation. This similarity is, perhaps, more evident in research that is qualitative and exploratory in style than in research that is quantitative and experimental. Task evaluation, then, can be seen as a way of developing our understanding of the ways in which tasks work and, in so doing, of contributing to both acquisition theory and pedagogic practice. It can also be seen as one way of carrying out action research.

10 What do teachers really want from coursebooks?

Hitomi Masuhara

Introduction

Since the 1980s learner variables have attracted a lot of attention in the research (Ellis 1994; Larsen-Freeman and Long 1991) and the findings have influenced pedagogy (Nunan, 1988). Textbooks seem to reflect this change and their blurbs these days often emphasise that their product is designed to satisfy learners' needs and interests.

On the other hand, teacher variables have received very little attention in the literature and discussion about teachers has centred around their roles in methods (e.g. the teacher as facilitator of learning, catalyst, language model provider: Richards and Rodgers 1986). In contrast to the range and number of studies on learner variables, studies of teacher variables seem hard to find. An investigation of the psychology of teachers in relation to security and involvement could reveal a lot about teaching which enhances language learning. An investigation into teaching styles and preferences could reveal how teachers react to and implement teaching materials. However, teachers often seem to be treated in both language learning and teaching studies as passive beings who are expected to adapt flexibly to the roles determined by the objectives of the method and by the learning theory on which the method is based.

The teacher training literature seems to reflect this tendency in that teacher development means preparing teachers for change. Even when individualistic aspects of teachers' needs and wants are brought to light (e.g. diary studies, classroom observation), they are often discussed in terms of how teachers can be helped to manage the success of the method as measured in terms of learner achievement (Richards and Nunan 1990).

This lack of a body of studies on teacher variables seems alarming because teachers are in a crucial position in language teaching and learning and are often expected to be in charge of vital stages of curriculum development. Teachers can even be said to be the central figures in materials development – for they are the ones who select materials (or, at least, have some influence in the selection process), who actually teach the materials and who sometimes have to rewrite

239

materials. The students come and go and so do materials but a large number of teachers tend to stay.

In this chapter, therefore, I intend to demonstrate some potential benefits of studying teacher variables. Specifically I would like to focus on how teachers' needs and wants from coursebooks can be identified and catered for in the processes of materials development.

Whose needs analysis?

Needs analysis has featured prominently in the literature of language teaching in the last 20 years (e.g. Hutchinson and Waters 1987; Robinson 1980 and 1990; Richards 1990; Johnson 1989) but most of what has been written has focused on learners' communicative needs. Teachers' needs are treated as a part of situation analysis (i.e. general parameters of a language program), if given any significance at all.

How are 'needs' defined in the literature? They seem to be defined in terms of: a) ownership (whose needs are they?) b) kinds (what kinds of needs are identified) c) sources (what are the sources for the need?). Table 1 summarises the needs which are identified in the literature.

Table 1: List of needs identified in needs analysis literature

ownership	kind	source
LEARNERS' NEEDS	personal needs	age; sex; cultural background; interests; educational background
	learning needs	learning styles; previous language learning experiences; gap between the target level and the present level in terms of knowledge (e.g. target language and its culture); gap between the target level and the present level of proficiency in various competence areas (e.g. skills, strategies); learning goals and expectations for a course
	future professional needs	requirements for the future undertakings in terms of: knowledge of language knowledge of language use L2 competence

TEACHERS' NEEDS	personal needs	age; sex; cultural background; interests; educational background teachers' language proficiency
	professional needs	preferred teaching styles; teacher training experience; teaching experience
ADMINISTRATORS' NEEDS	institutional needs	sociopolitical needs; market forces; educational policy; constraints (e.g. time, budget, resources)

Differentiating needs as in Table 1 seems useful in demystifying some of the unclear areas in previous survey studies in materials development. Take an example of a coursebook which claims to have been tested to satisfy the needs and interests of the students. In order for the claims to be valid, the data must be taken directly from the learners and their related documents by objective means (e.g. documents of future job specifications, the learners' strengths and weaknesses in L2 performance observed in class, achievement tests, etc.) as well as by subjective ones (e.g. questionnaires and interviews directed to the learners). Subjective data is informative but tends to be variable and thus vulnerable in terms of reliability. Therefore the claims of satisfying learner needs deserves criticism if they are based solely or largely on the questionnaires given to teachers asking if the coursebook has satisfied their learners' needs and interests; the survey has only measured teachers' perception of learners' needs, which do not necessarily represent the actual learners' needs (Masuhara 1994).

A summary of needs, as in Table 1, is also indispensable in describing how each different category of needs could influence the others. When teachers are asked what their needs from a coursebook are, for example, their responses may quite possibly be influenced by:

1 teachers' perception of administrative needs:
   e.g. The school is under-resourced and a very strict syllabus is set which the teachers are expected to obey.
2 measured learners' needs:
   e.g. The teacher has administered a diagnostic test at the beginning of the course and is aware of the learners' communicative needs.
3 teachers' perception of learners' needs:

e.g. The teacher believes that Japanese students are quiet and shy and thus require special training in speaking.

4 teachers' wants:

e.g. Even though ELT experts recommend a learner-centred approach these days and the other colleagues of the language centre follow the trend, the teacher prefers and also secretly believes in the value of a teacher-centred approach for certain learners.

In order to avoid such confusion, it seems vital to extract, from Table 1, only the teachers' *own* needs and wants, and to design a more refined framework which can facilitate our investigation. Figures 1 (see page 243) and 2 (see page 245) are an attempt to provide such a framework for the studies of teachers' own needs and wants.

Teachers' needs (see Figure 1) would consist of two general areas: one deriving from personal traits such as their age, sex, cultural and educational background and the other from their professional traits such as areas and levels of expertise, length and types of teaching experience.

I have differentiated three kinds of needs according to how they are identified:

a) Self-perceived needs – the needs which are reported by the teacher. These are what teachers themselves can articulate.

b) Needs perceived by others – the needs of the teachers which they are not aware of and thus cannot articulate themselves and which are identified by others (e.g. colleagues, teacher-trainers, researchers) in response to qualitative data (e.g. observation of the teacher's teaching, analysing the tendency in interview and questionnaire responses of the teacher).

c) Objectively measured needs – the needs which are identified in objective studies in which quantified data is collected, analysed and interpreted by a third party who tries to be detached, unbiased and accurate.

It would increase the validity and reliability of the study if subjective data of self-perceived needs was cross-referenced or validated by other kinds of data (i.e. needs perceived by others, objectively measured needs). For example, a teacher reported his lack of confidence in classroom management. His lack of confidence was confirmed in a series of classroom observation by others. The quantitative study of teacher-learner interactions revealed that the teacher seemed to have trouble especially when co-ordinating groupwork to facilitate open discussion. Further analysis revealed that in fact the textbook presupposes much smaller classes than the size of the classes this teacher faces every day. Therefore the solution for this case may not be teacher

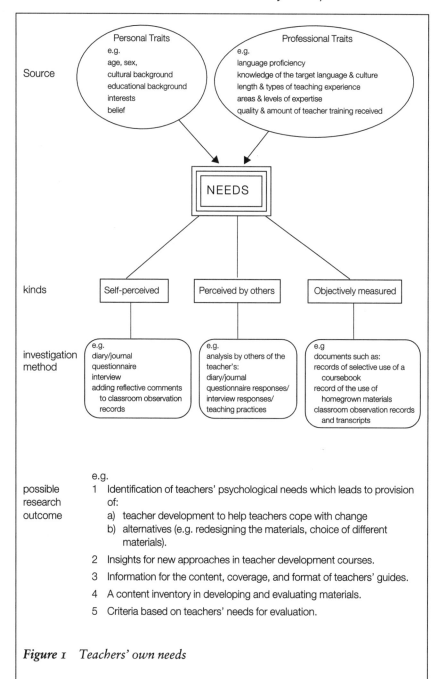

Figure 1   Teachers' own needs

training to help him to cope with the material but the provision of alternatives (e.g. a textbook which is appropriately designed for a large class situation).

The study of teachers' needs would provide useful information for the content, coverage and format for producing a teachers' guide. An inexperienced teacher might need more detailed instructions and suggestions on teaching methods in the teachers' guide compared to experienced teachers who might prefer a teachers' guide to supply a lot of different optional activities or interesting raw materials to be exploited.

The identification of needs could also make an interesting small project investigating which teachers' needs would predict the final selection of a coursebook, and which needs could be generalised, for instance, as an indicator for the popularity of a particular coursebook. Studies of teachers' needs may also provide a content coverage inventory in developing and evaluating materials.

In many cases, what may be identified by the teachers themselves and by a third party as their 'needs' could be their 'wants' as well. For example, an intermediate general English course may include an extensive reading class twice a week, based on the needs assessment of the learners and also on the pedagogical decisions by the administrator, but also because the teacher wants to promote an extensive reading approach because she firmly believes in the value of such an approach.

Teachers' wants (see Figure 2 on page 245), however, can be distinguished from needs when there is preference despite the fact it may not be necessary, obligatory, encouraged, or assumed. For instance I would call it a teachers' want if they prefer to employ a certain approach (e.g. teaching grammar with a discovery approach) even though it is not considered to be important or even suitable by their administrators and colleagues. Or teachers may want to set some creative writing activities in their speaking classes as consolidation even though it is not what is usually associated with oral classes. The study of teachers' wants in this sense may lead to discoveries of idiosyncratic aspects of teaching, of gaps in materials coverage, or even of innovative approaches to materials development. The study of teachers' wants may reveal that teachers' commitment and involvement due to their preference for materials and methods are keys to effective language learning. Figure 2 summarises the source and kinds of teachers' wants and possible research methods and outcomes.

The theoretical framework which Figures 1 and 2 try to provide should help untangle a seemingly unreconcilable past debate between the supporters and sceptics of coursebooks. Teachers' needs and wants from coursebooks have often featured on both sides of the debate as evidence. For example, Sheldon (1988) described quite persuasively the

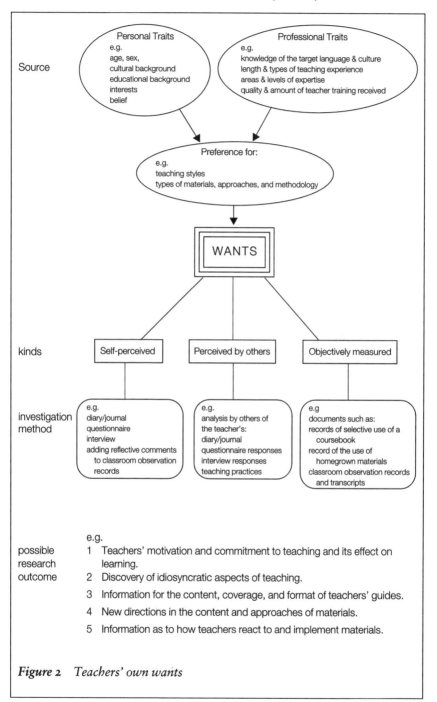

Figure 2   Teachers' own wants

teachers' needs for more theoretically and practically sound course-books and their frustration in not getting them. And he welcomed, as one future option of 'published' core materials, computer programs, which teachers could modify and supplement as required according to their local and on-the-spot needs. Hutchinson and Torres (1994), on the other hand, argued for the benefit of structured coursebooks, quoting the result of Torres' survey showing teachers' needs for security in classroom management. Reading both articles, the readers are left unsettled as to which exactly is the teachers' need for future course-books, a flexible coursebook which presupposes exploitation by the users or a structured and visible coursebook which is foolproof? The needs of teachers reported by Sheldon seem very different from those claimed by Torres. Solutions based solely on one claim would not solve the problems of teachers reflected by the other claim.

The theoretical framework (see Figure 1) is useful in putting each claim in perspective. When examined against the framework, the force of both claims starts to reduce. Firstly, in both cases teachers' needs are assumed and not defined. Secondly, the source and methods of how they identified the particular teachers' needs are not made explicit. For instance, Sheldon (1988) uses anecdotes to illustrate teachers' needs without specifying who they are or how the sampling was done. Hutchinson and Torres (1994) do base their claims on a questionnaire survey, but the non-representativeness of the sample seems to limit the generalisability of their arguments.

The framework (see Figure 1) is also helpful in locating where the source of conflict lies. Apparent contradiction between Sheldon and Hutchinson and Torres seems to me to derive, in fact, from the same root. In this case, the teachers' confidence and professional expertise influenced their perception of what they need from coursebooks. There-fore the real issue here is the necessity to explore how to cater for different needs which derive from varying degrees of teachers' profes-sional ability and confidence.

Teachers – an endangered species

Exploring teachers' needs and wants is crucial when the role division between the materials producers (e.g. professional materials writers and publishers) and the users (e.g. teachers, educational administrators and learners) seems to be becoming more and more evident. Remarkable technical advancement has brought sophistication and a great prolifer-ation of ESL/EFL coursebooks but it has also created a wider role division between materials producers and materials users. The sheer

246

scale and amount of time, energy and different expertise required in contemporary coursebook production seems to be alienating teachers as potential materials writers, because they often have a heavy workload in often under-resourced teaching contexts. The teachers' homegrown materials may be more finely tuned to the local classroom needs with valid methodological awareness but the colourful or glossy appearance of commercial coursebooks may be more eye-catching and may even seem to the learners to have more face validity.

The division between the producers and users has also affected the coherent linear sequence of curriculum development/course design processes to the level that concerns are being expressed that the materials could carry the threat of deskilling teachers by reducing the teachers' role.

Various different models of the process of course design (e.g. Johnson 1989; Dubin and Olshtain 1986; Richards 1990) suggest that materials design or selection should come at a later stage of the process. The sequence of course design recommended by experts may be summarised as the linear Model X in Figure 3.

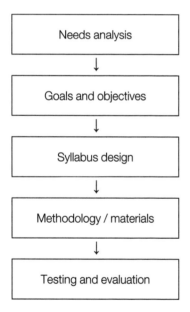

Figure 3 *Model X – course design procedures*

This Model X shows how the teaching contexts and the learners' needs provide a framework for the objectives and then, the decisions concerning the best methods and materials should be made accordingly.

Ideally teachers should be involved as major members of curriculum development teams to make the whole sequence coherent (as in Alderson and Scott 1992; Tomlinson 1995b).

Many practitioners, however, may find that this theoretical Model X does not represent the actual sequence that they experience in their ELT institutions all over the world. Instead, a more familiar sequence may be described in the following manner.

Firstly, the teachers and administrators draw up a very general framework of a particular class and learners. In this framework, the characteristics of the learners are defined in terms of the learners' preference for a course and the levels of their proficiency based on the tests administered at the beginning of the course. The goal of teaching is usually represented in the name of the course (e.g. First Certificate Preparation Course, Oral Communication I).

Materials selection holds an assertive position in the second stage in the sequence; the teachers and administrator select from commercially available coursebooks the one suitable for the class defined in the initial stage. The stages such as needs analysis, objectives specification, syllabus design, and selection of methodology which Model X presupposes to happen prior to materials selection are assumed to have been taken care of by the producers (e.g. materials writers and publishers). In fact producers provide prospective selectors (e.g. administrators and teachers) with information as to the target learners, objectives and methodology in the blurbs or in the introductions of the books. They may also provide a syllabus map indicating how units are integrated into a coherent course. This sequence of course design introduced above may be summarised as Model Y (see Figure 4 on page 249).

By contrasting Model Y with Model X it becomes apparent how crucial stages of the course design have been removed from the hands of the teachers and administrators to those of materials producers.

The careful analysis of learning and teaching situations recommended by the experts as a prerequisite in Model X may not seem appropriate to the teachers and administrators operating in the system represented in Model Y; loose specification of the learners' level and purpose is sufficient in selecting a coursebook from a limited number of available pre-designed materials.

The writers and publishers of a textbook may or may not have gone through the stages of needs analysis, specifications of the goals and objectives, designing the syllabus, and choosing the methodology but the teachers and administrators are even less able to oversee these processes than before, except through the selection of and the flexible use of the materials. In such cases, the materials writer and the publisher who produced the materials have more direct control of the course design

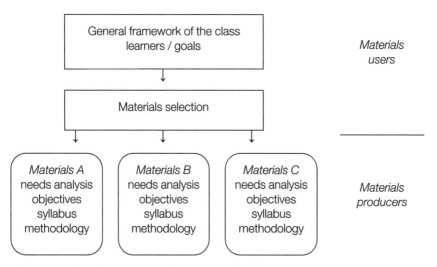

Figure 4   *Model Y – Course design procedures in practice*

processes than the teachers. The degree of dominance depends on how much and how closely the teachers choose to follow the coursebook or how much teachers take initiative in making flexible use of the materials.

In fact, this phenomenon of the coursebook possibly diminishing teachers has featured in the recent debate on whether the textbook could cause teachers to be over-dependent on books or not. Littlejohn (1992: 84) in his PhD thesis, reported in Hutchinson and Torres (1994: 315), expressed such concern by saying that 'the precise instructions which the materials give reduce the teacher's role to one of managing or overseeing a preplanned classroom event'. This concern is further supported from the perspective of teacher development by Richards (1993a, 1993b).

These views seem to me to testify to the negative manifestation of the conflicts inherent in the system depicted in Model Y above. It seems surprising that the theorisation of such widely practised procedures represented in Model Y does not seem to have been attempted, not to speak of the discussions on how best the procedures can be made use of without producing negative effects.

On a more positive note, the reversal phenomenon and the role divisions may be even described to be sensible and realistic procedures **provided** teachers' needs and wants are reflected in materials, that theoretical validity is pursued by the producers, and that the teachers have the overall control in the teaching. The crucial question is how can teachers' needs and wants be tapped and catered for in the materials production process. If the two contemporary phenomena of role division and reversal of the course design sequence were to stay and the final responsibility for successful teaching is still attributed to teachers, then efficient and effective systems must be established in order to empower teachers.

Empowerment of teachers

Four areas are recognised in which teachers' needs and wants could be reflected in the development and use of materials. Under each heading I have tried to acknowledge some of the past ideas and I have added suggestions of my own.

Quality assessment of published coursebooks

a) The need for objective measurements of the quality of published coursebooks.
   Sheldon (1988) has advocated several ways of realising this. They include:
   – desirability of introducing a *Which?* magazine for ELT coursebooks (Brumfit 1980: 30).
   – improvement and innovation in *ELTJ* reviews in order to enhance their validity, usefulness, and availability e.g. collaborative teachers' and learners' reviews.
b) Stricter and more systematic material selection procedures.
   Many checklists are now available which are designed to enable systematic selection of materials (e.g. Breen and Candlin 1987; Cunningsworth 1984; Hutchinson and Waters 1987; McDonough and Shaw 1993; Sheldon 1987; Sheldon 1988; Skierso 1991).
   It would be useful, I think, to have a survey review comparing these checklists. It seems to me that many checklists so far are based on criteria which derive from experts' intuitions, paying more attention to the theoretical construct of materials. It may also be valuable to extract criteria from empirical evaluation against learners' and teachers' needs.
c) Establishing methods and feedback routes of users' evaluation.
   Rea-Dickins (1994) summarises three kinds of evaluation:
   – pre-use evaluation which can be done prior to the use of a coursebook (for the purpose of checking the construct validity and the match with the needs),
   – in-use evaluation
   – post-use evaluation, measured in terms of learners' performance.
   She (like Daoud and Celce-Murcia, (1979) and Rea-Dickins and Germaine (1992)) advocates more attention being paid to in-use and

post-use evaluation (see Chapter 9 by Rod Ellis in this book for suggestions of how to do this).

It seems to me to be a pity that currently there are virtually no channels through which systematic whilst- and post-evaluation of published materials can be fed back to the materials producers to be reflected in future production.

I also believe that more whilst- and post-use evaluation should be published not only as articles but also as *ELTJ* reviews. In this sense, the post-use reviews in *MET* (*Modern English Teacher*) should be recognised for their pioneering efforts.

d) Establishing systems for teachers' needs and wants to be reflected in the production processes (see section below – *Opportunities for change* – for more discussion).

e) Wider perspectives in teacher development.

Inclusion in teaching development courses of components of materials evaluation, adaptation, and writing.

Also inclusions of research methodology training in postgraduate courses in TEFL/TESL and applied linguistics.

I also feel that institutions could make more use of staff meetings to provide opportunities for teacher development (see section below – *Opportunities for change* – for more discussion).

f) More acknowledgement of the teachers' non-teaching expertise and workload.

Johnson (1989) summarised in the table below stages, decision-making roles and products in curriculum development.

Table 2

Developmental stages	Decision-making roles	Products
1 curriculum planning	policy makers	policy document
2 specification: ends	needs analysts	syllabus
means	methodologists	
3 programme	materials writers	teaching materials
implementation	teacher trainers	teacher-training programme
4 classroom	teacher	teaching acts
implementation	learner	learning acts

In reality, however, such group cooperation of 'experts' may rarely happen except under highly privileged circumstances. In fact, a teacher may be expected to function as a course designer, needs analyst, methodologist and materials writer. Often these non-teaching activities seem to be considered as part of teachers' duties without them being properly appreciated or acknowledged. More systematic materials selection, for example, could really be achieved if teachers were given the time, a place and encouragement. Thus, it seems vital to encourage institutional support for all the above suggestions to be materialised.

Opportunities for change

Judging from the fact that the 'for and against coursebooks' debate recurs and persists, regular and successful communication between materials producers and users does not seem to be taking place. I, therefore, intend to go through the process of materials production and use, acknowledging current practice and suggesting some new angles in order to reflect teachers' needs and wants.

Table 3: Opportunities for reflecting teachers' needs and wants – production stage

stages of production	agent	kinds of investigation	methods
1 Planning	publisher in-house investigator materials writer(s) outside investigator	needs analysis market research	questionnaires interviews classroom observation
2 Drafting	materials writer(s) publisher	–	–
3 Evaluation	'readers' publisher	reading of the materials	criterion-referenced evaluation
4 Piloting	publisher teachers learners	trialling	questionnaires interviews classroom observation testing

	material writer(s)		
5 Production	publisher	consultation	–
	designer		
6 Post-production	reviewers	book reviews	evaluating
	researcher	sales record	analysing data
	analyst		

For more details as to current practice, readers may like to refer to publications by publishers on their needs analysis, market research and materials trialling. My efforts to locate such literature, however, has met with a lot of difficulty. Personal communication with those involved in past studies revealed that there is a considerable amount of study conducted by individual publishers but the actual reports often remain 'for-your-eyes only' for the insiders. More publications from the materials producers' side (as in the account of piloting by Peter Donovan in Chapter 7 of this book) would be a great step forward in promoting open and effective communication between the producers and users.

It is interesting to note that, in my personal communications, certain reservation and scepticism toward the value of questionnaire surveys was expressed by representatives of major publishers on the grounds that the teachers: a) do not seem to have many opinions, b) do not do what they say, c) are not cooperative in returning the questionnaires.

I think that the research methodology literature could give more detailed and user-friendly accounts of the strengths and limitations of questionnaire surveys (and of other research methods for that matter). In a survey, the questionnaire appears to be an obvious method to be employed: it is comparatively economical in terms of cost, time and personnel, and the ease of the control of the scale. Also it is potentially informative if it is used well.

However, less understood is the fact that getting generalisable results out of a questionnaire requires very careful and systematic thinking and monitoring. Research methodology books (e.g. Seliger and Shohamy 1989) warn that expertise is called for in each stage from its construct, distribution, administration, collection and analyses to the interpretation of its results.

In the construction stage, for instance, the designer must have clear objectives and strive to write precise and specific questions which will elicit informative responses. A vague question such as 'How do you feel about the format of the teachers' book?' would only bring forth a non-informative vague answer. Or a question like 'Would you like the coursebook to include systematic coverage of a learner training syllabus?' may puzzle some respondents who have little idea of what a 'learner training syllabus' is. Even if a respondent had general knowledge of learner training, 'systematic coverage' could mean many things.

The most difficult part of a questionnaire survey may be in fact obtaining a sufficient number of representative responses back. Unless the teacher has a stake in it, answering questionnaires is often perceived as a tedious extra chore which will at best bring very little reward and thus goes fairly low in the long priority lists of things to do. If the questionnaire is designed to elicit teachers' views about fundamental issues, answering such questions requires a lot of effort from the respondent: to articulate and to communicate complex thoughts is demanding in itself, even more so if you are asked to respond straight away after glancing at a question cold. As for providing innovative ideas for future coursebooks, the task may seem too much, especially without any guarantee of the idea being attributed to those who proposed it or of it being realised in the near future. In this sense, the questionnaire may not be the best means if we want feedback on delicate issues such as teachers' needs and wants and the future directions of coursebooks.

What has been lacking, it seems to me, is our awareness that probing teachers' needs and wants should be a major undertaking in the exploration of new directions. And this requires more creative thinking and new approaches; in order for the teachers to be willing to be involved, then the procedures in themselves should be intrinsically rewarding for them. So far, the feedback and piloting seem to me to have often been done as acts of, more or less, goodwill, and therefore, I suspect, accompanied an attitude of the less the burden, the better. I would like to put forward some other activities as possible alternatives or useful additions.

New opportunities: publishers' sponsored events involving groups of teachers

Example A: Evaluation meetings
Representative samples of teachers are invited to half a day lunch and coffee meeting with all expenses paid plus some payment on top if possible, in which:

a) the newest commercially available coursebooks are presented (better still, if demonstrated in a mock classroom situation)
b) what the teachers consider to be good and useful activities are identified
c) discussions as to why they are so are conducted with monitors and a facilitator (e.g. materials writer) organising the session.

Many variations of this kind are possible, depending on the objectives. For example, using one coursebook, teachers could be invited to select useful activities from the book. Then discussion could be held on why they are perceived as useful. Or teachers could focus on suggesting ways of improving the activities to suit their needs and wants. This would be especially suitable at an early stage of materials production to give indications to the materials writers as to what kinds of materials and approaches are needed.

Example B: 'Take your pick' sampling meetings
The materials writer produces three kinds of prospective mini-coursebooks (black and white copies of a few units, for instance, would be enough) in which a controversial point of choice is embodied. For example, three mini-coursebooks are all text-based with the same text but each one employs a different approach. One is structure-based, the second is explicit strategy training oriented and the third aims at implicit strategy training through tasks which first aim at global understanding then become language awareness activities.

Representative samples of teachers are invited to a half-day lunch and coffee meeting with all expenses paid plus some payment on top if possible, in which these three samples are presented (ideally demonstrated) and evaluation discussion on issues is conducted with monitors and a facilitator (e.g. materials writer) organising the session.

This would also be suitable at an early stage of materials production to give indications to the materials writers what kinds of materials and approaches are needed.

Example C: Users as producers (based roughly on the Namibian Textbook Project)
Representative and recommended samples from the target population of the teachers are 'contracted' for a certain period of time. During this period, brainstorming for the ideal coursebook they need (some stimulating workshops for ideas and approaches would be beneficial), syllabus design and raw materials searching, writing the units, giving feedback between groups and by facilitator, and editing are carried out under the supervision of a co-ordinator/facilitator. The materials are then taken back to their schools and tried out and the results inform the revision process. This option seems preferable to other suggestions in a sense that:

a) it provides solutions to many of the problems caused by the role divisions (e.g. materials not meeting the local needs, teachers not understanding the materials writers' approach).

b) the materials themselves address the teachers' needs and wants and the possible ways of satisfying them without actually having to go through intricate research procedures to identify them.

For those who are interested in this option, I would recommend Tomlinson (1995b) for a suggestion of how this system can successfully be materialised.

In all three examples, the criteria for success would be as follows:

- Teachers' work is acknowledged and time, place and reward are properly supplied.
- There is a substantial prospect that in the near future the teachers' efforts could result in lessening the frustration of not having the kinds of coursebook they want.
- It gives teachers opportunities to meet other teachers and discuss issues which are relevant and useful to their own development.
- The discussions are never held cold; there are interesting and useful stimuli first which are directly relevant to everyday teaching or are thought-provoking for future self-development.
- When asked an opinion, there are concrete examples in front of the teachers which they can react to.
- Before being asked for choice, options are provided and demonstrated.
- There is some possibility of career advancement and of social acknowledgement.
- The discussion analysing the reasons for the choice must only be held *after* the teachers have made selections. This is crucial: the facilitator/ organiser should be aware that he/she is probing for teachers' unarticulated needs and wants as well as teachers' self-perceived ones which are reported by teachers themselves in the discussion. Furthermore, provided that enough such meetings are held, the characteristics of popular principles or approaches may emerge by quantifying the teachers' choice through tallying the kinds of books or the kinds of activities chosen by the teachers – thus substantiating the study with more objective data.

What sort of opportunities, then, are there for reflecting the teachers' needs and wants through the stages of materials use? Table 4 illustrates the stages and various possibilities for reflecting the teachers' needs and wants.

I have tried to list some new approaches as well as those which are currently practised. Some of the new approaches will be exemplified in more detail.

Table 4: Opportunities for reflecting teachers' needs and wants – stages of use

stages of use	agent	kinds of investigation	methods
pre-use (materials selection)	teachers director of studies	collecting information about the books	ELT reviews reputation colleagues' opinion based on experience of use
		impressionistic pre-use evaluation	looking through the books for: overall impression syllabus topics/subjects illustrations
		systematic pre-use evaluation	a. making use of self-generated criteria b. making use of experts' checklists
whilst-use	teachers director of studies publishers	analysis of subjective data by the teacher and by others	the teacher's diary/journal
		quantitative and qualitative analysis	classroom observation data
		analysis of objective data	keeping records of: a. selective use of units and parts of units b. supplementary use of homegrown materials c. adaptation of the coursebook
after-use	teachers director of studies publishers	impressionistic post-use evaluation	questionnaire interview diary/journal
		systematic post-use evaluation	evaluation using evaluation sheet validation of pre-use evaluation record

New opportunities: institution-based evaluation

Example A: Pre-use evaluation of materials being timetabled as a staff meeting in teaching hours

It seems to me materials selection and materials evaluation should be given far more significance and a system should be set up with institutional support. For instance, in materials selection, a staff meeting could be held and teachers who will be in charge of certain courses or those who have been involved in the past could form groups. Firstly each group member reflects and lists criteria he/she thinks are important for the prospective course. Teachers may find it useful to take three steps in identifying the needs: firstly just listing the needs and wants, secondly categorising them (e.g. administrative needs, learners' needs and teachers' needs and wants), and lastly prioritising them. Then the criteria could be gathered and compared firstly in the group in order to discuss issues and problems and then each group could report to the whole group the most important issues for further discussion. Then groups could pick up candidates from the available collection of textbooks and new sample copies and start evaluating them against the criteria. The list of criteria produced can be filed as the criteria for post-use evaluation and also for similar future materials selection sessions in staff meetings.

Example B: Keeping records of use

It would make a very interesting study to keep records of which parts of a coursebook are used and which are not. Publishers may like to commission this kind of project and reward the participants for their extra work. Keeping records should be fairly simple if the teachers are asked to tick the parts used (with brief comments if possible). Teachers' meetings can be held to reflect and analyse why some parts of the same book get used and others discarded. Such study would be likely to reveal the hidden needs and wants of teachers. This exercise would offer a new angle for piloting based on objective data.

In the same way, the study of the production and use of supplementary home-grown materials may offer insights and suggest new directions for future materials. An indicator memo can be attached to the top of home-grown materials when produced. On the indicator the purpose, the target learners and the relationship with the main coursebook can be specified and kept in files. Such collections can then be analysed in terms of when, why and how teachers supplement the main coursebook. Another option may be a record of how teachers exploit the coursebook.

Example C: Post-use – validating the selection criteria at a staff meeting
It seems to me to be very productive to hold a post-use evaluation meeting. In such a meeting, the pre-use selection criteria which are produced prior to the course can be validated. The re-evaluation of the materials can be attached to the coursebook for later use and as a basis for publication of collaboratory post-use reviews in English teaching journals.

Publishers may benefit from establishing some systems under which this kind of post-use evaluation of coursebooks can be fed back to the materials writers and editors.

In all three examples, the criteria for success would be as follows:

- Materials selection and evaluation is acknowledged as an important aspect of teaching and teacher development. Therefore time and place is properly secured within teaching hours.
- It gives teachers' opportunities to discuss issues with colleagues, to share experience and expertise and to build teachers' resources in collaboration, thus reducing the amount of individual work.
- There is for teachers a substantial prospect of future benefit of:
  a) reducing the suffering from having chosen a wrong coursebook as a result of a rushed solitary decision.
  b) publications of materials evaluation and reviews since systematic group evaluation could give more depth and this could enhance the careers of those as a result of publication.
  c) having a good, accessible and user-friendly collection of evaluation comments for future reference.
- If institutions support and acknowledge such activities as those above, they may benefit from the positive gains of having a well-analysed bank of coursebooks and home-grown materials, (possibly) more useful contacts with publishers, and from more publicity for the name of the institute to be acknowledged in ELT journals.

Conclusion

To conclude, may I suggest to the reader a short activity designed to identify your own needs and wants from coursebooks? The activity is primarily meant for teachers. Even if you are not a teacher, say a materials writer, publisher or teacher trainer, you still might like to try it, modifying the activity to suit you. As a result you may decide to write an article on materials writers'/publishers'/teacher trainers' needs and wants.

On a piece of paper, specify a particular teaching context which is most relevant and important for you. Then list all the needs and wants you can think of. Then identify each of them according to the following categories:

1 administrator's needs
2 your perception of learners' needs
3 measured learners' needs
4 your own self-perceived needs
5 your own self-perceived wants

Then focus on 4 and 5 to see why they are so and think of how your needs and wants can be realised in your teaching, in your involvement with future teacher training, and in materials development.

I hope you find this activity rewarding.

Comments on Part C

Brian Tomlinson

The obvious link between the chapters in Section 3 is their insistence on the need for more feedback (and for more systematic feedback) from materials users to materials producers. All too often major decisions are made about the content, approach, procedures and design of learning materials based on assumptions of user needs and wants and on impressions of what 'works' in the classroom. Often these assumptions and impressions are misinformed or unrepresentative and mistakes are made which contribute to dissatisfaction and failure. One of the things that always amazes me is that, as I travel around the world meeting teachers at conferences and workshops, the impression I am given is that most teachers are dissatisfied with the materials available to them. Yet publishers and ministries tell me that their impression is that the teachers are basically satisfied with these same materials. I suspect that both impressions are wrong because they are based on unrepresentative samples of teachers and because of the ways in which the impressions were gained. Many teachers who come to conferences and workshops are untypically knowledgeable, enthusiastic and discerning. If given a chance to express their views to somebody like myself, who does not represent a publisher or authority and who is keen on the development of innovative materials, they are more likely to tell me what they do not like about their materials than what they do like. On the other hand, teachers when being interviewed by publishers or officials (or even when responding to their questionnaires) are more likely to be polite and/or cautious and to incline more towards the positive in their responses. Both my impressions and those of the 'authorities' are often not only misleading but they are also too crude to be informative. What we need is fine tuned information about the outcome of materials use in terms of what the teachers and learners actually did, what they felt about what they did and what the consequences were of what they did. As all the chapters in this section have pointed out, whilst-use and post-use evaluations can be extremely valuable but they are difficult to carry out as they require not only expertise but great investment of teacher energy and time. We can observe materials being used, we can test learners before and after use of materials and we can administer questionnaires to the users of materials. But it is the teachers who could tell us the most. They use materials every working day and they could participate in intensive and longitudinal studies of materials in use. But they would need to be trained and rewarded and to be supported by valid and reliable instruments of evaluation if they were to be valuably informative. This could be achieved if publishers, ministries of education and university departments of applied linguistics formed consortia to fund and develop research projects which aimed to record the actual outcomes of particular sets of learning materials. MATSDA would be more than willing to help set up such consortia and we intend to make a small start in this direction by holding a materials evaluation conference at which the participants will be helped to develop instruments for whilst-use evaluation and then to use these instruments in longitudinal studies of the materials they are using. The results of these studies will be reported in the MATSDA journal, *FOLIO*, and could form a basis for further, more extended studies and even for use by such consortia as suggested above.

One of the major problems of getting user feedback is that normally the users are not given choices to consider. They are asked to give their responses to a particular set of materials and therefore their feedback can only give information about the effectiveness and not the efficiency of the materials (see Chapter 9 by Rod Ellis in this book). It can only tell us about their evaluation of that set of materials in relation to their objectives and experience; it does not tell us about the relative value of the materials compared to other sets or types of materials. Also teachers can only express their needs and wants in relation to what they have experienced; they cannot be expected to be aware of all the materials options which could cater for their needs and wants. What I would like to see is a development of what Hitomi Masuhara suggests in Chapter 10 when she proposes meetings of teachers in which they give their responses to alternative versions of the same base materials. I would like to see teachers presented with a number of alternative versions of materials for pre-use evaluation. Each teacher would select two of the versions and then teach them to two comparable classes so as to be able to carry out whilst- and post-use evaluations of the materials. The teachers could then produce an efficiency evaluation comparing their two versions of the materials. Such a project could only be feasible if the teachers were rewarded or if the evaluations were carried out as part of the research component of a post-graduate degree. How about a number of universities cooperating in research which involves a group of PhD candidates developing such a project? Or how about universities including a teaching practice component on their MA in applied linguistics/TEFL courses so as to facilitate such research? In MATSDA we intend to make a contribution by including comparative evaluation as a component of the MATSDA materials evaluation conference mentioned above. Maybe we can then follow this up by helping some of the participants to carry out and write up whilst-use efficiency evaluations of comparable materials after the conference.

Another link between the chapters in this section is a plea for evaluation to focus on what actually happens as outcomes of material use rather than on the reactions of the teachers and the learners to the materials. Too often judgements about materials are based on considerations of interest and enjoyment. These are important factors in achieving learner engagement but it is possible for learners to enjoy using materials without learning very much from them and it is also possible to learn a lot from materials which are not particularly interesting or enjoyable to use. What we need to know is did the teacher and the learners do what the materials intended, were the learning objectives achieved and did unintentional learning take place? It is easy enough to produce a narrative of observable behavioural outcomes (by, for example, videoing lessons as a matter of routine); it is possible to work out a narrative of mental activity during the lesson (through, for example, speak aloud protocols, reflection tasks, questionnaires and interviews); it is possible to gain information about short-term learning gains (through administering pre- and post-use tests) but it is very difficult to find out what we really want to know about the long-term learning gains which are attributable to the materials. This could be done on a macro-scale by finding (or better still assembling) two classes which are comparable in level and motivation, which are taught by the same teacher and which have no contact with the target language outside the classroom. The two classes could be administered a series of pre-tests which focus on the performance objectives which two comparable sets of materials have in common. The two classes could then be taught with each class using a different set of comparable but crucially differentiated materials. At the end (or preferably after the end) of the course the two classes could be administered post-use tests and the differences in progress between the two classes could be measured.

Another, more manageable, procedure would be for the research to focus on the comparative progress towards a very specific and measurable objective made by two comparable classes using different materials. This could be done with learners living in the target language culture if both classes had equal access to relevant experience outside the classroom; or if no relevant experience was available to any of the learners. Examples of such areas of focus could be increase in the mean length of utterance in conversation, increase in the range of vocabulary in written story telling, increase in the range and appropriacy of exponents of a particular function, increase in the range and appropriacy of tense use in unplanned discourse.

In short we need much more research into the effects of types of materials if we are to contribute to the development of materials which not only attract and impress but which actually facilitate learning too.

11 Seeing what they mean: helping L2 readers to visualise

Brian Tomlinson

Introduction

There is currently much concern about the apparent mismatch between what learners are asked to do in published textbooks and the reality of language use; see, for example, the chapters in Part A of this book by Gwyneth Fox, by Jane Willis and by Ron Carter, Rebecca Hughes and Mike McCarthy. Many think that there is also a mismatch between some of the pedagogic procedures of current textbooks and what second language acquisition researchers have discovered about the process of learning a second or foreign language (see, for example, the Introduction to this book by Brian Tomlinson and Chapter 8 by Andrew Littlejohn). One type of textbook which seems to be largely exempt from such criticisms of mismatch is that which attempts to help learners to develop reading skills in an L2.

It seems to be accepted that current textbook activities designed to develop reading skills do to a large extent mirror the actual process of reading authentic texts. These activities are based on generally accepted models of the reading process which stress the active role of the reader in relating world knowledge to information in the text, the parallel interaction between low level decoding of words and high level processing of concepts and the way in which effective readers vary their reading techniques according to their purposes for reading. However it is arguable that there is one significant reading strategy which has been almost entirely neglected by both general EFL coursebooks and by EFL reading skills books too. That is the strategy of visualisation, the converting of words on the page into pictures in the mind. In a recent analysis of EFL textbooks published in the '90s I found no evidence at all of any systematic attempt to help L2 learners to develop visualisation skills except in *Openings* (Tomlinson 1994c) and *Use Your English* (Tomlinson and Masuhara 1994).

The following chapter focuses on the neglected reading strategy of visualisation as an example of how a combination of classroom experience, of informed intuition and of research can lead to the development of innovative materials which can help learners to learn more. It reports on how I have followed up intuitions about the salience of visualisation in L1 reading and its neglect in L2 reading by studying research on imaging, by conducting a series of experiments and by writing materials aiming to promote visualisation in L2 reading.

Do L1 readers typically visualise?

In my experiments a total of over a hundred proficient readers were asked to read a descriptive or narrative text. Some were asked to read a poem ('River Station Plaza' by Sheldon Flory 1990), some read an extract from *Closing Time* by Joseph Heller (1994) and some read the opening page and a half of *Brazil* by John Updike (1994). Ninety-six per cent of these readers reported that they visualised the content of the texts as they read them and all 23 proficient readers in an experiment at the University of Luton claimed that they saw pictures in their minds as they read the opening of *Brazil*. Stevick reports a proportion of 95 per cent of visualisers from his experiments with L1 listeners and readers and he states that: 'Words that have come into our heads from reading or listening commonly leave us with pictures, sounds and feelings in our minds' (1986). Other researchers have come to similar conclusions about the phenomenon of visualisation whilst reading in the L1. For example, Brewer (1988) showed that readers have 'phenomenal experience pre-, whilst-, and post-reading' and also that, 'descriptive texts and narrative texts . . . tend to produce imagery during reading'. Similar claims about the use of visualisation as an L1 reading strategy have been made by Bugelski (1969), Pylyshin (1973), Mowrer (1977), Paivio (1979) and Thompson (1987).

Although it seems that most people use visualisation to help them to read and to think in the L1, not all visualisers use visual imagery with the same vividness, frequency and effect; they can be placed on a cline from very low imagers to very high (or eidetic) imagers. For example, 95 per cent of L1 respondents to a questionnaire I gave to readers of an extract from *Brazzaville Beach* (Boyd 1990) reported visualising whilst reading and 100 per cent of proficient readers who were asked to read the first one and a half pages of *Brazil* reported visualising. But in both experiments some of the respondents reported only partial, rather vague visualisation whilst others reported differing degrees of detail and vividness. For example, some of those who read the extract from *Brazzaville Beach* saw the narrator (who was not described in the text) in clear detail, some saw her vaguely, and some did not see her at all. In another experiment 100 per cent of respondents to my questionnaire on the reading of an extract from *Closing Time* reported visualising but about 25 per cent of them only reported visualising occasionally. It also seems that visualisers vary in the way they respond to different texts in different circumstances, and that some of the facts which determine vividness of visualisation are motivation, topic familiarity, topic interest and relevance to previous experience. For example, some of those respondents who reported only occasional visualisation of the extract from *Closing Time* also reported lack of interest in the text and many of the respondents visualised most vividly those parts of the extract which coincided with their own interests and experiences. Another important factor is the perceived relevance of visualisation as a strategy for reading a particular text at a particular time; texts and tasks do not always require the use of visualisation, and when it is used it is normally because it is perceived as potentially rewarding.

The surprising thing is that despite the mass of data affirming the prevalence of visualisation in L1 reading (and especially in the reading of narrative and descriptive texts) most books on the reading process make little or no mention of the fact that L1 readers typically visualise before, whilst and after reading. Grellet 1982, Barnett 1989, Carr and Levy 1990 and Nuttall 1995 are examples of popular books on the reading process which do not deal with the reading strategy of visualisation.

It would seem that most L1 readers typically visualise when reading descriptive or narrative texts but do so with differing degrees of vividness. It would also seem that this phenomenon is not considered to be significant in books on the reading process.

Is visualisation functional in L1 reading?

Eysenk and Keane (1990) ask whether visual imagery has 'functional significance' or whether it is a 'mere epithenomenon'. Intuitions, introspections and research lead me to agree with Esrock when she asserts that, 'the reader's visual imagery can have unique cognitive and affective consequences that heighten the readers' experience' (1994). They also suggest to me that for many L1 readers visualisation plays a major role in helping them to achieve involvement, comprehension, retention and recall.

Many claims have been made for the functional significance of visualisation in L1 reading. It is claimed, for example, that L1 visualisation can help:

- whilst-reading retention of concepts and propositions originally represented by words which can remain in memory for no more than ten seconds (Swaffer 1988);
- post-reading retention of the content of a text (Kulhavy and Swenson 1975);
- 'recall by furnishing the learner with a meaningful representation of the material being studied' (Kulhavy and Swenson *op. cit.*; see also Thompson 1987 who states that 'there is evidence that persons with high imagery ability are able to recall . . . more . . . from texts than low imagers');
- to increase comprehension of a text (Anderson and Kulhavy 1972; Knight, Padron and Waxman 1985);
- to achieve interaction between old information (represented by images activated by the reader's schemata or knowledge of the world) and new information (instantiated from data in the text) (Enkvist 1981);
- to achieve the default inferencing needed to complete the gaps created by what Eysenk and Keane (1990) call 'the writer's logical implications and pragmatic implications';
- 'to achieve an aesthetic experience of the literary work' through 'concretization', that is through 'fleshing out the text' to complete the fictional representation' (Ingarden 1973);
- to achieve tolerance of ambiguity by enabling the reader to make hypotheses which can be retained visually until they are confirmed or revised as new information becomes available from the text (Tomlinson 1993);
- 'to create images endowed with a descriptive power capable of representing more upper levels of discourse, such as a paragraph, or a chapter, or a general theme' (Esrock *op. cit.*);
- to achieve affective impact (Esrock *op. cit.*);
- to personalise a text and make it relevant to the reader (Tomlinson 1993; and Sadoski (1985) who concludes that image elaborations are 'a means of personalising literary texts while also maintaining a core of shared meaning');
- to achieve a ludic, hedonistic, reading experience which gives the reader access to what Tierney and Cunningham (1984) call the 'wonder' of reading (see also Denis 1982)
- to achieve 'the "experiencing" of the text and not just the comprehension of information' (Esrock *op. cit.*);
- to contribute to the 'deep processing' of salient parts of the text and thus to achieve 'more elaborate, longer lasting and stronger traces' (Craik and Lockhart 1972) in the long-term memory.

There is little doubt that visualisation is functionally significant in L1 reading and there is a strong possibility that it could therefore play a beneficial role in L2 reading too.

Do L2 readers visualise?

In 1985 Knight, Padron and Waxman investigated the reading strategies reported by ESL and by monolingual students. They found that 'imaging was significant' for L1 readers but was not mentioned at all by the L2 readers, whose 'primary concern was with low level decoding skills'. In 1989 Barnett devised a questionnaire entitled, 'What do you do when you read?' She administered it to L2 readers and in her report she makes no reference at all to visualisation as a strategy used by anybody in her sample. This indication that L2 readers do not typically visualise is also supported by Stevick who, for example, refers to a woman who 'claimed to get pictures from words in her own native language, but not in a foreign language which she spoke very effectively' (Stevick 1986). My own experiments also suggest that most L2 readers do not seem to visualise very much whilst reading. Most of the lower intermediate to upper intermediate Japanese students who took part in nineteen experiments conducted at Kobe University and at Nagoya Women's University made no reference to visualisation or to mental imaging of any kind when asked to reflect on how they had read a text. For example, in one experiment only seven out of 41 students reported any visualisation when they were asked to say what they had done in order to try to understand the poem 'River Station Plaza'. The main strategies reported by the others were looking up difficult words, trying to translate the poem, reading the poem over and over again, trying to memorise the poem, and 'giving up'. In another experiment only three out of 16 students who had been asked to read an extract from *The Bonfire of the Vanities* (Wolfe 1988) and then predict the next scene reported using visualisation to help them to understand the passage and only two said they had used visualisation to predict the next scene. Likewise in another group of 19 students who were asked to read the poem 'River Station Plaza' and then to reflect on the process of reading it only four reported visualising and only the same four reported using visualisation as a strategy to help them to overcome the difficulties they encountered in trying to understand the poem. The interesting thing is that these four students performed better than the others when asked after an interval to recall words from the poem and to write a summary of it. A similar tendency not to visualise when reading in the L2 was indicated by questionnaires given to EFL students at the University of

Luton asking them to report on how they had read the first page of *A Pale View of Hills* (Ishiguro 1982), of *No Other Life* (Moore 1993) and of *Remembering Babylon* (Malouf 1993).

In all my experiments the few students who reported visualising tended to achieve greater comprehension and recall than those who did not. This was also the case when Padron and Waxman administered a reading strategy questionnaire to 82 Hispanic ESL students and found that one of the most frequently cited strategies by the successful students was 'imaging or picturing the story in your mind' (Padron and Waxman 1988). Of course this equation between visualisation and successful L2 comprehension and recall raises the question of whether imagery is 'an outgrowth/consequence of . . . reading skill, rather than a contributor to it' (Esrock: personal correspondence). My view (developed in Tomlinson 1993) is that increasing an L2 reader's ability to visualise can facilitate positive engagement with the text and can increase the reader's ability to comprehend and retain what is read. This in turn can further increase the ability to visualise in the L2.

It seems that L2 learners do not typically visualise when reading in the L2. The indication that those who do so tend to achieve greater comprehension and recall than those who do not would suggest that we should be trying to help L2 readers to visualise more.

What are the characteristics of L2 visualisation?

Anderson and Pearson (1984) point out that younger children are not predisposed to draw inferences spontaneously and they give the example of five-year-olds being less able to infer the instrument than eight-year-olds when reading the sentence, 'The man dug a hole'. My experience of L2 learners is that when they do visualise they are less likely to make default inferences than L1 readers are and that like the young L1 child they are reliant on the writer providing most of the information to be visualised. For example, when asked to visualise the poem *River Station Plaza* most of a group of Japanese students saw a yellow light described as shining on the plaza but, unlike L1 readers given the same task, they did not visualise its undescribed source. However this childlike state seems to be typical rather than inevitable, as groups of L2 readers who have become used to doing visualisation activities in reading classes have become easily capable of seeing what is not actually described. Thus a multinational EFL class at the University of Luton saw the sun, a car headlight and a shop window as the source of light in 'River Station Plaza'. In all my experiments in which L2 learners have been encouraged to visualise there have invariably been gaps in the mental pictures they have created. Thus when drawing what they had seen whilst reading the first two pages of *Brazzaville Beach* a group of Japanese students did not draw the topless sunbathers nor the working fishermen (sights not common on Japanese beaches) nor did they draw the itinerants and scavengers (words they did not know); but most of them did draw the volleyball players (beach volleyball is popular on Japanese television). Some of the students just left gaps in their pictures where they knew other activities should go, others compensated by seeing the volleyball game in vivid detail and many others compensated by imaging details not described in the text at all (e.g. birds in the sky and boats at sea). The L2 readers who are content to leave many gaps in their mental images of what a text represents seem to be those who achieve the least understanding of the text whereas those who try to fill in the picture by, for example, compensating from their visual schemata, seem to understand more. Another typical characteristic of L2 visualisers in this sample was the tendency to see only prototypical or stereotypical images suggested by key words and not to develop them into instantiated images on the strength of further evidence in the text. The 'debilitating effect of' this 'premature commitment to a particular schema' (Rumelhart 1980) was most in evidence in an activity in which a class of students at Kobe University were asked to draw the party which was about to happen in an extract they were reading from Harold Pinter's *Birthday Party* (1976). All the students drew young boys drinking soft drinks (the stereotypical image of a birthday party in a country where adults do not normally have birthday parties) even though the text made it clear that the characters were adults and the party was going to be a 'booze-up'. In the same way another class at Kobe University, when asked to read an extract from *Brazzaville Beach* and then 'draw Clovis', all drew a small boy because he is described as 'stupid'. When asked to read on and draw Clovis again they all drew a boy again because he is described as having a finger up his nose. When asked to read on and draw Clovis again they all drew a boy again even though by now the text had made it clear that Clovis was a monkey of some sort who swings away through the trees. A multinational class at the University of Luton (who had been given some prior experience of visualisation activities) all drew boys the first two times but some of them drew dogs and cats the third time and one of them drew a monkey. Native speakers drew boys and men for the first two extracts but all of them changed Clovis to a monkey after reading the third extract.

It seems that many L2 readers who do visualise tend to achieve only partial visualisation and to stick to their original images despite contradictory evidence from the text.

Can L2 readers be helped to visualise more often and more effectively?

There seem to be many reasons why L2 readers typically under-use or misuse visualisation. The main reason seems to be that they are conditioned from an elementary level to read using primarily bottom up strategies which focus on the low level decoding of words. Given their inevitable lack of vocabulary such a focus is initially unavoidable. But it is reinforced by the language teaching focus and the comprehension testing orientation of many of their textbooks and teachers. This insistence on understanding every word leaves little processing capacity for such high level skills as inferencing, connecting and visualising. So the pattern is set of relying on low level skills for reading in the L2 and there is little encouragement for global or interactive visualisation. Delaying the teaching of reading until learners have achieved a linguistic threshold level could help the learners to transfer their visualisation skills from their L1, especially if the initial focus is on using high level strategies to achieve global understanding of extensive texts rather than on achieving total understanding of each word in a short intensive text.

Stanovich (1980) in outlining an 'interactive compensatory model' claims that the strong use of one strategy can compensate for weakness in another. I have found this to be true in relation to encouraging L2 learners to use visualisation as a compensation for weakness in linguistic knowledge, as well as an aid to connection, inferencing, retention and recall. Like most other reading strategy use though, it only works well if it replaces cognitive activities rather than overloading the reader's processing capacity by adding to them, and if the learners are made aware that, 'Accepting appropriate tolerance of uncertainty is an essential part of being a good reader' (Brumfit 1986). In my experience L2 readers can be helped to visualise effectively by encouraging a 'tolerance for inexactness, a willingness to take chances and make mistakes, formulation of hypotheses before reading, then reading to confirm, refine, reject' (Clarke 1980). They can also be helped to visualise by materials which combine visualisation strategy instruction with visualisation strategy activities.

In 19 experiments conducted with over 600 L2 students, those students who visualised (mainly as a result of being instructed or induced to do so) were able to understand and recall slightly more of the text than those who did not visualise. Thus, for example, in experiments in which half the class were induced to visualise a text whilst the other half studied it, the visualisers always outscored the studiers on recall and comprehension tests. For example, in a sopho-more class at Kobe University the visualisers scored an average of 44 per cent whereas the studiers scored an average of 38 per cent. In these experiments also on average seven out of ten of the top ten scorers were visualisers and seven out of ten of the bottom ten scorers were non-visualisers (see Tomlinson 1997 for details of these experiments). In some of the experiments the initial visualisers were then asked to study a short story whilst the initial studiers were induced to visualise the story. Comprehension and recall scores for both groups on the second activity were very similar in all these experiments (possibly indicating that the initial visualisers continued to visualise when asked to study). In none of the experiments was there a statistically significant difference between the scores of the visualisers and the non-visualisers but there were indications that visualisation instruction and visualisation induction helped students to slightly improve their reading performance in a single task. Some of the classes which participated in these experiments then followed a reading course in which the emphasis was on developing their ability to achieve effective visualisation. It seemed that most students in these classes considerably improved both their reading confidence and their reading competence and that by the end of the semester they were able to read in English in ways much closer to the ways in which they read in Japanese. Of course, these classes were not conducted under experimental conditions, there were no control classes to compare improvements with and there were many uncontrolled variables which could have improved reading performance (e.g. rapport with the teacher, increased quantity of reading, increased acquisition of language). However the indications of increased use of visualisation as a causal factor in improved reading performance were strong enough to support the inclusion of visualisation activities in reading skills materials and were responsible for the emphasis given to the objective of developing visualisation skills in *Use Your English* (Tomlinson and Masuhara 1994). They were also strong enough to justify the idea of a controlled longitudinal experiment with a large sample of EFL learners in which experimental classes use materials designed to develop visualisation skills whilst control classes use conventional reading skills materials in which there is no systematic attempt to promote visualisation as a reading skill at all. Such an experiment is about to be conducted at the University of Seville.

The reading courses which my students at Kobe University and at the University of Luton followed included materials designed to help them to use visualisation effectively as follows:

Visualisation instruction

1 Students were told before reading a text not to study it or to translate

it but to imagine pictures as they read it and then to change these pictures as they found further information in the text.

2 They were also sometimes told to focus their images initially on what was familiar in the text and then to use these images to help them work out what was unfamiliar in the text.

3 Another frequently given instruction was to picture a summary of each section of the text immediately after reading it and also to attempt a pictorial summary immediately after finishing the text.

4 Students were also sometimes given reading texts which contained explicit visualisation instructions either just before the text or in the margins within the text. Often these were instructions designed to help them achieve interactive imaging which would facilitate interpretative connections between different parts of the text (e.g. 'Try to see Nanga's face in your mind. Compare your picture to the image of Nanga's face which you "saw" when you were reading page 17.').

5 Sometimes visualisation instructions were inserted into comprehension questions to help students to make connections (e.g. 'What does the narrator's description of Hannah tell you about his attitude towards her? Try to see a picture of Hannah and the narrator's father in the foyer of the cinema before answering this question').

Visualisation activities

I found overt visualisation instruction to have beneficial effects in aiding comprehension of demanding narrative and descriptive texts but agreed with Van Dijk and Kintsch that:

> a comprehension strategy which must be applied consciously is of limited usefulness, because in many actual comprehension situations insufficient resources would be available for the application of such a strategy. (1983)

I therefore also devised materials which featured visualisation activities designed to induce visualisation subconsciously, with the intention of establishing visualisation as something the students do habitually when reading narrative and descriptive texts in experiential ways. These activities included:

Drawing

I have found that pre-reading drawing activities help to make sure that the students have relevant images in their minds when they start to read the text. These images are activations of their schemata, or knowledge of the world. They enable them to read interactively straight away rather than being initially reliant on text data and running the risk of word dependence. These activities often involve drawing predictions of the characters, the setting or the narrative from a rapid sampling of the book or from the title, the blurb, the front cover or the introduction to the book. Or they might involve drawing scenes from the students' own lives connected to the title or front cover of a book. One such activity involved the students drawing a strange teacher they have known before reading a scene from Chinua Achebe's *Girls at War* (1972) which focused on an eccentric teacher; another asked them to draw their first day at school before reading Roger McGough's poem 'First day at school' (1979).

I have also frequently used whilst-reading drawing activities to facilitate interactive reading and thus help the students to relate data from the text to their knowledge of the world. Being asked to draw a picture of Chief Nanga whilst reading the first chapter of Achebe's *A Man of the People* (1988) helped students not only to visualise Nanga and to bring him to life but also to begin to develop and retain an understanding of his personality. Likewise, asking students to draw the two people in Wole Soyinka's poem 'Telephone conversation' (1963) as they read it helped them to 'see' the landlady for what she was and to appreciate the dilemma of the black student trying to find accommodation in London.

Post-reading drawings have also helped students to read visually and interactively, provided that they were told what they were going to be asked to draw prior to reading the text. Thus being told they were going to be asked to draw a picture to show what they understood of 'First day at school' helped students to gain access to the poem through focusing on what they could understand and see. It also helped them to use pictures in their mind to help them to reread the poem with greater understanding. Thus, for example, none of the students initially understood the word 'railings' in the following lines:

And the railings.
All around, the railings.
Are they to keep out wolves and monsters?

But when they visualised what could be all around a school they all began to draw railings without knowing the meaning of the word. In a similar way students who were asked to draw the scene in which the son discovers his father with a woman at the beginning of Nadine Gordimer's *My Son's Story* (1991) reread the extract with much greater understanding when they asked themselves what the characters looked like and what they were wearing.

In addition to writing visualisation materials which feature drawing activities I have also added drawing activities when using published coursebooks with classes. For example, I asked students to draw their prediction of what Paul McCartney's house looks like before reading the passage in Unit 1 of *Headway Intermediate* (Soars and Soars 1986) which describes the McCartney house and then asked them to describe the house that the family actually did live in. Also when using *Intermediate Matters* (Bell and Gower 1991) I asked students to draw the metal boxes (i.e. cars) which the whale family in *The Great Whale's Mistake* could see people throwing rubbish from on the beach (Unit 20) and to draw what the whales thought that the people did at night (i.e. continue their activities on the beach). Such activities appeared to facilitate a better understanding of the texts than just using the exercises in the books as they helped students to make connections and inferences that similar students did not make when not encouraged to visualise by drawing activities.

Connection activities

I have found that by asking learners to connect a text to an incident in their own lives or to one in another text they automatically visualise in order to achieve the connection. So if I ask a group of students to read the opening chapter of *A Man of the People* and to compare Chief Nanga to a politician they know as they read. Most of them will develop images of both politicians in their minds as they read. Likewise if I tell students to read the opening chapter of *Brazil* and as they read to compare the beach which is described to the beach they can remember from the opening chapter of *Brazzaville Beach* they are likely to develop images of Copacabana Beach as they read the text.

Illustrations

Illustration of texts often inhibit active visualisation because they impose a visual interpretation of the texts. However I have found that involving the students in relating given illustrations to their own visualisation of the text they are reading can facilitate interactive reading. For example, before reading Brian Patten's poem 'Little Johnny's letter home' (1967) the students were asked to predict the story of the poem from four pictures and then to draw their own pictures, first of all as they listened and then as they read the poem. Also students who were asked to draw a picture of the scene in the foyer of the cinema at the beginning of *My Son's Story* were then asked to compare their drawings to two illustrations depicting slightly different interpretations of the scene.

Other types of visualisation activities exploiting illustrations include the students:

- selecting from a number of possible illustrations of a text
- completing partial illustrations by relating them to a text
- re-drawing an illustration to fit their own interpretation of a text
- solving a jigsaw puzzle so that it provides a valid interpretation of a text
- reading a story in which the drawings continue the story told by the text rather than illustrating what the text says

Miming

I have also found miming to be an effective way of inducing visualisation. I have often mimed extracts from texts before asking students to read them, so that they start reading with pictures in their minds to relate the text to. I have also asked students to read a story in order to be able to mime it to another group, I have asked students to mime a story or poem as it is read aloud to them and then to read it silently, and I have asked students to mime a text as they are reading it. These activities seem to help to achieve a visual and kinaesthetic impact which aids involvement, understanding and retention.

Through these and other types of visualisation activities (e.g. making a video version of a poem) I believe I have helped many students to understand and enjoy texts which many teachers would consider to be beyond their linguistic level. This has been achieved by encouraging an appropriate balance between concept driven and data driven processing which has enabled the students to personalise, interpret and retain what they have read. For many students this has not only helped to develop their reading confidence and skills but has also seemed to result in a positive enrichment of language input and in the development of positive attitudes towards English and the educational opportunities it can open for them.

Conclusion

In first language reading the norm is experiential reading in which such high level skills as visualising, inferencing and connecting are employed automatically to deepen the reading process. In second language reading the norm is studial reading in which processing energy is often devoted to low level decoding and to cognitive strategies of comprehension. If learners do not see pictures in their minds of the texts they are reading then they will have great difficulty in achieving global understanding and their experience of the texts will be fragmentary and shallow. Not only will they not enjoy reading but they will not transfer reading skills which they have already developed in their L1 and their encounter with the language of the texts is unlikely to be deep and meaningful enough to facilitate language acquisition.

It is possible and desirable for materials to be developed which can help L2 learners to use visualisation to increase their understanding of the texts they are reading, to deepen their engagement with the texts, to improve their comprehension and retention skills and to facilitate language acquisition.

12 Squaring the circle – reconciling materials as constraint with materials as empowerment

Alan Maley

Introduction

A major dilemma faced by all writers of materials, even those writing for small groups of learners with well-defined needs, is that all learners, all teachers and all teaching situations are uniquely different, yet published materials have to treat them as if they were, in some senses at least, the same. A further problem for materials writers is that, although they are well aware that the course, the direction and the pace of learning are largely unpredictable, they have to predetermine all these things.

Prabhu (forthcoming) among others, has pointed out the constraining effects of materials on the freedom of action of teachers. In the interests of efficiency and quality (in one of its definitions at least), the writing of materials is delegated to a group of specialists, who produce centrally the materials to be used locally by another group: the teachers in their individual classrooms. By so doing, the materials can preempt all the important decisions which teachers themselves might otherwise be expected to make. The content is predetermined. The order of the content is predetermined. The procedures for using the content are also predetermined.

Clearly, what actually happens in classrooms using published materials, is that there is a complex trade-off between the three major elements in the equation: the materials, the teacher and the learners.

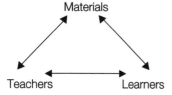

Materials

Teachers   Learners

Figure 1

In some cases there may be a relatively close fit between the three. This may occur when the materials have been designed for a relatively specific learning group. Even then, owing to individual differences among the learners and to teacher factors, there will never be a perfect fit. Such teacher factors include the teacher's:

- degree of language proficiency and confidence.
- previous personal learning experiences.
- own personality (introvert/extravert, open/closed, etc.)
- preferred teaching style (directive/consultative, etc.).

However, in most cases, for reasons to do with the economics of publishing among other things, the materials are intended to be used by the largest possible number of learners. An obvious consequence is that:

> The wider the area to be served by a given set of materials, the more varied the learners' states are likely to be . . . (Prabhu, *op. cit.*)

> In other words, the more extensive the user population, the more variety it will exhibit. All learners are different; the more of them there are, the more scope there is for difference. (Maley 1995b)

In cases like this, the materials can be conceived of as constituting a constraint upon the individual teacher's sense of what may be appropriate at a given pedagogical moment. The materials may also be far from the learners' capacity or sense of relevance at a given point:

> What typically happens in these circumstances is that the teacher has to bridge the gap between the materials and his/her sense of the learners' needs at that particular moment. So, the more widely used the materials, and consequently the more different and varied the learner need from the prescribed, pre-empted materials, the harder the teacher has to work to adapt the one to the other. (Maley, *op. cit.*)

The solution which is sometimes applied is to design materials with relatively specific groups in mind, with respect to cultural and cognitive content, local learning conditions, etc. But this still fails to address the central problem. What is needed is, 'not just a decentralisation of materials production, but a fundamental change in the design of materials' (Prabhu, *op. cit.*), in the direction of providing greater flexibility in decisions about content, order, pace and procedures.

The remainder of this chapter will look at two possible responses to this problem. The first of these is no more than a set of coping strategies which teachers adopt with the materials currently available. The second is in line with Prabhu's view that we need 'a fundamental change in the design of materials'.

Making the best of it – what teachers can do

Many teachers use some or all of the following strategies to make the published course bearable, or more effective:

Give it a rest

From time to time teachers will introduce additional material not in the coursebook to restore interest when it is flagging or to provide light relief. (The 'wet Friday afternoon effect'.) Such material typically includes songs, rhymes, games, cartoons, off-air recordings, video clips, etc. Although such activities involve setting the coursebook aside, they are generally no more than cosmetic entertainment. However, many teachers do manage to build such activities into their teaching in a principled way, for example by using them as 'warmers' for the more extended activities which follow, or as 'coolers' to promote reflection on a previous activity.

Change it

For the teacher who wishes to adapt the materials, a number of options are available:

- omission: the teacher leaves out things deemed inappropriate, offensive, unproductive . . . for the particular group.
- addition: where there seems to be inadequate coverage, teachers may decide to add material, either in the form of texts or exercise material.
- reduction: where the teacher shortens an activity to give it less weight or emphasis.
- extension: where an activity is lengthened in order to give it an additional dimension. (For example, a vocabulary activity is extended to draw attention to some syntactic patterning.)
- rewriting/modification: teachers may occasionally decide to rewrite material, especially exercise material, to make it more appropriate, more 'communicative', more demanding, more accessible to their students, etc.
- replacement: texts or exercise material which is considered inadequate, for whatever reason, may be replaced by more suitable material. This is often culled from 'resource materials' (see below).
- re-ordering: teachers may decide that the order in which the materials are presented is not suitable for their students. They can then decide to plot a different course through the materials from the one the writer has laid down.
- branching: teachers may decide to add options to the existing activity

or to suggest alternative pathways through the activities. (For example, an experiential route or an analytical route.)

For further discussion of such materials adaptation see Cunningsworth (1995) and McDonough and Shaw (1993).

Do It Yourself
a) Scissors and Paste:
i) Skills modules: Teachers may decide to abandon the idea of a single coursebook altogether and instead to erect their own course based on one or other of the several skills series now on the market. This gives teachers the freedom to choose material at different levels for different skills, according to the needs and level of the learners. This looks easier than it is. One of the main problems is the relative lack of coherence between skill modules. For example, if students are judged to be at level X in reading and at level Z in writing, it may be difficult to harmonise the modules in these two skill areas. It also requires an experienced teacher who can keep tabs on the overall shape of the course as it develops, and can make good any obvious omissions.
ii) Resource option: this is a more radical option in that teachers draw upon the whole range of available resource materials to put together a course they feel is in accordance with their students' needs. The materials available are now considerable and include resource book series with banks of texts/activities, materials culled from existing coursebooks, skills collections, collections of 'authentic' texts (printed, audio, video, Internet, etc.) and materials tailor-made by the teachers themselves.

Again, it takes a very skilled teacher to operate this option. It requires an encyclopaedic knowledge of existing resources, a sure grasp of the overview of the learning pathway for the group, and enormous energy. It is, for the present at least, most likely to be operated in the context of well-resourced private language teaching institutions working with relatively small groups on intensive courses. Most secondary school teachers would find it a daunting prospect, even were they to be permitted to cast away the coursebook in the first place. However, it can be done if teams of teachers from the same institution, city or area get together regularly to share ideas, techniques, materials and resources. (A good example of this in a high-tech context is the TELEC run from the Department of Curriculum Studies at the University of Hong Kong, which allows teachers all over the territory to share ideas on a computer network.)

b) The process option
This is an even more radical alternative: teachers may decide to eradicate pre-developed materials altogether. Instead they set the scene for a process to take place. It is the process which will generate its own content and learning activities. Examples of process approaches include:

i) Project work. In project work, the teacher simply sets up, or helps the learners decide on, a project they will work upon for an agreed period of time. For instance, they might decide to produce a booklet describing the facilities available to disabled people in the local community. To do this they will need to discuss and plan their activities, read documents, interview people outside the school (possibly having designed a questionnaire), discuss their findings, draft and redraft their booklet until it is in final format. The teacher's role is then to monitor and support the process as required. For further information about project work see Fried-Booth (1987) and Legutke and Thomas (1991).

ii) Community Language Learning (CLL). In this approach (Richards and Rodgers 1986), it is the learners who decide what they want to say. The teacher's role, initially at least, is to provide the foreign language equivalent of what a learner wants to say. Content is wholly in the hands of the learners, who gradually build their own 'syllabus'. The process is therefore unpredictable and precludes the use of preformatted materials.

iii) Drama techniques. Here too it is only the 'empty' shell of the technique which is provided by the teacher. Learners 'fill' the technique with their own spontaneously-produced, unpredictable language. (Maley and Duff 1980; Wessels 1987).

Clearly, process options too require great competence and skill, energy and self-confidence on the part of the teacher. They are therefore only ever likely to appeal to a minority of teachers, although elements of process approaches can and often are incorporated in more traditional, course-based teaching.

Incorporating choice – what materials writers can do

The previous section reviewed the options open to teachers for dealing with materials as they are. In this section I shall pick up Prabhu's proposal referred to earlier, for a radically different way of designing materials.

One of the main objectives of the proposal is to pass to teachers at least some of the control over four major factors in the classroom: Content (what), Order (when), Pace (how fast), Procedure (how).

Prabhu's proposals

The approach to materials production which Prabhu proposes would:

> Provide a range of possible inputs, without envisaging that they will be used in any one classroom or that all classrooms will use the same inputs. They may suggest different teaching agendas and lesson formats but are not themselves organised into lesson units. They may provide inputs at different levels of difficulty and in different quantities, leaving it to the teacher to select from the range in both respects. . . . the expectation is . . . that teachers will find it useful to draw on them in implementing the decisions they themselves make as teachers, being as faithful as possible to their own perceptions of learner states and learning processes. (Prabhu, *op. cit.*)

Prabhu suggests two possible ways of categorising such resource options:

a) Semi-materials. These can be of two kinds:
   – single-type activities such as listening comprehension, writing activities, reading skills exercises, vocabulary development work, role-play, etc. Such materials would still be 'centrally' produced, i.e. published, but it would be left to the teacher to decide on the order of presentation, the pace and the way in which they were combined with other materials.
   – collections of 'raw' input, i.e. collections/selections of written, spoken or visual texts which are presented without specifying how they are to be used (Maley and Duff 1976). It is left to the teacher to decide which procedures (grammar awareness-raising activities, vocabulary in context, role-play, comprehension questions, diagram completion, etc.) it is appropriate to use with a particular class at a particular moment.
b) Meta-materials. Essentially, meta-materials are 'empty' pedagogical procedures. For example, dictation is a meta-material. Other examples would include role-play, gap-filling, summary writing, jigsaw listening, drama techniques, etc.

The teacher decides on the nature of the input (the 'text') and applies the procedure to it. In this way, the teacher is in control of the content side of the teaching event.

To summarise:

Semi-materials
– single-type activities.	Teacher decides on order, pace.
– 'raw' input.	Teacher decides on choice of text, procedure, order, pace.

Meta-materials
– pedagogical procedures. Teacher decides content, pace, order.

Flexi-materials

It is possible to take these ideas of Prabhu a stage further. In fact, flexi-materials combine the notion of semi-materials with that of meta-materials.

In flexi-materials, teachers are provided with a set of 'raw' texts. (They are then encouraged to add further texts they find for themselves.) They are also provided with a set of generalisable pedagogical procedures (see Appendix 1) which may be applied to any/all of the texts in any combination (Maley 1994, 1995). Teachers are then free to decide on which texts to use, in which order, and with which procedures. This gives them control over content, order, pace and procedure.

The flexibility of such materials lies not only in the fact that teachers can decide on the factors listed above but also in the possibility of returning to texts for a second or third time; each time using a different procedure. For example:

Text-type	Procedure
One-line texts	Expansion
(Proverbs, headlines, etc.)	
Haiku	Reduction
Mini-texts	Media-transfer
Epitaphs	Matching
Diary entries	Selection/ranking
Short poems	Comparison/contrast
Prayers	Reconstruction
Programme notes	Reformulation
Mini-sagas	Interpretation
Short newspaper articles	Creating text
Nasruddin stories	Analysis
Short essays	Project work

The detailed description of the application of flexi-materials is set out in Appendix 1. Worked examples of different combinations of text plus procedure are to be found in Appendix 2.

Clearly the key idea of permutating text with procedure can be applied to pictorial material, audio-recordings and video as well as to printed text. It is clearly a powerfully generative idea which could be further developed.

The Sourcebook

An alternative strategy for developing choice is set out in *The Sourcebook* (Shepherd *et al.* 1992). In this case, the authors have attempted to reconcile choice within the covers of what feels more like a 'normal' coursebook.

There is a foundation unit, entitled 'Starting Out', which prepares the learners for the material in the course and offers orientation/learner training on how to use the rest of the book.

The rest of the material is divided into three main blocks: grammar, vocabulary and skills, each of which contains material for the teacher/learner to select from.

Like flexi-materials therefore, *The Sourcebook* is attempting to give a degree of choice to the teacher in the matter of order and pace, and to some extent content and procedure (in that the teacher can decide on the proportionate dosage of grammar, vocabulary and skills development).

Other possibilities

a) Computerised materials. Clearly the storage of multimedia materials both as text and exercises which can be rapidly and flexibly accessed offers enormous potential for the freeing of learners and teachers alike from the constraints of the coursebook. So far however, there has been only modest development of such materials, which are attended by a new set of problems (Eastment 1994). It is certain however that we now stand on the threshold of a new generation of materials based on CD-Rom technology, and its successors.

b) A Rattlebag of ideas. Further possibilities for offering choice include the following. As far as I know, none of them has so far been developed in published form. If I am wrong, I tender my apologies in advance!

   i) Develop a course which is specially designed to allow for different pathways through it. Guidance would be given to teachers on possible route maps (linear/branching, experiential/analytical, in-depth/ overview, etc.) but ultimately the choice would be their own. This might be a development of the Resourcebook idea but, rather than offering material in three major blocks, it would incorporate the choices within each unit. This would imply the inclusion of a great deal more material than is usual.

ii) Develop a set of texts roughly graded for length/difficulty. Alongside it, develop a set of varied activities at different levels of task difficulty (Nunan 1989, Skehan 1993). Teachers would then be able to choose texts at a suitable level of difficulty and match them with tasks at a corresponding level of cognitive/linguistic demand. This is a possible refinement of the flexi-materials concept (see Tomlinson's *Openings* (1994c), for one way in which this can be done).

iii) Develop a set of materials in which students are given instruction and practice in a particular strategy or set of strategies (e.g., for reading academic texts), after which they, or the teacher, choose a text from a resource bank to work with.

iv) Develop a course with a central core component which it would be essential for all teachers/learners to follow. This would be accompanied by a cluster of optional modules at a number of levels, focused on different aspects of the language: skills modules (to develop writing, listening, reading, speaking skills), vocabulary development modules, grammar awareness-raising modules, cultural awareness-raising modules, testing modules, project-based modules, thematic modules, games/fluency activities modules, etc. Teachers/learners would then be able to select modules appropriate to their interests, learning needs and level at any particular point.

Conclusion

Materials will always be constraining in one way or another, so that teachers will always need to exercise their professional judgement (or 'sense of plausibility') about when and how a particular piece of material is best implemented in any particular case. However, it must also be clear that there are alternatives to the relatively inflexible design of most currently available published materials.

It is heartening to learn of concrete examples of such alternatives being applied currently: a Bulgarian textbook project in which two different teams of writers are writing two different books for the same set of users so as to offer choice; a Namibian textbook project which gives encouragement and guidance to teachers on how to select and re-order the units from the new secondary textbooks produced by the project (Tomlinson 1995b).

Choice is important, not only for ideological reasons but also for the opportunities it offers teachers to exercise responsibility, and in the process to continue their own professional development.

Appendix 1 Twelve generalisable procedures

Each major category will be described. Examples of possible activities will then be given.

Although most of the procedures can be applied to most of the texts, they *need not all be used*. There is no point in wringing the text dry just for the sake of completeness. It is also often the case that a given text works better with certain procedures than with others. The detailed permutation of procedures and texts is in any case a decision only the teacher can properly make.

1 **Expansion**
   Key criterion – the text must be lengthened in some way.
   Examples:
   - Add one or more sentences/paragraphs to the beginning and end of the text.
   - Add specified items within the text (e.g. adjectives).
   - Add sentences within the text.
   - Add subordinate clauses within the text.
   - Add comment within the text.

2 **Reduction**
   Key criterion – the text must be shortened in some way.
   Examples:
   - Remove specified items (e.g. adjectives).
   - Turn it into telegraphese.
   - Combine sentences.
   - Remove clauses/sentences.
   - Rewrite in a different format.
   (see also 3 **Media transfer** and 8 **Reformulation**, below.)

3 **Media transfer**
   Key criterion – the text must be transferred into a different medium or format.
   Examples:
   - Transfer it into visual form (e.g. pictures, graphs, maps, tables etc.)
   - Turn prose into poem (or vice versa).
   - Turn a letter into a newspaper article (or vice versa).
   - Turn a headline into a proverb (or vice versa).

288

- Turn a poem into an advertising slogan (or vice versa).
- Turn a prose narrative into a screenplay.

4 Matching
Key criterion – a correspondence must be found between the text and something else.
Examples:
- Match text with a visual representation.
- Match text with a title.
- Match text with another text.
- Match text with a voice/music.

5 Selection/ranking
Key criterion – the text must be chosen according to some given criterion. (In the case of ranking, several texts must be placed in order of suitability for a given criterion.)
Examples:
- Choose the best text for a given purpose (e.g. inclusion in a teenage magazine).
- Choose the most/least (difficult, formal, personal, complex, etc.) text.
- Choose the text most/least like the original version.
- Choose words from a text to act as an appropriate title.

6 Comparison/contrast
Key criterion – points of similarity/difference must be identified between two or more texts.
Examples:
- Identify words/expressions common to both texts.
- Identify words/phrases in one text which are paraphrased in the other.
- Identify ideas common to both texts.
- Identify facts present in one text and not in the other.
- Compare grammatical/lexical complexity. (See also 11 **Analysis**, p. 290.)

7 Reconstruction
Key criterion – coherence/completeness must be restored to an incomplete or defective text.
Examples:
- Insert appropriate words/phrases into gapped texts.
- Reorder jumbled words, lines, sentences, paragraphs etc.
- Reconstruct sentences/texts from a word array.
- Reconstitute a written text from an oral presentation (various types of dictation).
- Remove sentences/lines which do not 'belong' in the text.

8 Reformulation

Key criterion – the text must be expressed in a form different from the original without loss of essential meanings.
Examples:
- Retell a story from notes/memory.
- Use key words to rewrite a text.
- Rewrite in a different format (e.g. prose as poem). (See also 3 **Media transfer**, above.)
- Rewrite in a different style/mood.

9 Interpretation

Key criterion – personal knowledge/experience must be used to clarify and extend the meaning(s) of the text.
Examples:
- What does this recall from your own experience?
- What does this remind you of?
- What images does this throw up?
- What associations does it have?
- What questions would you wish to ask the author?
- Formulate questions on the text beginning: what?, who?, where?, when?, why?, how? . . .
- What does the text *not* say that it might have said?

10 Creating text

Key criterion – the text is to be used as a springboard for the creation of new texts.
Examples:
- Write a parallel text on a different theme.
- Use the same story outline/model to write a new text.
- Quarry words from text A to create a new text B.
- Use the same title but write a new text.
- Add lines/sentences to the text to reshape it. (See also 1 **Expansion** and 8 **Reformulation**, above.)
- Combine these texts to create a new text.

11 Analysis

Key criterion – the text is to be submitted to some form of language-focused scrutiny.
Examples:
- Work out the ratio of one-word verbs to two-word verbs.
- How many different tenses are used? Which are most/least frequent?
- How many content (or function) words does the text contain?
- List the different ways in which the word X is referred to in the text. (Anaphoric reference)

- List all the words to do with (the sea, movement, ecology etc.) in this text.

12 Project work
Key criterion – the text is used as a springboard for some related practical work with a concrete outcome.
Examples:
- Use the text as a centrepiece of an advertising campaign. First decide on the product. Then design the campaign posters, advertising jingles etc. Finally present the product as a TV commercial (which must incorporate the text). If possible video it.
- This text is about the problem of X. Design a questionnaire on this problem for other groups to complete. Tabulate the results and present them to the rest of the class.
- This text presents a particular point of view. With a partner, prepare a brief magazine article which either supports or disagrees with this point of view. In both cases you will need to collect ideas and examples to support your own point of view.
  Display the articles on the class notice-board.

Classroom procedures
Unless otherwise indicated, the normal procedure to adopt with all the suggested activities is:

1 *Individual work* Each student first does the activity for her/himself. This ensures that everyone makes an initial personal effort.
2 *Pairwork* (or work in threes) Students work together to compare and discuss what they have produced individually.
3 *Classwork* The pairwork then feeds back into whole-class discussion as appropriate.

There are a few cases when *groupwork* is preferable to pairwork, especially in **12 Project work.**

Appendix 2   Examples of text + procedures

Space does not permit me to give a complete set of activities to demonstrate how any given text might be combined with any one or more of the procedures. I hope however that the following will be sufficient to set teachers going if this idea appeals to them.

Text 1   Haiku
Strange to think of you
Thirty thousand feet below
And five years away.

a) Expansion (NB. Instructions are written as if direct to students.)
   i) Rewrite the haiku 'in full'; that is, making clear what this is all about, e.g. I'm sitting in this aeroplane. We are flying over the city where I used to live five years ago and where we used to know each other. I suddenly think of you again . . .
   ii) Write a 'haiku paragraph' which might have come before this one, and one that could have come after it, e.g. When I got on the plane in Sydney, I fell asleep almost immediately. When I woke up, I realised we were over X . . . As soon as I get back home, I shall call you. Old friends are precious.

b) Media transfer
   i) Write out the incident from the haiku as a postcard to the person who was 'Thirty thousand feet below'.
   ii) Write an entry to the passenger's diary, recording this incident.

Here are some other haikus which could be worked on in similar ways:

> Bark-skinned crocodile
> One eyelid flickers open –
> Sharp sliver of flint.

> This sudden Spring squall
> Shags the daffodils with snow –
> Am I young or old?

> Sounds across the valley,
> In the early twilight:
> Eyes dim – ears sharpen.   *Alan Maley*

Text 2 Short poem

The adversary

> A mother's hardest to forgive.
> Life is the fruit she longs to hand you,
> Ripe on a plate. And while you live,
> Relentlessly she understands you.   *Phyllis McGinley*

a) Media transfer
   Rewrite the poem as a haiku (line 1 = 5 syllables; line 2 = 7 syllables; line 3 = 5 syllables). Use words taken from the original as far as possible. For example:

> Hardest to forgive
> Is a mother. She so longs
> To understand you.

b) Comparison/contrast
   Compare this poem with the original. Make a list of things the poems share and a list of the differences between them. Then compare your lists with another student. (E.g. Do they have any words in common? or ideas? Are the attitudes of the two 'speakers' the same? etc.)

   ### Sorry

   Dear parents,
   I forgive you my life,
   Begotten in a drab town,
   The intention was good;
   Passing the streets now,
   I see the remains of sunlight.

   It was not the bone buckled;
   You gave me enough food
   To renew myself.
   It was the mind's weight
   Kept me bent, as I grew tall.

   It was not your fault.
   What should have gone on,
   Arrow aimed from a tried bow
   At a tried target, has turned back,
   Wounding itself
   With questions you had not asked.   *R. S. Thomas*

c) Selection
   – Which is the most important word in the poem? Compare your answers in groups of four.
   – Decide on an order from most to least suitable for the purposes to which this poem might be put. Compare your answer with a partner:
   i)   as part of an advertisement for family counselling/advisory services.
   ii) as part of a letter from a daughter to her mother, with whom she is on bad terms.
   iii) as a poem for inclusion in an anthology for teenagers.
   iv) as the dedication on the first page of a book on the psychology of the family.

d) Interpretation
   – In pairs write out three questions you would like to ask the author of the poem.

- Does this remind you of any feelings you have had? Or that friends of yours may have sometimes had. Discuss this with a partner.
- The poet takes a rather negative view of mothers. Write a note to Phyllis McGinley in which you disagree with her views. Try to find at least three points in favour of your argument.

Text 3 Mini-text

He never sent me flowers. He never wrote me letters. He never took me to restaurants. He never spoke of love. We met in parks. I don't remember what he said, but I remember how he said it. Most of it was silence anyway.   *Lescek Szkutnik*

a) Reconstruction
   - Word Array

silence	was	he
never	love	of
I	sent	anyway
took	met	letters
me	don't	spoke
most	restaurants	flowers
wrote	parks	said
to	what	how
remember	we	it
in		

Make as many sentences as you can, using **only** the words from the word array. (You can use the words as many times as you like and you do not have to use them all.) Then work with a partner. Use some of your sentences to write out a short story. Then compare it with the text your teacher will give you.

b) Creating text
   - Imagine the couple in the text are meeting for the last time before they break up. With a partner, write the dialogue of what they say to each other.

c) Analysis
   - What is the grammatical subject of each sentence? Can you see a pattern from the beginning through to the end of the text? (NB. For teachers – it moves from HE to WE to I to IT. Food for speculation!)

13 Autonomy and development: living in the materials world

Julian Edge and Sue Wharton

Introduction

Our aim in this chapter is to look at the relationships between commercial materials, learner autonomy and teacher development. We do not provide arguments in favour of learner autonomy or teacher development, we accept both as appropriate goals towards which we aspire in our work. This is not to say that we think the concepts unproblematical, or that the issues involved are not worthy of continuing debate, it is simply that this chapter concerns itself with questions of *how* to act towards agreed goals, rather than with a discussion of the goals themselves.

Given these limitations, then, we begin with a discussion of some of the key aspects of learner autonomy and teacher development, and we consider the links between the two. We then go on to examine ways in which the principles we have discussed are expressed in a commercial coursebook.

Learner autonomy and teacher development

Learner autonomy can be thought of as primarily a matter of taking responsibility for one's own learning. It is a goal, but more importantly it is an ongoing process requiring both individual and collective effort in the classroom context. One of the most important aspects of the process is the acquisition both of study skills and certain attitudes towards study.

Study skills can be thought of as instrumental techniques, such as reading or vocabulary-learning strategies, which are relatively easy to concretise. Helpful attitudes towards study, like self-confidence and independence of mind, are more nebulous. So while it is clear that materials could be designed to help foster study skills, it is less obvious that they could foster helpful attitudes. And yet, it is important that they should try: even if a learner possesses instrumental skills, s/he will not be able to use them in an autonomous way unless the underlying attitudes are there as well. We will argue in this chapter that the most valuable way to promote a change of attitude alongside the acquisition of skills is to encourage the learner to reflect on what they are doing and why.

One way of encouraging reflection is to give learners the opportunity to develop their own record of the language system. For example, in Figure 3 on p. 306, learners are asked to match ways of labelling verb tenses with examples of such tenses. On one level, this is simply a grammar exercise, but if the teacher encourages learners to refer to it later, perhaps to use it to correct mistakes of verb form, then it becomes a resource for language development. The process of working on the record is at least as useful as the resulting product since, with careful planning on the part of the teacher, it will involve the learners in discussions about the language in the context of meanings they themselves have produced. Edge and Samuda (1981) stress the value of this kind of activity, especially where there is a problem-solving slant which encourages students to find new ways of thinking about language.

Skills and attitudes, then, are one important aspect of learner autonomy. Another important aspect is the encouragement given to learners to move steadily away from dependence on teachers, classrooms and coursebooks: to make the most of *all* the learning opportunities that they may find in their environment. To establish this purpose is in no sense to devalue the role of the classroom in helping towards it.

To encourage this process from within the classroom, we need to increase the extent of learner control over the meanings and interactions that are generated there. Language learning discourse communities like classrooms can provide a relatively safe environment for experiment, but the major goal is for learners to be able to transfer what they have learned to the world outside. It is therefore important for classrooms to include some features of outside communication. If learners in classrooms can initiate interaction patterns and create the meanings that they personally want to express, then there is more chance that they will be able to make use of such learning to exploit outside sources for learning when they find them.

We have seen that there are different aspects to the overarching idea of taking responsibility for one's own learning. If we now move on to consider teacher development, we will see that a number of issues raised by learner autonomy are also relevant here: learner autonomy can be encouraged, but not imposed, and in the same way teacher development, as we are using the term, is in the hands of the individual teacher concerned.

One key to teacher development is reflective practice (Schön 1983): examining what we do and then working on it. Examination of practice is partly a question of introspection, but it can most profitably be linked with informal or formal classroom research. Such research frequently begins with the identification of an issue which is salient for the teacher, and leads not only to perceived improvements in practice but, more importantly, to deeper understandings of the areas investigated. Opportunities for understanding can be increased still further if the research is carried out in collaboration with a colleague.

Certain skills may be seen as important elements of reflective practice. Richards (1993b) identifies some key skills for teaching: among these are decision-making skills and pedagogical reasoning skills. By decision making he refers both to the planning that teachers undertake before going into the class, and to the interactive decisions that are taken while a class is in progress. By pedagogical reasoning he refers to the process of 'turning content (e.g. grammar, vocabulary, reading skills etc.) into learnable form through the organisation and presentation of suitable learning activities' (p. 9).

It is clear that the development and improvement of such skills is both a basis for, and an outcome of, reflective practice. But reflective practice also implies a certain attitude on the part of the teacher. Critical thinking is part of such an attitude, and a desire to continue to learn is another part.

Continuing to learn means being open to new possibilities. So a commercial coursebook could be helpful, if it offered the teacher the opportunity to learn more about the language and about approaches to teaching. The goal, for the coursebook writer, is not to impart new methods via the equivalent of a transmission model, but rather to invite teachers to integrate possibly new ideas into experiences of reflective practice.

The synthesis of new perspectives and reflective practice assists the teacher in expanding and refining a wide variety of teaching-related schemata, and in being able to support their own, constantly evolving, critical standpoint. This standpoint will of course function as a point of departure for interaction with people, with ideas and with texts such as coursebooks. So a coursebook designed to encourage teacher development, if it is successful, will itself be the subject of evaluation, adaptation and critical use.

We have seen in this section that learner autonomy and teacher development have a great deal in common. It is possible to summarise the links between them under the twin headings of **choice** and **distribution of responsibility**.

Choice is the most obvious point of the two. It is a prerequisite to the sense of ownership which is necessary for people to take responsibility for their development and to engage their critical faculties. Distribution of responsibility is related to what work there is to do in the teaching/ learning process, and who can most profitably do it. Allwright (1981) argues that certain teaching situations and teaching materials may limit the amount of investment and involvement that learners can have in the learning process: for example, by limiting their participation in decision making. Such situations or materials tend to lead to teachers becoming overloaded with work that learners, in fact, would gain great advantage from doing for themselves. The implications of this argument are quite clear: if teachers can share some responsibility with learners, then not only will learners benefit, but teachers will be less burdened and more able to pay attention to their own development too.

This background discussion of learner autonomy and teacher development has of necessity been brief and selective. We will continue to explore the issues involved later on in this chapter, when we look at examples of materials. At that point, we will also make some suggestions for further reading. But now, having sketched out some of the goals of learner autonomy and teacher development, we need to consider whether a commercial coursebook can help us achieve them.

Are coursebooks a help or a hindrance?

In the ELT literature, views about coursebooks seem to polarise. Some writers, such as Richards (1993b), express the concern that a comprehensive, tightly structured coursebook encourages dependence on the part of the teacher, and fosters a situation where the teacher relies on the book to do the real work of teaching. He suggests that many coursebooks attempt themselves to do the work of decision making and pedagogical reasoning, and therefore do not encourage teachers to use them in a creative and personal way. Such a relationship between teacher and book effectively reduces the teacher's role in the teaching/ learning process. At worst, this reduction in role can result in the de-skilling of teachers. Here, again, we see a 'distribution of responsibility' parallel with Allwright's comments on learner autonomy, above.

Other writers, though, are more optimistic about the role that a coursebook can play, and even suggest that published materials can make a positive contribution to professional development. Hutchinson and Torres (1994) argue that participants in social interactions like lessons feel a legitimate need for structure; such a structure provides a safe base, a platform for negotiation and exploration. A coursebook, they claim, can provide this structure. It functions as a management aid for the lesson and gives students and teachers a secure base from which to depart. By doing a certain amount of routine work for teachers, it frees them to concentrate on planning effectively and on using their creative skills (for comments on Hutchinson and Torres 1994, see Chapter 10 by Hitomi Masuhara in this book).

Different views on the impact of coursebooks naturally lead to different proposals about the role they can play in teacher development. Richards (1993b) describes a series of workshop activities in which in-service teachers are encouraged to demystify coursebooks and to develop criteria for evaluating them. The teachers then go on to design materials and to discuss ways of monitoring materials in use. Richards' approach exemplifies valuable activities such as can be found on most teacher training programmes today. However, the assumption behind the approach seems to be that teacher development *vis-à-vis* course-books is a matter of being able to debunk them.

The position of this chapter, on the contrary, is that a carefully designed coursebook can *in itself* encourage development: it can carry the seeds of its own creative adaptation. Far from making the skills of decision making and pedagogical reasoning redundant, it can assist teachers to develop these skills further. Let us now consider which are the characteristics of coursebooks that give them the potential to play this developmental role.

The coursebook as ELT theory

Coursebooks are full of theoretical statements and positions. In order to convince ourselves of this idea, we have only to think of the ways in which coursebooks are typically used. New teachers may approach books in the first instance looking for practical guidance, but their interaction with the book also provides an opportunity for them to take on board some of the methodology behind the suggested activities and to apply it in other circumstances. Experienced teachers may recognise a book's theoretical position more quickly and interact with it more critically; they will evaluate it as they make their planning decisions. And learners, in asking more or less explicitly what the point of any activity is, are engaging in the debate about what the process of language learning actually consists of. In each case the reader is looking for the principles behind the practice of the book.

The design of a coursebook, and the way in which its authors intend it to be used, is an essential part of its theoretical position. It has been suggested (e.g. Nunan 1989: 145) that theory in teacher training should be derived from practice if it is to be meaningful, and Hutchinson and Torres (*op. cit.*) report on various pieces of research into coursebook use. They argue that use is both selective and flexible, that experienced teachers do not tend to follow the script of a coursebook inflexibly. They add, delete and change tasks at the planning stage, and they reshape their plans during the lesson in response to the interactions that take place.

In attempting to arrive at a design which specifically attempts to facilitate this kind of flexible use, coursebook writers can aim to capitalise on teachers' capacity for creativity and flexibility, and encourage a style of use that can lead to development.

We would not wish to suggest that only materials which have been designed for flexible use can be used flexibly. Such is clearly not the case. We would suggest, however, that a book with flexible pathways can be seen as modelling a certain approach to the use of any other materials, especially where the approach is relatively new to teachers using the book.

Materials as discourse

The ELT coursebook is a genre with the potential for mass communication. This is a source of constraints – the marketplace makes its own demands – but also one of its great strengths. The coursebook can enable its authors to enter into dialogue, albeit attenuated, with teachers and students on all of the issues which we have mentioned above and more. In order to achieve this, however, it must operate in a different language than the one we have used so far in this article. If we are living in the materials world, we must speak materials.

Let us explain what we mean by this. By proposing an activity where learners first work together on a task, and afterwards examine some language relevant to its completion, an author suggests that an initial focus on meaning rather than form can be helpful for language acquisition. Teachers and students may have varying responses. They may do the activities as suggested, and find them more, or less, useful. They may decide to change the activities radically. In these ways, they are responding to the author, even though the author will not be immediately aware of the response. The feedback loop is completed when they talk to others about their views of the book, and contribute to a body of opinion which eventually finds its way back to author and publishers. This body of opinion influences future publications.

The coursebook, then, is a genre whose goal is a dialogue about principle via suggestions for practice. In order to demonstrate this point clearly, it would be very tempting to take a page of a coursebook and unpack all the theory which the insiders involved in producing it know is locked in there. Tempting, but beyond the scale of this chapter. We

16 An interview

be: past tense. Dates.

⊙ET READY   **1** 🖥 **Bob wants a job. Listen to the interview. What does Bob say about his school subjects?**

DAVE: Tell me about school, Bob.
What were you good at?
BOB: Well, I was pretty ¹_____ at science.
DAVE: Hm... Were you good at math?
BOB: I was ²_____ at math.
DAVE: How about history?
BOB: I wasn't ³_____ at history.
DAVE: Were you good at English?
BOB: Yes, I was. In fact, I was first ⁴_____.

2 🖥 *Was* **has a strong form (wʌz) and a weak form (wəz). Listen again and underline the strong forms of *was*. Practice saying the sentences with *was/wasn't*.**

3 *Pair Work* **What school subjects do people study in your country? Make true sentences about *you*. Then role-play an interview.**

⊙ET SET   **4** **Can you complete the names of the months?**

January Feb_____ M_____ April
M_____ June J_____ A_____ September
O_____ November D_____

5 *Pair Work* **Take turns writing and saying dates:**

EXAMPLE:
A: (writes) 11/21.
B: (says) November twenty-first.

⊙o!   **6** *Pair Work* **Can you answer the police officer's questions? Ask and answer ten more questions.**

EXAMPLES:

Where were you Friday at 11 a.m.?

Where were you on June 5th at 6 p.m.?

I was here in an English lesson.

I can't remember. I was probably on the bus, on my way home.

35   CHOICES Talking, page 74 Grammar, page 86 ▶▶▶

Figure 1

shall, nevertheless, begin with a page of a coursebook (Adrian-Vallance and Edge 1994), albeit decontextualised, reduced in size, and devoid of colour.

As we discuss the ways in which this particular material attempts to facilitate learner autonomy and teacher development, it will be helpful to keep in mind two aspects of the larger pedagogic context in which we are operating.

First, the idea of including materials to help students work on their learning processes is by now well-established in EFL coursebooks. Ellis and Sinclair (1992) provide a review of this aspect of several courses, as well as an evaluative framework. Orienting teachers' manuals towards teacher education is also an acknowledged theme. Cunningsworth and Kusel (1991) discuss the issue, and Hopkins and Potter (1994) introduce a useful approach.

Second, materials are not capable of **making** learners autonomous or **making** teachers develop. No materials could achieve such aims. If it were possible to design materials which attempted to constrain students and teachers in directions which the materials writers considered to be developmental, the use of those materials would defeat their own declared purposes. Autonomy and development arise from a desire for autonomy and development, supported by awareness of what it is that one does already and from a perception that the possibility of choice exists. Materials can aspire to be facilitative, to lend themselves towards use(fulness) in this type of process. In order to achieve this, however, they have first to be acceptable in terms of what teachers and students are already familiar with.

Choices for teacher development and learner autonomy

We have situated the page of material shown above in its wider pedagogical context. We have have also explained that it is beyond the scope of our paper to unpack all the ELT theory which lies behind such a page. So we will now ask readers to switch focus, and to treat the page itself as a context, for one specific feature on which we wish to concentrate. In line with our argument about the importance of choice (and our comments regarding the scale of what is involved), we shall focus our attention solely on the 'Choices' section which appears at the bottom of each page.

Via the 'Choices' section, the authors of the coursebook are seeking the delicate balance between familiarity based on existing experience, and pedagogically motivated innovation. The materials presented are an attempt both to provide a practical response to classroom realities, and to make another contribution in the areas of teacher development and learner autonomy.

In the example given, the reader is directed towards supplementary materials in the areas of 'Talking' and/or 'Grammar'. In other words, towards more communicative activity, if that is what is needed, and/or more language awareness work, if that is what is needed. Each lesson-page offers similar alternatives. Other 'Choices' sections contain supplementary work in the areas of 'Pronunciation', 'Writing', and 'Learning to learn'.

Teacher development

The 'Choices' are presented to the teacher as being available in the following ways:

- If there is sufficient time in the course, teachers have relevant supplementary material available and can choose which is most appropriate for their students.
- If there is, unexpectedly, some time left at the end of a lesson, teachers can decide which of the 'Choices' it would be appropriate for their students to follow.
- If one or more pairs or groups in a class finish a task before the others, the teacher can assign relevant follow-up material according to their needs.
- Teachers can assign 'Choices' for homework.
- The 'Choices' sections can be left towards the end of a course and then taught as coherent mini-syllabuses for review work in the various areas.

This approach is declaredly *not* revolutionary nor, it is hoped, overly directive. Teacher development should not be (in fact, cannot be) forced on to people. But what is offered here are materials which can either be used quite conventionally for supplementary work or, for those teachers who are interested, as the basis for increased involvement in aware and sensitive decision making as they extend the range of their own responsibility for their actions. In other words, the materials invite teachers to become more engaged in the deployment of what they have available, according to their perception of their own situation.

Teachers who begin this kind of engagement will pursue it to the extent that it brings them increased professional satisfaction. They will also approach other materials with what we might call this developmental attitude. The attitude, of course, needs to be fostered and supported in other ways. Once again, and as with most forms of communication, the new is best communicated in the context of something familiar. The position towards which the teacher's manuals for these materials has moved introduces a developmental slant to the expected provision of alternatives and extras. Thus, the introduction to *Teacher's Manual 3* (p.1) states:

- The lesson notes frequently suggest alternative ways of using the material and/or extra activities you can try. These are marked **Teacher Development Option**. You can use these suggestions to work on your own development as a teacher: If you teach the same materials to different classes, you might try both alternatives and then think about what happened and why. If you have a colleague who teaches the same materials, you could agree to use the different options and talk afterwards about what happened. Even more interesting is when you introduce your own alternatives and discuss them with a colleague. And if you have a colleague whom you trust enough, invite him or her to watch you teach a particular lesson That will make your discussions more meaningful again. The main point is to reflect on our experience in cooperation with our colleagues, so that we can each improve our teaching in ways which suit our own skills and personalities.

In the context of this general approach, Farrell (1995: *Teacher's Manual 3*, Unit 8: 39) for example, draws attention to alternative ways of combining an illustration, a printed dialogue and a recording.

We have focused so far on issues of teacher development. Relevant sources in which to pursue these ideas would be Edge 1992, Edge and Richards 1993, Fanselowe 1992, Freeman and Cornwell 1993, Nunan and Richards 1990 and Wallace 1991. The issues raised and exemplified, however, have equally direct relevance to learner autonomy.

Learner autonomy

Our approach to teacher development is to make choices available and to indicate how they might be used. If we return specifically to the 'Choices' section of the materials we have looked at, we can see that, for those teachers who wish to develop their teaching in this direction, any or all of the decisions concerned can be handed over in a structured way to the students themselves. In other words, the 'Choices' become available in the following ways:

- If there is sufficient time in the course, students have relevant supplementary material available and can choose which is most appropriate for themselves.
- If there is, unexpectedly, some time left at the end of a lesson, students (individually or in groups) can decide which of the 'Choices' it would be appropriate for them to follow.

- If one or more pairs or groups in a class finish a task before the others, they can look for relevant follow-up material according to their needs.
- The 'Choices' are available for work outside class.
- The 'Choices' sections can be left towards the end of a course and studied as coherent mini-syllabuses for review work in the various areas.

Initially under guidance, but increasingly independently, students can be offered the opportunity to become more aware themselves of the purpose of what they are doing in class, of how they individually seem to learn best, and of how they can support their own learning outside the class and away from the coursebook.

For those wishing to pursue issues of learner autonomy and development, the exchanges between Rees-Miller (1993, 1994) and Chamot and Rubin (1994) highlight differing positions in this area, as well as giving a useful contemporary bibliography. Cotterall (1995) provides an interesting case-study of the integration of such ideas into a teaching programme. For our own purposes, at this point, it is time to look at examples of the 'Choices' materials themselves.

The 'Choices' materials

In this section, we exemplify the five types of 'Choices' material. We have added comments and questions which we hope might initiate a discussion of some issues of potential interest.

Talking

Extra vocabulary: scientist president king
                              queen artist writer musician

1 *Pair Work* **Take turns asking and answering about famous people from history.**

EXAMPLE:
A: Who was Albert Einstein?
B: He was a scientist. **or**
    I don't know. Who was he?

2 *Pair Work* **With your partner, write five *pairs* of people from history.**

EXAMPLE:
John F. Kennedy and Ferdinand Marcos
(two presidents)

Ideas for materials development

3 *Pair Work* **Find a new partner. Ask and answer like this:**

EXAMPLE:
A: Who were John Kennedy and Ferdinand Marcos?
B: They were presidents.

Figure 2

How successful is this exercise in balancing, on the one hand, the need to provide false-beginner/elementary students with something to say, and, on the other hand, the need to provide a framework which encourages the investment and expression of their own general knowledge? Is it at all valid to posit the need for such a balance?

Grammar

TALKING ABOUT VERBS AND TENSES
Match the words on the left to the examples on the right.

a) the simple present tense with a frequency adverb — I'm waiting; He's going.
— I usually walk to school.
b) the present progressive tense — Stop!
I can't.
c) the past tense of *be* — To be or not to be.
d) a modal verb — Yes, I do.
e) an auxiliary verb
f) an infinitive with *to* — Where were you yesterday?
g) an imperative

Figure 3

The theoretical position taken up here is threefold:

1 Given that the students concerned, even at a false-beginner/elementary level of ability to communicate in English, have several years' experience of learning about English grammar, it can be cognitively useful to engage this learning in the new, more communicative, overall context.

2 In the above situation, it is affectively important to show respect for students' previous learning and to link it to their current work.

3 The outcome of this exercise is a written record, produced by the students, exemplifying familiar grammatical terms: the production of such a record is useful as a process in its own right. The record itself is useful for reference purposes.

What do you think of this position? How well does this exercise represent the position?

306

Pronunciation

MORE VOWEL SOUNDS

1 Circle the vowel sound that is different.

a) one   cut   (go)   love
b) does   run   come   road
c) where   were   hair   pair
d) friend   clean   see   street
e) through   pool   show   true
f) door   four   more   hour
g) say   eye   great   rain

Figure 4

Providing free-standing pronunciation practice without an initial teacher or taped input is not easy! Here is one attempt. Can you come up with other suggestions? Is it perhaps not a good idea to try to provide such practice? This exercise also sets out to engage student creativity and encourage peer teaching. Are these valid purposes in this type of work, or would the second part of the activity cause more problems than it is worth?

Writing

The reading referred to ('Names', on page 8) provides short paragraphs by characters from the United States, Morocco, Japan and Taiwan. One part of the thinking here is to include accurate information across cultural backgrounds, making students more aware of other customs, and of the relative nature of their own. Is this a realistic contribution to such a goal? Is the goal worthwhile? Or is it just pretentious window-dressing?

In terms of its form, the writing exercise asks teachers to decide for students, or students to decide for themselves, how much support they want to avail themselves of in order to complete the task. So, the principles of choice, development and individual responsibility are also operating at this level. How else might they be realised?

First, read **Names** on page 8.

WRITING TASK

What is your name? What do people call you? In your country, what titles do people use for men, women and children, and for teachers and for the boss at work?

If you need help, start with this exercise:

Ideas for materials development

Figure 5

Learning to learn

Here, we are working explicitly towards the delivery of the ideas
regarding attitudes and skills discussed in our section on learner
autonomy above.

THINK ABOUT LEARNING

1 Match the things below to exercises in Unit 1.

What do we learn and practice?	Exercises (left-hand page) and CHOICES	Exercises (right-hand page) and CHOICES
listening	*1*	
speaking	*2, 3, 5, 6*	
reading		
writing		
grammar		
vocabulary		
pronunciation		
*useful phrases		

*Examples of useful phrases are:
Good afternoon. I don't know. Thank you.*

**2 *Group Work* Talk to other students in your
group. Which things do you like?**

EXAMPLES: I like listening. I don't like speaking.
Reading is OK.

Which things are important for you?

Figure 6

308

This is the opening exercise in the 'Choices' section. Its first aim is make an immediate start on encouraging students to think about the purpose of the work they are doing. The second aim is to make people aware of their own preferences and aims, and of the fact that other learners can be very different. The theory is that all three forms of awareness can be helpful to language learning. Specifically, they can help people develop a reflective attitude regarding what they are doing and why. What is your position on that?

LEARNING VOCABULARY (3)

1 A technique for remembering vocabulary:

Meriem's language is Arabic. When she first heard the English word *kitten* (= baby cat), it reminded her of the Arabic word *kitab* (= book). She imagined a picture of a kitten reading a book, and she never forgot the meaning of *kitten*!

Try Meriem's technique now!
Choose an English word. Which word in your language does it sound like? Imagine the two things together.

Figure 7

A very different sort of exercise (Figure 7), deals more directly with a technique for the learning of language items themselves. Vocabulary acquisition is an area of language learning more amenable than most to such techniques as this. It is important to get across the idea that there is no such thing as a good technique in its own right – there is a variety of techniques and students should try them out to see which work for them. Or do you think that there are some techniques which are definitely useful and which should be taught to everyone?

Conclusion

At a theoretical level, the 'Choices' materials, used in the context of a general, commercial coursebook, aspire towards sharing a commitment with the work of Earl Stevick (e.g. Stevick 1986, 1989) to the idea of growth by choice, and to the possibility of facilitating growth by choice.

The central argument which we are putting forward is that teaching materials can be written in such a way as to support teacher development and learner autonomy. We have supported the argument with examples from one of what we expect to be an increasing number of attempts in the area. We are only at the beginning of these possibilities, but they seem to indicate one fruitful way forward for material design.

Acknowledgements

We should like to acknowledge the work of all the people involved in the production of the above materials, most especially that of Damien Tunnacliffe, who first commissioned *Right Track*, and who did not lose faith. We take full responsibility for the interpretations offered in this article.

14 Lozanov and the teaching text

Grethe Hooper Hansen

Introduction

Georgi Lozanov MD is the creator of Suggestopedia, a revolutionary method of learning/teaching which surfaced in the late 60s. Concentrating on learner receptivity, it uses music and complex means of relaxation to mediate states of mind in which a very large volume of material can be absorbed with ease. The early reports were naturally received with some scepticism and opposite camps were established of the Faithful vs. the Ironists. The publication of Lozanov's book *Suggestology and Outlines of Suggestopedy* (1978), with its strange Iron Curtain scientific terminology and accounts of experiments which did not satisfy the research requirements of the time, met with critical censure from the American academic world. From that time on his work was committed to the 'fringe' of odd-ball methodologies.

However, a lot has happened in neuropsychology since Lozanov was branded with the all-too-well-remembered 'pseudo-scientific gobbledygook'. Thanks to the technology that produced positron emission tomography (PET) and magnetic resonance imaging (MRI), we now know how the two brain hemispheres react differently to particular stimuli, that neo-cortex functioning is inhibited by alarm and survival activity from the lower areas of the brain and that long-term memory relies heavily on circuits housed largely in the limbic (emotional) area.

The work in medicine of Hans Selye and his interpreter E. L Rossi (1986) brought to light the fact that both physical health and mental dispositions are hugely influenced by the biochemicals that we produce in the brain through our emotions, thoughts and responses to our physical activities and environmental stimuli. N. F. Dixon, doyen of the psychology of the preconscious, established the distinction between new learning, which is largely right-hemispheric and prior to awareness, and 'coding' or integrating the knowledge into our existing store (Dixon 1985). Most recently, the work of Antonio Damasio, head of Neurology at the University of Iowa Medical School, has shaken the foundations of what we always believed to be reason. According to Damasio (1994), Descartes' error was the assumption in *Cogito ergo sum* that thinking is the substrate of consciousness. Damasio establishes that this is not the case, showing that what we take to be reason is more likely to be based on a computation of representations of bodily states stored in memory and 'tagged' for future reference so as to assist in the prediction of probable outcomes when selecting alternative courses of action. This theory has been incorporated by linguists such as Bob Jacobs and John Schumann (1992) into studies of the neurological differences between 'deep learning' and that which teachers have traditionally offered to learners in educational institutions.

So it was neither pseudo nor gobbledygook, just ahead of its time. Lozanov worked on scientific intuition (based on a lifetime in medicine and psychiatry) and went to press before acceptable substantiation was available. Now his work forms the basis of what is filtering into education under the banner of Multi-Level Learning, and in the commercial world, Accelerated Learning. The unfortunately named Suggestopedia (a tribute to his imperfect English) may still be regarded as a 'fringe method' in EFL but it is the seed of revolution in general education. This chapter summarises Lozanov's ideas and reviews their implications for text writing and grammatical presentation.

Lozanov's fundamental discovery was that STATE of consciousness and mind is crucial to learning. In his medical work, he found that hypnosis could give rise to mental conditions in which it was clear that the mind not only controlled its own intake of information but could influence dramatically such physical processes as bleeding and healing. Applying this to education, he soon became firmly opposed to the use of hypnotic techniques but worked instead on ways to enable clients to achieve such effects autonomously. His teaching method is an attempt to build learner autonomy by subtle means (of which the most significant are non-directive teaching and techniques for raising expectation, self confidence and, with it, trust in others) to the point where learners can exercise control over their own ability to learn – and, conversely, imperviousness to unwanted influence.

Noting that the brain uses only a fraction of its capacity, he tested the hypothesis that this is partly due to negative expectation. He found that when conscious awareness of intake is inhibited, the absence of recoding (and with it, all the negative beliefs we have of our own limitations) enabled the mind to absorb infinitely more information. This has now been clarified by N. F. Dixon (*ibid.*), and is of course familiar to linguists as the acquisition process, when new language enters a mind which is concentrating on other matters. Turn up the volume of emotion to increase salience, introduce games and play to keep the mind relaxed (and receptive fields open wide), add music for right hemispheric stimulation, and learning increases proportionately.

Lozanov also observed that the whole brain is always working, right and left hemispheres, neocortex and subcortical areas. When we polarise our messages towards the intellectual centres of the brain only, the others will not close down but engage in competing activities. Lozanov attempts to harness all areas in the same endeavour, reducing interference to a minimum and making use of the various different learning strengths and means available. Montessori worked on similar lines and Experiential Learning makes use of the same basic principles, as did Gerald Edelman's work on perception in the sixties. Edelman's 1968 theory of perception is that groups of neurons in different areas of the brain oscillate in synchrony in response to pattern perceivement in the environment. From the teaching perspective, the notable point is that, rather than building incrementally, we receive the *gestalt* (for details of Edelman's theories see Edelman 1993). What Lozanov has done is to add a battery of techniques for intensification – which has led to the name Multi-Level Learning.

The conclusion to be drawn for constructing texts is that the material is aimed at unconscious, not conscious, learning (hence the form of the material normally used: a dramatic dialogue, not isolated chunks of prose), and the means of making it more memorable are all those things that attract the non-conscious mind. While the conscious mind opens to that which makes sense and closes to that which is not plausible, the non-conscious (like the rest of nature) is governed more by the pleasure principle. As advertisers know, colour, form, beauty, comfort and intimations of things we desire are magnets to the mind.

An example of the lesson cycle

Text: a comedy in 8–10 acts (1 act per cycle). Cycle 8–10 hrs, parcelled as appropriate: Role play: Ls choose name and profession in target lang and develop persona as course proceeds.

Presentation
1 Teacher (T) introduces story of act, using target grammmatical structures and vocabulary, 'Passive' learners (Ls) listen, intervening only if they want to.
2 First concert: T distributes text (1,000–2,000 words) with translation at beginner level, then reads the whole act aloud to accompaniment of classical music. Ls listen, read and follow the translation.
3 Second concert: T reads again to accompaniment of Baroque music. Ls listen, eyes closed, relaxed.

Elaboration

Activation of target structures and vocabulary. E1 involves (Ls) reading aloud, translation, occasional grammatical demonstration. E2 freer: activities, games, drama, songs. (VARIETY)

THE TEXT

is a play in 8–10 acts, each complete in itself.
The cast mirrors
an ideal suggestopedic learning group –
8 or more extraordinary people,
equal in humanity   equal in . . .
if not in material status,
involved in some way in the arts   involved in . . .
(to allow for artistic metaphors,
high aesthetic content,   allow for. . .
underlying search for self-realisation).   search for. . .
The plot typically involves
a situation which brings together
geographically scattered people.
It is important that the situation
not be too 'far-out' because
the intention is to show
that high-voltage living   intend to . . .
is only a small step,
an adjustment of mind,
from where we are now.
Mythical worlds appeal to writers   appeal to . . .
but may impose a dissociative framework.

Figure 1

The dialogue is written in column form, as above, with language presented in sense units, which makes it easier to learn. Key words may be underlined or emphasised (I don't like doing this). A grammatical feature is picked out and examples of it are listed in the right-hand column. Translation is used at beginner level, provided in a single column clipped over the grammar column, never printed in the text, since this would be a negative learning suggestion.

Since suggestopedic learning is based on text absorption, it is essential that all the grammatical structures chosen for emphasis or exposition are contained in the text. Ideally, texts would exist in floppy disk form rather than in printed books so that they can be changed and adapted for different circumstances, but Lozanov uses books for the sake of convenience and to include high-quality coloured illustrations (see the section on the aesthetic principle).

In addition to this constraint, the text must be full of cue words or phrases to trigger activities and 'spontaneous' grammatical presentation (for example, when in the first elaboration we chorus the phrase 'on the fourth floor' from my text, this is my cue to run through a quick routine on ordinal numbers – as if the idea had just popped into my head and was not a planned piece of linguistic work).

This is a need which does not exist within other methods, and will be explained in the section on grammatical presentation.

Language

The target structures and vocabulary must be worked into a natural, flowing dialogue. The more fluid and melodious it sounds, the more vivid in imagery and poetic the language, the better it will penetrate the (non-conscious) mind. Simplicity implies ease, and texts should delight the ear: ideally this would invoke a combination of Pinter and Eliot. But, to be sure of engaging the limbic brain, there is also a need for high emotional content. In addition, there are metaphors and images wherever possible to encourage global rather than analytical respond-ing, symbols and archetypes to rivet attention (water, trees, birds, animals of all kinds, sun, moon etc.), words stimulating the senses and motor system (sensori-motor learning) and a high concrete vocabulary to encourage imaging. To this we can add Assagioli's recommendations to fascinate the mind of paradoxes, wordplays and koans (apparently nonsensical word puzzles requiring right hemispheric, inferential solutions), as well as humour, tongue twisters, snatches of poetry, proverbs and sayings (Assagioli 1968).

Unlike most other methods, Lozanov's presents richness and com-plexity of structures right from the start; language is not limited to the structures which will be taught in that unit. The intention is to prime the mind for future learning and present the language as a *gestalt* in all its variety and multiplicity.

The most controversial issue in Lozanovian writing is the need for total positivity at all times. Negativity is avoided rather than denied (Lozanov includes various other means of discharging negative emotion, particularly through music) simply because, within this paradigm, it is obstructive to learning. Stress and anxiety tend to over-activate the left hemisphere and the sympathetic division of the auto-nomic nervous system, which reduces receptivity at the paraconscious level. With Lozanov's method, the mind must be soaring high and free.

Thus, texts avoid gossip, malice (even when hilarious), accidents, disasters, crime, manipulation in relationships and sex (because it can have very painful connotations for some people).

Texts are also peppered with symbols and suggestions of success – so that the mind is primed in this way. It is interesting that, although Lozanov was not aware of the work of Assagioli, they were contemporaries and thought on very similar lines. Another fellow spirit is Carl Rogers, whose dislike of 'didacticism' mirrors Lozanov's avoidance of the pedantic and erudite, which he refers to as 'philosophising' and regards as armouring against assorted emotional deficits. Rogers was one of the founding fathers of Humanistic Pschology and is famous for bringing its ideas into education and in particular for a lecture at Harvard University in the 50s in which he announced that education was not only a waste of time but was positively harmful to its recipients. For details of Roger's views, see Rogers 1983.

A final point is Lozanov's insistence on aesthetic content. He takes a Socratic view of art as uplifting to the mind: a work of art, which creates harmony among its elements, has the effect on the perceiver of drawing her mind into a similar harmony, which in turn makes her better able to perceive or respond to the implicit order of the world which surrounds her. This is a subtle effect which Lozanov tried and tested in his own psychotherapy long before he turned his attention to language teaching. According to him, it is sufficient simply to introduce into the text material about the artistic world, which will have the effect of adjusting the perceiver's mind in that direction. His own texts include poetry and high-quality colour reproductions of paintings: Turner, Gainsborough etc., for his as yet unpublished English text *The Return*.

Grammar

Contrary to what is often believed about Lozanov's method, he is meticulous in grammatical presentation and insists that if a structure is omitted from overt presentation it may never be learned. However, his methods of presenting are very different from the norm, aimed as they are at non-conscious rather than conscious reception.

The major slot for overt grammatical presentation in the Lozanov cycle is in the first elaboration during the choral reading of the text. After the repetition of a certain sentence, there will be a momentary and apparently spontaneous (but in fact carefully planned) focus on a grammatical item. This must:

a) come from the text, so that the learner's mind remains focused on the drama rather than the linguistic structure;

b) be BRIEF so that the learners do not get a chance to switch into analytical mode. For this reason, it is never followed by an exercise or drill, which will take place at a later stage.

c) be INCOMPLETE so that there is still material for the (unconscious) mind to puzzle over and sort out – given that the human mind is a compulsive pattern maker and is positively stimulated by challenge.

Grammar never appears to be dwelt upon for its own sake, but to arise spontaneously as a textual puzzle. Questions about it are typically mirrored back to the asker, albeit in a delicate and diplomatic way; at all levels learners are encouraged to do their own problem solving, and receive assistance only after persistent request, a gentle discouragement to most people.

'Explanation' is given in visual, auditory and kinaesthetic (bodily) modes to cater for different learning styles, although in fact the visual mode is the most useful in catering for predominantly right hemispheric reception because it allows a greater degree of mobility and freedom in perception. In an auditory message the listener has to follow the sequence of words and cannot back-track, whereas in a visual message the eye can leap about as it pleases.

To meet the needs of the right brain for whole pattern and *gestalt*, information is presented in volume and completeness and pattern picked out through colour change and through form. All those old-fashioned grammar books with page after page of tables would provide perfect material for the Lozanovian lesson if they could be reproduced in colour (which is especially meaningful to the non-conscious mind). The only difference is that old-fashioned grammar teachers forced students to track through the text in a way that makes global learning almost impossible, whereas Lozanov presents the material at speed and with only minimal verbal comment (relevant posters appear on the wall in advance of the lesson and will go back on the wall for a short time after it).

In this way, the learner's mind remains in the context of the drama and simply notices a brief interruption in which a potentially puzzling phrase is elucidated by being linked to the syntactic pattern inherent in it. Thus, the non-conscious mind remains responsible for sorting out the linguistic issues while the conscious mind concentrates on following the story, a more appropriate occupation for its reductive and much slower process. (I used to observe as a foreign language teacher how children, particularly at early teenage prior to the stage of development which facilitates interchange between the two hemispheres, would founder in the gulf between global language immersion and an analytical presentation of grammar. It was no wonder that they 'hated grammar'.)

Of course, there is no escaping from the fact that some repetition is necessary for learning ('Automaticity is a function of repetition' (Anderson 1980)). In the Lozanovian context, this occurs during the second elaboration when the learners are playing games. Typically, there will be a circulation game (I use a tambourine to make this more attractive and keep to tempo) in which learners ask each other communicative questions of their own devising; all Lozanov practice has always observed what we refer to as the communicative principle. Rote learning will take place in playful ways such as singing (e.g. irregular verbs – try this with movement in two teams, alternating, to the tune of the Big Ben clock chimes. Teams join hands; team A shouts out an irregular verb and team B walks forward and then back singing it; then Bs choose and As perform, etc.).

Puppets provide a wonderful means of giving verbal example and explanation while avoiding didacticism, and at the same time offer great potential for positive suggestion in the topics they talk about; nearly all learners automatically identify in some way with puppets, who seem to represent their secret thoughts when confronted by teachers and authority figures. (This could be analysed in the light of Robert Lang's work on the human's compulsive adaptive response to the boundary implications of verbal message (Smith 1991).) Puppets, being non-animate, do not communicate at a non-verbal level, and therefore offer unlimited possibilities to the imagination – as does the mask.

Given all his reasons for preserving globality at all times and at any cost, Lozanov has to introduce structures in a different sequence from that of 'normal' courses. For example, in the case of modal verbs, they are ALL introduced at once (and posters designed accordingly) so that it is immediately apparent that all conform to a single language pattern, which, in the Lozanov context, is all that the learners need to be told. Thus both semantics and order of simplicity are subordinated to FORM. For Lozanov semantics are a negligible issue since meaning should already be apparent in the text, and is something so fundamental to the unconscious mental search that it does not have to be presented twice.

Conclusion

Since he is not a linguist and is far more interested in psychological than linguistic matters, Lozanov has not written much about grammatical presentation, and the information has to be gleaned from study of his texts and activation notes. A great deal of work remains to be done, which opens up an exciting and rewarding area for graduate studies. His ideas are also applicable to all coursebook writing, not to be followed to the letter but to be borne in mind. The post-Dixon and Damasio academic world has to recognise that every human being is at all times hugely influenced by impressions occurring beneath conscious awareness. Study of factors which facilitate learning in this mode can only make our materials more effective and more appealing.

15 Access-self materials

Brian Tomlinson

Introduction

The stereotypical image of self-access materials is of exercises which enable the learners to work on what they need in their own time and at their own pace without reference to a teacher. Such materials attempt to achieve the desirable objective of learner centred, learner invested activity. Typically they are used to supplement classroom learning activities and usually they focus on providing extra practice in the use of specific language items or language skills which are problematic for the students. Thus in a recent *ELTJ* article the authors asserted that:

> we remain convinced of the value of single-focus material for self-access learners who have been trying to identify their particular problems and who are keen to improve their ability in specific points of language. (Lin and Brown 1994)

The development of such materials and their attractive accessibility in learning centres or learning packages has been a positive feature of foreign language learning pedagogy in the last decade. However the main strength of self-access materials has been their main weakness too. In order to make sure that learners can work entirely on their own and still receive useful feedback there has been a limiting tendency to restrict the activities to those which can most easily be self-marked by the learners themselves. Thus, although there are notable exceptions, most self-access materials have consisted of controlled or guided practice activities which have used cloze, multiple choice, gap-filling, matching and transformation activities to facilitate self-marking and focused feedback. Such activities can usefully contribute to the development of explicit declarative knowledge (i.e. conscious knowledge of the forms, meanings and systems of the language). But their predominance has meant for many learners that their experience of self-access materials has been restricted to basically closed activities requiring a narrow left brain focus and little utilisation of prior personal experience, of the brain's potential learning capacity or of individual attributes or inclinations. It has also meant that opportunities have been lost to help learners to develop procedural knowledge of the language (i.e. know-ledge of how it is actually used to achieve intended effects) and also that self-access materials have made little contribution to the development of implicit knowledge (i.e. knowledge acquired subconsciously). So much more could be achieved through the medium of self-access if only we could stop worrying about answer keys and self-marking.

Ironically, in order to achieve ease and reliability of self-marking, many self-access materials designed to individualise learning have in fact treated learners as though they are stereotypical clones of each other. The prevailing learning styles are analytical, visual and indepen-dent. This is fine if you happen to be a learner who likes to focus on discrete bits of language, who likes to see the language written down and who is happy to work alone. In other words, if you are a studial learner, then self-access is for you. But then if you are a studial learner you probably fit the stereotypical image of the 'good language learner' (see Ellis 1994a: 546–50) and you are making good progress anyway; because, let's face it, most coursebooks and lessons are designed for you. But what if you are an experiential, global, kinaesthetic learner (i.e. you like to learn by doing and you prefer to respond to the overall meaning of language which you encounter rather than to decode bits of it)? Then there is not much in most learning centres for you. And yet you probably need the extra opportunities to compensate for the unprofitable time you have had to spend engaged in form focused, analytic activities in the classroom.

The narrowing tendency described above has been reinforced recently by the economy led demand for cost effective open learning in institutes of higher education in the UK (for example, some of the new universities currently stipulate that 10–15 per cent of courses be delivered through 'open learning'). Of course, in order to be cost effective, open learning has to be closed enough not to require the participation of teachers during or after student activities. Self-marking keys are cheaper and more reliable than teachers and thus closed activities rule.

What I would like to advocate is not the replacement of closed self-access activities (after all the best time for individual language practice is when you are alone) but their supplementation by genuinely open activities which require learner investment of both the mind and the heart and which provide opportunities for the broadening and deep-ening of experience as well as for the acquisition of the target language. Such activities I shall distinguish by the descriptive label of **access-self** activities.

Principles of access-self activities

Access-self activities should:

1 Be self-access in the conventional sense of providing opportunities for learners to choose what to work on and to do so in their own time and at their own pace.
2 Be open-ended in the sense that they do not have correct and incorrect answers but rather permit a variety of acceptable responses.
3 Engage the learners' individuality in the activities in such a way as to exploit their prior experience and to provide opportunities for personal development.
4 Involve the learners as human beings rather than just as language learners.
5 Require a personal investment of energy and attention in order for learner discoveries to be made (as recommended in Tomlinson 1994a and exemplified in Bolitho and Tomlinson 1995).
6 Stimulate various left and right brain activities at the same time and thus maximise the brain's potential for learning and development (as recommended in Lozanov 1978).
7 Provide a rich, varied and comprehensible input in order to facilitate informal acquisition (as recommended, for example, in Krashen 1981) as well as providing opportunities for selective attention to linguistic or pragmatic features of the discourse (as suggested by Schmidt 1990).

In other words I am recommending a more humanistic approach to self-access activities which aims to develop both the declarative and the procedural knowledge of the learners as well as making a positive and broadening contribution to their education.

Features of access-self materials

1 The materials provide extensive exposure to authentic English through purposeful reading and/or listening activities.
2 Whilst reading listening activities are offered to facilitate interaction with the text(s).
3 The post-reading/listening activities first of all elicit global, holistic responses which involve interaction between the self and the text.
4 The focus of the main responsive activities is on the development of such high level skills as imaging, inferencing, connecting, interpreting and evaluating.

5 There are also activities which help the learners to fix selective attention in such a way that they can discover something new about specific features of the text and thus become aware of any mismatch between their competence and the equivalent performance of target language users.
6 Production activities involve the use of the target language in order to achieve situational purposes rather than just to practise specific linguistic features of the target language. These activities offer involvement in various types of personal expression (e.g. analytical, aesthetic, imaginative, argumentative, evaluative).
7 The learners are given plenty of opportunities to make choices which suit their linguistic level, their preferred learning styles, their level of involvement in the text and the time they have available.
8 Whereas self-access activities are typically private and individual, access-self activities include the possibility of like minded learners working together without reference to a teacher. That way the learners are able to choose between the tailor-made benefits of private work and the opportunity to pool resources and energy with fellow learners.
9 Feedback is given through commentaries rather than answer keys. The commentaries give the learners opportunities to compare their responses to those of the material developers and of other learners. They can be consulted at the end of the activities to gain summative feedback or during activities in order to help learners to modify or develop their responses as they proceed through the unit (as recommended in Dickinson 1987 and exemplified by Bolitho and Tomlinson 1995).
10 Learner training is encouraged through activities which involve the learners in thinking about the learning process and in experiencing a variety of different types of learning activities from which they can later make informed choices in determining their route through the access-self materials.
11 Suggestions for individual follow-up activities are given at the end of each unit.

Suitable texts for access-self materials

There are many types of text which can provide a base for access-self activities. What is common to them all is that they have the potential to engage the learners both cognitively and affectively. My own preferred genre is narrative whether it be in the form of novels, short stories, plays, poems, oral stories or songs (as used, for example, in Tomlinson 1994c). I find that narratives which engage the reader in interaction with characters, events and themes which are meaningful to them have the potential to utilise and develop personal experience as well to provide 'positive evidence' for language acquisition. And, as Ronnqvist and Sell (1994) say in discussing the value of literature in language education for teenagers, 'the reading of literary texts in the target language gives genuine and easily available experience in the pragmatics of relating formal linguistic expression to situational and socio-cultural contexts'. Of course, in order for this potential to be realised the learners have to want to interact with the text and therefore have to be provided with a wide choice of texts to choose from. It has certainly been my experience that, 'providing the learners have some say in the choice of texts and are not forced to "study", then literature can motivate even the most reluctant learners because of its appeal to their humanity' (Tomlinson 1994c). Other genres and text types with similar access-self potential are newspaper reports, editorials and articles, television and radio news broadcasts, advertisements, magazine articles and television discussion and documentary programmes. One of the obvious advantages of narrative though is that it can be written for any level of learner without any loss of authenticity.

An example of a unit of access-self material

Below is an example of a unit of access-self material based on extracts from *My Son's Story* (Gordimer 1991). It is designed for self-access use in a Learning Centre but could easily be adapted for a self-access period in the classroom or for a homework book. Note in particular the use of open-ended, holistic activities, the possibility of groupwork and the use of a Commentary which gives possible responses rather than answers as well as making use of previous learners' responses to the activities.

You could actually do the activities and experience what they involve or you could read through the materials and try to connect them to learners who you know. Either way it would be useful if you could then evaluate the materials. Ask yourself whether they put into practice the principles of access-self materials as outlined above and whether they would appeal to your learners. If you like the materials you could adapt them for use with your learners and you could also write other similar Samples for use with your learners. If you do, please write and let me know what the learner responses are.

An example of access-self material
Samples of modern literature
Sample 1 – *My Son's Story*

Introduction

This is one of a series of units which is based on modern literature and which is designed for learners who are at an intermediate level or above. Each unit introduces you to extracts from a book and aims to give you access to that book in such a way that will help you to develop your language skills and to acquire new language. It is also hoped that the extracts and activities will give you an interest in the book and that you will go on to read the book for yourself.

Try the unit and if you get interested in it carry on and do most of the activities (you don't have to do them all). If you then want to read the book for yourself take it out from the library. If you don't want to read the book, do another of these sample units and see if you want to read that book for yourself.

You can do this unit by yourself or you can work on it with other learners if you prefer.

Activities

1 You're going to read the beginning of a novel called *My Son's Story*. The novel begins:
   'How did I find out?
   I was deceiving him.'

   Think of different possible meanings for this beginning of the novel and then write answers to the following questions:
   a) Who do you think 'I' might be?
   b) What do you think the discovery could be?
   c) Who do you think 'him' might be?
   d) What do you think the deception could be?

2 Read the first paragraph of the extract from *My Son's Story* on page 1 of the Text Sheet (see page 328) and then answer questions 1 (a–d) again.

3 Check your answers to 2 above against those on page 1 of the Commentary (see page 330).

4 Read all of Extract 1 from the novel on pages 2–3 (see pages 328–29) of the Text Sheet and try to picture in your mind the people and the setting as you read.
   If you found the extract interesting go on to question 5. If

325

you didn't find it interesting choose a different Sample from the box.

5 Draw a picture of the narrator's meeting with his father. Don't worry about the artistic merit of your drawing (you should see my attempt); just try to include the important features of the scene.

6 Compare your drawing of the meeting with the drawings on page 1 of the Commentary (see page 330). What do all three drawings have in common? What are the differences between the drawings?

7 If you're working individually pretend you're watching a film of *My Son's Story* and act out in your head the meeting between the narrator, his father and Hannah. Try to give them different voices. If you're working in a group act out the scene together.

8 Compare your scene with the suggested film-script for the scene on page 2 of the Commentary (see page 331).

9 Imagine that the narrator is talking to his best friend the next day and that he's telling him about the meeting with his father. Write the dialogue between the two friends.

10 Compare your dialogue with the suggested dialogues on page 3 of the Commentary (see pages 331–32).

11 Write answers to the following questions:
   a) Why do you think the narrator is so disturbed by the encounter with his father?
   b) How old do you think the narrator was at the time of his encounter with his father and Hannah? Why?
   c) Who does 'us' refer to in 'Cinemas had been open to us only a year or so'?
   d) Explain in your own words the meaning of 'the moment we saw one another it was I who had discovered him, not he me'.
   e) Why do you think his father opened the conversation by saying, 'You remember Hannah, don't you –'? Why did he not ask him why he was not studying?
   f) When had the narrator met Hannah before? Why did he not recognise her when he first saw her outside the cinema?
   g) What does the narrator mean by, 'And the voice was an echo from another life'?

h) What does the narrator's description of Hannah tell you about his attitude towards her?

i) Why do you think the narrator mentions that his father was wearing 'his one good jacket'?

j) What does the narrator mean when he says he was 'safe among familiar schoolbooks'?

12 Compare your answers to 11 with the suggested answers on pages 3–4 of the Commentary (see pages 332–33).

13 Find examples in the text of the use of the past perfect tense. For each example say why you think the writer used the past perfect instead of the simple past.

14 Compare your answers to 13 with the suggested answers on pages 4–5 of the Commentary (see pages 333–34).

15 Later in the novel, the father asks his son to go on his new motorbike to Hannah's house to deliver an important parcel to her.

a) Write the dialogue in the scene in which the father asks the son to deliver the parcel.

b) Imagine that you are the narrator. Write the scene from the novel in which you deliver the parcel to Hannah's house.

16 Compare your answers to 15 to the answers on pages 5–6 of the Commentary (see pages 334–35). These are answers which were written by other learners.

17 Read Extract 2 from the novel on page 2 of the Text Sheet in which the narrator goes to Hannah's house on his motorbike (see page 329).

If you'd like any further feedback on any of the written work that you've done in this unit put your name on it and put it in the Feedback Box.

18 If you're still interested in the story, take the novel, *My Son's Story*, from the library shelf.

Write down what you think the significance is of the illustration on the front cover.

Read the novel in your own time and then, if you wish, talk about it with one of the other students who've already read the book (their names are on the back cover). Add your name to those on the back cover.

(Adapted from Tomlinson, B. 1994. *Openings*)

Extract 1

How did I find out?
I was deceiving him.
November. I was on study leave—for two weeks before the exams pupils in the senior classes were allowed to stay home to prepare themselves. I would say I was going to work with a friend at a friend's house, and then I'd slip off to a cinema. Cinemas had been open to us only a year or so; it was a double freedom I took: to bunk study and to sit in the maroon nylon velvet seat of a cinema in a suburb where whites live. My father was not well off but my parents wanted my sister and me to have a youth less stunted by the limits of an empty pocket than they had had, and my pocket money was more generous than their precarious position, at the time, warranted. So I was in the foyer waiting to get into a five o'clock performance at one of the cinemas in a new complex and my father and a woman came out of the earlier performance in another.

There was my father; the moment we saw one another it was I who had discovered him, not he me. We stood there while other people crossed our line of vision. Then he came towards me with her in the dazed way people emerge from the dark of a cinema to daylight.

He said, You remember Hannah, don't you—

And she prompted with a twitching smile to draw my gaze from him—for I was concentrating on him the great rush of questions, answers, realizations, credulity and dismay which stiffened my cheeks and gave the sensation of cold water rising up my neck—she prompted, Hannah Plowman, of course we know each other.

I said, Hullo. He drew it from me; we were back again in our little house across the veld from Benoni and I was being urged to overcome the surly shyness of a six-year-old presented with an aunt or cousin. What are you going to see? he said. While he spoke to me he drew back as if I might smell her on him. I didn't know. They managed to smile, almost laugh, almost make the exchange commonplace. But it was so: the title of the film I had planned to see was already banished from my mind, as this meeting would have to be, ground away under my heel, buried along with it. The Bertolucci—an Italian film—it's very good, he said, delicately avoiding the implications of the natural prefix, 'We thought. . .' She nodded enthusiastically. That's the one to see, Will, he was saying. And the voice was an echo from another life, where he was my father giving me his usual measured, modest advice. Then he signalled a go-along-and-enjoy-yourself gesture, she murmured politely, and they left me as measuredly as they had approached. I watched their backs so I would believe it really had happened; that woman: with her bare pink bottle-calves and clumsy sandals below the cotton outfit composed of a confusion of styles from different peasant cultures, him in his one good jacket that I had taken to the dry-cleaners for him many times, holding the shape of his shoulders folded back over my arm.

Then I ran from the cinema foyer, my vision confined straight ahead like a blinkered horse so that I wouldn't see which way they were going, and I took a bus home, home, home where I shut myself up in my room, safe among familiar schoolbooks.

Extract 2

I went on the motorbike. I had it by then. They gave it to me for my birthday. He said to me with that smile of a loving parent concealing a fine surprise, you can get a licence at sixteen now, can't you. So I knew he was going to buy me a bike I never asked for it but they gave it to me. With the latest, most expensive helmet for my safety; he must have had to promise my mother that.

I went with the helmet and chin-guard and goggles hiding my face. You can't see the place from the street, where he goes. Dogs at the gate, and a black gardener had to come to let me in; I suppose they wag their tails for someone who comes often, is well known to them by his own scent. There was a big house but that's not where he goes. She lives in a cottage behind trees at the end of the garden. Maybe there's even a private entrance from there I didn't know about, he didn't like to tell me. All open and above-board through the front entrance.

He must have told her, she was expecting me. Oh it's Will, isn't it—as if the helmet and stuff prevented her from recognizing me, from remembering the cinema that time. It also playfully implied, determined to be friendly, that I was rude, not taking the helmet off. So I did. So she could see it was me, Will, yes. I gave her whatever it was he'd sent me with. It was a package, books or something, he told me 'Miss Plowman' needed urgently.—You're the family Mercury now, with that wonderful machine of yours—off you go, son, but don't tear along like a Hell's Angel, hey.— A perfect performance in front of my mother.

This was where he came. It must be familiar as our house to him, where we live now and where we lived when we were in Benoni, because our house is where we are, our furniture, our things, his complete Shakespeare, the smells of my mother's cooking and the flowers she puts on the table. But this isn't like a house at all; well, all right, a cottage, but not even any kind of place where you'd expect a white would live. The screen door full of holes. Bare floor and a huge picture like spilt paint that dazzles your eyes, a word-processor, hi-fi going with organ music, twisted stubs in ashtrays, fruit, packets of bran and wheat-germ, crumpled strings of women's underthings drying on a radiator—and a bed, on the floor. There was the bed, just a very big wide mattress on the floor, covered with some cloth with embroidered elephants and flowers and bits of mirror in the design—the bed, just like that, right there in the room where anybody can walk in, the room where I was standing with my helmet in my hand.

So now I know.

Figure 1   Extracts from My Son's Story *by Nadine Gordimer*

Samples of modern literature
Sample 1 – *My Son's Story*
Commentary

3 a) 'I' is the narrator of the story. He or she was a pupil in a
       senior class at the time of the story and was about to take
       exams.
    b) That his or her father had been to the cinema with a
       woman. Maybe the father was having an affair.
    c) Probably the father.
    d) The narrator had pretended he or she was going to a
       friend's house to study but had gone to the cinema
       instead.

6 Look at the two drawings below of the meeting between the
   narrator and his father. How are they similar to each other

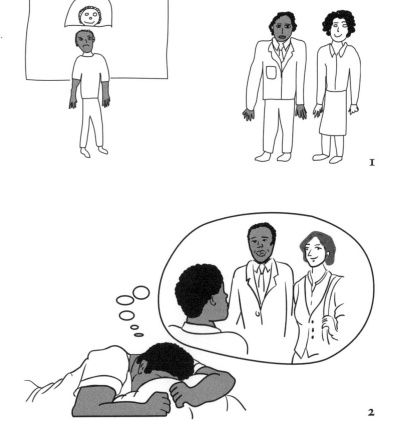

and how are they similar to your drawing. How are they different from each other and how is each one different from yours?

Go back and change any features of your drawing that you want to and add some extra details if you wish.

8

Here is one possible film script for the scene. How is it similar to and different from yours? Obviously there are many possible interpretations.

The son is standing in a queue in the foyer of a new cinema complex. He looks at the posters on the wall and then at his watch. People start to come out of a door across the foyer. At first he looks at them without much interest but then he notices his father coming out of the door with a white woman. He looks surprised and annoyed. His father sees him and looks guilty.

The son and the father stand where they are whilst people walk between them. Then the father and the woman walk towards the son. When the father gets close to the son he gestures towards the woman and speaks to the son.

Father: You remember Hannah. don't you . . .
Woman: (*smiling at the son*) I'm Hannah Plowman. Of course we know each other.
Son: (*after hesitating for a while*) Hello.
Father: (*moving away slightly from the son*) What are you going to see? (*The father and the woman smile at the son. The son doesn't answer.*)
Father: The Bertolucci – an Italian film – it's very good. We thought . . .
(*The woman nods enthusiastically.*)
Father: That's the one to see, Will.
(*The father signals for the son to go along and enjoy himself. The woman murmurs something politely and the two of them then walk away from the son.*)
(*The son watches their backs moving out of the cinema and down the road. Then suddenly he runs away from the cinema in the opposite direction.*)

10 This is a creative writing exercise and therefore has many possible 'answers'. Compare your dialogue with the two

versions below. How is yours similar to and different from each one?

a)
Tom: Heh. what's wrong Will?
Will: Nothing. Well nothing much.
Tom: What?
Will: It's my dad. He's having an affair.
Tom: Who with?
Will: A white woman. A do gooding white liberal.
Tom: Wow! Are you sure?
Will: I caught them together at the cinema yesterday.
Tom: Maybe they're just friends or . . .
Will: No way!
Tom: Or they're working on something together?
Will: I know. I could tell.
Tom: Are you going to tell your mother?
Will: What do you think? I can't.
Tom: Yeah. You're right. C'mon forget it. It won't last. Let's do some revision.
Will: OK. Let's try the English Lit.

b)
Will: Guess what?
Tom: What?
Will: My dad's got a girl friend.
Tom: Yeah. What's she like?
Will: Middle-aged . . . clumsy . . . white.
Tom: White?
Will: Yeah. Well bits of her are pink.
Tom: Why?
Will: The sun of course.
Tom: No. I mean why her?
Will: I don't know. She's some sort of a liberal, a social worker.
Tom: On our side, eh?
Will: She's not on my side. That's for sure. C'mon. Let's do some work.

12 Possible answers are:
  a) Probably because he had held his father in great esteem and he was shocked to find that he was not the perfect father after all. The father had deceived the son.
  b) Probably about eighteen. Because he was in a senior class

at school and was preparing for an important examination.

c) It refers to non-whites.

d) Although he had been caught deceiving his father he immediately realised that his father's deception was much bigger and that his father was aware of that.

e) Probably because he didn't want to antagonise his son and he wanted to pretend that the relationship with Hannah was as innocent as it was the last time they had met.

f) One interpretation is that it was when he was six years old. Obviously she had changed and probably he could not at first connect his father's 'lover' with his father's colleague or acquaintance.

g) It could be that he is thinking of the time when he was growing up 'in a little house across the veld from Benoni' when his father often gave him good advice. Or it could be that 'another life' refers to the time before this encounter when he respected his father and his advice – the implication being that now he doesn't respect his father.

h) Obviously it communicates a negative reaction. He picks on unattractive features and uses emotive words (i.e. 'clumsy': 'confusion'). He suggests that she's trying to be something that she really is not (e.g. the sunburn on her calves: the clothes borrowed from cultures which she doesn't belong to).

i) It suggests that his father had made a special effort to look good whilst Hannah had not. It also reminds him of how he'd taken the jacket to the cleaners for his father, presumably because it was needed for an important occasion and because he was proud of his father.

j) His world had suddenly changed and his security had been threatened. He needed to be somewhere which hadn't changed and which didn't threaten him.

14
i) 'Cinemas had been open to us only a year or so; . . .'
To stress the period of time rather than the particular time. To stress how short this period was and how relevant it was to the point of time in the narrative.
ii) '. . . it was I who had discovered him . . .'
Possibly to stress that there was no time in which the son was

guilty in comparison with the father. Right from the moment of recognition it was the father who was guilty.
cf. '. . . it was I who discovered him' (= I saw him and then realised he was guilty).
iii) '. . . the title of the film I had planned to see . . .'
To stress that the plan (although very recent) was now in the past and was irrelevant now.
cf. '. . . the title of the film I planned to see . . .' (= He still intended to see it).
iv) 'I watched their backs so I would believe it really had happened: . . .'
Possibly to stress that the incident was now in the past and he wanted to make sure that it was true that his father was having an affair. Possibly he was thinking of the future, when remembering the visual details would convince him it was true.
v) '. . . his one good jacket which I had taken to the dry-cleaners for him many times . . .'
Possibly to stress that such acts were now definitely in the past and to emphasise his emotional involvement in the memory.
cf. '. . . which I took to the dry-cleaners . . .' (= It leaves open the possibility that he might do so again).
The above examples seem to suggest that perfect tenses indicate more involvement of the speaker than simple tenses. The speaker seems to be more subjective when using perfect tenses and to be drawing attention to what is salient to him. Look for other examples in newspapers and books to see if this subjectivity is typical of the use made of perfect tenses.

16
a)
Below is one student's dialogue. How is yours similar to it and different from it?

Father: Will? Do you fancy a ride on your bike?
Will: Where to?
Father: To deliver an important parcel for me. I daren't send it by post.
Will: Where to?
Father: To Hannah Plowman's house.
Will: Do I have to?
Father: No.
(*Long pause in which Will looks at his father. His father looks away.*)
Will: Alright. Where is it?

Father: Here's the parcel. And here's a map to show you how to get there.
Will: OK. Give them to me.
Father: Don't forget to wear your helmet.

b)
Below is one student's scene. How is yours similar to or different from it?
I got off the bike across the road from her house. I took my helmet off and then tidied my hair in the mirror. Then I was annoyed with myself. What did it matter what I looked like?
I crossed the road hoping nobody would see me. There were some black kids playing at the end of the street. But they didn't bother about me. Trust her to live away from the other whites.
The house was small like the ones that black servants lived in. But hers needed painting and seemed to be falling down. The bell didn't work, so I knocked on the door. After a while she opened it and stood blinking into the sun. She was barefoot and wore only an African cloth.
Then she recognised me and asked me to come in. I saw into a room where my father must often have been and shook my head. I pushed the parcel at her, turned and ran. I heard her shout. 'Will. Will, come back!' just before I roared off down the road towards the frightened black kids without my helmet on.

Conclusion

The example demonstrated above shows how it is possible in self-access material to:

- give learners the responsibility of deciding what and how much to do (e.g. Introduction to Sample 1 and Activity 4);
- ask open-ended questions (e.g. Activities 1 and 11);
- encourage experiential reading (e.g. Activities 4 and 18);
- use previous learners' answers for comparison and feedback rather than imposing teacher answers (e.g. Activities 6 and 16);
- make use of creative drama (e.g. Activities 7, 8 and 9);
- set open-ended activities (e.g. Activities 5, 7, 9 and 15);
- make use of creative writing (e.g. Activities 9 and 15);
- ask 'think' questions (e.g. Activity 11);
- use extended texts for language awareness discovery work (e.g. Activity 13);
- provide opportunities for teacher feedback (e.g. Activity 17).

In addition, the sample unit shows how it is possible to engage the learner and to achieve depth of processing in self-access materials by activating both affective and cognitive responses and by respecting and challenging the learners. In my view, this is what all learning materials should be trying to do, and especially those which are designed to appeal to self-access learners who want something different and richer than what is conventionally offered in the classroom.

Comments on Part D

Brian Tomlinson

The chapters in this section offer very different views on materials development but have many things in common. One thing in particular that they have in common is their concern that different types of learners and different preferred styles of learning should be catered for in language learning materials. An analysis of any current global coursebook will reveal that it favours the analytic learner rather than the experiential learner, that it caters for the visual learner more than it does for the auditory learner and that hardly any provision is made for the tactile or kinaesthetic learner. Yet it seems that more learners are experiential than analytic and that the preferred mode for most learners is the kinaesthetic (Oxford and Anderson 1995). It is not difficult to work out why coursebook materials typically favour the analytic learner. The school cultures which the teachers, learners, publishers and textbook writers come from encourage and reward those who are primarily analytic. The learners who succeed in these cultures are those who can focus on discrete chunks of information, who can analyse and categorise, who can memorise and retrieve consciously, who are systematic and sequential in the ways that they learn. Most teachers, writers and publishers have been successful in such cultures; most learners expect to learn languages in the same ways that they have been made to learn other subjects at school; and most parents and adminis-trators want languages to be learnt in an analytic way which rewards effort and application and teaches the values of order and conformity. And it does not help when language acquisition researchers categorise the good language learner as someone who uses the appropriate learning strategies effectively, who monitors themselves and others, who pays attention to form and to meaning, who practises the language and who is aware of the learning process (Ellis 1994a: 546–50). In other words, someone who is flexible but who learns the language primarily by focusing attention on aspects of it. And, of course, such a learner is identified as a good learner by teachers who are following a primarily analytic course and is rewarded by language examinations which feature tasks which are primarily analytic too. In addition, it is much easier to write and design a book which requires analytic responses and

337

it is not easy to write and sell one which caters for the kinaesthetically inclined. But, as the chapters in this section demonstrate, it is possible to design materials which facilitate experiential learning and it is possible to cater for different learning styles by providing a variety of approaches, by providing opportunities for choice and by helping learners to take responsibility for their own learning. This, of course, does not mean that materials should stop trying to cater for analytic learning styles, it means that they should cater equally for other less language-focused styles too.

The stressing of the need to provide opportunities for learner choice is another of the common links between the chapters in this section and, of course, is one of the ways of catering for a diversity of preferred learning styles and modes. The problem for materials developers is how to offer useful choice to learners in such a way that they can make informed rather than purely intuitive decisions (see Tomlinson 1996a for further suggestions). This must involve encouraging learners to sample different potential learning routes and helping them to understand the objectives, principles and typical procedures of each of these routes. This risks the danger of becoming a course on language acquisition; but, if done experientially (e.g. an activity followed by learner reflection on and evaluation of the activity), it can give the learners a greater repertoire of learning styles and strategies, it can help them to make informed choices of routes and activities and it can help them to become more aware of the learning process (a characteristic identified by most researchers as being typical of the good language learner, and one which does not necessarily inhibit experiential learning). We really do need to give our learners more respect and responsibility and to pre-determine less of their decisions for them.

One of the surprising things about the chapters in this section is that none of them really stresses the potential role of the teacher's book in helping to cater for choice (and in contributing to teacher development too). At the moment teachers' books (because they do not sell many copies) receive little investment of time and energy in developing their contents and their design. They tend to provide just answer keys and obvious advice. As a result they are under used and their potential is under-exploited. If student books consisted basically of a large bank of texts and visuals to select from, teachers' books could include many different suggestions for activities which learners could choose from. If these activities were attractively designed and made photocopiable, then the teacher's book could become essential and profitably expensive: and everybody could gain.

Perhaps the most significant link between the chapters in this section is that none of them is proposing anything radically new but all of them are advocating approaches which are not commonly used by main-stream materials. The potential value of experiential learning, of peripheral learning, of engaging the senses and emotions in the learning process, of whole person approaches, of catering for different learning styles, of offering responsibility and choice to learners is supported by considerable research and is substantiated by the experience of teachers and learners all over the world. Yet very few current global coursebooks have made more than token efforts to incorporate these approaches. It would be difficult to persuade the consumers to buy a book which would conspicuously differ from their expectations, it would not be easy to engage the emotions of learners without risking giving offence, and it would be a demanding task to provide cost-effective choice. But I believe it would be possible to develop a global coursebook which could cater for experiential learners, for analytic learners and for analytical learners (those who, like myself, prefer to encounter language first of all in purposeful and engaging use but later enjoy analysing the 'text' to find out how the language was used). It would also be possible in the same book to provide activities involving visual, auditory, tactile and kinaesthetic responses and to offer choices both of major routes and of specific activities. Such a book could be extremely valuable to learners and teachers all over the world and could become a commercial success too. One of these days perhaps?

Conclusions

Brian Tomlinson

I would like to end this book by highlighting certain messages which seem to have been communicated throughout the book and to suggest ways in which we can gain from them.

We should be proud but not complacent about the progress made in materials development.
We have reached a situation in which high quality materials are available throughout the world to help learners to learn languages. These materials have taken advantage of recent developments in technology and of our recently increased knowledge of how languages are learned. But many learners still fail to achieve a satisfactory level of communicative competence and many teachers and learners are still not happy with the materials they are using. We must not sit back and say that what we have is good enough but rather continue to strive towards the development of materials which give even more learners the chance of satisfaction and success.

We need to find out more about the outcomes of existing materials.
There has been very little research into the actual learning outcomes of language learning materials. Publishers have been understandably reluctant to conduct longitudinal and expensive research into the effects of books which they have already published. Academics have been wary of undertaking research which would require massive expenditure of time and resources and which would involve great difficulty in controlling the variables in order to reach any conclusive results. But are we really being responsible and professional when we judge the effectiveness of a book by the number of copies it sells? Or by its popularity judged by responses to questionnaires? Or by a general impression that most of the activities in it 'work'? We need to (and could) find out more about the actual learning outcomes of types of materials if we want to help those learners who currently fail. We could make a start by encouraging more postgraduate students to do their research projects on materials development and we could undertake more ambitious projects in which consortia of experts actually

investigate the long-term effects of different types of learning materials on comparable groups of learners.

We need to find out more about what learners and teachers want from language learning materials.
Many of us are frequently guilty of saying things like, 'What most learners want is . . .' or, 'What teachers really want is . . .'. But do we really know? I have not seen any research which convinces me that teachers and learners actually want what they are being given by the materials they are using. (For example, do they really welcome the presentation, practice, production approach of the majority of global coursebooks on the market?) Nor have I seen any research which demonstrates their dissatisfaction. But I really would like to know what they want and I think that we really ought to make greater efforts to discover reliable and valid information about the sort of materials they really want to use. Such research requires cooperation between different types of experts and it requires the sort of funding which could only really be provided by a consortium of universities and publishers working with their own agendas but also towards a common goal.

We need to find out more about how we can develop more effective materials.
Providing learners and teachers with the materials they want could be extremely useful but it would not be enough. We do not know what the most effective types of materials are for learners in different types of situations and what the learners want might not always necessarily be the most effective materials for them. For example, a class of 80 unmotivated university students of engineering might want an easy book of practice exercises which can help them prepare for their compulsory English examination without requiring much investment of time, energy or attention. But a book of communication activities offering choice and involvement might be more useful to them. We just do not know.

What we need is not only reliable and valid information about what teachers and learners want and about the actual learning outcomes of current materials but also about what effects could be achieved by new types of materials. We need to innovate and experiment if we are really to find out how we could make language learning materials more effective. But why should publishers take risks when livelihoods are at stake? Why should ministries commit precious funds to projects which might not succeed? And why should learners risk failing to learn from experimental books? If only a large university (or group of universities) would cooperate with a publisher to produce and trial experimental materials, we might increase our knowledge about what contributes to the effectiveness of language learning materials.

We need to make more use of what we know about language learning in the development of materials.
If we are to develop more effective materials then we need to incorporate features into the materials which we know can facilitate language learning. In the Introduction to this book I have mentioned many such features. Of these I would particularly like to see more use made in materials development of what we know about the value of permitting a silent period at the beginning of learning a language or of learning a new feature of it and also of what we know about the value of engaging emotions in the learning process.

We need to find out more about how the target language is actually used and to apply this new knowledge to the development of materials.
As the chapters in Part A reveal, we are finding out more about how languages are actually used and this new knowledge is already being applied to the development of textbooks. But, of course, we need to go on finding out and applying. We need more knowledge about how languages are actually used in specific situations (e.g. when conducting business, when giving commercial presentations, when being questioned by the police), we need more knowledge about how grammatical principles (e.g. economy) are actually applied to language use in different situations and we need more knowledge of the patterns and norms of interaction between proficient non-native speakers from different backgrounds. And we need to find out to what extent exposure to reality is more or less valuable to learners than exposure to simplified samples illustrating idealised norms.

We need to find ways of developing materials which are flexible enough to offer choices and to cater for a variety of wants and needs.
This need has been expressed many times in this book already (e.g. my Comments on Part D) so I will just say that this is another area where we need actual information rather than subjective impressions. What are the effects of materials offering choice compared to the effects of materials offering no choice? How can we offer choice without increasing the processing load? Can we identify those learners who are likely to benefit from being offered choice and those who might gain from a more directed course? We need to know.

**We need to find ways of using textbooks to
contribute to teacher development.**
This is a need identified by Julian Edge and Sue Wharton in Chapter 13
and a need which is being addressed on textbook projects (such as the
Namibian Project) in countries where most teachers are untrained and
are often reluctant to experiment with new approaches. In my experience of contributing to teacher development and curriculum development in England, Indonesia, Japan, Nigeria, Vanuatu and Zambia for
any materials to contribute positively to teacher development they must
not be imposed, they must invite and facilitate reflection, evaluation and
adaptation by the teachers, and they must involve teachers in the
development and trialling of the materials. These factors are being
considered as important in many local projects but could also be taken
into account in the commercial development of global coursebooks too.

**We need to find ways of helping commercial publishers to take
advantage of new developments in methodology without
risking financial loss.**
This, I think, is our most urgent need if we are to really improve the
effectiveness of the materials which learners use. In the current
economic climate, and given the massive costs of global coursebooks
and the unprofitability of most supplementary materials, we cannot
expect publishers to be experimental and innovative. They need to
produce what they can expect to sell whilst, as Peter Donovan points
out in Chapter 7, striving as much as they can to ensure that their
materials are of value to their users. But is this enough? If the publishers
are not going to experiment, who is? And if we do not experiment, how
do we make progress? The answer has got to lie in more pooling of
expertise and resources so that we can help publishers to find out which
innovations might be well-received and ultimately profitable. And we
have got to help publishers to conduct more radical experimentation
without the risk of financial disaster. MATSDA would very much like to
be involved.

WE NEED TO FIND WAYS OF BRINGING TOGETHER RESEARCHERS,
TEACHERS, WRITERS AND PUBLISHERS SO AS TO POOL RESOURCES
AND TO TAKE ADVANTAGE OF DIFFERENT AREAS OF EXPERTISE IN
ORDER TO PRODUCE MATERIALS OF GREATER VALUE TO LEARNERS
OF LANGUAGES.
All the messages above are calling out for greater collaboration
between institutions with different types of resources and expertise in
relation to the development of L2 materials. What we would really like
to do in MATSDA is to find ways of helping to bring together experts in
language acquisition, in research methodology, in language data col-

lection and analysis, in language pedagogy, in materials writing, in materials design and in materials production and distribution. Only by pooling resources will we ever be able to answer some of the questions which we need to ask if we are to really increase the effectiveness of the materials which we produce.

I am looking forward to receiving approaches for MATSDA to help to arrange joint research projects aiming to inform materials development and I am looking forward to editing in the future a book reporting on the outcomes of such research.

Recommended reading

For further reading on materials development in L2 teaching the following are recommended:

Books

Byrd, P. 1995. *Materials Writers Guide*. Newbury House.
Cunningsworth, A. 1984. *Evaluating and Selecting EFL Materials*. London: Heinemann.
Cunningsworth, A. 1996. *Choosing Your Coursebook*. Oxford: Heinemann.
Dubin, F. and E. Olshtain, 1986. *Course Design*. New York: CUP.
Hidalgo, A. C., D. Hall and G. M. Jacobs. (Eds) 1995. *Getting Started: Materials Writers on Materials Writing*. Singapore: SEAMEO. Language Centre.
McDonough, J. and C. Shaw. 1993. *Materials and Methods in ELT: A Teacher's Guide*. London: Blackwell.
Projects in Materials Design. (Special edn.) 1987. Basingstoke: Macmillan.
Sheldon, L. E. (Ed.) 1987. ELT textbooks and materials: problems in evaluation and development. In *ELT Documents 126*. Modern English Publications.

Articles

Adaskou, K., D. Britten and B. Fahsi. 1990. Design decisions on the cultural content of a secondary English course for Morocco. *ELT Journal*, 44(1).
Allwright, R. L. 1981. What do we want teaching materials for? *ELT Journal*, 36(1).
Brumfit, C. 1983. Seven last slogans. In S. Holden (Ed.) *Second Selections from Modern English Teacher*. Harlow: Longman.
Candlin, C. N. and M. Breen. 1980. Evaluating and designing language teaching materials. In *Practical Papers in English Language Teaching*, 2. University of Lancaster: Institute for English Language Education.
Cunningsworth, A. and P. Kusel. 1991. Evaluating teacher's guides. *ELT Journal*, 45(2).
Hopkins, A. Out of Africa; reflections on materials writing. *FOLIO*, 1(1).
Kennedy, C. 1983. Exploiting a text. In S. Holden (Ed.) *Second Selections from Modern English Teacher*. Harlow: Longman.
Maley, A. 1994. 'Play it again Sam': A role for repetition. *FOLIO*, 1(2).

345

Mariana, L. 1983. Evaluating and supplementing coursebooks. In S. Holden. (Ed.) *Second Selections from Modern English Teacher.* Harlow: Longman.

Masuhara, H. 1994. But that's what teachers want! *FOLIO*, 1(1).

Moshback, G. 1990. National syllabus and textbook design on communicative principles: English every day. *ELT Journal*, 44(1).

O'Neill, R. O. 1982. Why use textbooks? ELT Journal. 36(2).

Sheldon, L. E. 1988. Evaluating ELT textbooks and materials. *ELT Journal*, 42(4).

Tomlinson, B. 1990. Managing change in Indonesian high schools. *ELT Journal*, 44(1).

Tomlinson, B. 1994b. Materials for TPR. *FOLIO*, 1(2).

Tomlinson, B. 1995a. What dialogues can do. *FOLIO*, 2(2).

Tomlinson, B. 1995b. Work in progress: Textbook projects. *FOLIO*, 2(2).

Tomlinson, B. 1995c. Dialogues – What are they for ? *FOLIO*, 2(1).

Tomlinson, B. 1996a. Choices. *FOLIO*, 3(1).

Tomlinson, B. 1996c. New directions in materials development. *ARENA*, 11.

References

Abbs, B. and I. Freebairn. 1980. *Developing Strategies*. Harlow: Longman.

Achebe, C. 1972. *Girls at War*. Oxford: Heinemann.

Achebe, C. 1988. *A Man of the People*. Oxford: Heinemann.

Adrian-Vallance, D. and J. Edge. 1994. *Right Track: Student's Book 1*. Harlow: Longman.

Aijmer, K. 1989. Themes and tails: The discourse function of dislocated elements. *Nordic Journal of Linguistics*, 12 (1), 137–54.

Alderson, J. C. 1985a. Is there life after the course? *Lancaster Practical Papers in English Language Evaluation*. University of Lancaster.

Alderson, J. 1985b. Evaluation. *Lancaster Practical Papers in English Language Education*, Vol 6. Oxford: Pergamon.

Alderson, J. 1992. Guidelines for the evaluation of language education. In J. Alderson and A. Beretta (Eds.)

Alderson, J. and A. Beretta (Eds.). 1992. *Evaluating Second Language Education*. Cambridge: Cambridge University Press.

Alderson, J. C. and M. Scott. 1992. Insiders, outsiders and participatory evaluation. In J. C. Alderson and A. Beretta (Eds.) *Evaluating Second Language Education*. Cambridge: Cambridge University Press.

Allwright, D. 1984. The importance of interaction in classroom language learning. *Applied Linguistics*, 5, 156–71.

Allwright, R. 1981. What do we want teaching materials for? *ELT Journal* 36 (1), 5–18.

Allwright, R. 1984. Why don't learners learn what teachers teach? The interaction hypothesis. In D. Singleton and D. Little (Eds.). *Language Learning in Formal and Informal Contexts*. Dublin: IRAAL.

Anderson, J. R. 1980. *Cognitive Psychology and Its Implications*. San Francisco: W. H. Freeman and Co.

Anderson, R. C. and R. W. Kulhavy. 1972. Imagery and prose learning. *Journal of Educational Psychology*, 62: 526–30.

Anderson, R. C. and P. D. Pearson. 1984. A schema-theoretic view of basic processes in reading comprehension. In P. D. Pearson (Ed.) *A Handbook of Reading Research*. New York: Longman.

Asher, J. 1977. *Learning Another Language Through Actions: The Complete Teacher's Guidebook*. Los Gatos. Calif.: Sky Oak Productions.

Assagioli, R. 1968. *Come si Imparano le Lingue per l'Inconscio*. Pamphlet available from l'Istituto di Psicosintesi Roberto Assagioli, Piazza Sta Maria degli Aldobrandi, Firenze, Italy.

References

Aston, G. 1988. *Learning Comity.* Bologna: CLUEB.

Barnett, M. 1989. *More Than Meets the Eye: Foreign Language Reading.* Englewood Cliffs. NJ: Prentice Hall Regents.

Batstone, R. 1994a. Product and process: grammar in the second language classroom in M. Bygate, Alan Tonkyn and Eddie Williams. (Eds.) *Grammar and the Language Teacher.* Prentice Hall International.

Batstone, R. 1994b. *Grammar.* Oxford: Oxford University Press.

Beck, I. L., M. G. McKeown and J. Worthy. 1995. Giving a text voice can improve students' understanding. *Research Reading Quarterly,* 30 (2).

Bell, J. and R. Gower. 1991. *Intermediate Matters.* Harlow: Longman.

Beretta, A. 1992. Evaluation of language education: an overview. In J. Alderson and A. Beretta (Eds.).

Berwick, R. 1990. *Task Variation and Repair in English as a Foreign Language.* Kobe University of Commerce: Institute of Economic Research.

Bialystok, E. 1982. On the relationship between knowing and using linguistic forms. *Applied Linguistics,* 3 (3), 181–206.

Bialystok, E. 1988. Psycholinguistic dimensions of second language proficiency. In Rutherford and Sharwood-Smith (1988).

Bolitho, R. and B. Tomlinson. 1995. *Discover English,* new edn. Oxford: Heinemann.

Boyd, W. 1990. *Brazzaville Beach.* London: Penguin.

Breen, M. P. 1987. Learner contributions to task design. In Candlin and Murphy 1987.

Breen, M. 1989. The evaluation cycle for language learning tasks. In R. Johnson (Ed.). *The Second Language Curriculum.* Cambridge: Cambridge University Press.

Breen, M. P. and C. N. Candlin. 1987. Which materials?: a consumer's and designer's guide. In Sheldon, 1987.

Brewer, W. F. 1988. Postscript: imagery and text genre. *Text.* 8: 431–8.

Brown, J. 1994. *The Elements of Language Curriculum: A Systematic Approach to Program Development.* Boston: Heinle and Heinle.

Brumfit, C. J. 1980. Seven last slogans. *Modern English Teacher.* 7 (1). 30–1.

Brumfit, C. 1986. Reading skills and the study of literature. In C. Brumfit and R. Carter (Eds.) *Literature and Language Teaching.* Oxford: Oxford University Press.

Brumfit, C. and R. Carter (Eds.) 1986. *Literature and Language Teaching.* Oxford: Oxford University Press.

Bugelski, B. R. 1969. Learning theory and the reading process. In *The 23rd Annual Reading Conference.* Pittsburgh: Pittsburgh University Press.

Burns, A., H. Joyce and S. Gollin. 1996. *I See What You Mean: a Handbook on Spoken Discourse in the Classroom.* Macquarie University, Sydney: NCELTR.

Bygate, M., A. Tonkyn and E. Williams. (Eds.) 1994. *Grammar and the Language Teacher.* London: Prentice Hall.

Canale, M. and M. Swain. 1980. Theoretical bases of communicative approaches to second language teaching and testing. *Applied Linguistics*, 11–47.

Candlin, C. N. and D. F. Murphy (Eds.) 1987. *Language Learning Tasks*. London: Prentice-Hall.

Capel, A. 1993. *Collins Cobuild Concordance Sampler 1: Prepositions*. London: HarperCollins Publishers.

Carter, R. A. and M. J. McCarthy. 1995. Grammar and the spoken language. *Applied Linguistics*, 16 (2), 141–58.

Carr, T. and B. Levy. (Eds.) 1990. *Reading and Its Development: Component Skills Approaches*. San Diego: Academic Press.

Chamot, A. and J. Rubin. 1994. Comments on Rees-Miller 1993. *TESOL Quarterly* 28 (4), 771–6.

Channell, J. 1994. *Vague Language*. Oxford: Oxford University Press.

Clahsen, H., J. Meisel and M. Pienemann. 1983. *Deutsch als Zweitsprache. Der Spacherwerb auslandischer Arbeiter*. Tubingen: Gunter Narr.

Clarke, M. 1980. The short circuit hypothesis of ESL reading – or when language performance interferes with reading performance. *Modern Language Journal*. 64: 203–9.

Cook, V. 1996. *Second Language Learning and Second Language Teaching*, new edn. London: Edward Arnold.

Coleman, H. 1992. Moving the goalposts: project evaluation in practice. In J. Alderson and A. Beretta (Eds.).

Corder, S. 1967. The significance of learners' errors. *IRAL* 9: 149–59. Also in S. Corder. 1981. *Error Analysis and Interlanguage*. Oxford: Oxford University Press.

Corder, S. 1973. *Introducing Applied Linguistics*. Harmondsworth, Middlesex: Penguin Books.

Cotterall, S. 1995. Developing a course strategy for learner autonomy. *ELT Journal*, 49(3): 219–27.

Craik, F. I. M. and R. S. Lockhart. 1972. Levels of processing: A framework for memory research. *Journal of Verbal Learning and Verbal Behaviour*, 11: 671–84.

Crowdy, S. 1993. Spoken corpus design. *Literary and Linguistic Computing*, 8 (2), 259–65.

Crookes, G. and S. Gass (Eds.). 1993. *Tasks and Language Learning: Integrating Theory and Practice*. Clevedon: Multilingual Matters.

Crystal, D. and D. Davy. 1975. *Advanced Conversational English*. London: Longman.

Cunningsworth, A. 1984. *Evaluating and Selecting ELT Materials*. London: Heinemann.

Cunningsworth, A. 1995. *Choosing Your Coursebook*. Oxford: Heinemann.

Cunningsworth, A. and P. Kusel. 1991. Evaluating Teachers' Guides. *ELT Journal* 45 (2), 128–39.

Damasio, A. R. 1994. *Descartes' Error*. London: Picador.

Daoud, A. and M. Celce-Murcia. 1979. Selecting and evaluating textbooks. In

M. Celce-Murcia and L. McIntosh (Eds.). *Teaching English as a Second or Foreign Language*. New York: Newbury House.

Davies, A. 1991. *The Native Speaker in Applied Linguistics*. Edinburgh: Edinburgh University Press.

Denis, M. 1982. Imaging whilst reading text: a study of individual differences. *Memory and Cognition*, 10 (6), 540–5.

Dickinson, L. 1987. *Self-Instruction in Language Learning* (pp. 83–4). Cambridge Cambridge University Press.

Dixon, N. F. 1985. *Preconscious Processing*. J. Wiley and Sons.

Doughill, J. 1987. Not so obvious. In Sheldon. 1987.

Dubin, F. and E. Olshtain. 1986. *Course Design*. Cambridge: Cambridge University Press.

Duff, P. 1986. Another look at interlanguage talk: Taking task to task. In R. Day (Ed.). *Talking to Learn: Conversation in Second Language Acquisition*. Rowley, Ma.: Newbury House.

Dulay, H., M. Burt and S. Krashen. 1982. *Language Two*. New York: Oxford University Press.

Eastment, D. 1994. CD ROM – An overview of materials. In *Modern English Teacher*, 3 (4), March 1994.

Edelman, G. 1993. *Bright Air, Brilliant Fire*. London: Penguin.

Edge, J. 1992. *Cooperative Development*. Harlow: Longman.

Edge, J. and V. Samuda. 1981. Methodials: The role and design of material and method *RELC Occasional Papers* 17: 50–67.

Edge, J. and K. Richards. (Eds.) 1993. *Teachers Develop Teachers Research*. Oxford: Heinemann.

Ellis, R. 1984. *Classroom Second Language Development*. Oxford; Pergamon.

Ellis, R. 1990. *Instructed Second Language Acquisition*. Oxford: Basil Blackwell.

Ellis, R. 1991a. *Second Language Acquisition and Second Language Pedagogy*, Multi-Lingual Matters.

Ellis, R. 1991b. Grammaticality judgements and second language acquisition. *Studies in Second Language Acquisition*, 13, 161–86.

Ellis, R. 1993. Second language acquisition and the structural syllabus. *TESOL Quarterly* 27: 91–113.

Ellis, R. 1994a. *The Study of Second Language Acquisition*. Oxford: Oxford University Press.

Ellis, R. 1994b. Second language acquisition research and teacher development: The case of teachers' questions. In D. Li, D. Mahoney and J. Richards (Eds.). *Exploring Second Language Teacher Development*. Hong Kong: City Polytechnic of Hong Kong.

Ellis, R. and M. Rathbone. 1987. *The Acquisition of German in a Classroom Context*. London: Ealing College of Higher Education.

Ellis, G. and Sinclair, B. 1989. *Learning to Learn English: A course in learner training*. Cambridge: Cambridge University Press.

Enkvist, N. E. 1981. Experiential iconism in text strategy. *Text* 1 (1): 77–111.

Esrock, E. 1994. *The Reader's Eye*. Baltimore: The Johns Hopkins University Press.

Eysenk, N. W. and M. T. Keane. 1990. *Cognitive Psychology. A Student's Handbook*. Hillsdale, NJ: Lawrence Erlbaum Associates.

Fanselowe, J. 1992. *Contrasting Conversations*. White Plains, NY: Longman.

Farrell, M. 1995. *Right Track Teachers Manual 3*. Harlow: Longman.

Flory, S. 1990. 'River Station Plaza'. London: The *Observer*.

Fotos, S. 1994. Integrating grammar instruction and communicative language use through grammar, consciousness-raising tasks. *TESOL Quarterly*, 28 (2), 333–51.

Fotos, S. and R. Ellis. 1991. Communicating about grammar: a task-based approach. *TESOL Quarterly* 25: 605–28.

Freeman, D. and S. Cornwell. (Eds.) 1993. New Ways in Teacher Education. Alexandra, Virginia: TESOL Inc.

Fried-Booth, D. 1987. *Project Work*. Oxford: Oxford University Press.

Freire, P. 1972. *Cultural action for freedom*. Harmondsworth: Penguin Books.

Gass, S. and C. Madden. 1985. *Input in Second Language Acquisition*. Rowley, Ma.: Newbury House.

Gass, S. and M. Varonis. 1985. Task variation and nonnative/nonnative negotiation of meaning. In S. Gass and C. Madden (Eds.).

Geluykens, R. 1992. *From Discourse Process to Grammatical Construction: On left dislocation in English*. Amsterdam: John Benjamins.

Glass, G. and N. Worthen. 1971. Evaluation and research: similarities and differences. *Curriculum Theory Network*, Fall: 149–65.

Gordimer, N. 1991. *My Son's Story*. London: Penguin Books.

Grellet, F. 1982. *Developing Reading Skills*. Cambridge: Cambridge University Press.

Halliday, M. A. K. 1985. It's a fixed word order language is English. *ITL Review of Applied Linguistics*, 67/68, 207/218.

Halliday, M. A. K. 1994. *An Introduction to Functional Grammar* 2nd edn. London: Edward Arnold.

Harmer, J. 1991. *The Practice of English Language Teaching*, 2nd edn. Longman.

Hasan, R. and G. Perrett. 1994. Learning to function with the other tongue: a systemic-functional perspective on second language teaching. In T. Odlin, (Ed.) *Perspectives on Pedagogical Grammar*, 149–226. Cambridge: Cambridge University Press.

Heller, J. 1994. *Closing Time*. London: Simon and Schuster.

Hidalgo, A. C., D. Hall and G. M. Jacobs. 1995. *Getting Started: Materials Writers on Materials Writing*. Singapore: SEAMO.

Hofland, K. and S. Johansson. 1982. *Word Frequencies in British and American English*. Bergen: Norwegian Computing Centre for Humanities.

Hooper Hansen, G. 1992. Suggestopedia: A way of learning for the 21st century. In J. Mulligan and C. Griffin. *Empowerment Through Experiential Learning*. Kogan Page.

Hopkins, A. 1995. Revolutions in ELT materials? In *Modern English Teacher*,

4 (3). An earlier version was first published in *MATSDA FOLIO* 1 (2) November 1994.

Hopkins, A. and J. Potter. 1994. *Look Ahead* series. Harlow: Longman.

Hutchinson, T. and E. Torres. 1994. The textbook as agent of change. *ELT Journal*, 48 (4), 315–28. Oxford: Oxford University Press.

Hutchinson, T. and A. Waters. 1987. *English for specific purposes*. Cambridge: Cambridge University Press.

Ingarden, R. 1973. *The Cognition of the Literary Work of Art.* (trans. R. A. Crowley, and K. R. Olsen.) Evanston: Northwestern University Press.

Ishiguro, K. 1982. *A Pale View of Hills.* London: Faber and Faber.

Jacobs, B and J. Schumann. 1992. Language acquisition and the neurosciences: towards a more integrative perspective. *Applied Linguistics* 13 (3).

James, C. and P. Garrett. 1991. *Language Awareness in the Classroom.* London: Longman.

Johns, T. and P. King. (Eds.) 1991. Classroom concordancing. *ELR Journal*, Birmingham University.

Johnson, J. 1995. Who needs another coursebook? *FOLIO*, 2 (1), 31–5.

Johnson, R. K. (Ed.). 1989. *The Second Language Curriculum.* Cambridge: Cambridge University Press.

Kennedy, G. 1973. Conditions for language learning. In J. Oller and J. Richards (Eds.) *Focus on the Learner.* Rowley, Mass: Newbury House.

Knight, S. L., Y. N. Padron and H. C. Waxman. 1985. The cognitive reading strategies of ESL students. *TESOL Quarterly.* 19: 789–92.

Krashen, S. 1981. *Second Language Acquisition and Second Language Learning.* Oxford: Pergamon Press.

Krashen, S. 1982. *Principles and Practice in Second Language Acquisition.* Oxford: Pergamon.

Krashen, S. 1985. *The Input Hypothesis.* London: Longman.

Kucera, H. and W. N. Francis. 1967. *Computational Analysis of Present-Day American English.* Providence, RI: Brown University Press.

Kulhavy, R. W. and I. Swenson. 1975. Imagery instructions and the comprehension of texts. *British Journal of Educational Psychology*, 45: 47–51.

Kumaravadivelu, B. 1991. Language-Learning tasks: teacher intention and learner interpretation. *ELT Journal* 45 (2), 98–107.

Kumaravadivelu, B. 1993. The name of the task and the task of naming: Methodological aspects of task-based pedagogy. In Crookes, G. and S. Gass (Eds.).

Larsen-Freeman, D. and M. Long. 1991. *An Introduction to Second Language Acquisition Research.* London: Longman.

Legutke, M. and H. Thomas. 1991. *Process and Experience.* Harlow: Longman.

Lin, L. Y. and R. Brown. 1994. Guidelines for the production of in-house self-access materials. *ELT Journal* 48 (2).

Littlejohn, A. P. 1992. *Why are ELT materials the way they are?* Unpublished PhD thesis. Lancaster: Lancaster University.

Littlejohn, A. and D. Hicks. 1996. *Cambridge English for Schools.* Cambridge: Cambridge University Press.

Littlejohn, A. P. and S. Windeatt. 1989. Beyond language learning: Perspectives on materials design. In. R. K. Johnson (Ed.).

Long, M. 1981. Input, interaction and second language acquisition. In H. Winitz (Ed.). *Native Language and Foreign Language Acquisition. Annals of the New York Academy of Sciences*, 379.

Long, M. 1983. Native speaker/ non-native speaker conversation and the negotiation of comprehensible input. In M. Clarke, and J. Handscombe. (Eds.) On *TESOL '82*. Washington D.C.: TESOL.

Long, S. A., P. N. Winograd and C. A. Bridge. 1989. The effect of reader and text characteristics on reports of imagery during and after reading. *Reading Research Quarterly*, 24: 353–72.

Lozanov, G. 1978. *Suggestology and Outlines of Suggestopedy.* London: Gordon and Breach.

Lynch, B. 1992. Evaluating a program inside and out. In J. Alderson and A. Beretta (Eds.).

McCarthy, M. J. and R. A. Carter. 1994. *Language as Discourse: Perspectives for Language Teaching.* London: Longman.

McCarthy, M. J. and R. A. Carter. 1995. Spoken grammar: What is it and how can we teach it? *ELT Journal,* 49 (3), 207–18.

McDonald, P., R. A. Edwards and J. F. D. Greenhalgh. 1984. *Animal Nutrition*: Chapter 16. Harlow: ELBS/Longman.

McDonough, J. and C. Shaw. 1993. *Materials and Methods in ELT.* Oxford: Blackwell.

McGough, R. 1979. 'First day at school.' In R. McGough and M. Rosen (Eds.) *You Tell Me.* London: Kestrel.

Mackey, W. F. 1965. *Language Teaching Analysis.* London: Longman.

MacLean, P. 1973. *A Triune Concept of the Brain and Behavior.* Toronto: University of Toronto Press.

Maley, A. 1994. *Short and Sweet 1.* London: Penguin.

Maley, A. 1995a. *Short and Sweet 2.* London: Penguin.

Maley, A. 1995b. Materials writing and tacit knowledge. In A. Hidalgo, D. Hall and G. Jacobs (Eds.) *Getting Started: Materials Writers on Materials Writing.* Singapore: SEAMEO Language Centre.

Maley, A. and A. Duff. 1976. *Words.* Cambridge: Cambridge University Press.

Maley, A. and A. Duff. 1980. *Drama Techniques in Language Teaching.* Cambridge: Cambridge University Press.

Malouf, D. 1993. *Remembering Babylon.* London: Chatto and Windus.

Masuhara, H. 1994. But that's what the teachers want! *Folio,* Journal of MATSDA (Materials Development Association), 1 (1), 12–13.

Meisel, J., H. Clahsen and M. Pienemann. 1981. On determining developmental stages in natural second language acquisition. *Studies in Second Language Acquisition,* 3, 109–35.

Mitchell, R. 1992. The 'independent' evaluation of bilingual primary education: a narrative account. In J. Alderson and A. Beretta (Eds.).

Modern English Teacher. Modern English Publications/Macmillan Publishers Ltd.

Moore, B. 1993. *No Other Life*. London: Bloomsbury.

Mowrer, O. H. 1977. Mental imagery: an indispensable psychological concept. *Journal of Mental Imagery*, 2: 303–26.

Murphy, D. 1985. Evaluation in language teaching: Assessment, accountability and awareness. In J. Alderson (Ed.).

Murphy, D. 1993. Evaluating language learning tasks in the classroom. In G. Crookes and S. Gass (Eds.).

Murphy, R. 1985. *English Grammar in Use*. Units 37 and 38. Cambridge: Cambridge University Press.

Norris, N. 1990. *Understanding Educational Evaluation*. London: Kogan Page.

Nunan, D. 1985. *Designing Tasks for the Communicative Classroom*. Cambridge: Cambridge University Press.

Nunan, D. 1988. *The Learner-Centred Curriculum*. Cambridge: Cambridge University Press.

Nunan, D. 1989. *Designing Tasks for the Communicative Classroom*. Cambridge: Cambridge University Press.

Nunan, D. 1991. *Language Teaching Methodology: A Text Book for Teachers*. Prentice Hall.

Nunan, D. 1993. Task-based syllabus design: selecting, grading and sequencing tasks. In G. Crookes and S. Gass (Eds.).

Nunan, D. and C. Lockwood. 1991. *The Australian English Course*, Cambridge/Sydney: Cambridge University Press.

Nunan, D. and J. Richards. (Eds.) 1990. *Second Language Teacher Education*. Cambridge: Cambridge University Press.

Nuttall, C. 1995. *Teaching Reading Skills in a Foreign Language*. Oxford: Heinemann.

On Target. 1995. Grade 10 English Second Language Learner's Book. Windhoek: Gamsberg Macmillan.

Owen, C. 1993. Corpus-based grammar and the Heineken effect: Lexico-grammatical description for language learners. *Applied Linguistics*, 14 (2), 167–87.

Oxford, R. L. and N. J. Anderson. 1995. A crosscultural view of learning styles. *Language Teaching*, 28, 201–15. Cambridge: Cambridge University Press.

Padron, Y. N. and H. C. Waxman. 1988. The effect of EFL students' perceptions of their cognitive strategies on reading achievement. *TESOL Quarterly*, 22: 146–50.

Paivio, A. 1979. *Imagery and Verbal Processes*. Hillsdale, NJ: Lawrence Erlbaum Associates Inc.

Palmer, A. 1992. Issues in evaluating input-based language teaching programmes. In J. Alderson and A. Beretta (Eds.) *Evaluating Second Language Education*. Cambridge: Cambridge University Press.

Patten, B. 1967. 'Little Johnny's letter home.' London: George Allen and Unwin.

Pennycook, A. 1994. *The Cultural Politics of English as an International Language*. Harlow: Longman.

Phillipson, R. 1992. *Linguistic Imperialism*. Oxford University Press.

Pica, T. 1994. Research on negotiation: What does it reveal about second language learning conditions, processes and outcomes? *Language Learning* 44: 493–527.

Pica, T. and T. Doughty. 1985. Input and interaction in the communicative language classroom: a comparison of teacher-fronted and group activities. In S. Gass and C. Madden (Eds.).

Pica, T., R. Kanagy, and J. Falodun. 1993. Choosing and using communication tasks for second language instruction. In G. Crookes and S. Gass (Eds.).

Pienemann, M. 1985. Learnability and syllabus construction. In K. Hyltenstam and M. Pienemann (Eds.) *Modelling and Assessing Second Language Acquisition*. Clevedon, Avon: Multilingual Matters.

Pinter, H. 1976. *The Birthday Party*. London: Eyre Methuen.

Potts, P. 1985. The role of evaluation in a communicative curriculum, and some consequences for materials design. In J. Alderson (1985).

Poynton, C. 1989. The privileging of representation and the marginalising of the interpersonal: a metaphor (and more) for contemporary gender relations. In A.Cranny-Francis, and T. Threadgold. (Eds.) *Feminine/Masculine and Representation*, 231–55. Sydney: Allen and Unwin.

Prabhu, N. 1987. *Second Language Pedagogy*. Oxford: Oxford University Press.

Prabhu. N. S. (Forthcoming) *A Sense of Plausibility*. Oxford: Oxford University Press.

Prodromou, L. 1990. English as cultural action. In R. Rossner and R. Bolitho. (Eds.) *Currents of Change in English Language Teaching*, 27–39. Oxford: Oxford University Press.

Pylyshyn, Z. W. 1973. What the mind's eye tells the mind's brain: a critique of mental imagery. *Psychological Bulletin*, 80: 1–24.

Quirk, R. *et al.* 1985. *A Comprehensive Grammar of the English Language*. Harlow: Longman.

Rea, P. 1983. Evaluation of educational projects, with special reference to English language education. In C. Brumfit (Ed.).

Rea-Dickins, P. 1994. Evaluation and English language teaching. *Language Teaching*, 27, 71–91. Cambridge: Cambridge University Press.

Rea-Dickens, P. and K. Germaine. 1992. *Evaluation*. Oxford: Oxford University Press.

Rees-Miller, J. 1993. A critical appraisal of learner training: Theoretical bases and teaching implications. *TESOL Quarterly* 27 (4), 679–90.

Rees-Miller, J. 1994. The author responds. *Tesol Quarterly* 28 (4), 776–81.

Richards, J. C. 1990. *The Language Teaching Matrix*. Cambridge: Cambridge University Press.

Richards, J. C. 1993a. Beyond the textbook: the role of commercial materials in language teaching. *Perspective*, 5 (1), 43–53.

Richards, J. C. 1993b. Beyond the textbook: the role of commercial materials in language teaching. *RELC Journal* (Singapore). 24 (1), 1–14.

Richards, J. and C. Lockhart. 1994. *Reflective Teaching in Second Language Classrooms*. Cambridge: Cambridge University Press.

Richards, J. C. and D. Nunan. 1990. *Second Language Teacher Education.* Cambridge: Cambridge University Press.

Richards, J., J. Platt, and H. Weber. 1985. *Longman Dictionary of Applied Linguistics.* London: Longman.

Richards, J. and T. Rodgers. 1986. *Approaches and Methods in Language Teaching.* Cambridge: Cambridge University Press.

Robinson, P. 1980. *English for Specific Purposes.* Oxford: Pergamon.

Robinson, P. 1990. *ESP Today.* Hemel Hempstead: Prentice Hall.

Rogers, C. 1983. *Freedom to Learn.* Merrill (Macmillan).

Ronnqvist, L. and R. D. Sell. 1994. Teenage books for teenagers: reflections on literature in language education. *ELT Journal* 48 (2).

Ross, S. 1992. Program-defining evaluation in a decade of eclecticism. In J. Alderson and A. Beretta (Eds.).

Rossi, E. L. 1986. *The Psycho-Biology of Mind-Body Healing.* Norton.

Rumelhart, D. E. 1980. Schemata: the building blocks of cognition. In R. J. Spiro, B. C. Bruce and W. F. Brewes (Eds.). *Theoretical Issues in Reading Comprehension.* Hillsdale, NJ: Lawrence Erlbaum Associates.

Rundell, M. 1995a. The word on the street. *English Today,* 11 (3), 29–35.

Rundell, M. 1995b. The BNC: A spoken corpus. *Modern English Teacher,* 4 (2), 13–15.

Rutherford, W. 1987. *Second Language Grammar: Learning and Teaching.* Harlow: Longman.

Rutherford, W. and M. Sharwood-Smith. 1988. (Eds.) *Grammar and Second Language Teaching.* Rowley, Mass: Newbury House.

Sadoski, M. 1985. The natural use of imagery in story comprehension and recall: replication and extension. *Reading Research Quarterly,* 20: 658–67.

Saville-Troike, M. 1988. Private speech: evidence for second language learning strategies during the 'silent period'. *Journal of Child Language,* 15, 567–90.

Schmidt, R. 1990. The role of consciousness in second language learning. *Applied Linguistics* 11 (2), 129–58.

Schmidt. R. 1992. Psychological mechanisms underlying second language fluency. *Studies in Second Language Acquisition,* 14, 357–85.

Schmidt, R. and S. Frota. 1986. Developing basic conversational ability in a second language: A case study of an adult learner of Portuguese. In R. Day. *Talking to Learn: Conversation in Second Language Acquisition.* Rowley, Mass.: Newbury House.

Schön, D. 1983. *The Reflective Practitioner.* London: Temple Smith.

Seliger, H. 1979. On the nature and function of language rules in language teaching. *TESOL Quarterly,* 13, 359–69.

Seliger, H. W. and E. Shohamy. 1989. *Second Language Research Methods.* Oxford: Oxford University Press.

Sharwood-Smith, M. 1981. Consciousness raising and the second language learner. *Applied Linguistics* 2, 159–69.

Sheldon, L. E. (Ed.). 1987. ELT textbooks and materials: problems in evaluation and development. *ELT Documents* 126. London: Modern English Publications and The British Council.

Sheldon, L. 1988. Evaluating ELT textbooks and materials. *ELT Journal,* 42 (4), 237–46.

Shepherd, J. *et al.* 1992. *The Sourcebook.* Harlow: Longman.

Skehan, P. 1993. A framework for the implementation of task-based learning. *IATEFL 1993 Annual Conference Report.*

Skehan, P. 1994. Interlanguage development and task-based learning in M. Bygate, Alan Tonkyn and Eddie Williams. (Eds.) *Grammar and the Language Teacher.* Prentice Hall International.

Skierso, A. 1991. Textbook selection and evaluation. In M. Celce-Murcia (Ed.). *Teaching English as a Second or Foreign Language.* Boston: Heinle and Heinle.

Slimani, A. 1989. The role of topicalization in classroom language learning. *System* 17: 223–224.

Slimani, A. 1992. Evaluation of classroom interaction. In J. Alderson and A. Beretta (Eds.).

Smith D. L. 1991. *Hidden Conversations: An Introduction to Communicative Psychoanalysis.* London: Routledge Kegan Paul.

Soars, L. and J. Soars. 1986. *Headway Intermediate.* Oxford: Oxford University Press.

Soyinka, W. 1963. 'Telephone conversation.' In G. Moore, and U. Beier (Eds.). *Modern Poetry from Africa.* London: Penguin.

Stanovich, K. E. 1980. Towards an interactive-compensatory model of individual differences in the development of reading fluency. *Reading Research Quarterly,* 16: 32–71.

Stenhouse, L. 1975. *An Introduction to Curriculum Research and Development.* London: Heinemann.

Stern, H. H. 1989. Seeing the wood AND the trees: some thoughts on language teaching analysis. In R. K. Johnson, 1989.

Stevick, E. 1976. *Memory, Meaning and Method.* Rowley, Mass.: Newbury House.

Stevick, E. 1986. *Images and Options in the Language Classroom.* Cambridge: Cambridge University Press.

Stevick, E. 1989. *Success With Foreign Languages.* Hemel Hempstead: Prentice-Hall International.

Swaffer, J. 1988. Readers, texts and second language: the interactive processes. *Modern Language Journal,* 72: 123–49.

Swain, M. 1985. Communicative competence: some roles of comprehensible input and comprehensible output in its development. In S. Gass and C. Madden. (Eds.) 1985. *Input in Second Language Acquisition.* Rowley, Mass.: Newbury House.

Swan, M. 1980. (rev. edn). *Practical English Usage,* 606 and 632.2. Oxford: Oxford University Press.

Svartvik, J. and R. Quirk. (Eds.) 1980. *A Corpus of English Conversation.* Lund: Lund University Press.

Tarone, E. and G. Yule. 1989. *Focus on the Language Learner.* Oxford: Oxford University Press.

Thompson, G. 1994. *Collins Cobuild English Guides 5: Reporting.* London: HarperCollins Publishers.

Thompson, G. 1995. *Collins Cobuild Concordance Sampler 3: Reporting.* London: HarperCollins Publishers.

Thompson, I. 1987. Memory in language learning. In A. Wenden and J. Ruben (Eds.) *Learning Strategies in Language Learning.* Englewood Cliffs, NJ: Prentice Hall.

Tierney, R. J. and J. W. Cunningham. 1984. Research on teaching reading comprehension. In P. D. Pearson (Ed.) *Handbook of Reading Research.* White Plains, NY: Longman.

Tomlinson, B. 1990. Managing change in Indonesian high schools. *ELT Journal,* 44 (1).

Tomlinson, B. 1993. Do we see what they mean? Unpublished PhD paper. University of Nottingham.

Tomlinson, B. 1994a. Pragmatic awareness activities. *Language Awareness,* (3&4), 119–29.

Tomlinson, B. 1994b. TPR materials. *FOLIO,* 1 (2), 8–10.

Tomlinson, B. 1994c. *Openings.* London: Penguin.

Tomlinson, B. 1995a. What dialogues can do. *FOLIO,* 2 (2), 14–17.

Tomlinson, B. 1995b. Work in progress: textbook projects. *FOLIO,* 2 (2), 26–31.

Tomlinson, B. 1996a. Choices. *FOLIO,* 3 (1), 20–23.

Tomlinson, B. 1996b. Helping L2 readers to see. In T. Hickey and J. Williams. *Language, Education and Society in a Changing World.* Clevedon, Avon: Multilingual Matters.

Tomlinson, B. 1997. The Role of Visualisation in the Reading of Literature by Learners of a Foreign Language. Unpublished PhD thesis. University of Nottingham.

Tomlinson, B. and H. Masuhara. 1994. *Use Your English.* Tokyo: Asahi Press.

Tribble, C. and G. Jones. 1990. *Concordances in the Classroom.* London: Longman.

Updike, J. 1994. *Brazil.* London: Hamish Hamilton.

Van Dijk, T. and W. Kintsch, 1983. *Strategies of Discourse Comprehension.* New York: Academic Press.

Van Lier, L. 1995. *Introducing Language Awareness.* London: Penguin.

Wallace, M. 1991. *Training Foreign Language Teachers: A Reflective Approach.* Cambridge: Cambridge University Press.

Waters, L. 1994. How to be a Coursebook author. A 12-point guide to becoming a publisher's paragon.' In *MATSDA FOLIO* 1 (2) November 1994.

Weir, C. and J. Roberts. 1994. *Evaluation in ELT.* Oxford: Blackwell.

Wenden, A. 1987. Conceptual background and utility. In A. Wenden and J. Rubin (1987).

Wenden, A. and J. Rubin. 1987. *Learner Strategies in Language Learning.* Hemel Hempstead: Prentice Hall.

Wessels, C. 1987. *Drama*. Oxford: Oxford University Press.
White, L. 1990. Implications of learnability theories for second language learning and teaching. In M. Halliday, J. Gibbons and H. Nicholas. (Eds.) *Learning, Keeping and Using Language*, 1. Amsterdam: John Benjamins.
Widdowson, H. 1979. The authenticity of language data. In H. Widdowson. *Explorations in Applied Linguistics*. Oxford: Oxford University Press.
Willis, D. 1990. *The Lexical Syllabus*. Collins Cobuild.
Willis, D. 1993. Syllabus, Corpus and Data-Driven Learning. *Proceedings of IATEFL Conference.*
Willis, J. 1996. *A Framework for Task-based Learning*. Harlow: Longman LHLT.
Willis, J. and D. Willis. 1988. *Cobuild English Course 1*. London: Collins.
Willis, J. and D. Willis. 1996. *Challenge and Change in Language Teaching*. Oxford: Heinemann ELT.
Wolfe, T. 1988. *Bonfire of the Vanities*. London: Jonathan Cape.
Woods, E. 1994. *Introducing Grammar*, London: Penguin.
Wright, T. and B. Bolitho. 1993. Language awareness: a missing link in language teacher education. *ELT Journal*, 47 (4).

Index

References in italic indicate figures or tables.

Index

Index

control 296
coursebook writing factors 125
    questionnaires 234, 235
    needs 240, 240-1
    pressures from 126
    self-investment 11
    student's targets vs. teaching
        objectives 228-9
learning measures, piloting 169-70
learning styles xi, 17-18, 111, 321, 337,
    341
'learning to learn' materials 308-9, 308,
    309
levels of analysis 194-202, 195, 197,
    199, 200-1, 203
    examples 205-13
'linguistic features' principle 13-14
'Little Johnny's letter home' 276
Lozanov, G. 20-1, 311-19
'L2 languages' xi
Luton University, 266, 270, 271

macro-evaluation 217-18, 219
Man of the People, A 275, 276
manuals, teachers' 244, 303-4, 338
marketing 140
    piloting benefits 186-7
matching procedures, flexi-materials
    289
'materials' xi, 2
'materials adaptation' xi
'materials development' 2
Materials Development Association vii,
    351-2
MATSDA (Materials Development
    Association) vii, 343-4
media transfer procedures, flexi-
    materials 288-9, 292
men, words typically used of 31
meta-materials 284, 285
methodology, coursebooks, 127-8,
    192
micro-evaluation 217, 218-20, 219
    see also communicative task
    evaluation
miming activities 277
modelling data 82

models of course design sequences
    247-50, 247, 249
Multi-dimensional Model 11-12
Multi-Level Learning 312, 313
multimedia materials xi
    piloting 188
My Son's Story 275, 276, 324-35,
    328-9

Nagoya Women's University 269
Namibian Textbook project 10, 23, 146,
    147, 255-6, 287
narratives, as access-self materials
    323-4
    example 324-35, 328-9
naturalness of language 68-70, 86, 87,
    88-9
    coursebook case study 123
needs analysis 240-1, 240-1, 341
    identification 90-1, 97, 98, 110, 111,
        113, 146-7
    case study examples 98, 104
    exploration 91-2, 97, 98, 113
    case study examples 98, 104
    teachers' 240-6, 240-1, 243, 245
Nottingham University Corpus 67-8
noun phrase concordance exercise
    50-1, 51

objective quality measurement 250
objectively measured needs 242, 243,
    245
objectives, task 28-9
objectives model 222-3, 224, 225
observation approach 73-7, 80
On Target 23, 146, 147
open learning 321
'operation' questions, task analysis 199,
    200-1, 210, 211
'organisation' feedback, piloting 185,
    186
others' perceptions of teachers needs
    242, 243, 245
outcome descriptions 228, 233
outcome feedback 21-2, 340-1
outcome vs. reaction evaluation 263
outside evaluators 224, 225

Index

reconstruction procedures,
flexi-materials 289, 294
records
coursebook usefulness 258
developing own 296
reduction procedures, flexi-materials
288
reflective practice 296–7
reformulation procedures, flexi-
materials 290
'relevance' principle 10–11
repetition, in Lozanov's method 318
reported speech, in corpus data 32
research 5–7
basic SLA principles 7–22
classroom 297
evaluation compared 237–8
making use of 342
resource options, 'scissor and paste'
strategies 282
responsibility distribution 297–8
responsive evaluation 222–3, 224, 225
'rest it' strategy 281
reversal of course design sequence
247–50, 247, 249
review materials, coursebooks, 124,
127
revision concordance activities 57–9, 58
'River Station Plaza' 269, 270–1
Rogers, Carl 316
role analysis 194, 199, 201–2, 216
role division, course design 246–50,
247, 249
rules, variable 80, 84–5

sampling meetings 255
schools, pressures from 126
'scissors and paste' strategies 282
scope of evaluation 223, 225, 233
scripted vs. authentic dialogues 68–70,
123
Second Language Acquisition see SLA
'second languages' xii
selection procedures, flexi-materials
250, 289, 293
self-access materials xii, 320–1
see also access-self materials

'self-investment' principle 11
self-marking 321
self-perceived teachers' needs 242, 243,
245
semi-materials 284, 285
senses of words, frequency 27–9, 29
sequence analysis 196, 197, 214, 215
'set in' concordances 31, 31
'silent period' principle 19–20
'simplified texts' xii
skills modules, 'scissors and paste'
strategies 282
SLA (Second Language Acquisition)
definition xii–xiii
research 5–22
software piloting 188
Sourcebook, The 294
'specific analysis' concordance
exercises 52–5, 53, 54
spoken language
grammar 67–70, 79–86, 87–8
tails 70–8, 73–7
word frequency 47, 64, 65, 66
'start/begin/commence' frequency 26–7
strong communicative approaches viii
students see learners
study skills 295–6
success symbolism, Lozanov method
316
suggestopedic learning 20–1, 311–19,
314
summative evaluation, 224, 225
'supplementary materials' xiii
support for piloters 166–7
syllabus-driven approach 147

tail structures 70–78, 81–4
evaluating materials 77–8
examples, 70–1
sample materials 73, 73–7
'take' concordances 35
'take your pick' meetings 255
'talking' materials 305, 305–6
tasks
analysis 198–201, 200–1, 205–13
communicative 227–38, 219, 228,
230, 235